POLITICAL ECONOMISTS
AND THE ENGLISH POOR LAWS

Political Economists and the English Poor Laws

A Historical Study of the Influence of Classical Economics
on the Formation of Social Welfare Policy

For Dick,

Ray

RAYMOND G. COWHERD
Professor of History, Lehigh University

Ohio University Press: Athens

ISBN 0-8214-0233-1
Library of Congress Catalog Number 76-8301
Printed in the United States of America.

For Phyllis Louise

Contents

Preface   ix

Introduction   xi

I.   The Humanitarian Reforms   1

II.   The Growth of Natural Law Opposition   27

III.   The Natural Law Reforms   49

IV.   The Origins of Radical Opposition:
        Part I. Jeremy Bentham   82

V.   The Origins of Radical Opposition:
        Part II. James Mill and David Ricardo   102

VI.   The Growth of Radical Opposition:
        Part I. Rural Unemployment   127

VII.   The Growth of Radical Opposition:
        Part II. Urban Unemployment   154

VIII.   The Growth of Radical Opposition:
        Part III. The Riots of 1830   182

IX.   The Radical Investigation of 1832   204

X.   The Radical Reform of 1834   244

Conclusion   283

Bibliography   287

Index   297

PREFACE

THIS is a study of the application of economic thought to social policy, especially to the reform of the old Poor Law. It seeks to appraise the influence of the political economists from Adam Smith to John Stuart Mill on the formation of social welfare policy. As a political and social historian, I have attempted an exposition of economic thought only insofar as administrators and other political leaders evoked the authority of the economists to explain or justify their decisions. As a general historian I have been concerned with the biographies of the thinkers in order to determine their possible influence on policy-makers. I have tried, moreover, to describe the economic and political contexts which evoked their writing. Before proceeding very far with the history of social policy, one needs to ask questions about conditions in order to determine, if possible, the relevance of both thought and policy to contemporary affairs.

A work so broad in scope places one in debt to more scholars than it is possible to acknowledge. I am aware, however, of my indebtedness to O. H. Taylor's observations on the ambiguities of moral philosophy which permeated an age when men modelled their thought after the natural sciences. I am even more indebted to Elie Halévy's exposition of the doctrines of natural and artificial harmony of interests. The major themes of these historians of thought have served to illuminate the differences between political economy and Bentham's science of legislation. Without the illumination which their studies have given to the ambiguities and complexities of political and economic thought, this history of social policy could not have been written.

In addition to the collaboration of scholars, the general historian has many servants assisting him and easing the burdens of his labors. Scores of librarians, archivists, and bibliographers serve in the maturing of every work of history. I wish to acknowledge the valuable assistance of several library staffs, especially the research librarians of Lehigh University, the University of Pennsylvania, the Kress Library of Harvard Graduate School of Business and Economics, and the Goldsmiths' Library of London University. I wish to thank my colleagues at Lehigh University for many fruitful comments and suggestions; in particular, I am grateful to the late Lawrence H. Gipson and to Richard M. Davis for their constant encouragement and advice. I wish to thank Virginia Frey and Terry Racosky who have faithfully typed the manuscript.

Some portions of the chapter on "Humanitarian Reform of the Poor Laws" have been previously published in the *Proceedings of the American Philosophical Society*. I am grateful for permission to republish the material; I must also thank the Society for financial assistance which enabled me to search public documents and other materials in the several libraries of London. I wish to thank the Lehigh Institute of Research for financial aid and Lehigh University for leaves of absence which enabled me to bring this work to completion.

INTRODUCTION

BETWEEN the years 1776, when Adam Smith wrote *The Wealth of Nations*, and 1848, when John Stuart Mill first published his *Principles of Political Economy*, England went through what historians have subsequently called the industrial and agricultural revolutions. In addition to the gyrations of these changes, England fought two major wars against France. In the midst of conditions that must be called catastrophic, several different groups of social reformers tried to modify the existing Poor Laws in order to improve the welfare of the working classes.

Inasmuch as agriculture was still the principal occupation of a majority of the families of England, the drastic changes attending the agricultural revolution affected more people adversely than did the simultaneous changes in industry.[1] The Poor Law reformers of the time were much more concerned with the social problems of the rural areas than with those of the industrial towns and cities. One aspect of the agricultural revolution which adversely affected many farm laborers was the enclosing of the open fields. This improvement in agriculture deprived many laborers of the use of land. Some lost their garden plots; others lacked access to wasteland for fuel and game. Rural laborers, therefore, became dependent on daily wages for their subsistence; and increasingly there was a lack of employment during winter months. In prosperous years of good harvests and high prices, which were rare in the areas of heavy clays of the South and Southeast, the farmer could employ the surplus hands to make repairs and to fertilize the soil. But in years of bad harvests or low prices, the farmer lacked capital and had to postpone improvements. The winter surplus of hands, however, turned to a scarce supply during spring planting and summer harvests.

Inherited from the days of subsistence agriculture was the expectation that all members of a family be employed. Even children five or six years old were employed under parental supervision. The laborer of good fortune was the man with a large family of children above ten years old; on the other hand, the laborer who won the sympathy and assistance of his neighbors was the father of several small children whose mother was too busy nursing them to contribute to the family income.

If the agricultural revolution brought more food to the table and eliminated the threat of famine, the larger supply had to be distributed among an increasing rural population. The increase in unemployment became identified in the minds of many with the growth of population. In the context of the agricultural revolution, notwithstanding the greater productivity, the problems of rural welfare became as intractable as the clay soils in the vales.

The simultaneous revolution in industry, which created its problems of congestion, health, and sanitation, alleviated rural unemployment in some areas and aggravated it in others. The industrial revolution applied science and technology to the production of textiles, metals, and many other commodities. In the underdeveloped counties of the North, steam and water supplied power that multiplied a hundredfold the harnessed strength of man and beast. As if following Adam Smith's command to divide and subdivide labor, the factory brought diverse processes of production under one roof. New towns and cities were built around the factories, providing a multitude of opportunities for the laborers in the adjacent countryside. The new industries provided better pay at less arduous labor than the farm. While new industries, power driven, were flourishing, the older domestic industries and many handicrafts fell into decline. Handloom weavers struggled on to their extinction; even if the whole family worked longer hours they could not earn their subsistence. The technological unemployment in Lancashire and other industrial areas increased relief expenditures. Trade fluctuations in the cotton industry might even threaten the towns with bankruptcy. In rural areas remote from London and industrial towns, the farm laborers lost their household industries. Without the winter employment provided by handicraft industries, the rural laborer's family descended to the ignominy of parish relief. Adding to the laborer's humiliation was the refusal of many parish officials to recognize the existence of unemployment, and some could not refrain from charging the pauper with the improvidence of marrying before he had an income sufficient to support his family.

In these confused and complex circumstances, the doctrines of political economy provided few guidelines for those who had to determine social policy. The economic maxims, inherited from the Age of Reason, had been systematized by Adam Smith in his *The Wealth of Nations*. By the beginning of the nineteenth century the axioms of political economy had, in the minds of some policymakers, achieved the scientific status of Newtonian laws of nature. Dugald Stewart, the most influential teacher of political economy during the 1790's, did not hesitate to exalt his distinguished progenitor to the pinnacle occupied by Sir Isaac Newton. The *Inquiry into the Nature and Causes of the Wealth of Nations* became a textbook for statesmen seeking to avoid the twin specters of famine and destitution.

While in the throes of economic revolutions, England had to wage two wars against France. The war against the French Republic, lasting from 1793 to 1802, divided the nation ideologically. The reaction to, and repression of, the French sympathizers made precarious the lives of most political reformers. Famines, food riots, and naval mutinies added to the pessimism of losing the war. During these dark days of defeatism, the humanitarian reformers undertook the amelioration of the Poor Laws. They abolished compulsory indoor relief in workhouses and established outdoor relief for both the impotent and the able-bodied poor.

When the war was resumed against Napoleon in 1803, the nation was no longer divided by ideologies; it was now clear that a dictator, at the head of a redoubtable army, threatened to conquer Europe. Huge appropriations were made to wage war and to subsidize the allies. The costs of recruiting militiamen added to the growing expenditures for relief. Wartime expenditures and deficits stimulated prosperity, providing opportunities for employment and increased wages.[2]

The peace of 1815 brought with it economic calamity. The wartime boom was followed shortly by a postwar depression which reached a nadir in 1818.[3] As a result of the depression, relief expenditures rose to the highest peak for the years 1815 and 1832. Industry began to recover in the following year and continued an upward climb to the financial crisis of 1825. The agricultural depression, however, persisted until 1824; rural relief expenditures kept pace with unemployment. During the depression, agricultural distress was spread unevenly over rural England. The areas with light sandy soils might prosper in a wet season that brought destitution to the areas of heavy clays. While the outcry was against the imports of foreign grain, the real competition was between the areas of sandy soil and those of heavy clays.[4]

The farmers themselves were caught between the millstones of high rents and low prices. Only by cutting costs could they remain solvent. They could let the poor soils return to grass; they could postpone improvements of soil and buildings until the return of higher prices. The oversupplies of laborers, so necessary for planting and harvest, were thrown on the parish chest during the winter months and the other seasons of agricultural unemployment.

During these gloomy years of wars, revolutions, and depressions, three different groups of Poor law reformers attempted to change the system of welfare inherited from the sixteenth century: the Evangelical humanitarians, the Benthamite Radicals, and the advocates of the natural law doctrines of the political economists.

The humanitarian reformers of Pitt's time were Evangelical Christians who had come to prominence and influence as a result of the revivals conducted by John Wesley and George Whitfield. In a recent book, Professor Kitson Clark has treated the Evangelical Revival as a counterpart of the romantic movement in literature and art. Whatever its defects, romanticism gave men the power to act. As initiated by John Wesley, the Revival was practical, moral, and conservative. "Yet for all its force and reality, it showed the inherent weakness of all romanticism, the inclination to value emotion for the sake of emotion."[5] The romanticism of the Evangelicals brought them into conflict with the natural law reformers who were strict rationalists. This difference in values and attitudes contributed to the controversy over the Poor Laws. The rationalist attitude was expressed by Sir Frederick Eden in his influential history, *The State of the Poor*, when he disparaged the Evangelicals with the remark that their "humanity exceeded their good sense."

As Christian moralists the Evangelicals accepted the ethics of self-denial and sought to act upon Christ's commands to feed the hungry, clothe the naked, and visit the sick and those in prison. The new Evangelical morality penetrated all levels of English society, from the highest to the lowest. Professor Asa Briggs has made this observation on Evangelical influences: "It is impossible to understand the tide of the new morality without relating its movements to the social contours of the changing age. The future victories of Evangelism could scarcely have been anticipated. . ., yet before the nineteenth century had progressed very long, London was invaded far beyond the spearhead of Clapham; and Bath and Brighton, like other popular watering places, became great Evangelical centers."[6]

The new morality of the Evangelicals became conspicuous in their effort to reform the Poor Laws. Identifying themselves with the weak members of society, they shed tears over pathetic and needy paupers. They wept over foundlings, unnursed and undernourished, dying in London workhouses. Pauper orphans, apprenticed as chimney sweeps, were the objects of their penitent sorrow. The moral attitudes of the Evangelicals increased their alienation from the Utilitarians who held to the ethics of self-love as the best guide for public policy.

The Evangelical leaders of the humanitarians who reformed the Poor Laws were members of the Clapham Sect. These pious men, known as "the Saints in politics," worshipped together in the Clapham village church on Sunday, and during the week took time from their affairs of business and finance to promote a multitude of good causes.[7] In the promotion of their benevolent projects, they won the support of many others who shared their enthusiasm for reform without sharing their particular religious beliefs.

The Evangelical humanitarians were stoutly opposed by the political economists, who confidently believed they had discovered laws of nature comparable to Newton's law of gravity.[8] The natural law reformers were as eager to improve society as were the Evangelicals, but they wanted to improve it in keeping with the natural laws of economics. These reformers preferred to repeal the Poor Law, not reform it, in order to allow wages and prices to reach their natural level.

The Radicals, who reformed the Poor Laws in 1834, were not only political economists, they were also Benthamite lawyers. As followers of Jeremy Bentham, they were prepared to use legislation as a positive means of achieving economic ends. Elie Halévy has observed that there was a difference among the Utilitarians, some believing in the natural harmony of interests and others believing in the artificial identity of interests.[9] Guided by the natural law principles of political economy, the Radical reformers were able to abolish the humanitarian Poor Law reforms of Pitt's time; and guided by the legislative principles of Jeremy Bentham, they were able to erect the new poor Law on the ruins of the old.

The old Poor Law dated from the time of Elizabeth I. This comprehensive measure, which passed in 1601, provided a constitution for a national system of welfare. Under this law Queen Elizabeth delegated the responsibility of assessing the poor rates and administering relief to the principal unit of local government, the Church of England parish. Its governing body, the vestry, assessed the rates, appointed the overseer of the poor, and held him accountable for expenditures. The vestry, in turn, was accountable to the justice of the peace, who was the most important official in the county and the effective link between the national government and the local community. By 1800 there were some fifteen thousand parishes, townships, and corporations with primary jurisdiction for welfare. Even at this late date most parishes had unpaid overseers of the poor, who were elected to serve in the office for one year. The magistrates, or justices of the peace, supervised the Poor Laws, and if the overseer refused to relieve a pauper, they could order the parish to do so.

Associated with the Elizabethan law was the Law of Settlement. The original law assumed that a person was legally settled at the place of his birth or where he had resided for three years. Much ignominious litigation over settlement began with the law of Charles II's reign which enabled the parish to remove a person within forty days of his arrival if it appeared likely that he would become an applicant for relief. To prevent a pauper from obtaining a legal residence, the parish frequently instigated legal proceedings to remove him before he became chargeable. Settlement might also be obtained on other grounds. The common law provided settlement for those inheriting estates and for wives whose husbands had residence. Such was the old Poor Law which the humanitarians undertook to reform during the ministries of the younger William Pitt.

NOTES

[1] J. F. Chambers and G. E. Mingay, *The Agricultural Revolution 1750-1800*, (New York, 1966.) This distinguished work brings up-to-date Lord Ernle's *English Farming Past and Present.*

[2] *Ibid.*, p. 119.

[3] *Ibid.*, p. 130.

[4] G. E. Fussell and W. Compton, "Agricultural Adjustments after the Napoleonic Wars," in *Economic History*, IV (Feb. 1939), 202-3. See also F. M. L. Thompson, *English Landed Society in the Nineteenth Century*, (Toronto: University of Toronto Press, 1963), pp. 232-33.

[5] G. Kitson Clark, *Our Expanding Society* (Cambridge, England, 1967), p. 119.

[6] Asa Briggs, *The Age of Improvement*, (1959), p. 73.

[7] Ford K. Brown, *Fathers of the Victorians* (Cambridge, England, 1961), Chapter IX.

[8] O. H. Taylor, *A History of Economic Thought* (New York, 1960), pp. 9-12. Taylor's concept of natural law is a guiding principle of my study.

[9] Elie Halévy, *The Growth of Philosophic Radicalism*, (New York, 1949), pp. 498-99.

POLITICAL ECONOMISTS
AND THE ENGLISH POOR LAWS

I

THE HUMANITARIAN REFORMS

ENGLAND has had a national policy of social welfare since the time of Queen Elizabeth I. Broad in scope and paternal in spirit, the Elizabethan Poor Law provided work for the unemployed, education for the children, relief for the impotent, and punishment for those able but unwilling to work.[1] The Poor Law assumed that the government had a responsibility for the welfare of the working classes. With the disruption of royal authority during the seventeenth century, the parishes, which were the primary units of administration, neglected their obligation of setting the poor to work, of binding pauper children as apprentices, of suppressing vagrancy, and of relieving the infirm.[2] Social responsibility reached a nadir in the Poor Law of 1722 which enabled the parishes to build workhouses and to deny relief to anyone refusing to enter them, even though it meant the separation of families and the loss of individual freedom. Many parishes abandoned their responsibilities under the law of 1722 by farming their poor to contractors. This mistreatment of the poor continued until the time of the younger William Pitt, when humanitarian reformers sought to restore the Elizabethan Poor Law to what they thought was its original purity.[3]

To understand William Pitt's policy of social welfare, one must penetrate the confusion of terminology. Who were the poor people of Pitt's time? They were all people without income from prop-

1

erty or profession and, therefore, dependent upon their manual labor for a living. The poor were not mere paupers (in the modern sense of the word) but all the working people.[4] Poverty meant the necessity of having to work for a living. Not until the nineteenth century did the term poverty come to mean destitution and dependence upon charity or public assistance.

During the eighteenth century the natural law theory of labor prevailed. According to this doctrine, poverty was essential to the progress of civilization, for only under the spur of hunger would man bear the heavy burdens of progress and do all those irksome tasks which society needed done. The natural law theorists deduced their labor theory from certain self-evident propositions which they deemed to be laws of nature.[5] These theorists thought all the able-bodied poor should be set to work, and those refusing to work should be punished.

Fortunately, there arose in opposition to the natural law reformers a group of benevolent men, under the leadership of the Clapham Evangelicals, who had a determination to ameliorate the harsh conditions of the working classes. The last decades of the eighteenth century, and especially the years of the French Wars, constituted a remarkable age of humanitarian reform. This was the period when William Wilberforce aroused evangelical sentiment to abolish slave trade, when John Howard and Elizabeth Fry strove to improve conditions in prisons, when Samuel Romilly agitated for softening of penal laws, when the elder Sir Robert Peel effected the first factory reform, and when Hannah Moore and Joseph Lancaster began a popular movement for the education of the working classes.[6] Motivated by religious zeal, the Evangelicals sought to remove all those obstacles — ignorance, sloth, intemperance, and prodigality — which hindered the individual's salvation. They were alike in their desire to lift the lower classes to a new life of industry, frugality, honesty, and temperance and to bring to the upper classes a new sense of social responsibility commensurate with their wealth and privilege. During the critical period of the wars against France, the Evangelicals, adding patriotism to their religious fervor, strove to improve moral conditions in time to merit the blessings of Providence upon Church, Crown, Aristocracy, and the whole superlative constitution.[7]

The humanitarian reform of the Poor Law was begun by Jonas Hanway, whose evangelical activities and religious writings created a new sympathy for the wretched working people of London.

2

Born in 1712, Jonas Hanway spent the first part of his mature life as a merchant, trading in Russia and the area of the Caspian Sea.[8] Upon his return to England in 1750, after having travelled extensively in the Near East, he gained distinction by writing an account of the British trade over the Caspian Sea. The wealth which he had acquired as a merchant, added to an inheritance, enabled him to retire from business and to devote the remaining thirty-six years of his life to uplifting the most neglected and wretched of London's poorer classes.

The more helpless and pitiable the people the more warmly Hanway identified himself with them, with infants born in workhouses, with orphan boys wandering homeless in the streets, with pauper children bound to harsh masters, with prostitutes who had known no other employment — all these wretches became the objects of his sympathy and the "righteous causes" for which he conducted pious crusades. His seventy books and pamphlets on the most mournful subjects, shocking and appalling to the upper classes, were the means of creating a more sensitive social opinion and of obtaining financial support for the benevolent institutions which he founded and promoted.[9]

As a result of Hanway's agitation against keeping infants at workhouses, where many died, Parliament enacted laws protecting the pauper infants of London. The law of 1761 required the parish clerk to record the names of pauper children under four years old, the names of the nurses who kept them, and the date of the death or discharge of such children.[10] When the parish registers indicated a high death rate among babies born in the workhouses of London, Hanway obtained a law in 1767 requiring the Metropolitan parishes to maintain their pauper children in the country until the age of six and then to pay some master to take them as apprentices. To assure better treatment for parish apprentices, Hanway's Act required the parish to pay the master £4.2s., half of the amount to be paid at the time of binding the child and the rest after three years. The same law placed parish apprentices on the level of "free" children by limiting the time of apprenticeship to seven years or the age of twenty-one instead of twenty-four.[11]

Of all the apprentices of London the most wretched and ill-treated were the chimney sweepers. These unwashed and half-clothed waifs of London, so urgently in need of a guardian, attracted Hanway's attention, and his tracts on their behalf initiated the reforms for the better regulation of the master sweepers. But a

3

business so essentially brutal could hardly be regulated, and a class of masters so callous were scarcely amenable to moral admonition. The "climbing boys," consequently, continued to be inadequately protected for another half-century, until the trade itself was abolished and machines substituted for boys.[12]

When Hanway died in 1786, he left behind not only the institutions which stood as monuments to his humanitarianism but also scores of people zealous to carry on the reform of the Poor Law that he had initiated. Hanway's contemporary, Thomas Gilbert, labored assiduously for many years to ameliorate the conditions of the working classes. While Hanway's reforms pertained primarily to the children of the Metropolis, the provisions of the Gilbert Act of 1782 and the recommendations of his benevolent bill of 1787 extended the new humanitarianism to other parts of England. Although the Gilbert Act of 1782 was limited in its application, and although the bill of 1787 was defeated in Parliament, Thomas Gilbert did much to ameliorate the Poor Law.[13]

A country gentleman of Straffordshire, Thomas Gilbert was familiar with local problems. His intimate knowledge of the affairs of rural parishes and his devotion to the improvement of their conditions made him an influential legislator in six successive Parliaments. He first directed his attention to the improvement of country roads by creating turnpike trusts. He also assisted the construction of canals and was one of the promoters of the Grand Trunk Canal. Because of Gilbert's fruitful activities, William Pitt, upon coming to office in 1784, appointed him chairman of the influential Ways and Means Committee.[14]

Early in his career Thomas Gilbert tried to improve the administration of the Poor Laws and to increase the benefits which the working classes derived from them. In order to achieve these ends, he thought that it was necessary to circumvent the inefficient parish system. Gilbert, therefore, created statutory authorities, similar to the turnpike trusts, to handle the specialized problems of employing the able-bodied and relieving the infirm. By combining a number of rural parishes under the new authority, he thought, it would be possible to employ salaried officials instead of the unpaid overseer. His bill of 1765 to incorporate parishes into Poor Law unions passed the House of Commons but was defeated in the Lords.[15]

Facing strong opposition, Gilbert patiently collected information to prove the need for drastic reform. Under his direction a

4

census of expenditures and the number of persons receiving public assistance was taken in 1776.[16] Prepared with greater and more accurate information than anyone had possessed heretofore, Gilbert introduced in 1781 three Poor Law bills. Embodying the new humanitarian attitudes towards the working classes, his bills made provisions for three classes of people. His first concern was the unemployed. To meet the need of unemployment he proposed to facilitate the movement of workers from rural parishes to industrial towns and to create more jobs by public works.[17]

A second class of people — the rogues, vagabonds, and sturdy beggars — Gilbert regarded in a new light. Since the time of Elizabeth, the parish official had punished vagrancy, but Gilbert now tried to understand the cause of wandering. The lack of employment in the communities where the vagrants had their legal residence, he thought, was the primary cause of their leaving home. Desiring to return the wandering fathers to their families, he recommended the issuance of a royal proclamation, setting aside for a time the penalties of vagrancy.[18] After the period of clemency had expired, however, the vagrant was to be sent, not to the workhouse, but to the house of correction. When his bill became law in 1783, the counties were empowered to build houses of correction and to levy a rate for that purpose.[19] Thus Gilbert tried to separate criminal rogues and vagrants from the rest of the poor, leaving the workhouses for the aged, sick, and infirm.

When proposing his Poor Law reforms in 1781, Gilbert was anticipating the end of the American War. To provide jobs for the disbanded army, he recommended the creation of a public authority to drain wastes and reforest barren lands. A promoter of roads and canals, he was aware that public works were a means of employment, especially in rural areas where there was seasonal employment.[20]

One of Gilbert's primary objectives was the repeal of that part of the Poor Law which required people to enter the workhouse to obtain assistance. Based upon the Poor Law of 1722 was the contract system, a kind of forced labor, by which many parishes escaped from their responsibilities by farming their poor. He struck another blow at the contract system by shutting the door of the workhouse on the able-bodied poor and leaving it as a residence for the infirm. He encouraged outdoor relief to all types of needy people so long as they had their own homes or relatives to care for them. He exercised more benevolence in prohibiting the removal

5

of sick persons and pregnant women.[21]

That such comprehensive provisions of welfare could not be carried out by many rural parishes Gilbert fully recognized. He therefore planned to create a new statutory authority to administer the law, leaving to the parish officials only the duties of levying and collecting the rates. Already a score and more of towns and cities had created, by the Local Acts of Parliament, the Guardians of the Poor, who hired salaried officials to administer the Poor Laws and who supervised their work.[22]

The Gilbert Act of 1782, an omnibus law, although comprehensive and benevolent in its aims, was limited in its application. In the first place, it did not apply to the towns and other places with incorporated Guardians of the Poor. In the second place, it was not compulsory; it merely enabled country gentlemen and other persons of wealth to initiate the union of several adjacent parishes for the better administration of the Poor Law.

Encouraged by the passage of the Act of 1782, Gilbert laid plans to extend more widely its benevolent provisions. Expecting to show that the union of parishes, under efficient management, had reduced expenditures, Gilbert obtained in 1786 a national census of Poor Law expenditures for the years 1783 to 1785.[23] With evidence of the reduced expenditures in those hundreds of Suffolk and Norfolk that had united their parishes, Gilbert went before Parliament with a plan to establish county-wide statutory authorities.[24] The proposed authorities, however, by circumventing the justices of the peace, would have reduced the political influence of both the Anglican clergy and the country gentlemen. Consequently, when Gilbert's bill reached its second reading on April 17, 1788, the House of Commons summarily rejected it. Speaking on behalf of the clergy and gentlemen who served as magistrates in many places, William Young declared: "The bill would reduce the magistrates in being throughout England to an insignificant and unworthy situation by creating a board of commissioners paramount in power. . . ."[25]

Outside Parliament the principal opponent of Gilbert's reforms was the Reverend Joseph Townsend. This Anglican clergyman, who was keenly interested in geology and a member of the Royal Society, produced a lengthy essay on the Poor Laws in 1785 and another, three years later, condemning Gilbert's bill of 1787. Townsend thought poverty was both necessary and inevitable. "It seems to be a law of nature," he said, "that the poor should be to a certain degree improvident that there may always be some to fulfull the most servile, the most sordid, and the most ignoble offices in the community. The sum of human happiness is thereby increased. . . ." Poverty, he insisted, was the necessary spur also for the soldier and the sailor, otherwise they would not risk their lives. Since in the progress of society some must want, Townsend thought it natural that "the prodigal, slothful, and vicious should suffer rather than the provident, diligent, and virtuous."[26]

The natural law assumption that poverty was the necessary motive for labor led Townsend to conclude that voluntary charity should be substituted for compulsory Poor Laws. "To promote industry and economy," he declared, "it is necessary that the relief given to the poor be limited and precarious." Townsend's objections to Gilbert's benevolent reforms stemmed from other natural law assumptions. Whereas Gilbert wished to organize the generosity of "gentlemen and men of substance" into a more benevolent system of relief, Townsend preferred to defend the parsimony of the overseers and to use the workhouse test as a shield against increasing Poor Law expenses.

Like other natural law reformers, Townsend derived his social and political philosophy from self-evident propositions about soil, climate, food, and population. A country's population, obviously, could never advance beyond its food supply. "If natural remedies are rejected," he admonished, "it remains only for the poor to expose their children, as is the horrid practice adopted by the richest country of the world [China]."[27] Notwithstanding poor relief, there were effective checks, Townsend thought, on the growth of population. These were lack of cottages and the workhouse test. Although he did not advocate the immediate abolition of the Poor Laws, he defended the workhouse test and the pulling down of cottages as necessary checks on an excessive population.[28]

Townsend's natural law arguments and the defeat of Gilbert's bill in 1787 delayed but did not prevent the humanitarian reform of the Poor Laws. Upon the retirement of Gilbert as the Parliamentary advocate of Poor Law reform, Sir George Rose took up the work of improving the conditions of the working classes.[29]

Born in 1744, George Rose spent several years of his youth in the Royal Navy before beginning his political career. In 1772 he was appointed the Keeper of Records at Westminster with the task of supervising the publication of the Journals and Rolls of Parliament. Showing ability to handle a complex body of information, he was appointed Secretary of Treasury with the duty of revising and consolidating the customs in order to prevent smuggling. In this office he served so efficiently that he continued to hold it from 1784 to Pitt's resignation in 1801. Upon Pitt's return to office in 1804, he appointed Rose Vice-President of the Board of Trade and Joint-Paymaster General of the Forces. Pitt highly esteemed him for his tact and thoroughness.[30] For sixteen years Rose kept a careful hand on the purse strings. His assiduousness in matters of commerce and finance made him indispensable, not only to Pitt, but also to other Tory Governments. His ability to assimilate quantities of statistical information made him an authority on budgetary matters at a time when the nation had to marshal its resources in war against France.[31]

Sir George Rose's benevolent attitude toward the working classes led him to espouse the reform of the Poor Laws. The first measure which he proposed — subsequently identified as the George Rose Act — was designed to encourage and protect Friendly Societies. These benefit clubs had long existed among the working classes to provide fellowship and financial assistance in times of emergency. As the practice of life insurance spread among the upper classes, several benevolent persons developed plans to bring group security within the reach of working people. As early as 1772 a bill providing life annuities for the poor passed the House of Commons but was rejected by the Lords. The several plans for life insurance were proposed as a means of reducing the poor rates as well as a benefit to the working classes. In 1787 John Rolle, when proposing in the House of Commons his plan for a universal benefit society, said "it would reduce expenditures for the poor, relieve distresses, give a spur to industry, and encourage population."[32] Rolle's bill failed to pass the Commons, however, because it attempted too much. Although Gilbert had supported the bill when it was first introduced, he abandoned it "after much deliberation and conversation with many members of the House. . .from an apprehension that it could not be executed on so hazardous a scale."[33]

The George Rose Act of 1793, more modest in its conception than the Rolle plan, provided protection and encouragement for Friendly Societies in the raising of funds voluntarily for the mutual relief and maintenance of members in sickness, old age, and infirmity.[34] The new law placed the Societies under the guardianship of the justices of the peace and endowed them with the power

8

to sue and be sued. It freed them from the stamp tax and other legal fees imposed by the courts on similar corporate bodies. Rose proposed his reform with the benevolent intention of improving the conditions of the working classes and with the prudent intent of reducing Poor Law expenditures.[35]

During the rest of his life, George Rose showed a solicitude for the Friendly Societies. When he persuaded Parliament to obtain the Poor Law Returns of 1803, he inquired about the number of Societies and their total membership. Throughout England and Wales there were 9,672 Societies with a membership of 704,350;[36] and by 1815 the membership had grown to 925,264.[37] By the end of the French Wars the Friendly Societies had proven their usefulness in ways not anticipated by Rose. When other types of political and social organizations were denied to the working classes by the Anti-Combination Acts, the Friendly Societies remained open to them as a means of sharing their miseries and articulating their grievances. Alarmed by the growth of the Societies, Parliament appointed in 1825 a committee to investigate their activities, and the committee confirmed the suspicion that the Friendly Societies had facilitated combinations to raise wages.[38]

While Sir George Rose did not intend to assist the formation of labor unions, he did wish to increase the mobility of labor. Like other humanitarians, he desired to help the poor to help themselves in becoming sober, frugal, and industrious. He was keenly aware of, and optimistic over, the rapid expansion of industry and the increasing demand for labor in the thriving factory towns.[39] To encourage workers to move to these opportunities and to give them greater security in their new residences, he provided in his law that no member of a Friendly Society should be removed until he became actually chargeable. Two years later this provision of the law was extended beyond the Friendly Societies to all the working classes so that parish officials could remove no one until he became dependent upon the parish for relief.[40]

By changing the Law of Settlement, which had empowered the parishes to remove poor persons to their place of legal residence, Sir George Rose went far in eliminating a perennial criticism of the Poor Law. Since the time of Adam Smith, the natural law theorists had objected to the Laws of Settlement and Removal on the grounds that they immobilized the working classes.[41] In addition to increasing the migration of labor to places of employment, Rose and the humanitarian reformers wished to reduce the expenditure of money on litigation and to prevent the removal of sick persons and pregnant women. Subsequent laws were enacted forbidding the removal of any pregnant woman or any family with a sick member.[42]

The laws to improve the mobility of labor were enacted in conjunction with an increase in outdoor relief. By providing casual relief the Friendly Societies had already prevented some of their members from becoming chargeable. The law of 1795 commanded the justices of the peace to grant relief to everybody in time of sickness or "temporary distress."[43] Previously, the Gilbert Act of 1782 had repealed the workhouse test in all those parishes united under its provisions. The law of 1795 extended this benevolent provision of the Gilbert Act to all parishes by repealing the law requiring the poor to enter workhouses to obtain assistance. The preamble of the new law declared the Workhouse Act (9 Geo. I c.7) to be "inconvenient and oppressive inasmuch as it often prevents an industrious person from receiving such occasional relief as is best suited to the peculiar case of such poor persons."[44] The new law granted to the "industrious poor" the right to be relieved in their own homes even though they refused to be lodged in workhouses and even though the parish had contracts with persons to provide relief and employment.[45]

According to the law of 1795 one justice of the peace could order relief for one month "and from time to time as occasion shall require." The policy of giving casual relief to persons in their own homes was maintained during the period of the wars against France. The Militia Act of 1803 granted parish relief to the families of men serving in the army. A later reform empowered the justice of the peace to order outdoor relief for more than one month but not exceeding three months.[46] The same law limited the amount of relief to three shillings a week or to three-fourths of that necessary to maintain a person in the workhouse.[47]

The extent of the benefits derived from the new policy of granting casual relief outside the workhouses was revealed by the Poor Law Returns of 1803. The total number of people in England and Wales receiving assistance in that year was 1,233,768; and of this total, 956,248 persons received outdoor relief, while only 83,468 were relieved in workhouses. Of the number receiving outdoor relief in 1803, 194,052 persons did not belong to the parishes which helped them.[48]

Both Pitt and Rose thought of the modification of the Laws of Settlement and Removal as one of their most beneficial reforms.

Rose believed that the Friendly Societies benefited not only working men, but also manufacturers and tradesmen.[49] In Pitt's thinking, the immobilizing of labor was the principal evil of the Elizabethan system. "The poor laws of this country," he said, "had contributed to fetter the circulation of labor. . . ." They had prevented the workman "from going to that market where he could dispose of his industry to the greatest advantage. . . ." By increasing the circulation of labor, Pitt felt that "the wealth of the nation would be increased, the poor man rendered not only more comfortable but more virtuous, and the weight of the poor rates. . . greatly diminished."[50] Granting relief according to the number of children in the family, preventing removals at the caprice of the parish office, and compelling the poor to subscribe to the Friendly Societies — these reforms, he said, "would tend, in a very great degree, to remove every complaint to which the present partial remedy [a minimum wage] could be applied."[51]

The reformation of the Poor Laws had to give ground to the more crucial problems of waging war on a foreign front and marshalling economic resources at home. Early in 1793 England declared war on France. To equip the army and navy and to subsidize the allies, the Government's expenditures greatly exceeded its revenues. Wartime inflation, the dislocation of trade, and a bad harvest brought the country to a crisis in 1795. Rioting, hungry mobs seized grain in transit and threatened to disrupt the flow of military materials.[52]

When Parliament convened in October, 1795, the King's speech expressed alarm over the high price of provisions. To cope with the emergency Pitt obtained a committee to investigate the price of wheat.[53] The Evangelicals on the Committee, William Wilberforce and Dudley Ryder, introduced in Parliament and obtained the adoption of a resolution calling for the formation of an association among the upper classes, which would take pledges from them, to reduce their consumption of wheat flour by one-third. Familiar with the dietary experiments of Count Rumford, Ryder and Wilberforce recommended also the making of bread from other than wheat flour.[54]

The Tory government, however, could not rely upon voluntary measures to obtain an adequate food supply during the dearth of 1795. It placed bounties on the importation of food including sugar, grain, and potatoes, and repealed the bounties on the exportation of sugar. It legalized the making of bread flour of mixed

11

grains and potatoes. To increase further the supply of food, it prevented the distilleries from making wines and spirits from all types of grain, malt, and potatoes.[55]

Since the rising prices of 1795 brought the Guardians of the Poor, which had been incorporated under the Gilbert Act and numerous Local Acts, to virtual bankruptcy, it was necessary for Parliament to enact legislation enabling them to remain solvent.[56] With the expectation that efficient management would reduce Poor Law expenses, Gilbert previously had placed a ceiling over the assessment of poor rates. After the Poor Law Returns for the years 1783 to 1785, he had established the medium expenditures of those years as the maximum for future assessments. While thus limiting the Guardians' revenues, the law enabled them to borrow money to build workhouses and made them responsible for the repayment of the loans as well as for the administration of relief.[57] Parliament now came to the rescue of the Guardians by raising the ceiling on assessments. The law, enacted late in 1795, enabled them to increase the assessments in proportion to the rise in the price of wheat but not more than double the average expenditures for the years 1783 to 1785. One clause placed a new ceiling over assessments by requiring that, after January 1, 1798, "the sum to be assessed. . .shall never exceed in any one year the amount double the sum at present raised by virtue of this Act." The cost of living, however, continued to rise, and when the harvest failed in 1799, Parliament again raised the ceiling on assessments in proportion to the rise in the price of wheat. The permission to increase assessments according to the rise in the price of wheat was limited to January 1, 1802. But even this ceiling was not high enough to allow the adjustment of rates to prices, and Parliament consequently removed the ceiling "to enable the Guardians to pay debts on workhouses."[58]

During the crisis of 1795 the Foxite Whigs, a small but outspoken minority, continually harassed the Tory Government, demanding the restoration of peace and plenty.[59] During this crisis Samuel Whitbread proposed a minimum wage as the proper remedy for the ills of wartime inflation. Using Richard Price's index of the cost of provisions, he estimated that prices over a long period of time had far outdistanced wages. While conceding the natural law doctrine that prices and wages, like water, should be left to find their own level, he insisted that something be done to lessen the hardships of the working classes. His remedy was a minimum wage. From the time of Elizabeth I the magistrates had power to regulate wages, and this power they occasionally used to prevent the combination of workers by setting a maximum wage. Whitbread, on the other hand, proposed that the magistrates use their power to benefit the working classes by fixing a minimum wage in proportion to the rise in the price of wheat.[60]

The Whig leaders, Fox and Sheridan, who supported Whitbread's bill for a minimum wage, weakened their case by making concession to the natural law doctrine of noninterference, and Pitt was quick to exploit their concession. In refuting the arguments for a minimum wage, he invoked the name of Adam Smith against such interference.[61] To strengthen the natural law doctrine that wages and prices should be left to find their own level, it was necessary for Pitt to discredit Richard Price's cost of living index. He doubted the reliability of the index, because the people's habits of consumption had so changed that the price of wheat was no longer a reliable guide to the cost of living. Although readily granting the severe conditions of the working classes, Pitt was unwilling to interfere with manufacturing and trade by regulating wages. Parliament, therefore, rejected the minimum wage.

Outside Parliament the principal defense of the Whig's minimum wage was made by the Reverend John Howlett. While acknowledging Pitt's eminent abilities, Howlett deigned to refute him because "some of his leading ideas were directly opposed to those he had long imagined to be so clear and evident as to be kind of first principles altogether indubitable."[62] "An indubitable maxim and of universal application," Howlett thought, is "that everything will be dear or cheap as it is scarce or plentiful." From this self-evident proposition he had no difficulty in deriving the policy of regulating wages: "If hands be numerous and demand for labor comparatively small, labor will be cheap." It was clear to Howlett that there was "a superabundance of hands" coming from an ever-increasing population. The only alternative to the Providential checks on the supply of laborers was an increase in demand for labor. He would increase the demand for labor by fixing a minimum wage that would break up the combination of employers.[63] If this were done, he reasoned, wages would return to their natural level and England would escape from the Providential visitation of sword, famine, or pestilence, otherwise necessary to wipe out the surplus labor.

13

All the arguments for the minimum wage left Pitt unconvinced. But he desired to do something to reduce the obvious miseries of the working people. Rather than interfere with wages, he preferred to reform the Poor Laws. In general, his proposed reforms continued the humanitarianism of Thomas Gilbert. Pitt's first desire was to increase the mobility of labor by relaxing the Laws of Settlement and by granting casual outdoor relief. He wished to reward large families by giving relief, as a right, to those having more than two children and to widows with more than one child. He proposed schools of industry to educate the children of the poor. He would repeal the law requiring workers to give up their last shilling of property before obtaining relief, and he would grant occasional relief to people with property worth less than thirty pounds. He also proposed the granting of credit to the poor for the purchase of a cow or other capital which would help them to help themselves. In making these benevolent proposals, Pitt assumed that he was restoring the Elizabethan law to its original purity.[64]

Early in 1796 Pitt printed his Poor Law Reform Bill. Comprehensive in scope and humanitarian in spirit, it attempted so much that it aroused opposition in many quarters.[65] The provisions calling for larger expenditures and greater capital outlays alarmed parish officers who were already overwhelmed by the increasing demands for relief. Confronted with strong opposition, Pitt abandoned his omnibus bill but he did not relinquish his principles nor relax his purpose. The reforms which he had suggested were enacted bit by bit during the next decade, and even after his death his closest friends, as a tribute to his memory, wrote into the law several reforms which he had proposed in 1796.[66]

To overcome the opposition to Pitt's Bill, the Evangelicals organized the Society for Bettering the Condition of the Poor. William Wilberforce took the initiative in the formation of this Society, as he had done on other occasions to promote good causes. An intimate friend of Pitt, Wilberforce was the leader of the Clapham Saints in Parliament and the national leader of the movement to abolish the slave trade.[67] After communicating with his Clapham friends, he invited a group of Evangelicals to meet at his house in December, 1796, to form an organization similar to the Abolitionist Society. The original meeting was summoned by a circular letter signed by Wilberforce, Edward Eliot, and Thomas Bernard. The purpose of the Society, as stated in the letter, was "to remove the difficulties attending parochial relief and the discouragement of industry and economy by the present mode of distributing it, to correct abuses of workhouses, and to assist the poor in placing out their children in the world."[68] To uplift the people morally was the ultimate object set forth: "in proportion as we can multiply domestic comforts in the same degree we can hope to promote the cause of morality and virtue."[69]

Organized after the pattern of a score of Evangelical societies, the new institution had Shute Barrington, the Bishop of Durham, as its President; William Wilberforce as one of its Vice Presidents; and Thomas Bernard as its Secretary and spokesman.[70]

The leader of the new Society, Thomas Bernard, was the son of Sir Thomas Bernard, who had served as colonial Governor of New Jersey and later of Massachusetts. Born in 1750, the younger Thomas Bernard was educated at Harvard College before he began the study of law at Lincoln's Inn. After marrying into a wealthy family, Bernard quit law and devoted the rest of his life to charity. Like Jonas Hanway, he served as treasurer of the Foundling Hospital. As chairman of the Petty Sessions for the Hundred of Stoke in Bucks, he zealously watched over the administration of the Poor Laws.[71]

Who were the poor people to whose welfare Bernard dedicated himself? "We mean by the poor," he said in a charge to the overseers of Stoke, "those who have not the advantage of any profession, trade, property, or income, nor other means of support except their daily labor."[72] What did Bernard expect the overseers to do for the poor? He charged them to be "the guardian and protector of the poor and as such to provide employment for those who can work and relief and support for those who cannot; to place the young in a way of obtaining a livelihood by their industry and to enable the aged to close their labours and their life in peace and comfort." He entreated overseers to educate the young outside the workhouse and warned them against defaulting their duties by farming the poor to contractors. He also exhorted the overseers not to remove laborers lacking a legal settlement, when "all they want is a little temporary relief."[73] Such was the humanitarian spirit of Thomas Bernard and the character of the reforms which he advocated for more than a decade.

Although Bernard and the Society for Bettering the Condition and Increasing the Comfort of the Poor did not prevent the defeat of William Pitt's bill, they took it up piece by piece and helped to enact into law many of its provisions. In its benevolent activities on behalf of Pitt's Bill, the Society met with opposition from the natural law theorists.[74]

One of the ablest and best-informed natural law opponents of Pitt's Bill was Sir Frederick Morton Eden. When he published his three volume history, *The State of the Poor*, he included Pitt's bill, with Howlett's criticism of it, in his appendices. In the preface to his work, which he wrote in December, 1796, he summarily rejected the humanitarian reforms of both Pitt and Gilbert.

The low wages and rising prices of 1795 induced Eden to investigate the condition of the laboring classes. The alarming conditions which he discovered and reported in his three volumes convinced him that the main cause of these bad conditions was the "profusion" of the poor rates.[75]

In his remarkable history, *The State of the Poor*, it was clear that Eden much preferred agriculture to industry and rural labor to urban. Whereas Gilbert's reforms had been designed to apply to rural parishes the efficient management of the urban Guardians, Eden began by denying that the farm worker was worse off than the urban laborer. From what classes do paupers come, he asked; and replied confidently "that paupers, comparatively speaking, are but rarely found among those employed in agriculture. . . ." If manufacturing labor earned higher wages than workers in agriculture, the fair inference seemed to be that it is "the result of that marked favor shown to commerce in preference to the landed interest which many suppose to have long prevailed in our national councils."[76]

Whereas the Evangelicals were determined to abolish the system of contracting the poor, Eden pronounced it "the greatest improvement of modern times" because its reduction of the rates "must be confessed to have been extraordinary." At the same time he pointed out the failures of the incorporated places under the Gilbert Act; he found their houses of industry experiencing "the common fate of all the plans hitherto attempted for the management of the poor. . . ."[77]

Although Eden amassed considerable practical information about the living conditions of the poor, he did not draw all of his conclusions from such information. His condemnation of the Poor Laws was *a priori*; for example, his objections to public provision of employment stemmed from his economic theory. The Elizabethan requirement that the parishes provide employment for the able-bodied, he said, "proceeded from the supposed existence of

16

facts in political economy, which was doubtful at the time, but which experience has since proved to be mistaken. It is a most satisfying circumstance. . .to show that the capital stock of the public cannot enter into competition with the capital and well-exerted industry of individuals. . . ." [78]

Invoking Adam Smith's wages-fund theory, Eden redirected the natural law criticism of the Poor Laws. Previously the principal argument had been against the Law of Settlement, which supposedly immobilized labor. Eden frankly denied that the Poor Laws had restricted the movement of labor. He preferred to argue from the wages-fund theory that all compulsory payments to the poor came from employers' funds available for the payment of wages and for the employment of additional workers. [79] From this doctrinaire position he fired at Pitt's Bill. He even objected to the public provision of education as a calamitous waste of the nation's wealth. The maxim *pas trop gouverner*, he concluded, was fully illustrated by the operation of the Poor Laws, for "the system has insinuated itself into every crack and aperture of the edifice and, like spreading ivy, has at length overshadowed the building that supported it. . . ." Since "the plans and schemes of Poor Laws were costly beyond all calculation," Eden concluded that the only remedy was a definite limit to expenditures, looking forward to the substitution of Friendly Societies for the Poor Laws. "The inveteracy and malignity of the malady has been such that the best medicine had only checked it; a radical and complete cure is within the competency only of the legislature." [80] Eden's natural law remedy for the disease was the substitution of voluntary charity and self-help for the Poor Laws.

While Eden was resisting the Government's measures to improve the conditions of the poor, the prosecution of the war with France increased the inflation that aggravated the miseries of the working classes. Continued deficit spending and the rapid expansion of commercial credit compelled the Government, in 1797, to suspend the payment of specie. [81] When the harvests failed in 1799 and 1800, the nation was again threatened by famine. With the news of a bad harvest the price of wheat rose from 48s. a quarter in 1798 to 79s. in October, 1799. [82] To meet this crisis, the Government again stopped the distilleries, prohibited the exportation of food, and placed bounties on the importation of wheat, flour, and rice. [83]

At this crisis Samuel Whitbread introduced a second bill calling for a minimum wage; and Pitt again refused to accept his measure

17

because "it was legislative interference into that which ought to be allowed to take its natural course."[84]

In the second controversy over the minimum wage, Thomas Bernard produced a tract in support of Pitt's position. He arrayed statistics on the price of wheat and the wages of labor to demonstrate — at least to his own satisfaction — the impossibility of regulating wages in proportion to the price of wheat. According to his estimation, rural wages remained in 1800 at 9s. a week or about at the level of 1780; over the same period of time the quartern loaf of bread rose from 6d. to 1s. 9d. To have increased wages proportionately would have brought them to a level of 25s. per week, a rate far above what Bernard thought manufacturers could afford to pay. He concluded that it was fortunate, indeed, that the price of labor depended upon supply and demand rather than upon "laws and lawgivers."[85]

The famine years brought forth a new natural law opponent of Pitt's Poor Law policy. In 1800 Thomas Robert Malthus wrote a tract, "An Investigation into the Present High Price of Provisions." Having already published his *Essay on Population*, he turned now to apply the principles of population to explain lagging wages and rising prices. The growth of population, he thought, was "the real cause of the continued depression and poverty of the lower classes of society and of the total inadequacy of all the present establishments in their favour to relieve them, and to the periodical return of such seasons of distress as we have of late experienced."[86] Malthus pointed to the Poor Law "allowances in proportion to the price of corn" as the "sole cause which has occasioned the price of provisions to rise so much higher than the degree of scarcity would seem to warrant. . . ."[87]

Only the Government and the grain dealers knew the extent of the dearth in 1799 and the grave threat of starvation that came with another bad harvest in 1800. The price of wheat fluctuated so widely during these years that no guardian or overseer could have granted relief in proportion to the price of bread and have remained solvent. To deal with the famine conditions, the Government appointed a Committee on the High Price of Provisions. Its reports revealed the extent of the famine. During the preceding decade the annual average consumption of wheat had been seven million quarters, and the domestic yields 6.7 million. The Committee estimated the harvest of 1800 as only five million quarters. With so large a deficiency the Government, even if it were able to import more than ever before, would have to find substitutes for wheat bread.[88]

In the House of Commons Dudley Ryder, the Chairman of the Committee on the High Price of Provisions, recommended several of the practices of the Society for Bettering the Conditions of the Poor. The Committee recommended the making of bread from coarse and mixed flour. It encouraged the fishing industry by supplying duty-free salt. These recommendations of the Committee were adopted by the Tory Government to meet the dire threat of famine.[89]

Out of the crisis caused by high prices came the proposal to enumerate the people. Whether population was increasing or decreasing had become a hot political controversy. Believing that the population was declining, the Whigs censured the Tory Government for waging war against a country so powerful and populous as France.[90] To put an end to the controversy, Charles Abbot introduced a census bill. "In times like these," he said, "when the subsistence of the people is in question, this knowledge becomes of the highest importance. It is surely important to know the extent of the demand for which we are to provide a supply."[91] With the assistance of Wilberforce, Abbot's bill became law. The census of 1801, showing a population of about nine million people in England and Wales, seemed to confirm the arguments of those who feared the consequences of an increasing population.

Chief among those fearing the increase in population was the Reverend Thomas Robert Malthus. In 1798 Malthus published *An Essay on the Principle of Population as it Affects the Future Improvement of Society with Remarks on the Speculation of Mr. Godwin, M. Condorcet, and other Writers.* The *Essay* had been written especially to refute William Godwin's optimistic view of social progress. In the preface to his *Essay*, Malthus apologized for a view of life with such a "melancholy hue" but he had held the view because he thought "these dark tints. . .are really in the picture." He further thought that the gloomy picture accounted for "much of that poverty and misery observable among the lower classes of people in every nation and for those reiterated failures in the efforts of the higher classes to relieve them."[92]

When Malthus wrote the *Essay*, he was situated in a country parsonage with only three or four books at hand. Among these was Adam Smith's *The Wealth of Nations*. Malthus developed at length Smith's observation: "Every species of animals naturally multiplies in proportion to the means of their subsistence, and no species can ever multiply beyond it." Malthus also assumed Smith's wages-fund theory. Wages should be naturally determined, Malthus thought, and if the rich paid poor rates they would have less for wages and employment. Although Malthus had derived his principle of population *a priori* before the first census had been taken, he nevertheless confidently applied it to society. In the second edition of his *Essay*, published in 1803, he turned the principle of population against the Poor Laws. Their first obvious tendency, he said, is to increase the population without increasing the food for its support; since the Poor Laws encourage early marriage, "they may be said to create the poor which they maintain." [93]

The bold and sweeping attacks of Eden and Malthus upon the Poor Laws threw the humanitarian reformers on the defensive. To meet the new criticism, greater factual information was needed. Acting with his customary prudence and caution, George Rose, who had helped to initiate the first census of population, called for an inquiry into the Poor Laws. Complying with his request, Parliament ordered in 1803 the fifteen thousand parishes and places to return information relating to the conditions of the poor. A careful administrator, Rose requested information directly bearing on policy. Always interested in the welfare of the Friendly Societies, he inquired about the number of such Societies and the number of their members. Seeking a clue to the mobility of labor, he asked how many persons were relieved occasionally and how many of those relieved were without a legal residence. Desiring more light on Gilbert's policy of encouraging outdoor relief, Rose asked for the number of people permanently relieved inside and outside the workhouses; and how many of those permanently relieved were aged, infirm, or children. His systematic investigation supplied more information on the operation of the Poor Laws than had ever been available before — knowledge accurate enough to correct some of the misrepresentations of the natural law reformers.

Neither an eloquent speaker nor a fluent writer, Rose spoke in the House of Commons briefly and rarely, but as a devoted civil servant he wrote occasional tracts, based upon Treasury statistics, to inform members of Parliament and to refute the criticism of Pitt's policies. His knowledge of the growing national wealth gave him the optimism of a prosperous businessman, and his optimism sustained the less sanguine Pitt during the dark years of war and famine.[94] With similar optimism, Rose produced a tract, based upon the Poor Law Returns of 1803, to defend Pitt's Poor Law policy. In considerable detail he answered the criticisms of Malthus and Eden, both of whom had advocated a total, though gradual, abolition of the Poor Laws. Malthus had recommended that no child born a year after the enactment of his reform be given relief. Eden had proposed to substitute the self-help of Friendly Societies for compulsory relief. Although opposed by able critics, Rose defended the Elizabethan system as coming from the "wisest councils. . .in any period of our history." If the lapse of time and the progressive improvement of the country might call for changes in detail, "yet it is believed the general principles are still founded in wisdom and its regulations suited to the unvarying rules of human nature and the ordinary course of political society."[95]

Somewhat disturbed by the increase in Poor Law expenditures, Rose compared the growth of expenditures with the increase in population and the rise in the cost of living. Moreover, he was aware that the "fluctuations in manufactures, risks attendant on trade. . .must reduce many to indigence." By the Returns of 1803, he also attempted to refute the charge of "profusion" and to correct the misinformation about the increase in poor rates. That there were hardships in certain parishes Rose did not deny, but he knew that many cases of hardship were due to low assessments. By the Returns of 1803 he was able to show that the rated rentals were generally three-fourths, or less, of the actual rentals. From the returns made to the Tax Office (on which national taxes were based), Rose calculated the actual rate in the pound as 2s. 10d.[96]

The Returns of 1803 showed the success of Gilbert's policy of transforming the workhouses from places of employing the able-bodied to residences for children, the aged, and infirm. By 1803 most of the workhouses had become mere poorhouses. Of more than a million recipients of relief, only eighty-three thousand received assistance indoors, and although 3,765 places reported having workhouses, they had spent less than fifty thousand pounds on the purchase of materials to put people to work. The contract system, which had been widespread before Gilbert's reforms, had been abandoned in all but 293 places.[97]

The Returns of 1803 encouraged Pitt and subsequent Tory Governments to continue the humanitarian reforms of the Poor Laws. Subsequent reforms increased the policy of granting outdoor relief to the able-bodied poor.[98] Finding the contract system still in

21

existence, the humanitarian reformers struck another blow at it in 1805 by requiring the contractor to be a resident of the parish where the poor were maintained, to have his contract approved by two Justices, and to give security that the provisions of the contract would be fulfilled.[99]

The death of Pitt in 1806 did not put an end to the humanitarian reform of the Poor Law. When Samuel Whitbread introduced his Poor Law Bill in 1807, Sir Thomas Bernard censured him for proposing reforms less benevolent than those of Pitt's bill. At the same time, he approved of the provisions which were common to both bills. Bernard approved of boarding infants with friends or relatives rather than maintaining them in workhouses. He approved of allowing occasional relief to laborers without dispossessing them of their small property, and he specified that such relief should not be restricted to times of sickness. Pitt had recommended in 1796 the rewarding of families who reared more than two children, and Bernard preferred this provision to Whitbread's proposal to reward families having reared six or more children to the age of fourteen. It is clear from Bernard's letter to the Bishop of Durham that the Society for Bettering the Condition of the Poor was still seeking in 1807 to enact the benevolent reforms that Pitt had recommended ten years earlier.[100]

The conflict between the Evangelicals and the natural law reformers extended even to the detailed administration of the Poor Laws. Nearly all the reforms from 1782 to 1800 had been designed to increase the authority of the magistrates over the parish officers. The natural law reformers, on the other hand, preferred the parsimony of the overseers to the benevolence of the magistrates, whom they pictured as warm-hearted, seeking to do good, but not alert to the long-run consequences of their "profusion." Undoubtedly, both groups of reformers, in their eagerness to justify their particular reforms, exaggerated the benevolence of the magistrates and the parsimony of the overseers.

That a system so comprehensive as the Elizabethan Poor Laws collided again and again with the tough mind of avarice should be readily conceded. The critics of the Poor Laws, conscious of paying the costs, were always more articulate than the working classes who derived benefit from them. It was fortunate for the English working classes that the Evangelical reformers advocated their welfare and ameliorated some of the harsh conditions of the Poor Laws. At a time of rapid industrialization, the humanitarian reforms made it easier for the workers to move to places of employment and be more secure in their new residence. The granting of outdoor relief to the sick and to large families lessened somewhat the harsh conditions during the years of wartime inflation. Although the benevolent reforms mitigated conditions somewhat, they also serve to emphasize the enormous amount of misery which the working people endured during the period of the French Wars.

NOTES

[1] Sidney and Beatrice Webb, *English Local Government: English Poor Law History:* Part I: *The Old Poor Law* (1927), VII, 54. The statute, 43 Elizabeth I, c. 2, established the Old Poor Law system which lasted to 1834.

[2] Dorothy Marshall, *The English Poor in the Eighteenth Century* (1926), p. 22.

[3] Sir George Nicholls, *A History of the English Poor Law*, 2nd ed. (1898) II, 15. The first edition of this famous history appeared in 1854. The principal historians of the Old Poor Laws, Nicholls, Marshall, and the Webbs, have looked at the Evangelical reformers through the unsympathetic eyes of the natural law and Radical reformers. Nicholls, of course, was hostile to the Old Poor Law and to the Evangelicals who had reformed it. Dorothy Marshall, who emphasizes the early eighteenth century, gives little attention to the later decades. The Webbs, in their haste to reach the Radical reforms of 1834, call the period from 1792 to 1832, "a generation of legislative failure" (vol. VIII, 32).

[4] Patrick Colquhoun, *A Treatise on Indigence* (1906), p. 7. Nicholls, vol. II, p. 24, distinguishes poverty and indigence: Poverty is "the state of one who in order to obtain a mere subsistence is forced to have recourse to labor." The indigent were those who received charity. Thomas Bernard, the Secretary of the Society for Bettering the Condition of the Poor uses *the poor* interchangeably with the *working classes*. See his *Letter to the Bishop of Durham*. (1807).

[5] A famous statement of this doctrine is Bernard de Mandeville, *The Fable of the Bees* (1714). This work was reprinted in 1793. "The poor have nothing to stir them up but their wants which is wisdom to relieve but folly to cure." Adam Smith differed somewhat: "It is but equity, besides, that they who feed, clothe and lodge the whole body of people should have a share of the produce of their own labor as to be themselves tolerably well fed, clothed, and lodged." *The Wealth of Nations* (ed. by Edwin Caunan, Modern Library, 1937), p. 79.

[6] In my book, *The Politics of English Dissent*, I have analyzed the religious aspect of these Evangelical reform movements.

[7] William Wilberforce, *A Practical View of the Prevailing Religious System* (1797) and Thomas Gisborne, *Enquiry into the Duties of Men in the Higher and Middle Classes* (1794) are the two most influential Evangelical works of this period. Both Wilberforce and Gisborne wished to revive a sense of responsibility among the upper classes as well as to uplift morally the lower classes.

[8] John Harold Hutchins, *Jonas Hanway, 1712-1786* (New York, Columbia University Press, 1940) is a useful study of Hanway's career.

[9] John Pugh, *Remarkable Occurrences in the Life of Jonas Hanway* (1787).

[10] 2 Geo. III, c. 22. Also, Hanway, *Serious Considerations on the Salutary Design of the Act of Parliament for a Regular, Uniform Register of the Parish Poor* (1762).

[11] 7 Geo. III, c. 39. Also, Hanway, *An Earnest Appeal for Mercy to the Children of the Poor Particularly those Belonging to the Parishes within the Bills of Mortality. . .* (1766).

[12] George L. Phillips, *England's Climbing Boys* (Cambridge, Mass., Harvard University Press, 1949).

[13] There is no adequate study of Thomas Gilbert's many benevolent activities. For my knowledge of him, I have depended mainly upon his four tracts on the Poor Laws.

[14] *Gentlemen's Magazine* (1798), Pt. II, pp. 1090, 1146.

[15] Thomas Gilbert, *Plan for the Better Relief and Employment of the Poor . . .* (1781), p. 2. Hereafter cited as *Plan* (1781).

[16] *Gentlemen's Magazine* (1798), Pt. II, p. 1146.

[17] Gilbert, *Plan* (1781), pp. 4-7.

[18] *Ibid.*, p. 18.

[19] 23 Geo. III, c. 51.

[20] Gilbert, *Plan* (1781), p. 18.

[21] 22 Geo. III, c. 83. See S. and B. Webb, vol. VII, p. 151 and Marshall, *op. cit.*, p. 159 for expositions of the law. The Poor Law historians recognize the humanitarianism of the Gilbert Act. The Webbs call it "the most influential for both good and evil" of all the scores of statutes between 1601 and 1834. Vol. VII, p. 171. But later say "for years it scarcely worked at all." Under the Act of 1782, 67 unions were formed comprising 924 parishes. Vol. VII, p. 275.

[22] Gilbert was familiar with the Poor Law Unions established in Norfolk and Suffolk. The Webbs have treated these in their study of *Statutory Authorities*, pp. 121-37.

[23] 26 Geo. III, c. 56.

[24] Thomas Gilbert, *Considerations on the Bills for the Better Relief and Employment of the Poor. . .Intended to be offered to Parliament this Session* (1787).

[25] *Parliamentary History*, XXVI, 266.

[26] Joseph Townsend, *Dissertation on the Poor Laws* (1785), p. 35.

[27] *Ibid.*, p. 51.

[28] Townsend, *Observations on Various Plans Offered to the Public for the Relief of the Poor* (1788), pp. 4-10.

[29] *Gentlemen's Magazine*, 1819, p. 529.

[30] J. Holland Rose, *William Pitt and National Revival* (1911), p. 286.

[31] G. F. Vernon-Harcourt, ed., *The Diaries and Correspondence of the Right Hon. George Rose* (1860), II, 505-18.

[32] *Parliamentary History*, XXVI, 1062.

[33] *Ibid.*, 1280.

[34] 33 Geo. III, c. 54.

[35] George Rose, *Observations on the Act for the Relief and Encouragement of Friendly Societies* (1794), p. 10.

[36] *Abstract of Returns Relative to the Expense and Maintenance of the Poor* (1804), p. 715.

[37] *Abstract of Returns Relative to the Expense and Maintenance of the Poor* (1818), p. 629.

[38] *Report from the Select Committee on the Laws Respecting Friendly Societies* (1825), p. 8.

[39] Rose, *Diaries*, II, 525.

[40] 35 Geo. III, c. 101. This law partly circumvented the old statute, 13 and 14 Car. II, c. 12, which had empowered the parishes to remove persons lacking a lawful residence.

[41] Adam Smith, p. 135. Howlett and Eden did not think that the laws of Settlement had immobilized labor.

[42] 49 Geo. III, c. 124. Nicholls, II, 142, says: "This was a humane provision and calculated to prevent great hardship."

[43] 36 Geo. III, c. 23. "An Act to Amend so much of an Act made in the ninth year of George I. . .as prevents the occasional relief to poor persons in their own houses. . . ."

[44] J. Holland Rose, *Pitt and Napoleon: Essays and Letters* (1912), p. 84, felt obliged to apologize for Pitt's weakness in giving aid to the "industrious poor."

[45] This Act of 1795 had no connection with the "Speenhamland system," as the Hammonds supposed in *The Village Labourer*, pp. 162-64. "Speenhamland" is not to be found in the literature for the next two decades, other than the journalistic account in F. M. Eden's, *The State of the Poor*. The Assistant Commissioners of 1832 were instructed to identify the origins of the practice, but they were unable to do so. (This point will be treated at length in Chapters IX and X.) Working independently, Poynter and I have reached similar conclusions about "Speenhamland". J. R. Poynter, *Society and Pauperism* (1969), p. 78. In this connection, it should be remembered that William Pitt, in the debates with Samuel Whitbread, objected to the magistrates' fixing a minimum wage because he thought the price of bread was not an adequate index of real wages.

[46] 43 Geo. III, c. 47. See Nicholls, II, 135.

[47] 55 Geo. III, c. 137.

[48] *Abstract of Returns* (1804), p. 716. For an analysis of the statistics on the indigent population of 1803, see J. D. Marshall, *The Old Poor Law, 1795-1834* (1968), pp. 54-55. After the Returns for the years 1813-1815, there was no census taken of the pauper host, but thereafter an annual accounting of expenditures was made.

[49] Rose, *Observations of Friendly Societies*, pp. 10-15.

[50] *Parliamentary History*, XXXII, 709.

[51] *Ibid.*, 710.

[52] Asa Briggs, *The Age of Improvement* (1959), chapter III.

[53] *Parliamentary History*, XXXII, 235.

[54] *Ibid.*, 690.

[55] 36 Geo. III, c. 20.

[56] 36 Geo. III, c. 10.

[57] 22 Geo. III, c. 83.

[58] 42 Geo. III, c. 74. The law applied only to incorporated places.

[59] *Parlimentary History*, XXXII, 239.

[60] *Ibid.*, 701-3.

[61] *Ibid.*, 706.

[62] John Howlett, *Examination of Mr. Pitt's Speech. . .Relative to the Condition of the Poor* (1796), p. 2.

[63] *Ibid.*, 21.

[64] *Parliamentary History*, XXXII, 707-9.

[65] George Rose, *Observations on Banks for Savings* (1816), p. 2.

[66] Thomas Bernard, *A Letter to the Bishop of Durham. . . .* (1807), p. 60.

[67] J. H. Rose, *William Pitt and the National Revival*, 294, and R. Coupland, *Wilberforce* (1923), pp. 257-64.

[68] Society for Bettering the Condition and Increasing the Comforts of the Poor, *Reports*, Fifth Edition (1805), I, 390.

[69] James Baker, *The Life of Sir Thomas Bernard* (1819), p. 17.

[70] *Reports*, I, 4.

[71] George Jacob Holyoake, *Self-Help A Hundred Years Ago* (1888), pp. 14-15.

[72] *Reports*, I, 381.

[73] *Ibid.*, 387.

[74] Bernard, *Letter to the Bishop of Durham* (1807), pp. 60-62.

[75] Frederick Morton Eden, *The State of the Poor* (3 vols., 1797), I, 580.

[76] *Ibid.*, I, ix.

[77] *Ibid.*, I, v.

[78] *Ibid.*, I, 586.

[79] For Adam Smith's wages-fund theory, see *The Wealth of Nations*, p. 69.

[80] Eden, *op. cit.*, I, p. xxv.

[81] Thomas Tooke, *A History of Prices* (1838), p. 213. See also Arthur D. Gayer, W. W. Rostow and Anna J. Schwartz, *The Growth and Fluctuation of the British Economy, 1790-1850* (2 vols., 1953), I, 54.

[82] The peak of 136 shillings was reached in July, 1800. See the *First Reports of the Committee to Consider the High Price of Provision* (1800), pp. 9-10.

[83] *Parliamentary History*, XXXV, 791.

[84] *Ibid.*, 1439.

[85] Society for Bettering the Condition of the Poor, *Reports*, V, 154-57.

[86] Malthus, *An Investigation of the Present High Price of Provisions* (1800), p. 27.

[87] *Ibid.*, pp. 4-5.

[88] *Parliamentary History*, XXXV, 825.

[89] 41 Geo. III, c. 12.

[90] *Parliamentary History*, XXXI, 1354.

[91] *Ibid.*, XXV, 598.

[92] Malthus, *Essay* (2nd ed., 1803), p. III.

[93] *Ibid.*, p. 410.

[94] Rose, *A Brief Examination into the Increase of the Revenue, Commerce and Manufactures of Great Britain from 1792 to 1799* (1799).

[95] George Rose, *Observations on the Poor Laws and on the Management of the Poor* (1805), p. 1.

[96] *Ibid.*, p. 41.

[97] *Abstract of Returns* (1804), p. 716.

[98] 50 Geo. III, c. 50.

[99] 45 Geo. III, c. 54.

[100] Bernard, *Letter to the Bishop of Durham*, pp. 60-62.

II

THE GROWTH OF NATURAL LAW OPPOSITION

DURING the difficult years of the Napoleonic War, the policies affecting the welfare of the working classes, as we have seen in the previous chapter, were established by the humanitarian reformers. While the humanitarians were occupied with the amelioration of the Poor Laws, the natural law reformers were steadily adding weapons to their formidable arsenal of opposition. When the wars against France came to an end in 1815, they were fully prepared to open their attack upon Pitt's benevolent system of social welfare.

The increasing strength of the natural law reformers, in terms of their ability to command public attention, was evident during the controversy over Samuel Whitbread's bill to reform the Poor Laws. As a leader of the Whigs in the House of Commons, Whitbread had assumed responsibility for those measures affecting the welfare of the working classes. On two occasions during Pitt's ministries, he proposed a minimum wage as the proper answer to the wartime problems of increasing prices and lagging wages. A constant advocate of the welfare of the working classes, he had acquired a reputation for philanthropy. It was indeed unfortunate that Whitbread was unable to improve the conditions of the lower classes at a time when the humanitarians, under the leadership of Wilberforce, were successfully abolishing the slave trade.

When Samuel Whitbread introduced his comprehensive bill in 1807, he promised to make the Poor Laws obsolete in fifty years by enabling the lower classes to help themselves.[1] His primary means of achieving this goal was public support for education. While there was general agreement among several groups of reformers on the need of education, there was little agreement as to the kind of education that should be given. Reformers also agreed as to the benefit of savings banks, but they differed on how to organize such institutions.

Whitbread incorporated in his Poor Law bill some of the reforms which had long been advocated by the Evangelical humanitarians. From the time Pitt had first introduced his bill, his friends advocated the allotment of funds to build cottages for farm workers and to provide them with a small plot of ground for a garden and a cow. The natural law reformers, however, were strongly opposed to this provision. They firmly held that such public expenditures of capital were wasteful, and that public expenditures could never be as efficient as private expenditures of capital. On the same grounds, they objected to Whitbread's provision for public works to aid the unemployed.

Although Whitbread was primarily seeking the humanitarian reform of the Poor Laws, he was willing to make concessions to the natural law reformers. With respect to Poor Law administration, he preferred to restrict the authority of the magistrates and to increase the power of the parish vestry and the overseers. While professing to uphold the Poor Laws, he criticized them in the language of the natural law reformers when he declared that the Poor Laws aggravated the disease which they were designed to remedy. He also assumed the natural law doctrine of acceleration, namely, that every grant made to the poor increased the demand for relief. Whitbread's defense of his bill makes it clear that by 1807 new arguments had entered into the debates on the Poor Laws. By this time there was little anxiety that the Laws of Settlement would immobilize labor, which had been the main concern of the reformers ten years earlier. Moreover, the reformers had to accommodate their arguments to the population principles of Malthus, whereas ten years earlier Pitt had to accommodate his arguments only to the free trade principles of Adam Smith.

"One philosopher has arisen among us," Whitbread declared, "who has gone deeply into the causes of the present situation. I mean Mr. Malthus. His work, I believe, has been generally read; and it has completed that change in opinion with regard to the Poor Law. . . . I have studied the work of this author with as much attention as I am capable of bestowing upon any subject. I am desirous of doing justice to the principles on which he proceeds. I believe them to be incontrovertible. But in many of the conclusions to which he comes, I materially differ with him."[2]

Whitbread's tribute to Malthus was both a recognition of the growing prestige of the natural law reformers and a confession of the weak position of the Evangelicals who could offer only sentiment or expediency in opposition to principle. Whitbread should have learned from his earlier defeat that he could not abandon principles with impunity. His earlier concession, that prices should generally be left to find their own level, had weakened his case for a minimum wage. His present concession, that the Poor Laws were contrary to Malthus's "incontrovertible principle," weakened his case for ameliorating the conditions of the working classes.

The natural law reformers continually reproached the humanitarians as "soft-headed men of good intentions." Whitbread tried to anticipate their scornful retort by declaring: "I am no visionary enthusiast, seeking after universal perfection. I know the laws of God to be immutable. . . . I believe man to be born to labor as the sparks to fly upwards; and that all the plans for lodging, clothing, and feeding mankind. . . . are quite impossible in practice." While rejecting the labels of "utopian" and "enthusiast," Whitbread attempted to show that Malthus's principles, although incontrovertible, did not apply to England. He would not admit Malthus's contention that the misery of the working classes arose from a redundant population. "After the most anxious and patient research into the state of society in these kingdoms. . .," he said, "I believe the situation of the lower and more useful classes to be better in every respect than in former times."[3]

Whitbread did not charge Malthus with brutality even though he recognized that the abolition of the Poor Laws, as Malthus recommended for the able-bodied, would be exceedingly brutal. Knowing that the Parliament would refuse to enact a law denying relief to any child born a year after the adoption of such a reform, Whitbread warned against the dangers of Malthus's principle of population: "I believe the design and intention of the author to be most benevolent. . . I think any man who reads them ought to place a strict guard over his heart, lest in learning that vice and misery must of necessity maintain a footing in the world, he give up all attempt at their subjugation."[4]

Malthus promptly replied to Whitbread's speech which warned against the consequences of the principle of population. The ostensible purpose of Malthus's letter to Whitbread, written on March 27, 1807, was a defense of his own character. The charge of cruelty, coming from a member of Parliament, "can not but give me pain," but "to those who know me I feel that I have no occasion to defend my character from the imputation of hardness of heart." [5] The central purpose of the letter, however, was to remonstrate against the proposal to use parish rates for building more cottages. The building of more cottages, according to Malthus, was the most dangerous reform of the Poor Laws that had been proposed. He argued that the Poor Laws tended to increase the population and that they had not done so was due to the lack of cottages. If more cottages were built, he thought, "we should soon see the proportion (of births and marriages to the whole population) increase to a much greater degree and the increase in population would render the condition of the independent poor absolutely helpless." [6]

Malthus also strongly objected to Whitbread's plan to tax personal property, especially the capital of tradesmen and manufacturers, because he feared the spiraling effects of increasing the funds available for relief. Above all else, he wished to see the working classes self-respecting and independent of public relief. If the laborers were not prudent and sufficiently disciplined to restrain their passions, they would continue to multiply their numbers and aggravate their own miseries. [7]

It is doubtful that Malthus's letter had a decisive influence, for many Poor Law reformers were already familiar with his *Essay on the Principle of Population*. In the midst of war Parliament had little inclination to adopt any extensive measure that would transform domestic institutions. Hopeful of making some progress in the amelioration of social conditions, Whitbread divided his original plan into four parts, separating general education from poor relief. His bill to provide national education passed the House of Commons, only to be rejected in the House of Lords because it had proposed to take education out of the hands of the National Church. [8] Since the Whigs were badly divided on the question of poor relief and too weak to remain in office, the question of reforming the Poor Laws reverted to the Tory followers of William Pitt, who continued the social policy which he set forth in his bill of 1796.

The controversy evoked by Whitbread's bill revealed the humanitarians' inability to refute Malthus. The most systematic attempt to refute the principle of population was made by John Weyland. A magistrate in the counties of Oxford, Berks, and Surrey and a member of the Board of Agriculture, he was well-acquainted with the operations of the Poor Laws. In 1807 he published his tract, *A Short Inquiry into the Policy, Humanity and Past Effects of the Poor Laws*, in which he defended the Poor Laws on the grounds of Biblical teachings. During the same year he also published his *Observations on Mr. Whitbread's Poor Bill. . . .*, in which he praised Whitbread for using his talents "to the disinterested purposes of philanthropy."[9]

At the same time, Weyland denounced Malthus's principle of population as "utterly subversive of this country and the moral and political welfare of its inhabitants." He was confident that Malthus's principles "are themselves visionary and contradicting to the usual and acknowledged laws of Providence."[10] Where Malthus had explained the increase of misery in terms of a redundant population, Weyland was content merely to reply that "a redundant population is necessary to our welfare." Weyland's tract apparently had little influence beyond the narrow circle of Evangelicals who were content to appeal to Biblical teachings and their practical knowledge of the utility of the Poor Laws.

The failure of the Evangelicals to refute Malthus in 1807 was manifested by Sir Thomas Bernard's letter to the Bishop of Durham, and to the members of the Society for Bettering the Condition of the Poor. As spokesman for the Society, Bernard approved of Whitbread's bill but objected to the provisions which were less generous than those in Pitt's original bill. He went on to suggest that Whitbread should have attended "to all points of Mr. Pitt's bills" and thus have perpetuated "our gratitude to the memory of the greatest statesman this country has ever possessed."[11]

Even while defending Pitt's humanitarian reform of the Poor Laws, Sir Thomas Bernard was making concessions to Malthus's principle of population. Professing to reject "remote and metaphysical calculations of consequences," he nevertheless accepted Malthus's doctrine that the Poor Laws tended to encourage a redundant population. "Political wisdom should never forget," he wrote, "that if these habitations (parish cottages for the poor) were supplied in full extent, a vicious injurious population would ensue. I am far from presuming to contravene the primary com-

31

mand, 'Be fruitful and multiply'. But there is such a thing as forcing an extraordinary population that leads to nothing but vice and misery."[12]

The fatal Malthusian pessimism, that the Poor Laws aggravated the misery which they were designed to remedy, began to take possession of some Evangelicals. The Christian's willingness to accept Malthus can best be understood in terms of theology. Evangelicals among both Churchmen and Dissenters held the belief that the present life was a place of trial, a probation for a better future life. If passion between the sexes, like original sin, brought upon man the retribution of plagues, wars, famines, and death, he could escape from this divine punishment through moral discipline.

Malthus's *Essay on the Principle of Population* was heavy with connotations for the Christian theologian and the preacher of stern morality. In the first place, Malthus was careful to accommodate his principle of population to Biblical teaching by insisting that there was no conflict between the natural law of population and the moral law of the Bible. The moral law of the Bible, a particular and subsequent revelation, he held, supplemented but did not contravene the original and universal revelation of nature. The moral man, Malthus insisted, should obey the revelations of God in nature as well as the revelations of the Bible. The moral man could comply with the principle of population, which was God's natural law, by practicing prudence and foresight. Exercising prudence, a man should postpone marriage until he could afford to support a family; exercising foresight, he could save a part of his income to provide for the misfortunes of accident, sickness, and old age. Malthus thus gave to the Christian theologian a new commandment to keep and a new set of morals to teach. He enabled the preacher to dramatize daily living as a moral struggle in which man could escape from poverty and social degradation.

Malthus did more than provide the theologian with a new commandment. He restored to the Christian church the primary responsibility for charity. The Christian preacher admonished that it was a blessing to give as well as to receive. As a result of such preaching, there were Christians ready to believe that the Poor Laws, which made charity compulsory, interfered with their religious duties. The Evangelical Christians, in particular, found in Malthus's principle of population a justification for the multitude of voluntary agencies which they had designed for the education and the improvement of the working classes.

It is well known that Malthus employed the principle of population to refute Godwin's egualitarianism, but it is not so well known that he turned the principle against the Christian Evangelicals who were seeking to reform the Poor Laws. Malthus objected to nearly all the humanitarian reforms on the grounds that they tended to increase an already redundant population and so to multiply misery and vice. In his attack upon the Evangelicals, he first refuted the theological criticism of his principle of population. "The first great objection that has been made of my principles," he said, "is that they contradict the original command of the Creator to increase and multiply and replenish the earth." To this objection he replied as follows: "I am fully of the opinion that it is the duty of man to obey this command of his Creator. . . . Every express command which is given to man is given in subordination to those great and uniform laws of nature, which he had previously established; and we are forbidden both by reason and religion to expect that these will be changed in order to enable us to execute more readily any particular precept."[13] Such was the argument by which Malthus, to his own satisfaction and apparently to the satisfaction of other theologians, removed the conflict between the moral laws of the Bible and the natural laws of science.

Malthus did more than refute the theological critics of his *Essay*, for he was earnestly concerned with the application of its principles to the Poor Laws. Convinced that England had reached the state of a redundant population, he was eager to reduce the number of working-class people who were already pressing beyond the means of subsistence. He was also convinced that he had a scientific explanation of the increasing misery of the working classes and that the misery could be lessened only by a drastic reform of the Poor Laws. He therefore scrutinized each humanitarian proposal to reform the Poor Laws, approving or disapproving in terms of the principle of population.

When remonstrating with the Evangelicals, whom he professed to esteem, he insisted upon the application of general principles to the improvement of social conditions. Practical reformers, however benevolent, were often poor theorists, and Malthus explained at length why practical men should not be trusted with the reform of the Poor Laws. "When a man relates faithfully the facts of his experience, he adds to the sum of knowledge; but when from a limited experience, he draws a general inference, he at once erects himself into a theorist and is dangerous, for many people fail to understand that partial experience is an inadequate basis for theory." [14]

Malthus did not hesitate to rebuke Sir Thomas Bernard, William Wilberforce, and other distinguished members of the Society for Bettering the Condition of the Poor. While conceding that Bernard and the members of his Society were aware of the difficulties of relieving the poor, he pointed out that they had made the error "of drawing general inferences from insufficient experience." [15] Although his rebuke was gentle, he made it clear that he thought the benevolent members of the Society were very bad theorists and their proposed reforms of the Poor Laws most inadequate.

Sir Thomas Bernard and other Evangelical reformers had supported William Pitt's plan of granting capital to build cottages on waste land for agricultural laborers. Arthur Young, after his religious conversion, was an advocate of this plan. Against the plan Malthus raised the following objection: Assuming that a farmer built additional cottages, "his laborers will live in plenty and be able to rear up larger families and the farmer would soon have more laborers than he needed." [16]

We have seen already that Jonas Hanway, one of the earliest and most influential of the Evangelical reformers, had devoted his efforts to the Foundling Hospital of London. In retrospect it seems strange to find Malthus objecting in principle to both foundling and lying-in hospitals. "Foundling hospitals. . .in every view," he said, "are hurtful to the state." [17] Such institutions were objectionable, he believed, because they encouraged early marriage and large families. He further believed that such institutions weakened family ties by lessening the father's responsibility for rearing his children. [18]

If such Evangelical writers as Hanway and Bernard supplied the humanitarian motivation for ameliorating the conditions of the working classes, Count Rumford's experiments with the dietary habits of the working classes of Munich provided them with the practical knowledge of how to improve the people's health. Under the leadership of the Evangelicals of the Church at Clapham and the Quakers of London, the humanitarians sought to improve the people's diet by subsidizing the importation of fish, the planting of potatoes, and the sale of cheap cuts of meat. In order to increase the supply of fish, they conducted a campaign to reduce or abolish the salt tax. In times of famine they established kitchens where wholesome soups could be bought at prices less than the cost of the ingredients. During the emergency of 1799 and 1800, their object was to save people from starvation, but beyond this they intended to improve the people's diet according to the information disseminated by Count Rumford.

Malthus had serious misgivings about Count Rumford's experimenting with the people's diet. Although he readily allowed that potatoes and soups, "as occasional resources," might prevent famine, he did not wish to see such a diet universally adopted by the poor, for then the price of labor would be regulated by cheap food. "The desirable thing is, with a view to the happiness of the common people, that their habitual food should be dear and their wages regulated by it; but in a scarcity, or other occasional distress, the cheaper food should be readily and cheerfully adopted."[19]

A charitable man himself, Malthus opposed the social reforms of the most distinguished philanthropists of his time because he was completely confident that the principle of population afforded the scientific basis for social policy. Yet he did not wish to see his principle used to discourage charity, for he knew of cases "in which the good resulting from the relief of the present distress may more than overbalance the evils to be apprehended from the remote consequences." He did not object to relieving occasional distress "not arising from idle and improvident habits," but he earnestly resisted "that kind of systematic and certain relief on which the poor can confidently depend, whatever may be their conduct. . . ." Hence, it followed that the "systematic and certain relief," as provided by the Poor Laws, was worse in consequence than the evil which it remedied.[20]

That the poor had no legal claim on society for relief or employment was a position carefully taken and closely guarded by Malthus. "Our laws indeed say that he has this right and bind society to furnish employment and food to those who cannot get them in the regular market; but in so doing they attempt to reverse the laws of nature; and it is in consequence to be expected, not only that they should fail in their object, but that the poor who were intended to be benefited, should suffer most cruelly from the inhuman deceit that is practised upon them."[21]

Malthus's continuous exhortation that the laws of nature are the laws of God persuaded some Evangelicals to accept his principle of population as a Providential discipline for the working classes. Not only did the Evangelicals come to abandon their earlier reform of the Poor Laws, but they also accepted as "scientific philanthropy" the Christian doctrine of charity.

Apart from the reform of the Poor Laws, there was no slackening of Christian philanthropy during the Napoleonic War. The voluntary agencies for the redemption of mankind, morally and physically, seemed to multiply at a Malthusian rate. There were societies to abolish slavery and the slave trade, societies to reform prisons and the penal laws, societies to suppress vice, blasphemy, and sedition. Missionary, tract, and Bible societies carried the message of salvation to the ends of the Empire. The British and Foreign School Society and the National Society, which were established to educate the poor, supplanted the earlier Society for Bettering the Condition of the Poor. If the Evangelicals were losing confidence in the direct relief of poverty, they were doubling their efforts to help the poor to help themselves by means of education.

The Christian philanthropists did not slacken their efforts during those difficult years when Napoleon's commercial blockade of the Continent threatened England with starvation. England's countermeasures, the Orders in Council, further blocking the flow of goods, seriously curtailed such industries as cotton and iron and caused many business failures and widespread unemployment.[22] In addition to the stagnation of trade, the poor harvests of 1810 and 1811 brought the nation again to the brink of famine. During the severe crisis of 1799 and 1800, the Government had acted promptly to subsidize the importation of grain, to curtail the distillation of grain, and to encourage the substitution of other food, especially fish and potatoes, for bread. Although the Government of 1811 was equally aware of the extent of distress, it would not undertake relief measures other than providing loans to businesses about to become bankrupt. Upon receiving a petition from forty thousand unemployed cotton workers of Manchester, a committee of the House of Commons recommended that there be no interference with the freedom of trade nor with the liberty of the individual to dispose of his labor according to his own interests.[23]

While the Government was meeting economic distress by suppressing the Luddite frame-breakers, the Evangelicals organized relief in London and elsewhere to supply the workers with food. Returning to the relief method originally recommended by the Society for Bettering the Condition of the Poor, the philanthropists of London first encouraged the substitution of rice and fish for wheat bread. They reorganized the Spitalfields Soup Society to feed hundreds of families in the slums of East London. The Society bought meat and barley at wholesale prices, made soup of these and other ingredients, and sold the soup at a penny a quart. During the severe winter of 1811 and 1812, the Society fed as many as seven thousand persons daily.[24]

As the distress increased among the working classes, the Soup Society expanded its activities by organizing the Spitalfields Association for the Relief of the Industrious Poor. With the financial help of commercial companies, bankers, and merchants of the City, the Spitalfields Association bought supplies of fish and rice and sold them at less than the market price. They provided relief for the working classes in the Metropolitan area, which included Bethal Green, Shoreditch, a part of Whitechapel, and the hamlets of Mile End New Town and Mile End Old Town. Many of the residents of these places were employed in the silk industry, which had been badly depressed by the Napoleonic blockade. Other workers, who were employed in the docks, had come into the area to find cheap housing. The consequent rise of the slum made the Poor Laws ineffective. A member of the Spitalfields Association, Thomas Fowell Buxton, observed that the Poor Laws were no longer adequate to meet the needs of the changing industrial conditions of the Metropolis. "The City," he said, "had the man so long as he could work; the country had him when he could not. Spitalfields was the drain for the distresses of the Capital — a kind of metropolitan workhouse, to which all that is wretched resorts." [25]

Alert to the inadequacy of the Poor Laws to relieve the misery during the years of scarcity, the London Evangelicals further expanded their activities in 1812 by organizing the Association for the Relief and Benefit of the Manufacturing Poor. This third relief organization, broader in scope than the earlier agencies which it supplemented but did not supplant, had the primary purpose of encouraging the formation of local associations in other parts of the kingdom. The London Association granted financial help to fifty-two communities to initiate local relief associations. The London Association also undertook the procurement of a greater quantity of fish by agreeing to buy the entire catch if the price should fall below a profitable level. As a result of these voluntary relief measures, suffering was mitigated during the winter of 1812.[26]

Fortunately for the working classes, the good harvest of 1812 and the relaxation of trade restrictions brought a return of prosperity in 1813 and lessened the need for the special relief agencies. During the last three years of the Napoleonic War, England enjoyed relative prosperity, and in this period of prosperity, there was no major effort to reform the Poor Laws. Increasingly the Evangelicals spent their energies and resources promoting voluntary education as the best means of helping the poor. By the end of the war some Evangelicals had come to accept Malthus's opinion that the Poor Laws were the greatest obstacle to the improvement of the moral conditions of the working classes.

The most important Evangelical magazine was the *Christian Observer*. Started in 1802 by the Reverend Josiah Pratt, it was edited by Zachary Macaulay until 1816. With the financial subsidy of the Thornton family, this Evangelical monthly attained a wide circulation among both Anglicans and Dissenters. It promoted those benevolent objects — education of the poor, abolition of the slave trade, prison and factory reform, and a dozen or more societies — through which the Evangelicals strove to improve the conditions of the working classes. During the early years of its publication, the *Christian Observer* supported Sir Thomas Bernard and the Society for Bettering the Condition of the Poor. By 1807 the magazine had acquiesced in Malthus's principle of population without accepting his conclusions on the Poor Laws. From this moderate position, it went on to become a zealous defender of Malthus and an equally firm foe of the Poor Laws. In the issue of 1812 it held that Malthus's views of population were not inconsistent with the Christian conception of Providence, and that the idea of redundancy was not more mysterious than the existence of pain. When John Weyland, attempting to refute Malthus, argued that the adaptation of means to ends, or food to population, was grounds for belief in Providence, the *Observer* was content simply to quote Malthus: "I believe it is the intention of the Creator that the earth should be replenished, but certainly with a healthy, virtuous, and happy population, not an unhealthy, vicious and miserable one. . . ."[27]

Why did the *Christian Observer* abandon the reform of the Poor Laws and come to accept Malthus's conclusion that those Laws aggravated the condition that they were supposed to remedy? For one thing, the growth in population, as shown by the census of 1811, seemed to confirm Malthus's principles.[28] Undoubtedly the stern morality which Malthus preached appealed to many of the Evangelical readers of the *Christian Observer*. But whatever the explanation may have been, some Evangelicals did accept Malthus as "an enlightened philanthropist" and came to prefer his doctrine of "moral restraint" to the "compulsory charity of the Poor Laws." With compunction to uplift the morals of the working classes, the *Christian Observer* felt obliged to inculcate the voluntary abstinence from marriage "as a very great virtue."[29]

The Evangelicals' acceptance of Malthus was quickened in 1816 by the publication of John Bird Sumner's *Treatise on the Records of Creation and the Moral Attributes of the Creator*. This major work of theology, by invoking the principle of population, attempted to prove that revealed religion had the confirmation of the latest scientific knowledge. Taking Malthus as his principal authority, Sumner did not expect to see any diminution of evil in the world, for the evil appeared to be in keeping with divine ordinances and not the result of "accidental inconvenience or human institutions." As he stated in his Preface, his main purpose was "to inquire if possible into the final cause of that provision for replenishing the world. . .and to show that the present and actual state of the world is not only consistent with the wisdom and goodness of God but affords perpetual testimony of both."[30] Sumner's problem of reconciling Providence with the existence of poverty was the same as the traditional theological problem of reconciling a wise and good Creator with the presence of evil in the world. The solution of both problems was the same: Man's life here and now was a state of probation, preparatory to a better life in a better world.

According to Sumner, Malthus had gone far toward explaining the existence of evil in the world, since he had "clearly proved that the greater part of these evils are the necessary consequence of a cause universally operating, viz., the natural tendency of mankind to increase in a quicker ratio than their substance." In the bright, scientific language of Malthus, Sumner restated the traditional problem of evil: "Why must our poverty contribute to another's prosperity? Cannot Omnipotence provide general good except by the expense of individual misery?" To this newly stated question he gave the traditional answer: Life is a state of discipline in which the faculties are to be exerted and "moral character formed, tried, and confirmed, previously to their entering upon a future and higher state of existence."[31]

Once satisfied that poverty was in accord with the plan of Providence, Sumner could join Malthus in defending the "inequality of ranks and fortunes." He could also agree with Malthus that equality fixes man "in stationary barbarism." Inequality of condition, he averred, demonstrated Providence, for it "offers not only the best improvement of the human faculties, but the best trial of human virtue."[32]

Sumner thus gave religious sanction to the natural law doctrine that poverty is "the necessary spur of civilization." He followed Patrick Colquhoun in distinguishing poverty from indigence. "Poverty is both honorable and comfortable," he said, "But indigence can only be pitiable and is usually contemptible." Whereas poverty was the natural lot of many, "indigence is not the natural lot of any but is commonly the state into which intemperance and want of prudent foresight push poverty." While indigence was God's punishment of the lower classes for "thoughtless and guilty extravagance," degradation was the moral punishment of the higher ranks. The tendency to sink in social rank, unless one exercised prudence and industry, was taken by Sumner as evidence of a moral universe.[33]

Like other disciples, Sumner pushed the principles of population beyond the intention of Malthus. Nevertheless, Malthus promptly accepted his new ally and recognized the *Records of Creation* as a useful exposition of the moral and theological implications of the principles of population.[34] That Sumner's book provided an answer to those theologians who had objected to the principle of population as an impeachment of Providence was asserted by the *Christian Observer*. When it reviewed Sumner's volumes in 1817, it reached the gloomy conclusion that "Providence has constituted society upon such a model which renders a certain degree of poverty and dependence in a great number of its members essential to its healthy condition. . . ." If only the poor were properly submissive and the rich properly benevolent, the resulting harmony and happiness would prove the goodness of the Creator.[35] But such harmony would never be realized; because society is under a curse, the remedy for all its evils will remain infallible.

Along with the repudiation of the earlier Christian view of Providence, the Evangelicals of Clapham abandoned the reform of the Poor Laws, which they had previously accepted as a righteous cause. In keeping with the principle of Malthus, the *Christian Observer* enunciated in 1817 its policy of social welfare as follows: "The diffusion of general education, exalting the character of the poor; the institution of provident banks, enabling them to better their condition; and the cultivation of larger Christian charity which binds the whole body together and provides a ready corrective for temporary distress."[36]

In 1818 the Reverend Charles Jerram's tract, *Considerations of the Impolicy and Pernicious Tendency of the Poor Laws. . .*, which was favorably reviewed by the *Christian Observer*, indicated the extent to which some Evangelicals had gone in abandoning the reform of the Poor Laws. An Evangelical clergyman, Charles Jerram, dedicated his tract to Samuel Thornton, for, as he said, "I know of no family to which the poor are so much indebted as to that of the Thorntons." Whether or not the sagacious and benevolent Samuel Thornton approved of the tract is uncertain but it is certain that Jerram thought it neither benevolent nor sagacious to defend the Poor Laws. He set forth his views in three propositions: "(1) that the hope of removing the evil of poverty is vain, (2) that the present administration of the Poor Laws tends greatly to aggravate the evil, and (3) that the best means of improving their condition lie with the poor themselves." Although Jerram expounded these propositions at some length, he demonstrated their truth only by referring to "the celebrated work of Mr. Malthus on population."[37]

Malthus's views of Christian charity and the Poor Laws were also accepted by the *Philanthropist*. When this magazine first appeared in 1811, it carried the subtitle, "Repository for Hints and Suggestions Calculated to Promote the Comfort and Happiness of Man." With the first issue it was designed to promote among the Dissenters the same benevolent causes which were being promoted among the Anglicans by the *Christian Observer*. As an organ of the Dissenters, it advocated religious toleration and was generally more Whig than Tory in politics. It was edited by William Allen, the leader of the London Quakers and the Secretary of the British and Foreign School Society. In addition to advocating schools for the working classes, the *Philanthropist* urged the building of more cottages, each one provided with a plot of ground for a garden and pasture for a cow.

In its first issue the *Philanthropist* stated its purpose as follows: "to stimulate to virtue and active benevolence. . .those who have the disposition and the means. . .and to show that all, even the poorest, may render material assistance in meliorating the condition of man."[38] To justify so noble a purpose it was sufficient to simply quote the Christian commandments to feed the hungry and clothe the naked, to visit the sick and imprisoned. The *Philanthropist* began its first article with an optimistic conception of Providence. "When we reflect on the attributes of the Creator. . . we shall be convinced that his purpose shall be the happiness of his creatures and that it is the duty of his rational beings to cooperate with him in producing this desirable end."

The London Quakers, like the Evangelicals of the Established Church, had a sentimental attachment to the poor. It seemed strange to many, no doubt, to find Quaker bankers and merchants professing esteem for the misery of Lazarus, rather than for the bounty of the rich man. In the midst of London's conspicuous misery, the Quakers could believe that the poor had Providential blessings not possible for the rich. For example, there was the case of Rusticus, with a large family and sickly wife, who, although he could not know the joys of contributing to charity, was endowed by his Creator with tenderness and sympathy; and as for the sick wife, she derived more benefit from her husband's look of tenderness than from the help of ten physicians.

If the poor were endowed by Providence with tenderness and a genuine piety whose brow was unclouded by "scowling discontent," the rich also had Providential blessing peculiar to their state. "To a mind of sensibility, the very sight of an object it has been instrumental to relieve is a source of secret joy," and the tear of gratitude brings a "glow of satisfaction" which is unknown to those who indulge in self-gratification.[39]

The Quakers' sentimental attachment to the poor, as shown in the pages of the *Philanthropist*, not only influenced their conception of charity and the obligations of the rich but also determined the manner in which they organized their benevolent enterprises. Charity is more than giving money, they earnestly believed: "we must also devote a portion of our time to select the objects of our bounty — to discriminate between the idle and profligate, and the industrious and deserving, and to inquire into their condition and to see that what we bestow is properly applied. . . ."[40] Such sentiments and beliefs, of course, were not peculiar to the Quakers and the Evangelicals of the Church of England. But it is true that the London Quakers and the Clapham Evangelicals supplied much of the money and most of the leadership for the many organizations designed to ameliorate the conditions of the poor.

Although a common faith and sentiment made it possible for the Quakers to cooperate with the Evangelicals of the Anglican

Church, they differed from the Anglicans in politics. Like other Dissenters, the Quakers preferred the Whig policy of religious toleration and this became a major political issue during the first quarter of the nineteenth century. The Quakers were also unlikely to agree with the Evangelicals of the Establishment that the social orders were divinely ordained. Such basic differences in social and political attitudes made cooperation increasingly difficult after the end of the Napoleonic War.

The different social and political attitudes of the Dissenters and the Anglicans — at least, as expressed in the pages of the *Christian Observer* and the *Philanthropist* — appeared in the long controversy over the Poor Laws. The effect of the Poor Laws, the Quakers believed, "is to oppress the classes upon whom the contribution to them falls and to ruin the character and morals and impair the comforts of those for whose benefit the contribution is ostensibly made."[41] But the malignant tendency of the Poor Laws did not alone cause the degeneracy of the working classes. The upper classes should be censured for setting a bad example by "striving to become eleemosynaries of the state." Instead of seeking public pensions, the upper classes, according to the *Philanthropist*, should be striving to "make the poor more productive members of society and more agreeable associates." [42]

As shown in the pages of the *Philanthropist*, some Quakers did not follow Malthus in attributing the increased misery of the working classes to a redundant population. Some attributed the growth of poverty to the waste of capital during the war; others preferred to honor Jeremy Bentham as one who has "advanced further in the science of legislation than all the philosophers, taken together, who have gone before him."[43] Some writers recommended the application of Bentham's model prison, the *Panopticon*, to the building and management of workhouses. Stringent discipline under central inspection, the main features of the *Panopticon*, undoubtedly appealed to the Quakers' sense of frugality and business efficiency. [44]

But it was Malthus, not Bentham, who dominated the thinking of the Poor Law reformers at the end of the Napoleonic War. Some leaders among both the Whigs and Tories were inclined to accept Malthus as a scientific authority on questions of social policy. The Whigs of the *Edinburgh Review* early recognized the importance of his principle of population.[45] In the first issue of October, 1802, the Reverend Sydney Smith reviewed Samuel Parr's

Spital sermon attacking Godwin's doctrine of universal benevolence.[46] In his celebrated sermon, Parr employed the principle of population to deprecate the optimism of universal benevolence. When reviewing Parr's sermon, Sidney Smith recognized Godwin's inability to refute the principle of population.[47]

The Whigs who sponsored the *Edinburgh Review* had appointed themselves the guardians of Adam Smith's economic doctrines, and since it was their habit to argue from self-evident propositions, they were disposed to accept Malthus's principle of population. By 1807 they were trumpeting Malthus as "the eminent philosopher" who has "enlarged the boundaries of science." They not only adopted his principle but they also accepted his conclusion that the Poor Laws "were a most fertile source of misery to the poor." They agreed with Malthus in preferring private charity, for it would never flow "so certainly as to draw after it any sort of dependence."[48] As is often the case, these disciples were more zealous than their teacher. They would not merely cooperate with nature by repealing the Poor Laws, but they would go further by enacting a law to prohibit every kind of charity to the common laborer. With the utmost confidence in their doctrine they concluded that "it is much safer to fall short than to exceed in relieving distress by public charity."[49]

The *Edinburgh Review*, however, did not represent the opinions of all the Whigs, nor did the *Quarterly Review* represent the views of all the Tories. There were writers for the *Quarterly* who favored Malthus and others who opposed him.

Among the writers of *Quarterly Review*, Robert Southey thought Malthus's *Essay* was bad arithmetic, bad morals, and bad theology. That "population increases in a geometrical series but food only in an arithmetical one" was the first of his fallacies — "the fundamental sophism of his book." Southey fiercely objected to Malthus's doctrine of moral restraint or, as he interpreted it, sexual continence: "He reasons as if lust and hunger alike were passions of physical necessity and the one equally with the other independent of reason and will." Malthus's picture of "nature's feast," where there was no cover for poor and where the rich were called on for no sacrifice was contrary to Southey's faith in Providence. Against Malthus's harsh view, he invoked the first commandment of the Creator, "Be fruitful and multiply." He ridiculed the Malthusian view that "the Mosaic account cannot be permitted to stand in the way of a demonstration."[50]

With the aid of John Rickman, an able civil servant who supplied him with statistical information, Southey continued his opposition to Malthus. When favorably reviewing John Weyland's *Principles of Population* in 1816, he used the occasion to endorse the benevolent reforms which had long been advocated by the Society for Bettering the Condition of the Poor. The reforms endorsed by Southey were the abolition of the Game Laws, the reform of factories, and a system of parochial schools connected with the Established Church. If such reforms should be adopted, Southey believed, "the poor rates would diminish and in no long time disappear." But standing in the way of the adoption of these causes was the great adversary: "Mr. Malthus's discovery must be remembered," he exclaimed, "and the 'new science of population!'"[51]

Southey's humanitarian reforms were like those advocated earlier by William Pitt and his friends Harrowby, Rose, Vansittart, and Wilberforce. Although the friends of Pitt were still influential in the councils of the Tory Government, their power had diminished somewhat after the death of Spencer Perceval. Under Lord Liverpool, younger men such as George Canning and William Huskisson preferred the natural law doctrines of economics to the sentimental benevolence of the Evangelical humanitarians. Lord Liverpool himself was more doctrinaire than Pitt in his attachment to the ideas of Adam Smith.[52]

In 1817, when the Poor Laws were again under discussion, the *Quarterly Review* called on Sumner to review the fifth edition of Malthus's *Essay on the Principle of Population*. After apologizing for the *Quarterly's volte face* on Malthus, Sumner proceeded to praise his book as one "which has taken such a firm hold of the public attention and which in the judgment of its partisans, is likely to effect a greater change in public opinion than any which has appeared since the *Wealth of Nations*."[53] Although Sumner viewed Malthus's principle of population as an unproven assumption, he accepted his conclusion that there was a redundant population and that the Poor Laws were a cause of the redundancy.[54]

Sumner's article in the *Quarterly Review* marked the end of a decade during which the natural law doctrine respecting the Poor Laws had come to be widely accepted. The majority of Poor Law reformers, both Whig and Tory, conceded that drastic change was necessary to stop the moral degeneracy of the working classes. By the end of the eighteenth century the natural law doctrine had

45

come to mean that poverty was the necessary spur to civilization. Underlying this attitude toward labor was the more elementary assumption that self-interest was the only adequate guide for social policy. Since individuals should be allowed to pursue their own interests, the state must not interfere with wages and prices. If left alone, wages and prices would find their level as surely as water seeks its own level. It was also assumed that the individual, guided by his interests, would invest capital more efficiently than the state. Since capital determined the amount of funds available for wages, any waste of capital tended to decrease the demands for labor. According to this doctrine, the building of workhouses to employ the poor wasted capital and so defeated the object of increasing the demand for labor.

Malthus greatly strengthened the natural law doctrine by adding to it the principle of population. If man did not exercise moral restraint, vice, misery, wars, famine, and plagues, which arise from the laws of nature, would indubitably check the growth of population. As all long-established countries, such as England, had a redundant population, misery and vice were operating to keep the number of people in balance with the supply of food. The only effective means of reducing vice and misery, according to Malthus, was the moral restraint of refraining from early marriage. Because the Poor Laws encouraged early marriage and granted allowances to large families, he concluded that they added to the misery which they were designed to relieve. By the end of the Napoleonic War, the natural law doctrine, which now included the principle of population, induced many Poor Law reformers to think in terms of the moral education of the working classes. At the same time, some reformers were of the opinion that the Poor Laws needed a drastic revision to prevent the further moral degeneracy of the working classes.

NOTES

[1] Samuel Whitbread, *Substance of a Speech on the Poor Laws*, (London, 1807), p. 2.
[2] *Parliamentary Debates*, VIII, 869.
[3] Whitbread, *op. cit.*, p. 9.
[4] *Ibid.*, p. 10.
[5] T. R. Malthus, *A Letter to Samuel Whitbread. . .on the Proposed Bill for the Amendment of the Poor Laws*, (London, 1807), p. 11.

[6] *Ibid.*, p. 18.
[7] *Ibid.*, p. 26.
[8] *Parliamentary Debates*, IX, 493.
[9] John Weyland, *Observations on Mr. Whitbread's Poor Bill and On the Population of England* (London, 1807), p. 2.
[10] *Ibid.*, p. 64.
[11] Thomas, Bernard. *A Letter to the Bishop of Durham on the Measures Now Under the Consideration of Parliament for Promoting and Encouraging Industry and for the Relief and Regulation of the Poor*, (London, 1807), p. 62.
[12] *Ibid.*, p. 56.
[13] T. R. Malthus, *An Essay on the Principle of Population*; (4th ed.; London, 1807), II, 430-31.
[14] *Ibid.*, II, 389.
[15] *Ibid.*, II, 394.
[16] *Ibid.*, II, 391.
[17] *Ibid.*, I, 342.
[18] *Ibid.*, I, 365-68.
[19] *Ibid.*, II, 383.
[20] Malthus, *Essay* (5th ed., 1817), III, 292. In the fourth edition, see Vol. II, 345-62.
[21] *Ibid.*, III, 154.
[22] For history of this business fluctuation, see: Arthur D. Gayer, W. W. Rostow, and Anna J. Schwartz, *The Growth and Fluctuation of the British Economy 1790-1850*, (Oxford; Clarendon Press, 1953), I, 85. Also, Thomas Tooke, *A History of Prices and the State of Circulation From 1793 to 1837.* (London, 1838), I, 319-28.
[23] William Smart, *Economic Annals of the Nineteenth Century, 1801-1820*, (London, 1910), pp. 272-73. Also, J. Steven Watson, *The Reign of George III, 1760-1815*, (Oxford, Clarendon Press, 1960), pp. 469-70.
[24] *Philanthropist*, II (1812), p. 342.
[25] Thomas Fowell Buxton, *The Distress in Spitalfields* (London, 1816), p. 7.
[26] *Report of the Association Formed in London, May 23, 1812, for the Relief and Benefit of the Manufacturing and Laboring Poor* (London, 1813), pp. 1-7. The several relief agencies were financed and promoted by the London Evangelicals, many of whom also belonged to the Strangers' Friend Society, which had been organized in 1785 to visit the sick and poor in their homes.
[27] *Christian Observer*, XV (1816), 738.
[28] *Ibid.*, XI (1812), 63.
[29] *Ibid.*, XV (1816), 798.
[30] John Bird Sumner, *A Treatise on the Records of Creation and on the Moral Attributes of the Creator* (6th ed.; London, 1850), p. XIII.
[31] *Ibid.*, p. 184.
[32] *Ibid.*, p. 214.
[33] *Ibid.*, p. 224.
[34] Malthus, *Essay* (5th ed., 1817), III, 425.
[35] *Christian Observer*, XVI, (1817), 110.
[36] *Ibid.*, 189.
[37] Charles Jerram, *Considerations of the Impolicy and Pernicious Tendency of the Poor Laws*, (London, 1818), p. 6.
[38] *Philanthropist*, I (1811), 2.
[39] *Ibid.*, 5.
[40] *Ibid.*, 4.
[41] *Ibid.*, II (1812), 309.

[42] *Ibid.*, 335.
[43] *Ibid.*, 321.
[44] *Ibid.*, 129.
[45] John L. Clive, *The Edinburgh Review 1802-1815* (London: Farber and Farber, 1957), p. 131.
[46] *Edinburgh Review*, I (1802), 19.
[47] *Ibid.*, 26.
[48] *Ibid.*, XI (1807), 105.
[49] *Ibid.*, 113.
[50] *Quarterly Review*, VIII (1812), 322.
[51] *Ibid.*, XV (1816), 235.
[52] W. R. Brock, *Lord Liverpool and Liberal Toryism* (Cambridge; University Press, 1941), p. 41.
[53] *Quarterly Review*, XVII (1817), 375.
[54] *Ibid.*, 400.

III

THE NATURAL LAW REFORMS

THE divisions within the Tory party and the diversity of opinion respecting the reform of the Poor Laws which prevailed at the end of the Napoleonic War did not prevent the establishment of the savings bank. Virtually all groups of reformers agreed on the utility of savings banks — since in principle they were institutions of self-help — but they differed among themselves on how the banks should be organized and what purposes they were designed to serve.

When Sir George Nicholls wrote his famous history of the Poor Laws at the middle of the nineteenth century, he described the savings banks of 1817 as "receptacles for the small savings of the industrious classes."[1] What they ultimately became — and their present commonplace reality — hides from view the ideas and the moral purpose that originally brought them into being. The originators of the savings banks preferred to call them frugality banks or provident institutions. They envisaged the banks as shrines where the lower classes could exercise the virtues of prudence and foresight.

Malthus thought that the savings banks would demonstrate the moral lessons taught by nature and Providence. Indeed, the savings banks were essential for the effective exercise of moral restraint, otherwise a young man could not practice prudence during the years when he was postponing marriage, nor could the mature man use foresight to prepare for the lean years of sickness and accident. The only rational remedy for indigence, or the misery of poverty, so far as Malthus could see, consisted of "whatever has a tendency to increase the prudence and foresight of the laboring classes."[2] From his confidence in the principle of population and his faith in self-interest as a sufficient guide, Malthus derived his views of the savings banks. "To facilitate the saving of small sums of money . . .," Malthus wrote in 1807, "and encourage young laborers to economize their earnings with a view to a provision for marriage, it might be extremely useful to have country banks, where the smallest sum would be received and a fair interest paid for them."[3] Malthus proposed the savings bank as a substitute for the "cow and the cottage system" by which the parish would have been able to lend or give money to large families for the purchase of a cow and a cottage.[4]

A decade or more before Malthus recommended the savings bank as an institution of moral regeneration, various philanthropists had started banks to assist poor workers and especially children. The Reverend Joseph Smith started a bank at Wendover, in Bucks, to receive the savings of his parishioners. Two pence and upwards were received every Sunday evening during the summer months, and the amount saved was repaid at Christmas, plus a bounty of one-third of the amount saved. The farm laborers could receive the bounty on their thrift even though they resorted to parish relief in times of illness and unemployment. The rural workers, quick to take advantage of this generous bargain, brought the venture to a speedy end.[5]

At Tottenham, Priscilla Wakefield organized in 1798 a Female Benefit Club to provide a loan fund for working people and to receive the earnings of children. The success of the loan fund led in 1804 to the establishment of the Charitable Bank of Tottenham. Under the patronage of several wealthy ladies, the bank had one of their number to keep the books and six others to serve as trustees. Each trustee of the bank assumed the liability of repaying the amount of one hundred pounds with a guaranteed interest of 5 per cent. As more funds were accumulated, an additional trustee was appointed for every hundred pounds. Apparently the losses were not considerable, for trustees were found willing to bear the risk in order to encourage thrift among the working classes.[6]

The most important of the early charity banks was founded in 1808 at Bath. Eight benevolent persons, four of whom were ladies, undertook the management of the funds of servants, guaranteeing them a return of 4 per cent. No individual could accumulate more than fifty pounds, and the total of all savings was not to exceed two thousand pounds. Five years later this small bank was superseded by the Provident Institution of Bath. The new charity bank began operations when a committee of twenty-five gentlemen contributed two thousand pounds to protect the trustees against possible losses. The savings of the working classes were invested by the trustees in government funds and guaranteed against falling prices. Distinguished philanthropists among the framers of the Provident Institution of Bath were Lord Lansdowne, one of its patrons, and Sir George Rose, who served as president of the board of trustees.[7]

Following the example of Bath, the philanthropists of London founded the Provident Institution for savings to serve the western part of the Metropolis. Sir George Rose, who guided the formation of the new bank, was assisted by the Society for Bettering the Condition of the Poor, which contributed two hundred pounds to start its operations. The bank accepted the savings of the working classes in deposits as small as six pence and invested them in government funds. Its trustees and managers served without pay. The bank was extraordinary in bringing together as its managers such enthusiasts as Bernard, Rose, and Wilberforce, as well as such rationalists as Malthus, Ricardo, and Hume.[8]

In Scotland the early savings banks were organized as Friendly Societies. The Reverend Henry Duncan established in 1810 the Parish Bank Friendly Society at Ruthwell, Dumfries. Under the approval and inspection of the magistrate, the Ruthwell bank prospered without patronage. Duncan organized similar mutual savings banks at Kelso and Dumfries. The critics of these early banks accused Duncan of attempting to erect a system calculated to excite the vice of miserliness among the lower orders. Duncan replied to this criticism that the vice of miserliness was possible only to those people "who are already blessed with independent fortunes." He intended his banks only for the use of the lower orders, in whom "industry and frugality are moral virtues of the first class." There was something "noble and affecting," he thought, "in the poor man's struggle to maintain his independence."[9]

The most important Scottish savings bank was formed in 1813 by the Edinburgh Society for the Suppression of Beggars. The members of the Society sanguinely expected the bank to have the good moral effects of reducing the consumption of intoxicating liquors and diminishing the number of early and improvident marriages.[10] Although the savings bank of Edinburgh had a moral purpose like the provident institutions of England, it differed from them in its organization. The savings bank of Edinburgh cooperated closely with the commercial bank, the former receiving deposits under ten pounds, and the latter receiving none below this amount. For this accommodation the commercial banks paid 1 per cent above the normal rate for all deposits of savings.[11]

After a score or more of savings banks had been established in England and Scotland, the Tory Government decided to promote them on a general scale. Early in 1816, Sir George Rose introduced a bill to protect and encourage provident institutions or banks for savings.[12] It is clear that he intended to give to the savings banks the same legal protection which he had previously provided for the Friendly Societies. For twenty-five years he had assumed, along with William Wilberforce, the responsibility of ameliorating the condition of the working classes, and like his benevolent colleague, he had given of time and money to promote institutions designed to improve their condition. The savings banks were, in his view, merely another institution to help the poor to help themselves.[13] His bill, therefore, extended to the whole kingdom the principles of the provident institutions which he had helped to administer at Bath, London, and Southampton. It enabled trustees and managers to receive deposits of the lower orders and to invest them in government funds. Like Friendly Societies, the savings banks were allowed to register with the justice of the peace without paying the stamp tax. Rose also made it possible for the poor to receive parish relief even while they possessed small savings in the bank.

Although supported by the Tory Government, Rose's bill aroused so much controversy that its opponents succeeded in delaying it for a year. The opponents objected to two clauses of the bill. The Scottish members especially opposed the requirement that savings be invested in government bonds, inasmuch as the practice in Scotland was to invest the savings in the commercial banks. This particular hurdle was removed by restricting the operation of the bill to England.

It was more difficult to satisfy the objection of the natural law reformers who held tenaciously the principle, as they had done for twenty-five years, that relief be granted only to the poor who were also destitute. They decried the clause which allowed the poor to receive parish relief while they had savings in the bank. The humanitarians, on the other hand, wished to retain this provision. Wilberforce, in particular, wanted savings banks to be provident institutions "to teach the poor what they were capable of doing by their own exertions."[14] After consulting with "many country gentlemen" who supported him, Rose accepted a compromise. He made it optional for the magistrate to order relief for the poor person who possessed as much as thirty pounds in a savings bank. When the foes of the bill demanded a division on this clause, they were defeated by sixty votes to twenty-seven.[15] They were successful, however, in eliminating that clause which granted a premium from the poor rates to those poor persons who had saved consistently for a period of three years.

Sir George Rose did not live to see the consequences of the Act to Encourage the Establishment of Banks for Savings in England, and his death weakened the followers of William Pitt who had labored so long to ameliorate the condition of the working classes. Influenced by Pitt's benevolence, the banks guaranteed 4.5 per cent on the savings, which were securely invested in government funds. The founders of the savings bank, however, did not anticipate that the institution designed to teach thrift would draw large deposits from wealthy persons who needed neither encouragement nor protection.[16] From August, 1817, to March, 1818, persons of means had deposited 657,000 pounds in the savings banks. Knowing that large deposits had come from persons for whom the banks were not designed, the Tory Government proposed in 1818 to amend the Savings Bank Act of the previous year. The amendment limited the amount that an individual could deposit to one hundred pounds during the first year and to fifty pounds in any year thereafter.[17] In 1824 another amendment set a new maximum of fifty pounds in the first year and thirty pounds in any subsequent year, and it further provided that no interest be paid on deposits above two hundred pounds. The Savings Bank Consolidated Act of 1828 reduced the interest on deposits to 3.5 per cent, but the continuation of large deposits indicated that persons other than the working classes were among the beneficiaries of the savings banks.[18]

The adoption of the savings bank as a serious remedy for poverty — coming as it did in the midst of a grave postwar depression — indicated the inadequacy of natural law doctrine in dealing with business fluctuations. Peace brought economic chaos.[19] When the war ended, industrial production declined, goods accumulated, prices fell, and businesses went into bankruptcy. Poor Law expenditures kept pace with the increase in unemployment. The discontent of the jobless, especially in London and the new industrial cities of the North, provoked political and social reformers to renewed activity. The political reformers, such as the Westminster Radicals, had willing and eager audiences for their proposals to reform Parliament. Meanwhile, in Parliament the natural law reformers scornfully ignored political reform as a remedy for economic discontent. They took the occasion to demand the resumption of specie payment and the repeal of the income tax. The Tory Government, consequently, abandoned the economic measures which it had so long defended as wartime necessities.

The incompetence of all reformers to deal with the postwar depression may be seen in the resumption of the debate over the Poor Laws. In May, 1816, John Christian Curwen introduced a motion in the House of Commons requesting the appointment of a committee to inquire into the Poor Laws.[20] As spokesman for the Whigs on social questions, Curwen had become responsible for the reform of the Poor Laws after the death of Samuel Whitbread. A country gentleman of Cumberland, Curwen had gained fame for his experiments in agriculture and for his attempts to improve the lot of the working classes at Carlisle.[21] Like his distinguished predecessor, he demanded a thorough reform of the Poor Laws, "because the radical defects of the system were not to be cured by palliatives." He also followed Whitbread in recommending national education as the ultimate means of abolishing the Poor Laws, but before that could be achieved he thought it necessary to equalize the poor rates. He therefore recommended national assessments and a tax on personal property, especially on income from stocks and bonds.

Although Curwen's motion passed the House of Commons, the committee of inquiry was never appointed. As the depression deepened during 1816, unemployment increased and greater demands than ever before were made upon the poor rates. When it appeared to Curwen that the rates "would swallow up the whole revenue and industry of the country," he again appealed to the Tory Ministers to appoint a committee of inquiry. The Tories were unwilling to accept his proposed reforms, but they did consent on February 21, 1817, to the appointment of a committee. The leader of the Tories in the House of Commons, Lord Castlereagh, promised to lend the committee "all the assistance in his power," but at the same time he clearly indicated his opposition to such reforms as the equalization of rates and the property tax. Since Castlereagh had devoted most of his time to the Foreign Office, he lacked Curwen's intimate understanding of the industrial transformation that had been going on during the war. Hence he could reply only in doctrinaire terms. Using the often repeated argument of Adam Smith, he objected to the property tax because of the inquisitorial methods necessary to collect it, and using the more modern authority of Malthus, he opposed the equalization of rates because he thought any increase in the funds for relief would encourage extravagance. He blithely assumed that Ireland was happier without Poor Laws, and that Scotland was better off than England because its laws were more stringently administered. However doctrinaire his reply, Castlereagh had at least one practical opinion, "that he would rather employ the poor to dig a hole one day and make them fill it up the next, than to allow them to remain idle. . . ."[22]

Curwen's motion for a committee of inquiry and the appointment of the committee in 1817 evoked a national controversy over the welfare of the working classes. Malthus contributed to the controversy by publishing the fifth edition of his *Essay.* The supplementary materials of the new edition, consisting of the practical applications of the principle of population, were published separately as *Additions.* Malthus was quite clear on what ought to be done: "We must diminish the proportion of paupers in order to give greater wealth and happiness to the mass of laboring classes."[23]

Malthus carefully reviewed and criticized Curwen's plan of reform. He rejected the scheme to equalize the rates between the wealthy parishes and the poorer ones, because such an equalization would increase relief funds and consequently the number of paupers. He rejected the income tax for the same reason.[24] He wanted the poor rates to be levied solely on landed property, for the farmers "had a very strong interest in keeping them down." Finally, he rejected Curwen's plan for a national insurance fund to assist the working classes in times of sickness and old age. Any system of social welfare nationally compulsory, Malthus argued, was self-defeating, as its tendency would be to increase the population.[25]

At least on one point Malthus found himself in agreement with Curwen. Both reformers rejected public responsibility for providing employment. Malthus agreed with his opponent "that the want of employment must furnish no claims on society; for if this excuse were to be admitted, it would most probably be attended with the most pernicious consequences."[26]

Why did Malthus, a benevolent man, refuse relief to the jobless in time of a depression? To understand the profound pessimism which led him to reject Curwen's plan of social reform, we must look at his picture of England. He saw a mature country, fully populated, existing at a subsistence level so that any increase in population meant the starvation of some. Although he perceived the grimness of this picture, he thought the principles of population, from which he had derived it, were a new science. With the confidence of a surgeon cutting away cancerous tissue, he felt obliged to cut away the pauperism of a redundant population.

Malthus deserves the sympathy and respect of all students of society who have sought a scientific basis for social policy. Although he was confident that his principles were scientific, he applied them with great caution, for he realized that moral and political philosophy was "confined within such narrow limits" when compared with physical science.[27]

Not all of Malthus's disciples, however, shared their master's sense of inferiority and his reluctance to apply the principles of population. Some were trumpeting the arrival of a new science. Mrs. Marcet, who had won fame as a popularizer of chemistry, published in 1816 her *Conversations on Political Economy in which the Elements of that Science are Familiarly Explained.* Other disciples of Malthus, the natural law reformers of the Poor Laws, were loudly insisting that a redundant population had to be limited to prevent the further moral degeneracy of the working classes.

The natural law reformers wrote into the Poor Law Report of 1817 the new science of population. The House of Commons appointed in February, 1817, a committee to inquire into the Poor Laws. With William Sturges Bourne as chairman, it carried on investigations for four months, calling witnesses with long experience in administering the Poor Laws. The evidence compiled by the Committee was the most important body of social information which had been collected since the Poor Law Returns of 1803. However, when the Committee settled down to the difficult task of writing its report, reputed to be the work of T. Frankland Lewis, it did not assimilate the evidence which it had so laboriously collected. Ignoring its own information, the Committee incorporated in its Report the policies advocated by various natural law reformers from Joseph Townsend to Thomas R. Malthus.[28]

A salient feature of the Report of 1817 was the doctrine of the secular increase in Poor Law expenditures — a doctrine which had become the stock-in-trade of the natural law reformers. The doctrine was explicitly stated: "Your Committee cannot but fear. . . that the system is perpetually encouraging and increasing the amount of misery it was designed to alleviate."[29]

The Committee also wrote into its Report Malthus's moral condemnation of the Poor Laws: "As every system of relief founded on compulsory enactments must be divested of the character of benevolence, so it is without its beneficial effects; as it proceeds from no impulse of charity, it creates no feelings of gratitude. . . . The results appear to be highly prejudicial to moral habits and consequent happiness of a great body of the people, who have been reduced to the degradation of a dependence upon parochial support. . . ."[30] On the positive side of the question, the Committee set forth Malthus's view that independence of parochial support, on the part of the working classes, was a great moral achievement.

In addition to Malthus's moral condemnation of the Poor Laws, the Committee incorporated in its Report Adam Smith's theory of wages. According to the views set forth, the rate of wages, like other prices, was determined by the natural laws of supply and demand. Since the demand for labor depended upon the funds available for its support, the rate of wages would be adjusted by the proportion that demand bears to supply. The happiness of labor, it was thought, depends absolutely on "the degree of nicety in which supply is adjusted to demand."[31] If the demand increases faster than the supply, higher wages will enable the laborer to rear a larger number of children, and an increasing supply of laborers will follow an increasing demand. On the other hand, if demand falls, because of the waste of wealth, wages will fall and marriage will be discouraged until "the supply is gradually adapted to the reduced demand." The Committee further assumed that any compulsory expenditure of the wealth, on which the demand for labor depended, would be spent "less profitably than it would have been if left to the interested superintendence of its owners," and that all such inefficient public employment of capital reduced wages and the demand for labor. Hence, they concluded that the Poor

Law expenditures wasted the capital on which the demand for labor depended and so actually increased the misery which they were designed to alleviate.

As it was not within the power of the state to provide work for everybody, that part of the Elizabethan Poor Law requiring the able-bodied to be set to work should not be fully executed. The Committee recommended that, as the demand for labor should revive, the parish should cease to provide work for the able-bodied, beginning with those between eighteen and thirty years of age. "The money thus restored to natural channels," they believed, "cannot fail to assist in increasing the natural demand for labor."[32]

According to the natural law theory of wages which the Committee had derived from Adam Smith, all payments from the poor rates reduced wages and decreased the demand for labor. Since they assumed that it was the first duty of Parliament to reduce relief expenses, the Committee proposed a check on expenditures which would be "the foundation of a better system" and "perfectly consonant with the nature of things." They also proposed that the poor rates be limited in any one year to the average expenditure of the previous ten years. Concentrating on the reduction of expenditures, the Committee refused to consider Curwen's schemes for equalizing rates and taxing personal property. The ideas of a county or national assessment for the poor, even if more adequate and equitable, were rejected as taking away from the wages of the independent laborer and giving to the dependent poor. To all proposals for increasing relief revenues, the natural law reformers had this confident reply: "Unless some efficacious check is imposed, the amount of assessment will continue to increase until it has absorbed the profits of property, producing neglect and ruin."[33]

Because the Committee desired to halt the assumed secular spiral of poor relief expenses, they went beyond the negative check of a legal maximum. They recommended a return to a system of workhouses as a means of keeping the poor off the relief rolls, for they found that the workhouse had acted for a long time "very powerfully in deterring persons from throwing themselves on relief."[34] To restore the workhouse as an effective deterrence, they recommended the repeal of those laws, which had been enacted by the Pittite humanitarians, enabling the justices of the peace to order relief outside the workhouses. Whereas the humanitarians Gilbert, Rose, and Wilberforce had struggled for thirty years to transform the workhouses into homes for the impotent, the natural law reformers in 1817 recommended that they be re-established as a shield to protect the parish from the idle and profligate.

To restore the virtuous independence of the working classes the Committee recommended the elimination of the allowance system, which granted relief to families in proportion to the number of children. The system had become as commonplace as feeding sheep by the size of the flock. This rule of thumb had prevailed in nearly all the rural parishes long before the high prices of the Napoleonic War began to push the low wage-earners below the level of subsistence. Before Malthus wrote his famous *Essay*, the struggling laborer who supported a large family had engendered sympathy among the more barren or fortunate families of his village. The magistrates nearly everywhere esteemed large families, but they differed greatly as to the size of the family meriting relief. During the famine years of the war, when prices were outrunning wages, William Pitt recommended that families of two children, and widows with one, be granted a parish allowance. Many parishes, however, preferred to celebrate large families by giving prizes to the largest families fully supporting their children. But as the fame of Malthus spread, the celebration of large families ceased. The poor man who brought into the world more children than he could support was increasingly deprecated as having failed to practice the virtues of prudence and foresight.

The Poor Law Committee of 1817 hastened to apply Malthus's new moral principles. Assuming that wages were sufficient to support a family of two children — this was the natural law doctrine that wages tended to subsistence level — the Committee recommended that the parish take from the families the redundant children, ages three to fourteen, and set them to work in schools of industry. The Committee expected much from these pauper schools. They expected to free the mothers for more useful labor, to inure the children to industry from their infancy, and to keep the fathers from spending relief on ale. In addition to teaching the children industry, which would enable them to pay their own way, the schools would teach morals and religion. The schools would feed the children as well as educate them. In summer the children would be fed bread and water, and a "little warm water gruel in winter, for the same fire that warms the room may be made use of to boil the pot." [35]

59

The efficient management of the schools of industry and the elimination of the allowance system depended upon the adoption of a new type of administration. The natural law reformers had been contending for some time that the justice of the peace, motivated by benevolence rather than self-interest, had been guilty of profusion in administering relief. The Committee, therefore, recommended that authority for ordering relief be taken from the justices and placed in the hands of a vestry elected from the largest occupiers of property in the parish. Whereas the humanitarian reformers had worked to circumvent the parsimony of parish officials, the natural law reformers were convinced that the only safeguard against profuse poor relief was the self-interest of the property owner and his tenants.

The Poor Law Report of 1817 was too doctrinaire to reflect the opinions of all the members of the House of Commons Committee. The wide diversity of opinion was disclosed in a letter written during the Easter Recess by one member, Thomas P. Courtenay, to Sturges Bourne. A permanent member of the Board of Control, Courtenay was a practical and well-informed civil servant. He was critical of the doctrinaire approach to social reform. "It does not appear to me," he wrote, "that an adherence to what is styled the doctrine of Mr. Malthus respecting population leads to a condemnation of the whole code of Poor Laws actually in operation."[36] Rather than abandon a system so "interwoven with our political constitution," Courtenay preferred to mitigate its evils by a "mild combination of palliatives." To prevent the hasty writing of a doctrinaire report, he detailed the conflicting opinions of several influential members of the Committee.

Since the Tory party was badly divided on questions of social policy, the Government decided to delay action on the Poor Laws. On May 9, while the House of Commons was busy with its investigation, Lord Liverpool recommended that the House of Lords undertake a similar inquiry. He justified his request for a second inquiry with the following words: "However general the coincidence of opinion was as to the effects of the system, and the evils that resulted from it, there was very considerable difference of opinion as to the proper remedies."[37] In compliance with the Prime Minister's request, the House of Lords appointed a Committee to investigate the operations of the Poor Laws. With Lord Hardwicke as chairman, the Committee called witnesses, compiled and published copious testimony, but refrained from recommending extensive reform of the Poor Laws.

When Lord Hardwicke reported to the House of Lords on July 10, only two days before the end of the session, he said the Committee had not examined the subject fully enough to have "any decided opinion as to what ought to be done."[38] Lord Liverpool further indicated there would be no general reform at present and "whatever measures might ultimately be adopted, much would be found to depend on the due administration of the existing laws."[39]

The Poor Law Report of the House of Lords, unlike that of the House of Commons, consisted of observations on the conditions attested to by many witnesses. The Lords observed what was surely the true postwar situation; viz., that with the fall of demand for manufactures "the most serious distress has ensued; without employment the poor suffer as never before."[40] They also found in manufacturing districts "where population of late has greatly exceeded demand for labor, the burden of rates has been particularly severe, notwithstanding the large subscriptions raised by private benevolence." In view of the widespread unemployment and the increasing burden of the rates, the House of Lords Committee were "decidedly of the opinion that the general system of those laws ought. . .to be maintained." Since the Lords were primarily interested in more efficient management of the Poor Laws, they recommended that the rates should be levied on "those who are immediately interested in the disbursement and who have personal knowledge of the situation." [41]

The Poor Law Report of the House of Lords clearly differed from that of the Lower House, for there was no bias of reformism. Whereas the Lords generalized from the testimony of witnesses, the Report of the House of Commons cited examples to prove a hypothetical case. While generally ignoring the testimony of the magistrates and the parish officials, the Committee of the House of Commons placed in the Appendix of their Report memorials, petitions, and other information marshalled to corroborate their preconceived plan of reform. Having deduced from their natural law doctrine a system of social welfare, they boldly recommended a drastic reform of the Poor Laws as a panacea for the economic ills of the postwar depression.

By piecing together the invaluable testimony compiled by the two Poor Law inquiries, one can picture the grim conditions of the working classes during the hard times that came at the end of the Napoleonic War. During the long period of wartime inflation, while wages were lagging behind prices, the slums of London,

Manchester, and other industrial places arose to appall and confound the social reformers. The testimony also supports the common knowledge of hindsight that there was great mobility of labor during the period of high wartime demand in spite of the Laws of Settlement.

While the Friendly Societies may have encouraged the laborers to move during the period of prosperity, they were not sufficiently strong to provide them security during the depression.[42] When the Friendly Societies collapsed under the financial strain of the depression, the need for relief exceeded all previous expenditures. The costs of relief in Manchester and Birmingham doubled between March, 1816, and March, 1817.[43] In the slums of East London the burden of poverty was far too great for the parishes to bear from their traditional revenues.[44]

The substantial economic conditions of the postwar depression were not comprehended by the natural law reformers who wrote the House of Commons Report. They had long accepted as inevitable the upward secular trend of Poor Law expenditures. To prove that the Poor Laws increased rather than lessened poverty, they compared the gross expenses of 1815 with the returns for 1776, 1785, and 1803.[45] The natural law reformers, however, did not take the pains to deflate the expenditures nor to compare them with the increase in population. They were so confident that the growth of expenditures meant ultimate national ruin that they inserted an account of the parish of Wombridge, Salop, where the annual rental, including the royalties of the mines, was not enough to pay the cost of poor relief.[46] The practical administrator of the Poor Laws, however, was not frightened by the specter of national ruin, for he realized that while the poor rates had doubled during the long period of war, actual rents had also risen.[47]

From the time of Adam Smith, the natural law reformers had preferred the welfare policies of Scotland to those of England. The failure to enforce the Poor Laws in Scotland, it was believed, made the morals of the working classes superior to those in England. In many rural parishes of Scotland, voluntary contributions were taken in place of legal assessments. The relief funds, whether voluntary or assessed, were administered by the elders of the Kirk and the landlords. To indicate the superiority of this voluntary system to the English compulsory system, the House of Commons Committee inserted in the Appendix of its Report a statement by the General Assembly of Edinburgh averring the success of the Scottish system.[48]

Although the General Assembly favored voluntary charity under the Kirk's management, it disclosed that the problems of relieving the working classes of Edinburgh were not unlike those of Manchester and Birmingham. In the populous parish of St. Cuthbert, for example, voluntary contributions were inadequate and it was necessary to resort to legal assessments. The General Assembly, however, neglected to say anything about the conditions which led to the formation of the Society for the Suppression of Beggars.

The Society for the Suppression of Beggars was organized at Edinburgh in 1813, when the combination of poor harvests and Napoleon's commercial blockade brought virtual starvation to the working classes. According to its *First Report*, the Society found that "unfavorable seasons and high prices had driven many to beg", so many, in fact, that it was difficult to distinguish "the really necessitous" from the habitual beggars. The avowed purpose of the Society was to suppress habitual beggars and rehabilitate the "really necessitous." During the first year of its operations, from March to October, 1813, the Society handled 501 cases; among these beggars were 180 widows and 135 married women who were seeking help for themselves and 481 children.[49] The Society continued its operations for several years without successfully suppressing the mendicants of Edinburgh. During the depression year of 1817, it reported the appearance of 227 new supplicants; of this number one hundred were put to work, forty-seven ordered to leave town, and eighty were retained for further investigation.[50]

The voluntary system, which was highly esteemed by the natural law reformers, had obviously failed to meet the needs of Edinburgh. It had also failed in Glasgow. The city of Glasgow had assumed public responsibility for relief as early as 1733, when it built the Hospital, an institution resembling the English workhouse or poorhouse.[51] The Directors of the Hospital levied rates to care for those permanently dependent upon the city. They also cooperated with the Kirk Session in administering outdoor relief. From time to time, when employment lagged or harvests failed, the Directors of the Hospital levied additional rates to supplement the funds of the Kirk Sessions; in the depression year of 1817, for example, the Hospital spent £10,602 for relief, while the Kirk Session spent only £3,313.

The division of authority between the two institutions led to inevitable conflict between the Kirk and the Hospital over the raising and distribution of relief funds. In 1817 a sharp conflict arose between them. The Reverend Thomas Chalmers, a zealous minister of Glasgow, was the leader of the Kirk's campaign against legal assessments. Chalmers wished to grant no public relief beyond the existing generation of paupers and to apply "the disengaged funds" to building additional churches. He piously believed that the strengthening of religion would invigorate benevolence so that voluntary collections would be sufficient. The Directors of the Hospital, however, after reviewing his plan, rejected it as "not suitable to the fluctuating parishes of a great city."[52] The Directors, consequently, proceeded with their plans to build the New Hospital to care for 478 needy persons, including adults and children, the able-bodied and the impotent. To employ those able to work and to educate the children, the Directors attached to the New Hospital a house of industry and a school of industry.[53]

Although Edinburgh and Glasgow were thus moving in the direction of legal assessments for poor relief, the natural law reformers continued to extol the Scottish system of voluntary contributions. But the House of Lords, reluctant to accept the alleged superiority of the voluntary system, called two Scottish M.P.'s for testimony. One of these witnesses attested to large amounts raised by the rates in Glasgow; another testified that many of the parishes of southern Scotland were supported by legal assessments.[54]

Although the testimony compiled in 1817 by the two Parliamentary inquiries was an invaluable source of information, it attracted little attention and was generally disregarded during the controversy over the Poor Laws. The House of Commons Report, on the other hand, attracted wide attention. Printed first in July, 1817, it was reprinted in March of the following year. It was thoroughly reviewed by the influential political magazines, and it provoked a new tractarian controversy over the reform of the Poor Laws.[55]

The *Quarterly Review*, with two major conflicting articles, one appearing in January, 1818, and the other in April, represented the diversity of opinion within the Tory party. The two articles were written jointly by John Rickman and Robert Southey, the first article being primarily the work of Rickman and the second primarily the work of Southey. A competent civil servant and compiler of population statistics, Rickman supplied Southey with detailed information on the Poor Laws, but the former had little influence on the latter's moral and religious philosophy. Although a life-long friend of Southey, Rickman was an avowed foe of the Evangelicals. His hatred of what he deemed "mock philanthropist humanity" was catholic and consistent enough to include Wilberforce, Perceval, and Romilly. While Southey was advocating the work of the Society for Bettering the Condition of the Poor, Rickman was trying to persuade him to take a stand against the Poor Laws. The appointment of the House of Commons Committee gave him the opportunity to send Southey an outline of the kind of article which he thought should be published by the *Quarterly Review*. "As to the poor rate question," he wrote on May 8, 1817, "pray prepare a good commonplace in the praise of selfishness, the only mover of large beneficial action. . . . A rule of reasonable duress must be general, mere sustenance of the cheapest kind, whereupon in walks industry, care and thrift in the poor; genuine humanity — alms judiciously bestowed — circles of endeared dependents — active and passive happiness to the rich. The poor must attain good character or fall upon the legal sustenance. . . . But you must steel your soul for a short time for future good. Bread and water and straw for all who have not character to elicit, or industry to acquire better maintenance."[56]

That Rickman was not able to put steel into Southey's soul nor place it in "a temporary severity for final good purposes" is shown by the two contradictory articles that appeared in the *Quarterly Review*. In the January article Rickman endorsed the House of Commons Report and especially approved of its "clear and concise expression of general principles previously understood only by authors."[57] Among the principles endorsed by Rickman was "the simple principle that no pauper shall have the right to insist on relief in any other form than as the magistrates or parish officers shall think his conduct and situation deserve. . . ."[58]

Although some of Rickman's economic analysis was retained in the second article, which appeared in the April issue of the *Quarterly*, Southey reaffirmed the Evangelicals' faith in Christian education and the building of more churches as the proper means of stopping the moral decay of the working classes. Far from trusting in the natural law of self-interest as a reliable guide, Southey thought it was the paramount duty of government to give "hope and good principles" to the people.[59]

While rejecting Malthus's doctrine of a redundant population, Southey declared: "Give us an educated population — fed from

65

their childhood with the milk of sound doctrine, not dry-nursed in dissent — taught to fear God and honor the king, to know their duty toward their fellow creatures and their Creator — the more there are of such a people the greater will be the wealth and power and prosperity of a state. . . ."[60]

Although Rickman had praised the Poor Law Report in the January issue of the *Quarterly*, Southey in the April issue continued to support the reforms advocated by the Society for Bettering the Condition of the Poor. He also took time to praise the Methodists as "the first persons in this country who appear to have felt any compassion for the sufferings of guilt."[61] He had praise, too, for "Mrs. Fry and those generous Quakers who have effected so great a change in the condition of female prisoners at Newgate."[62]

While the *Quarterly* was speaking with two voices, the *Edinburgh Review* had a single voice of abundant praise for the House of Commons Report. Thomas Chalmers, who had been embroiled in a struggle with the city fathers of Glasgow for the control of relief funds, published two lengthy articles on the "Causes and Cure of Pauperism." The first of these appeared in March, 1817, as a review of the report of the Mendicity Committee, and the second appeared in February, 1818, as a review of the Poor Law Report.

With more care for accuracy, Chalmers might have entitled his articles, "The Dangers and Follies of Charity." A century and a half later, one is amazed to discover a devout and distinguished clergyman declaiming against charity. Should not the clergy better spend their time exhorting their congregation to benevolence? This momentary aberration from Christian tradition can be understood best in terms of the natural law doctrine to which Chalmers adhered. He believed self-interest to be a better guide than benevolence. He believed that beneficence could never banish poverty from the world, for the fullness of the rich was not sufficient to fill the vacancy of the poor. Since he was confident that the benevolence of the rich did not relieve the poor but only augmented their number, he demanded a strict supervision of all charitable funds.[63] He stated the "principle of acceleration" in the precise language of mathematics, "every extension of the poor's funds is in general sure to be followed up by more than proportional increase in actual poverty."[64] The principle convinced him that the Poor Laws "ought to be entirely abolished."[65]

66

Although Chalmers accepted the principles of the House of Commons Report, he offered a different remedy for the cure of pauperism. His remedy was like Southey's. He would depend upon religious education, under the direction of the national church, to teach the people the virtues of prudence, frugality, and industry.[66]

Thomas Chalmers was no solitary figure among devout clergymen who, under the influence of Malthus, came to look upon the Poor Laws as a curse rather than a blessing. The pious editors of the *Christian Observer* favorably reviewed the Poor Law Report and praised the Committee for "unmasking the evils of the Poor Laws." In the midst of the postwar depression, they saw in the system of compulsory relief "the origin of a great proportion of our national distress."[67] Although the Clapham Sect continued to promote national education as the proper remedy for the "alarming decay" of the working classes, they were now willing to abandon the able-bodied poor to the caprice of private charity.

The Evangelical Dissenters were just as vociferous as the Clapham Saints in denouncing the Poor Laws as "ruinous and demoralizing." Their most important magazine, the *Eclectic Review*, accepted the wages-fund doctrine. Assuming that wages tended toward the level of subsistence, the editors solemnly concluded that casual labor would constantly be in danger of indigence.[68] Preferring a total, but not an immediate, abolition of the Poor Laws, they proposed the fixing of a maximum for relief expenses and the reduction of the limit annually by 10 per cent.[69]

In the House of Commons Report the natural law reformers wove economics, morals and theology into one fabric. These theorists had such confidence in their self-evident propositions that they either discounted or misused the testimony of experience. They selected from their own testimony those cases which illustrated the doctrines deduced from self-evident propositions. Moreover, they did not think it necessary to wait for that great mass of statistical evidence made available by the Poor Law Returns for the years 1813 to 1815.

To answer the natural law critics of the Poor Laws, the Tory Government in 1815 ordered a census of paupers and the amount of expenditures similar to the enumerations that had been made in 1776, 1785, and 1803.[70] The returns for the years 1813 to 1815, however, were so slowly made that they were not abstracted and printed until March, 1818. The Poor Law Committee, which had reported to the House of Commons almost a year before, had little opportunity to use this body of statistical information, the only one on which a reliable estimate might have been made.

The Poor Law census of 1815 was an enormous enterprise. More than fourteen thousand places returned answers to the compulsory questionnaire; those places making returns were 10,593 parishes and 4,047 other localities, being either townships, tythings, or hamlets. The questions asked by the Home Secretary concerned primarily the amounts and types of local expenses and the numbers and classes of persons receiving relief.

Every social reformer at that time wanted to know how much relief expenses had increased, for the high cost of relief was the argument most frequently used to justify additional reform. The census showed that gross expenditures had increased since the last returns had been made in 1803, and, indeed, the growth was enormous when compared with the returns of 1776. But B. P. Capper, who had been appointed by the Home Department to abstract the returns for 1815, pointed out that poor relief had not increased faster than other types of Poor Law expenditures. While poor relief expenses had increased four times during the period of forty years, expenses under the heading, "For Law, Removals, and Expenses of Officers," had increased eleven times. The most rapid increase occurred in the category, "Church rate, County rate, Highway rate, Etc." [71]

The natural law reformers had long been alarmed over the rapid growth of the poor rates, which they feared would devour the whole rental of land and the profits of property. Malthus, for example, confessed to having had more anxiety over the growth of rates than over the size of the national debt accumulated in the war against France. Again, Capper tried to quiet the criticism of the theorists by comparing the costs of relief with the increased rental value of land and other real property. The costs of maintaining the poor had increased from £4,077,891 in 1803 to £5,421,168 in 1815, an increase of 33 per cent. Meanwhile, the rental of real property, as recorded by the national Tax Office, had increased from £38,000,000 to £51,000,000, an increase of 34 per cent. [72]

If the poor rates were growing in proportion to the rental of land when viewed nationally, the diversity of assessments from county to county indicated that the burden of the poor rates had become exceedingly heavy in some places. The heaviest burdens were borne by mining and manufacturing parishes during periods of depressed trade, when unemployment had increased the number of persons on parish rolls. In such communities personal property, including merchandise, machinery, and even a canal in one place, was exempt from paying the poor rates. Moreover, the assessments of real property fell on the occupier rather than on the owner. The tenements in which the working classes lived were also frequently exempted from the poor rates, since they rented for less than ten pounds annually. The adverse relationship between needs and resources seemed to threaten some parishes with bankruptcy. Although the parishes escaped from such a fate when trade revived, they continued to express their alarm in strident voices. Such a parish was Wombridge, Salop, which was cited by the Poor Law Committee to exemplify the general tendency of the poor rates to devour the whole rental of land and profits of property. That Wombridge was not typical of the fourteen thousand places paying the poor rates was made amply clear by the returns of 1815.[73]

Since the natural law reformers had used the upward secular trend of expenditures as the principal weapon against the Poor Laws, they did not take into view the short run changes which came with the fluctuations in trade. The economics of the day had no business cycle theory to aid the understanding of these changes, but the administrator of social welfare could not fail to see the connection between relief and unemployment. The returns of 1815 revealed the influence of the business cycle on relief expenditures. With the repeal of the Orders in Council and the return of good harvests, business began to revive in 1813 and continued to flourish until the end of the war. During these prosperous years, gross expenditures fell from £8,865,838 in 1813 to £7,508,853 in 1815, a decrease of 15 per cent. Of the five categories included in the gross expenditures, all declined except Church rates and highway rates. The costs of maintaining the poor fell from £6,676,105 in 1813 to £5,418,845 in 1815, a decrease of 19 per cent.

In addition to the amount of expenditures, the Tory Ministers who had ordered the returns of 1815 wished to know the number and types of paupers receiving relief, and whether it was received indoors or out, permanently or occasionally. Since the Government continued to think of the working classes as composed of the independent and the dependent poor, they wanted to know also the number of persons belonging to the Friendly Societies.

69

The growth of the Friendly Societies, composed of the independent poor, was the Government's chief criterion of social progress. According to the Poor Law Returns of 1803, there were 9,672 Societies having 704,350 members; according to the Poor Law Returns of 1815, which did not enumerate the Societies, the total membership had risen to 925,439, an increase of 31 per cent, and the later returns also showed that during the years of prosperity, 1813 to 1815, the members of the Friendly Societies increased as the number of the dependent poor diminished.[74]

More significant than the size of the Friendly Societies was the increasing number of people being relieved. In 1803 the total number of paupers (not including children of families outside workhouses) was 725,566; by 1815 this number had grown to 895,973, or an increase of 24 per cent.[75] However, the number of paupers varied with business conditions, fewer being relieved in 1815 than in 1813. Even the number of persons receiving indoor relief declined during the prosperous years.

The Poor Law Returns of 1815 indicated that the Tory Government had continued to pursue the main lines of social policy initiated by William Pitt and the humanitarian reformers. The Friendly Societies continued to receive the protection and encouragement of the magistrates. Poor relief continued to be administered outside the workhouses, and these institutions were being gradually transformed into poorhouses to receive children and impotent persons who had no relatives to care for them. In 1803 there were 3,765, and in 1815 there were 4,194; meanwhile the number of inmates had grown from 83,468 to 88,115.[76]

The Tory Government of 1815, apparently, was no longer anxious about the mobility of labor, as Pitt had been twenty years before. In 1815 the Government did not inquire about the number of paupers who were not parishioners; in 1803 there had been one hundred and ninety-four thousand such persons. That there were many more non-parishioners receiving relief at the end of the Napoleonic War than there had been in 1803 was pointed out by B. P. Capper in his *Observations*: "This class of persons must have contributed very largely to the increase of expenditures since that period, from the operation of the war, in assisting families of the military and navy to proceed to their different homes, particularly from the Metropolis and the different seaport towns, including a large portion of the natives of Ireland."[77] Although there was no longer anxiety over the mobility of labor, there was very great concern over how to return the Irish and the Scots to their native lands and how to prevent the residents of rural parishes from migrating to the towns in search of employment.

Even though the Returns of 1815 offered the most reliable information on which to legislate, few members of Parliament made use of them. Only the permanent administrators at the Board of Trade, the Board of Control, the Treasury, and similar offices, had sufficient training in statistics to grasp the significance of so vast a body of information. Among those seeking to apply the information was Thomas P. Courtenay, the permanent secretary of the Board of Control. A member of the House of Commons Poor Law Committee, Courtenay led the opposition to the doctrinaire aspects of the Poor Law Report. In the spring of 1817, as we have seen previously, he wrote his first letter to William Sturges Bourne asserting that the latter's views did not reflect the opinions of all the members of the Committee. In a second letter addressed to Sturges Bourne on March 23, 1818, he presented to him his *Treatise on the Poor Laws*, with the following introduction: "It is, in fact, my dissent from some of the doctrines laid down and my repugnance to some of the measures recommended in the Report of the Committee over which you presided that I have been led to this publication."[78]

Courtenay's primary purpose was to refute the natural law doctrine of acceleration, viz., that the Poor Laws did not relieve paupers but merely increased their numbers. He was one of the few reformers who tried to deflate the rates. Using the Returns of 1815, he attempted to show the relation between the price of wheat and the growth of population on the one hand, and the increasing costs of relief on the other hand. He calculated the proportion of paupers to the population as 7.7 per cent in 1803, and 8.2 per cent in 1815. "If we reduce to sums assessed at various periods into quarters of wheat at the respective prices, the proportion of assessments to each thousand of population would be as follows: 1802, 145 quarters; 1815, 116 quarters."[79] He added to this calculation Capper's observation that the Church, county and highway rates had increased faster than the poor rates. Courtenay asserted throughout his *Treatise* that the poor rates had not increased faster than other prices and that the Committee had furnished "no fact in proof of the progressiveness of assessments."

Courtenay took issue with the Poor Law Report on a second major doctrine, viz., that the partial payment of wages out of the rates tended to keep wages low. Admitting that wages were being paid, in part, from the rates, he thought the cause of low wages had to be sought elsewhere. "The great occasional fluctuations in trade over the past twenty-five years," he said, "were the real cause of the disparity between prices and wages, since the rise of prices always occurs more rapidly and disappears more slowly than the advance of wages."[80]

Courtenay's remonstrances, however, did not deter Sturges Bourne from proceeding with legislation in keeping with the natural law doctrine of the Poor Law Report. On March 12, 1818, he introduced two bills which were a drastic departure from the policies initiated by Thomas Gilbert thirty years before and which had been perpetuated by Sir George Rose.[81]

Sturges Bourne's Poor Law Amendment Bill was designed to abolish the allowance system by taking children from parents who could not support them and placing them in workhouses or schools of industry. In keeping with Malthusian morals, the bill authorized the parish officers "to discriminate in the relief they offered and to regulate its amount and nature by the character and habits of those to whom it was granted." Moreover, the bill would enable the magistrates to remove the Irish and Scots, who had come to England in large numbers during the war, and send them to the seaport nearest their homes.[82]

During the debates on the bill, Curwen, as leader of the Whig opposition, objected to the bill because of the cruelty of separating children from their parents. When the House of Commons voted on this particular clause it was adopted by a vote of forty-six to fourteen.[83] The House of Lords, however, rejected the clause and refused to take further action on the other aspects of the Poor Law Amendment Bill.[84]

Sturges Bourne's second bill, which was passed by Parliament without much debate, became known as the Parish Vestry Act.[85] The new law enabled the parish to elect a vestry from the ratepayers, granting to each member voting rights in proportion to the amount of rates paid. Under the new law, the vestryman paying fifty pounds would have two votes; seventy-five pounds, three votes; one hundred pounds, four votes; one hundred and twenty-five pounds, five votes; and one hundred and fifty pounds, six votes, the largest number of votes to be cast by any ratepayer. In proposing this law Sturges Bourne frankly wished to follow the example of the Kirk Sessions of Scotland, which gave to the wealthier classes the greater influence in managing the affairs of the poor.

Moreover, the measure was in keeping with the natural law principle of self-interest, those having the most interest in keeping the rates low being vested with the authority to do so. Although the Whigs objected to a system of plural voting, they were unable to prevent the bill from becoming law.[86]

On April 30, 1818, Sturges Bourne introduced a third bill proposing a general revision of the Laws of Settlement.[87] Since he wished to increase the authority of the parish officials and to reduce the costs of appealing to the magistrates, he thought it necessary to clarify and strengthen the Laws of Settlement. He proposed, therefore, to restrict the ways of obtaining a legal settlement. He would prevent apprentices under sixteen from obtaining a settlement, and he would prevent acquiring a settlement by renting a tenement for forty days. In place of these liberal provisions, he would require a residence of three years. Although little progress was made on this bill during 1818, a modified version of it was adopted the following year. Under the new law it was not possible for the working man to obtain a legal residence by renting a tenement; it was now necessary for him to rent a separate house for a year at not less than ten pounds annually.[88] Under the law of 1819 persons who had migrated from Scotland, Ireland, and the Channel Isles were liable to removal. Henceforth the parish officials might return such migrants to the seaport nearest their home.

Although Sturges Bourne had suffered defeat in 1818 at the hands of the leaders of the Tory Government, he returned to the reform of the Poor Laws early in the next session of Parliament. He obtained the reappointment of the Poor Law Committee, having about the same members as the previous Committees. Since the Tories were still badly divided on the question, it was necessary for Sturges Bourne to enlist the support of the Whigs by appointing a Committee. Henry Brougham, who had no inclination to lessen the embarrassment of the Tory Ministers, insisted that a commission be appointed and that the Government undertake legislation on so important a question. But failing to make the reform of the Poor Laws a party question, Brougham refused to serve on the Poor Law Committee and left the leadership of the opposition in the hands of John C. Curwen.

Sturges Bourne's second parliamentary maneuver was to divide the Poor Law question into two bills, one containing the controversial provisions and the other including those measures which had been accepted the year before. The Poor Laws Amendment Bill became law without much debate, but the Poor Rates Misapplication Bill, which separated children from parents who could not support them, again aroused controversy.

The Poor Law debates of 1819 revealed that the Whigs were as seriously divided on the question as the Tories — not that they were willing to defend the existing system, but that they were unable to agree on a remedy. Curwen worthily carried on the Whig humanitarian tradition of Whitbread and Fox. Well-informed and sympathetically identified with the working classes, he did not follow the dogmas of either the theologians or the natural law reformers. He held the opinion that the cost of living had doubled during the war, while wages had risen by only 50 per cent. If this were so, then the proper answer was to raise wages. He thought the factory workers could improve their own conditions if they were left free to combine. As for agricultural workers, who were too scattered to combine, he thought the magistrates should set a minimum wage to maintain a family. He rejected such measures as badging the poor and the use of the workhouses, *in terrorem*, to deter people from parish relief.[89] He rejected Sturges Bourne's proposal to abolish the allowance system by separating children from their parents. To take the children away from the working classes, he said, would rob them "of the chief and greatest of happiness. . .I am not for interfering with their affections or comforts. I am not willing to offer them a temptation which, however reluctant their feelings would yield to, their necessities might compel them to comply with — such is my view of the bill."[90]

The Whig humanitarian tradition was also defended by Lord Milton. According to Milton, there were three groups of reformers. One group, agreeing with the principle of Malthus, would abolish the Poor Laws entirely. A second group would retain them and improve their administration, and in this class he placed himself and Curwen. A third group, in which he placed Sturges Bourne, would confine the benefit and operation of the Poor Laws to the old and impotent.[91]

There were some Whigs, however, who opposed Sturges Bourne's reforms because they were not extreme enough to deter paupers from seeking relief. Among this small group of doctrinaire reformers, Henry Brougham was the most vocal. Joseph Hume was as doctrinaire as Brougham. If Hume could have had his way, he

74

would have enacted at once Malthus's remedy, "that from and after the passage of this act, no child, legitimate or illegitimate, should be entitled to a maintenance from the parish."[92] Another natural law reformer, David Ricardo, opposed Sturges Bourne's bill "principally on the ground that it tended to increase population. He thought the bill was like the plan of Mr. Owen, in a worse shape and carried to a greater extent."[93]

The Whig opposition, however, was too divided to prevent the Poor Rates Misapplication Bill from passing the House of Commons, but in the Upper House the Whigs and Tories united to defeat it. Lord Lansdowne, a leader of the Whigs, objected to the building of industrial schools for children. "Taking away children from their parents," he said, "tended directly to destroy those ties of affection which knit together the families of the poor."[94] Among the Tory defenders of the bill, one who did not think it too harsh, was Lord Harrowby. This devout Evangelical, who had supported many humanitarian reforms, preferred to educate the children as useful members of society than to leave them with "profligate parents." The opposition of Lord Liverpool was decisive. He ridiculed the principle of spending more money now to save more later; the cost of building schools of industry in which to house the children would increase rather than reduce the poor rates.[95]

Inasmuch as the controversial proposal to end the allowance system by placing children in schools of industry had been incorporated in a separate bill, the Poor Laws Amendment Bill was pushed through Parliament without much debate. Far more comprehensive than the Parish Vestries Act of the previous year, the Act to Amend the Laws for the Relief of the Poor embraced all the reforms that Parliament was willing to accept.[96] Although it was later called the Select Vestry Act, it did much more than change the administration of the Poor Laws.[97]

The primary objects of the new law were to curtail relief expenditures and to restore the independence of the working classes. According to the natural law doctrine, these objects could be achieved by increasing the authority of the parish ratepayers who had the greatest interest in reducing expenses. Moreover, the parish officials, who alone knew the recipients of relief, were in best position to distinguish between the profligate and the deserving poor. Hence, the select vestry was clothed with the duty of rewarding the virtuous poor and punishing the idle and improvident. To effect the moral regeneration of the working classes the select vestry was enabled to appoint a salaried assistant overseer. That the select vestry failed to achieve its purpose, even with the help of a salaried official, shows the fallacy upon which it was based. It was a fallacy to assume that the self-interest of the rate-payers would effect a more efficient management than the alleged benevolence of the magistrates.

The controversy over administration set the natural law reformers against the humanitarians. The natural law reformers, on one hand, insisted that the magistrates, guided by benevolence rather than self-interest, were profuse in granting relief; the humanitarians, on the other hand, assuming too readily that the parish officials always strove to keep the rates low, wished to enlarge the power of the justices of the peace, enabling them to order relief. Moreover, the humanitarian reformers clothed the justices with authority to grant relief to needy persons in their own homes. Hence, the 36 Geo. III. cap. 23, which repealed an earlier law forbidding relief to persons in their houses, authorized two justices to order relief for a period of three months. The later 55 Geo. III. cap. 137 enabled one justice to order relief to persons in their homes for three months and empowered two justices to order relief for six months, "and so on from time to time as occasion shall require."

The Poor Law reformers of 1819 fully intended to curtail this "profuse benevolence" of the justices. Under the new law the justices could order relief only after the pauper had proven that he had applied to a select vestry which had refused to act.[98] In places lacking a select vestry two or more justices might order relief for one month, but only after they had carefully investigated "the character and conduct" of persons applying for relief. "This is a considerable curtailment of the power in ordering relief," Sir George Nicholls declared. "The impolicy of conferring a large discretionary power in cases notoriously open to misrepresentation and of the real merits of which the justices, from their social position, would almost necessarily be incompetent judges. . . ."[99]

A much larger duty than the curtailing of expenses was conferred upon the substantial property holders who constituted the select vestries. The select vestry was to meet once in fourteen days "to inquire into and determine upon the proper objects of relief and the nature and amount of the relief to be given and in each case shall take into consideration the character and conduct

76

of the poor person to be relieved and shall be at liberty to distinguish between the deserving and the idle, extravagant or profligate
poor." With this obligation the select vestry was more than a welfare agency; it was to be henceforth a society for the suppression
of vice and the reward of virtue.

Since the law of 1819 assumed that many of those on relief
were extravagant or improvident, it authorized the select vestry to
offer loans instead of relief. If the person failed to repay the loan
to the parish, and if he were guilty of "extravagance or neglect or
wilful misconduct," two justices could commit him to prison "for
any time not exceeding three months." Adding to this humiliation of the poor, the law of 1819 enabled the parishes to lay claim
to the pensions of soldiers and sailors and to the wages of merchant seamen if they failed to support the members of their family, including children, parents, and grandparents.

The Poor Law reformers of 1819 asserted the original intention
of Elizabeth I by commanding the parishes to set the people to
work, keeping them "fully and constantly employed." In order to
provide employment instead of relief, the parishes were empowered to lease land and to build workhouses.

Since unemployment had increased relief expenditures, the
Poor Law reformers wished to discourage immigration into England from Ireland, Scotland, and the Channel Isles of Man, Jersey,
and Guernsey. Large numbers of persons had come into England
during the war to find employment, and because they were not
subject to the Laws of Settlement, they could not be removed.
The Law of 1819 remedied this deficiency by allowing the parish
to return such persons to the seaport nearest their homes.

Without fully comprehending what they saw, the reformers of
1819 took notice of still another aspect of the social transformation
that had occurred during the Napoleonic War. Inasmuch as the
working classes were gathering into the areas where they could find
cheap housing, they were paying rents too low to be taxed. The new
law, consequently, enabled the parishes to rate the owners rather
than the occupiers. But this was not an adequate response to a situation which required either a county or national rate. An adequate
reponse to a new industrial situation could not be made so long as
the reformers continued to hold the belief that more relief funds
would only increase the number of people and multiply their misery.

It is difficult to estimate the consequences of the new Poor Law
of 1819, but it is clear that in some places authority was trans-

ferred from the magistrates to the parishes and concentrated in the hands of the richest ratepayers. Hundreds of parishes, the largest and wealthiest, elected select vestries and appointed paid overseers. Since the new law enabled them but did not compel them to act, the vast majority of the parishes did not comply with it. However, that aspect of the law was effective which curtailed the authority of the justices in ordering relief. The majority of the justices were undoubtedly willing to have this onerous burden removed from their shoulders.

We have called the new Poor Law of 1819 a triumph of the natural law doctrine. The natural law tradition of the eighteenth century viewed poverty as a necessary spur to labor. Because labor was unpleasant, people must be made to work. The natural law reformers, holding this view, wanted to use the workhouse to deter the pauper and to shield the parish rates from the demands of the idle and profligate. Malthus inherited this tradition and used it in the debate with Godwin and Paine to refute their arguments for equalitarianism. He greatly invigorated the eighteenth-century tradition by interpreting it in terms of the principle of population. Since he assumed that England had a redundant population, he believed that whatever encouraged early marriage and large families among the working classes aggravated misery. He offered moral restraint, the exercise of prudence and foresight, as the alternative to vice and misery.

Why did the Evangelicals of Clapham who had labored for three decades to ameliorate conditions, capitulate to the natural law reformers and abandon to them the reform of the Poor Laws? Some did so because they accepted the natural law theology of Malthus and Sumner. Some Evangelical preachers began to speak of poverty as God's probation and of self-help as His plan for a better life here and hereafter. Malthus's morals and theology appealed to those pious clergymen who were already busy promoting voluntary schools and churches. The preachers of Biblical doctrines needed little persuasion to believe that charity was better than compulsory poor relief — because giving blessed the giver as well as the gift. Moreover, the signs of the times seemed to confirm Malthus in his teaching that the population was redundant and misery constantly increasing.

NOTES

[1] Sir George Nicholls, *A History of the English Poor Laws* (2nd ed., 1898), II, 192.

[2] T. R. Malthus, *An Essay on the Principle of Population* (5th ed., 1817), III, 275.

[3] *Ibid.* (4th ed., 1807), II, 401.

[4] Arthur Young in the *Annals of Agriculture*, as well as the Society for Bettering the Condition of the Poor, frequently advocated the "cow and cottage system."

[5] *Quarterly Review*, XVI (1816), 98-99.

[6] *Philanthropist*, VI (1816), 15. This bank was also publicized in the *Reports of the Society for Bettering the Condition of the Poor.*

[7] *Ibid.*, IV (1814), 76-84. Also, *Quarterly Review*, XVI (1816), 100.

[8] Joseph Hume, *An Account of the Provident Institution for Savings Established in the Western Part of the Metropolis* (London, 1816), p. 8.

[9] *Quarterly Review*, XVI (1816), 111.

[10] *Philanthropist*, VI (1816), 8.

[11] *Quarterly Review*, XVI (1816), 107. For the history of this and other early savings banks, see William Lewins, *A History of Banks for Savings* (London, 1866), pp. 24-33.

[12] *Parliamentary Debates*, XXXIII, 841.

[13] George Rose, *Observations on Banks for Savings* (London, 1816), pp. 1-3.

[14] *Parliamentary Debates*, XXXV, 225.

[15] *Ibid.*, p. 835.

[16] Albert Fishlow, "The Trustee Savings Banks," *Journal of Economic History*, XXI (1961), pp. 26-40.

[17] *Parliamentary Debates*, XXXVII, 1157.

[18] John H. Clapham, *An Economic History of Modern Britain*, (Cambridge; University Press, 1926), I, 300.

[19] Gayer, Rostow, and Schwartz, *The Growth and Fluctuation of the British Economy 1790-1850*, I, 113-17. See also, Thomas Tooke, *A History of Prices and the State of the Circulation from 1793-1837*, II, 8-13.

[20] *Parliamentary Debates*, XXXIV, 878-901.

[21] *Gentlemen's Magazine*, XCIX, Pt. I, 178.

[22] *Parliamentary Debates*, XXXV, 525.

[23] Malthus, *Essay* (5th ed., 1817), III, 265.

[24] *Ibid.*, 265.

[25] *Ibid.*, 272.

[26] *Ibid.*, 267.

[27] *Ibid.*, 323.

[28] Sidney and Beatrice Webb, *English Poor Law History*: Part II, *The Last Hundred Years* (London: Longmans, Green, 1929), I, 40-43.

[29] *Report from the Select Committee on the Poor Laws, House of Commons*, 1817, p. 4. The full Report may be found in the *Annual Register*, (1817).

[30] *Ibid.*, p. 5.

[31] *Ibid.*, p. 17.

[32] *Ibid.*, p. 18.

[33] *Ibid.*, p. 8.

[34] *Ibid.*, p. 9.

[35] *Ibid.*, p. 15.

[36] Thomas P. Courtenay, *Copy of a Letter to the Right Honorable William Sturges Bourne, Chairman of the Select Committee of the House of Commons Appointed for the Consideration of the Poor Laws*, (London, 1817), p. 17.

[37] *Parliamentary Debates*, XXXVI, 298.

[38] *Ibid.*, 1365.

[39] *Ibid.*, 1366.

[40] *Report from the Committee on the Poor Laws, House of Lords*, 1817, p. 8.

[41] *Ibid.*, p. 10.

[42] *Report. . . . .on the Poor Laws, H. of C.*, 1817, p. 133. The Reverend John W. Cunningham, Vicar of Harrow, gave evidence of the failure of Friendly Societies. He also found that savings banks were of little benefit to the poor of London and throughout Middlesex and Hertfordshire because their wages were too low to permit them to save.

[43] *Report. . .on the Poor Laws, H. of L.*, 1817, for the testimony of Paul M. James relating to Birmingham, see pp. 176-81. For the testimony of William D. Evans relating to Manchester, see pp. 155-64.

[44] For Beriah Drew's testimony relating to Bermondsey, see *Ibid.*, pp. 79-83. For John Heaver's testimony relating to Spitalfields, see the H. of C. *Report*, pp. 34-40. Perhaps no one was better informed about working class conditions in London than William Hale. For his testimony, see the H. of C. *Report*, pp. 41-48.

[45] H. of C. *Report*, Appendix C., pp. 155-56.

[46] *Ibid.*, Appendix C., p. 158.

[47] For example, see the testimony of Nicholson Calvert, who had been a magistrate in Hertford for thirty years, *Ibid.*, p. 120.

[48] *Ibid.*, Appendix A., p. 147.

[49] *The First Report of the Society for the Suppression of Beggars* (Edinburgh, 1814), p. 23.

[50] *Fifth Report of the Society for the Suppression of Beggars* (Edinburgh, 1818), p. 40.

[51] *Report for the Directors of the Town's Hospital of Glasgow on the Management of the City Poor. . .* (Glasgow, 1818), p. 21.

[52] *Ibid.*, p. 41.

[53] *Ibid.*, p. 104.

[54] *Report from the Committee on the Poor Laws, House of Lords*, 1817, p. 134.

[55] I am indebted to Frank W. Fetter for the identification of the Authors of economic articles in both the *Quarterly Review* and the *Edinburgh Review*: for the former, see the *Journal of Political Economy*, LXVI; and for the latter, see *Ibid.*, LXV.

[56] Orlo Williams, *Life and Letters of John Rickman* (New York: Houghton, Mifflin, 1912), p. 193.

[57] *Quarterly Review*, XVIII (January, 1818), 280.

[58] *Ibid.*, 307.

[59] *Ibid.*, XIX (April, 1818), 85.

[60] *Ibid.*, 97.

[61] *Ibid.*, 104.

[62] *Ibid.*, 115.

[63] *Edinburgh Review*, XXVIII (March, 1817), 4.

[64] *Ibid.*, 13.

[65] *Ibid.*, XXIX (February, 1818), 271.

[66] *Ibid.*, 283.
[67] *Christian Observer*, XVII, (1818), 42.
[68] *Eclectic Review*, 2nd Ser., X (1818), 205.
[69] *Ibid.*, 422.
[70] 55 Geo. III, c. 47.
[71] *Abstract of Returns Relative to the Expense and Maintenance of the Poor* (London, 1818), p. 638.
[72] *Ibid.*
[73] *Ibid.*, p. 630.
[74] *Abstract of Returns* (1804), p. 715; *Abstract of Returns* (1818), p. 630.
[75] *Abstract of Returns* (1818), p. 637.
[76] *Ibid.*, p. 629.
[77] *Ibid.*, p. 638.
[78] Thomas P. Courtenay, *A Treatise on the Poor Laws* (London, 1818), p. 1.
[79] *Ibid.*, p. 165.
[80] *Ibid.*, p. 108.
[81] *Parliamentary Debates*, XXXVII, 1055.
[82] *Ibid.*, 1057.
[83] *Ibid.*, XXXVIII, 578.
[84] *Ibid.*, 916.
[85] 58 Geo. III, c. 69.
[86] *Parliamentary Debates*, XXXVIII, 574-75.
[87] *Ibid.*, XXXVIII, 420.
[88] 50 Geo. III, c. 50.
[89] *Parliamentary Debates*, XL, 466.
[90] *Ibid.*, 468.
[91] *Ibid.*, 1126.
[92] *Ibid.*, 472.
[93] *Ibid.*, 471.
[94] *Ibid.*, 1514.
[95] *Ibid.*, 1515.
[96] Sir George Nicholls, *op. cit.*, II, 181.
[97] Sidney and Beatrice Webb have underestimated the importance of the legislation of 1819. See their *English Poor Law History: Part I. The Old Poor Law*, p. 151-52.
[98] 59 Geo. III, c. XII.
[99] Sir George Nicholls, *op. cit.*, II, 183.

IV

THE ORIGINS OF RADICAL OPPOSITION:
Part I. Jeremy Bentham

THE natural law reform of the Poor Law, as we have seen in a previous chapter, triumphed with the publication of the Poor Law Report in 1817 and with the passage of the Sturges Bourne Select Vestry Act in 1819. The triumph came in opposition to the humanitarian reformers, who had done much to ameliorate the Poor Law during the Napoleonic War. The natural law reformers succeeded because they had accumulated a powerful arsenal of weapons against the Poor Law. The most powerful of these weapons was Malthus's principle of population which accounted for indigence in terms of surplus population.

During the 1820's another group of reformers, the Benthamite Radicals, augmented the growing hostility to the Poor Law. The major Radical weapon against the Poor Law was the economic doctrine that greater freedom for capital investment was necessary to supply employment for a redundant population. Added to this doctrine of freedom for capitalistic enterprise was the doctrine of the natural corruption inherent in the existing system of Poor Law administration. The Radical doctrines against the Poor Law, which had gone unheeded until the 1820's, can best be understood in the light of Jeremy Bentham's career and teaching.[1]

Trained as a lawyer, Jeremy Bentham early forsook the practice of law to pursue the career of moral philosopher and reformer. Throughout his long life as a reformer, he always applied his general principles to practical problems. His enthusiasm for reform was so persistent and his knowledge of the law so extensive that he rarely lacked the patience and ingenuity to find a remedy for the abuse which at any time claimed public attention.

Once Bentham had formulated his central principle, he continued to apply it to the most complex social situations. The principle of utility was set forth in the preface to his first major work, *A Fragment on Government*, which he published in 1776. In this work he defined what he called his "fundamental axiom" as follows: "It is the greatest happiness of the greatest number that is the measure of right and wrong. . . ."[2] Bentham confidently expected that by the careful application of his axiom he could accomplish in the moral science something comparable to what was being done in the physical sciences.[3]

In his second major work, *An Introduction to the Principles of Morals and Legislation*, printed in 1780, he expanded his discussion of the principle of utility to what he felt was a major contribution to social science: "Nature has placed mankind under the governance of two sovereign masters, pain and pleasure. It is for them alone to point out what we ought to do, as well as to determine what we shall do. On the one hand the standard of right and wrong, on the other the chain of causes and effects are fastened to their throne. They govern us in all we do, in all we say, and in all we think: every effort we can make to throw off our subjection, will serve but to demonstrate and confirm it. In words a man may pretend to abjure their empire: but in reality he will remain subject to it all the while."[4]

Bentham assumed that the principle of utility was like an axiom in mathematics, for, as he said, "that which is used to prove everything else cannot be proved: a chain of proofs must have their commencement somewhere."[5] Having assumed a self-evident proposition and having attributed to it the certainty of mathematics, Bentham spent the rest of his long life applying it to the reformation of social and political institutions.[6]

The longer Bentham applied his principle of utility to the existing society, the more convinced he became that he had found the key to the mysteries of government. "Now for some years past," he wrote in 1822, "all inconsistencies, all surprises have vanished; everything that has served to make the field of politics a labyrinth has vanished. . . . A clue has been found, it is the principle of self-government. Man, from the very constitution of nature, prefers his own happiness to that of all other sensitive beings put together; but for this self-interest, the species could not have had existence."[7]

The principle of utility, like other self-evident propositions, was a double-edged sword; it could be used to defend as well as to attack. In Bentham's hands the principle was a weapon of attack; but William Paley used the same principle to defend the institutions of church and state. By applying the principle of utility conservatively, William Paley won popularity for his major work, *Moral and Political Philosophy*, and pre-empted the field so that Bentham gained little recognition for his views during the decades when England was at war with France.[8]

While Paley was capturing an English audience for his version of utilitarianism, Bentham gained some recognition for his doctrine on the Continent. He became so well known in France that the National Assembly, in 1792, declared him a citizen of France, along with other such celebrated reformers as Thomas Paine, Joseph Priestly, William Wilberforce, Thomas Clarkson, and James Mackintosh.[9]

The French Revolution and the wars which followed it mark the period of Bentham's life when he was better known as a philanthropist than as a political reformer.[10] In an age of humanitarian reform, when Hanway, Wilberforce, and others were being celebrated, it was possible for one to gain national recognition as a philanthropist. Because of his primary interest in penal law, Bentham undertook the promotion of prison reform, a movement which had already brought fame to John Howard. During the war against the French Republic, while liberal political reform was being suppressed in England, the amelioration of social conditions was the only door left open to one who, like Bentham, had a desire for drastic reform.

Bentham spent more than twenty years promoting prison reform. His plan of reform was the Panopticon. While in Russia in 1785 visiting his brother Samuel, who was in command of a regiment of Russian troops, Jeremy conceived the principle of central inspection.[11] He derived the principle from an example so simple and vivid that he held it to be scientifically demonstrated. The example was Samuel's method of encamping his military regiment for the night. Whenever he bivouacked, he pitched his own camp on the knoll of a hill and had his troops camped in aisles radiating from the knoll. From this vantage Samuel was able to inspect his men at a glance without their being aware of his supervision. This military experience gave to Samuel and Jeremy the idea of constructing a building that would incorporate the principle of military inspection. Such a building, they thought, could be economically constructed for all types of public institutions, including prisons, schools, hospitals, and workhouses.[12]

Following the example of a military camp, Jeremy and Samuel designed the Panopticon, a circular building with partitions radiating from the center. Workmen, prisoners, students, or patients might be placed in separate cells or apartments at the circumference of the building, while at the center, the lodge, raised above the level of the first floor, would conceal the supervisor. From this vantage the inspector could see the people in his charge without their knowing it. Such was the building embodying the principle of central inspection. Rigorous and military in its efficiency, the Panopticon was applied successively to prisons, workhouses, and schools.[13]

The details of the Panopticon were set forth in a series of letters written while Bentham was in Russia and sent to a friend in England. When these letters were reprinted in 1791, Bentham added two postscripts which explained his principles of prison management. In addition to the principle of central inspection were the principles of contract-management and industrial management.

Bentham had adopted the principle of contract-management as early as 1778, when he published the pamphlet, *View of the Hard Labour Bill.* This pamphlet was a criticism of the government's plan to build workhouses in which prisoners, who could no longer be sent to the American colonies, might be profitably employed. The government incorporated in the Hard Labour Bill some of the ideas of John Howard. In one section of the bill it was proposed "that the salary of the governor bear a direct proportion to the quantity of labour performed in each house and to arise chiefly, and if possible, totally from that source." Bentham preferred the principle of contract-management to the principle of trust-management because the former "joined the interest of the governor with his duty of seeing that all persons under his custody be regularly and profitably employed." Believing this principle to be a scientific discovery, Bentham called it the stroke of genius that distinguished the true legislator from "shallowness and empiricism."[14] Although Bentham had discovered the principle early in his career, he spent more than a half-century seeking to substitute contract-managers for trust-managers.

Bentham's principles of efficient industrial management were closely related to his doctrines of economic liberalism. After becoming a disciple of Adam Smith, he applied the doctrine of natural liberty to the laws of usury. In his pamphlet *The Defense of Usury*, which he wrote in 1787, he attempted to show how the legal restraints on borrowing restricted the progress of inventive industry. He argued at length the case for freer business enterprise. Happiness, he thought, could not be greatly increased without improving the opportunities for capital investment: "In a word, the proposition I have been accustomed to lay down to myself on this subject is the following one, viz., that no man of ripe years and of sound mind, acting freely and with his mind opened, ought to be hindered, with a view to his advantage from making such bargains in the way of obtaining money as he thinks fit. . . ." [15]

In the *Manual of Political Economy*, Bentham idealized the businessman's profit motive and held that the same motive, if allowed to operate, would improve the management of public institutions. Bentham also idealized the role of the inventor. Living at a time of technological improvement, he advocated greater freedom for the promoter of new enterprises. He even imagined himself, in cooperation with his brother Samuel, to be an inventor and a promoter of new enterprises.

In developing his plan of scientific management of prisons, Bentham enunciated the principle of industrial management. He entitled Letter XIII of the *Panopticon*, "Means of Extracting Labour." [16] In this letter Bentham held that the prison contractor must have a free hand in extracting the maximum effort from the convicts in his care. Moreover, he was even enthusiastic over the prospect of employing economically the willfully idle and criminal elements in society.

Since it was central in Bentham's doctrine that men would endure the pain of physical labor only to satisfy their need for food and shelter, he visualized the workingman as a calculator of pain and pleasure, carefully balancing the pain of labor against the pleasures of satisfying thirst and hunger. Assuming the utilitarian motivation of labor, he thought the prison contractor was in a good position to obtain the greatest amount of labor at a minimum cost. His formula for the efficient management of prisons was rigorous and clear: "Bread, though as bad as wholesome bread can be, they shall have then, in plenty; this and water and nothing else." [17]

If the rigorous regimen of cheap bread and water sounded too harsh to the "brethren of the would-be-reforming tribe," Bentham reminded them that under his plan the prisoners would be paid for their labor, and their wages would enable them to buy additional food and drink. He further reminded his critics that if prisoners were allowed to pursue their economic interests, it would not be necessary to punish them physically.

Bentham had so much confidence in the profit motive as a reliable guide for conduct that he had no anxiety lest the prison contractor starve the convicts in his charge. He argued simply that the warden would derive no advantage from such an economy. If a safeguard against prison brutality were needed, it would be adequate, he thought, to penalize the contractor for a high death rate among his charges and reward him for a low one. [18]

Inasmuch as Bentham universalized his principles of prison management, extending them to schools and workhouses, it is well to summarize the plan of the Panopticon for which he sought government support. First, the principle of central inspection would enable the warden of the prison to maintain a constant watch over the prisoners; at the same time, the government and the public could readily see that the prisons were properly managed. Second, the principle of contract-management would enable the keeper of the prison to share in the profits derived from prison labor. Third, the principle of industrial management would enable the keeper to extract the maximum amount of labor from the prisoners at a minimum cost. This careful balancing of the inputs of food and drink against the outputs of labor would, in Bentham's language, enable the contractor to maximize efficiency. By paying wages, rewarding the worker by the piece or task, it would be possible for the contractor to refrain from other types of punishment. Such were the principles of management which Bentham deduced from the self-evident proposition that men avoid pain and pursue pleasure.

After designing the Panopticon and clearly defining the principles of efficient management, Bentham resolved to demonstrate them in practice. In March, 1792, he requested the Tory government to allow him to undertake the management of one thousand convicts. [19] He proposed to build a Panopticon penitentiary house

and to substitute its principles of management for the unaccount-
able management of the hull-masters, who were incarcerating their
prisoners in abandoned ships. He requested of the government
only the cost of the subsistence of the convicts and the right to
retain any profit that he could derive from their labor. The government accepted Bentham's proposal and by an act of Parliament
authorized the purchase of a tract of land at Battersea Rise.[20]
Bentham, however, was unable to purchase the land because the
owner, Lord Spencer, feared that the building of a prison would
depreciate the rest of his property.

The failure to purchase Battersea Rise was one of many frustrating delays which prevented Bentham from building a model
prison. Still hopeful of success, Bentham spent twelve thousand
pounds of his own money for the purchase of lands at Tothill
Fields, but the government was now unwilling to proceed with its
original agreement. This decision left Bentham with a heavy loss
on the property purchased and without recompense for his time
and effort.

Not until 1811 did another Tory ministry redress the grievance
done to Bentham by compensating him for his losses. In an effort
to do justice to Bentham, the House of Commons appointed a
Select Committee on Penitentiary Houses, which fully reviewed
his plan of prison management. The Committee finally rejected his
plan because they preferred trust-management to contract-management. In their *First Report* to the House, the Committee declared
"that under a system in which pecuniary advantage is thus made
the most prominent object of attention the experiment of reformation would not be fairly tried."[21] That the government com-
pensated Bentham twenty-three thousand pounds for his capital,
time, and effort did not satisfy him, for he was denied the recognition which he had so long sought, and he was deprived of the
opportunity of demonstrating the feasibility of his cherished principles. The personal bitterness of this frustrating experience remained with him the rest of his life.

In the last years of his life Bentham wrote an old man's memoirs of the Panopticon scheme which he entitled, *History of the
War between Jeremy Bentham and George III.*[22] The war was not,
in fact, with George III but with the chief ministers of William
Pitt's government. Trouble arose primarily because Bentham was
of such a temperament that he could not refrain from ridiculing
those who disagreed with him and upon whom he depended for

assistance. Among his few friends at Court were the Clapham Evangelicals who, from the days of John Howard, had been deeply interested in prison reform. His most patient defender was William Wilberforce.[23]   It was in part due to Wilberforce's persistence that Bentham finally received compensation for his misspent effort.

"But for George the Third," Bentham declared in his *History*, "all the prisoners in England would, years ago, have been under my management. But for George the Third, all the paupers in the country would, long ago, have been under my management."[24] In retrospect, it is difficult to comprehend why Bentham had been so eager to undertake the management of all the paupers and prisoners of England. That he was eager to do so can scarcely be doubted. The Hard Labor Bill, for example, evoked the intense activity that led eventually to the Panopticon scheme of prison reform. Similarly, Pitt's Poor Law Bill of 1796 induced him to apply utilitarian principles to the problems of pauperism.

Bentham first gave his attention to the Poor Law in 1797 when he undertook the refutation of Pitt's Poor Law Bill, which he viewed as a gross violation of utilitarian principles.[25] If happiness were to be increased for a greater number of people, workingmen would have to labor longer and harder to produce more wealth.[26] According to Bentham, Pitt's bill reduced the laboring man's incentive by granting relief to idle and profligate persons. It blurred the line which separates sloth from industry. The poor man's interest — his claim to subsistence — was his ability to work, and since work was painful, no man would endure it except under the spur of necessity. Such was the law of nature, with which the legislator should comply.[27]

Bentham's main objection to Pitt's Poor Law Bill was profusion, by which he meant waste and corruption. In place of profusion, Bentham wanted "efficacious, unmischievous relief", a relief that should not be at the expense of the whole community. "It was not within the power of parishes to give kingdoms," he said, and to banish indigence, "it would be necessary to banish not only misfortune but improvidence."[28]

Bentham also stoutly opposed the system of outdoor relief recommended by Pitt's Poor Law Bill. He called outdoor relief the home provision or the small-establishment system; he preferred, instead, the large establishment, or the Panopticon-type workhouse, where subsistence could be carefully measured in order to obtain the greatest amount of labor.

Besides granting relief at home to the aged, infirm, and infants, Pitt proposed to relieve families who were burdened with small children under the age of employment. The family allowance, or "the extra-children clause," as Bentham called it, provided relief for "fathers having two children under the ages of five years and part of the family unable to maintain themselves," and it provided relief for widows with one child. The allotment to families with two children under five years of age was to be one shilling a week. In Bentham's estimate it was extravagant to increase the allotment for dependent children from sixpence to one shilling.[29]

Bentham was even more severe in his indictment of that section of the Poor Law Bill, which he ridiculed as "an opulence relief clause." Had this clause been enacted, an individual possessing property worth as much as thirty pounds would have remained eligible for relief. Against this new system of relief, Bentham defended the old system which he defined in these words: "come in and give up all, or stay out and starve."[30]

The hostile criticism of Pitt's Poor Law Bill was only the beginning of Bentham's effort to improve the Poor Law. The utilitarian principles, which he had applied to the management of prisoners, were to be applied also to the management of paupers.

Bentham's plan of pauper management was incorporated in a series of letters written to Arthur Young with the expectation that they would be published in the *Annals of Agriculture*. In the introductory letter to Arthur Young, written in September, 1797, Bentham inserted a "Pauper Population Table" with the instructions that it be circulated among the readers of the *Annals of Agriculture* and returned to him. Such returns, Bentham thought, would provide the information for the further development of his plan. The questions for which he sought an answer were deduced from a careful classification of paupers and from a clear analysis of the problems of pauperism. The returns which he sought, however, were not forthcoming, even though Arthur Young had made an urgent plea for cooperation. They were not forthcoming because the parish records did not contain answers to the questions which had been asked.[31]

In his classification of paupers and his analysis of the problems of pauperism, Bentham distinguished indigence from poverty. He estimated that poor people comprised nineteen-twentieths of all the population. Poor people were all the working classes who lacked income from property and the professions. The working classes included both independent and dependent poor; among the latter were the indigent poor, or in modern terms, the paupers. He explained indigence in terms of internal (personal) and external causes. Among the external causes of indigence he recognized several types of unemployment, including casual, cyclical, and technological unemployment. Although factual information for the measurement of unemployment was lacking, Bentham was still fully confident that the Panopticon was the right answer for every type of indigence.[32]

The needs of so large a segment of the population required a mammoth institution, and Bentham's plan was commensurate with the needs. He proposed to delegate authority over the indigent population to a joint stock company. This national charity corporation was to be an organization like the Bank of England. The National Charity Company, as conceived by Bentham, was not a business corporation free to pursue an unregulated course; rather it was a public authority to which certain functions were delegated by the state and which was kept under careful public scrutiny. Thus, in effect, he was extending to the national level the principles of the Gilbert Act, which had created Poor Law authorities for certain districts within the counties.

Bentham, however, greatly differed with the principles of the Gilbert Act when he substituted contract-management for trust-management. Believing in the principle of utility, Bentham could not rely upon the benevolence of rich men to manage public institutions efficiently. Indeed, it was central in his doctrine that the duties of public officials must be made to coincide with their interests. The National Charity Company, then, should be a means of joining interests with duties. The stockholders in the Company were to be paid interest on the capital invested, as well as dividends on profits. If the Charity Company could manage the paupers more efficiently than they were being managed under the trustee system, a portion of the savings (40 per cent) would be retained by the Company for distribution among the stockholders and the rest of the savings (60 per cent) would be returned to the parishes to reduce the poor rates.

The National Charity Company was only one aspect of Bentham's plan of pauper management. But because the plan was never completed, it was only a partial application of utility to the problems of inspection and control at the national level.[33] Bentham devoted most of his time, as shown by the letters on pauper management, in applying the principles of the Panopticon to the efficient management of workhouses at the local level. Under his plan, he expected to build 250 workhouses, or houses of industry, each having accommodations for two thousand persons to care for an estimated five hundred thousand paupers.[34]

The architectural design of the workhouses was identical to the Panopticon prison, being circular or polygonal in form. The wards to receive paupers lay at the outer edge of the building and were separated by partitions radiating from the central lodge where the inspector resided.[35] Such a building, as Bentham envisioned it, was a house of many public functions readily adaptable as hospital, prison, workshop, bank, inn, and poorhouse. Indeed, it needed to be a house of many facilities, since he delegated to the National Charity Company power to arrest and detain in it all persons without means of livelihood. The destitute were to be retained in the workhouse until employment could be found for them. Children whose parents could not support them should be detained at the workhouse and provided education and employment. All indigent children were to be apprentices to the Charity Company and retained as apprentices until they reached the age of twenty-one.

The workhouse was thus designed with magnificent proportions; it was also grandiose in the scope of social change which it envisioned. It necessitated a host of salaried officials and trained technicians whose duties, in keeping with utilitarian principles, would be identified with their interests. The new salaried official would supplant the country gentleman as the guardian of the poor. That the country gentleman was honorable in his conduct and beneficent in his intentions Bentham never denied, but he charged the country gentleman with negligence, ignorance, and indolence. When the country gentleman, in his capacity as Justice of the Peace, was measured against the plumb line of bookkeeping efficiency, Bentham found him quite inadequate.[36]

Bentham's plan of pauper management incorporated not only the businessman's standard of bookkeeping efficiency but also the military man's authority to manipulate those under his command. The inspector of workhouses was vested with the authority to regulate the input of pains and pleasures in order to increase the output of goods. The inspector also had the authority to control the inmates according to the principles of separation and aggregation.

In the Panopticon type of workhouse, Bentham made provision for the separation of the paupers into several different wards in order to protect their health, morals, and decency. If there were obvious advantages in separating people, there were also advantages in bringing them together for family life, education, and religious worship. The new principles of separation and aggregation, which Bentham set forth in meticulous detail, were the hallmarks of his system of pauper management; these principles were adopted later by his disciples and incorporated in their plans of dispauperization.[37]

The principles of industrial management, which Bentham had devised to obtain the maximum amount of labor from convicts, were applied also to the management of paupers. The manager of a workhouse should be free to exact labor "to as great a value as may be, consistently with the regard due to health, customary relaxation, and the observance of religious duties." He directed the manager of a workhouse to use food and drink as rewards for labor; if laziness were detected among the inmates, food should be withheld until the tasks had been performed.[38]

Bentham also recognized the desire for liberty as a motive among paupers. Hence, he would give no relief outside the workhouse and free no pauper from it until he had worked out the cost of his maintenance. The twin principles of earn-first and self-liberation provided the motives for the efficient management of paupers. These motives, however, would be ineffective unless conditions inside the workhouse were worse than those outside the workhouse. If the conditions inside were better, the motive of self-liberation would be weakened and the house would be overrun. To reduce the number of paupers in the workhouse, it was necessary merely to lessen the quantity of food and increase the quantity of labor. The diet of the workhouse, Bentham thought, should always be carefully controlled so that "charity-maintenance, or maintenance at the expense of others, should not be made more desirable than self-maintenance." Only the cheapest fare should be served in the house; an ample fare might be served only if it did not "render the condition of the burdensome poor more desirable than that of the self-maintaining poor."[39]

Besides lower wages and poorer diet, the conditions in the workhouse should be made worse than the conditions of free labor by the kind of employment it provided. Employment in the workhouse should be provided as a last resort and should be temporary in nature. If workers in this kind of employment were paid wages inferior to the rates paid outside, then free labor would always appear superior to the work provided by the public authority.[40] Thus in applying utilitarian principles to the management of paupers, Bentham clearly formulated the principle of less-eligibility, which his later disciples made the central aspect of the Poor Law of 1834.

Bentham detailed the principle of less-eligibility in his plan to extirpate mendicity. He assumed that the condition of the beggar was more eligible than the condition of the pauper maintained in idleness, otherwise the beggar would become a pauper. In order to clear the city streets of beggars, he recommended that the Poor Law officials be authorized to apprehend them and incarcerate them in the workhouse. To render the workhouse less eligible than begging, it should afford nothing more than the barest maintenance — "maintenance in the most frugal and least luxurious shape."[41] In his grim view of life, society could prevent mendicity only when it left no alternative between the workhouse and starvation.

To assure the prevention of begging, Bentham proposed to reward the persons apprehending beggars, as was done in the case of felons. Once safely in the custody of the workhouse, the beggar was charged with the expense of his arrest and was not granted freedom until he had paid this amount and had also obtained the assurance of employment.

Even though his later disciple, Edwin Chadwick, wrote the principle of less-eligibility into the Poor Law of 1834, Bentham received little recognition at the time he wrote the *Plan of Pauper Management.* At that time he was seeking financial assistance from the government to build the Panopticon prison, and he could scarcely insist on his ability to manage paupers until he had demonstrated that he could manage convicts. Moreover, the Clapham Evangelicals, who supported his plan of prison reform, had already rejected the major part of his plan for managing paupers. After the time of Thomas Gilbert, the Evangelicals had become fully committed to outdoor relief for all persons having friends or relatives to care for them. They were especially opposed to farming the poor, or to the contract system of management. Their Society for Bettering the Condition of the Poor, which did so much to ameliorate the condition of the poor during the following decade, supported legislation which was contrary to Bentham's plan of Poor Law reform.[42]

Bentham was also at odds with the group of natural law reformers who were seeking to reduce Poor Law expenditures. Some of these, such as Frederick Morton Eden, favored a contract system of pauper management, but many despaired in believing that paupers could be profitably employed. Thus, while Bentham was recommending that the poor be set to work, other natural law reformers were rejecting such a policy. To have accepted Bentham's plan would have required large outlays of capital for workhouses; such a policy, according to Eden and others, would divert capital from individuals who could employ it more profitably.

In the great controversy over the Poor Law, other social philosophers carried the field against Bentham. As William Paley had become recognized as the foremost utilitarian philosopher, so Thomas Robert Malthus gained similar pre-eminence over Bentham as a reformer of the Poor Law. About the same time that Bentham's letters on pauper management appeared in the *Annals of Agriculture*, Malthus published his *Essay on the Principle of Population*. So great was its success that Malthus published a much enlarged second edition in 1803. As long as the war against France lasted, Malthus's use of the principle of population as a defense of social inequality enabled him to achieve an unrivalled prominence as a social philosopher.

In such circumstances, Bentham's plan of pauper management had to wait for a more favorable season. He failed to gain a sympathetic audience for his reforms because they were such a drastic departure from the current humanitarian policies. Although he had published the work *Introduction to the Principles of Morals and Legislation* as early as 1789, he was still relatively unknown as a philosopher. During the first decade of the century he was widely known as a philanthropist and as the creator of the Panopticon. But even his plan of prison reform, based upon the principle of contract-management, was rejected in 1811. It is little wonder that Bentham, feeling like an alien in his own country, contemplated moving to the more congenial climate of Mexico.[43]

Although still feeling rejected by his countrymen, Bentham, now at the age of sixty, was actually on the threshold of the recognition which he had long sought. In his own neighborhood of Westminster, the radicals in politics and the dissenters in religion were ready to receive him. His neighbors, who had already turned a sharp sword of criticism against the unreformed House of Commons and the privileged Established Church, now began to celebrate Bentham as their philosopher. These earnest supporters at Westminster were not merely working-class agitators, but also middle-class business men and professional groups who were hostile to aristocratic domination of Church and State.

Ever sensitive to opportunities for reform, Bentham was disturbed in 1807 by the fall of the Talents Ministry. In the elections which followed, the only evidence of a popular opinion favoring reform was the return of Sir Francis Burdett and Lord Cochrane for Westminster. Their victories prompted Bentham to undertake the task of reinforcing their efforts. In 1809 he wrote a pamphlet, *The Elements of the Art of Packing,* to publicize the baneful influence of the libel laws which restricted the freedom of the press, but his attack on the laws was so extreme that his friend, Sir Samuel Romilly, entreated with him not to publish it, lest he be prosecuted under the very laws which he condemned.[44] The following year he completed another pamphlet, *Plan of Parliamentary Reform,* which he sent to William Cobbett with the hope that it would be published in the *Political Register.* Cobbett, however, returned it to him, and Bentham was unable to find a publisher for it during the period when England was at war with France.[45]

The end of the Napoleonic War brought not only the blessings of peace but also the calamities of an economic depression. The hungry discontent of the unemployed working classes expressed itself in mass demonstrations and in a renewed agitation for Parliamentary reform. In Westminster Sir Francis Burdett and Sir John Cartwright, the leaders of Parliamentary reform, were more loudly acclaimed than ever before. In the midst of this popular agitation for reform, Bentham published his *Plan of Parliamentary Reform,* and the pamphlet immediately won the attention of the Westminster reformers.[46]

In the social convulsions of a postwar depression, Benthamite Radicalism was born. True to his economic liberalism, Bentham blamed the extravagance of the Tory government for the economic ills of the time, and he offered as a remedy his *Plan of Parliamentary Reform.* The drastic reform of Parliament was, according to Bentham, the only way of checking excessive government expenditures. The Tory extravagance, he thought, would continue so long as particular interests, "monarchical and aristocratical" were adverse to the universal interests of the people. Since the members of Parliament had become a "sinister interest" opposed to general welfare, it was necessary to restore to the people a full control over their representatives. To achieve popular control over Parliament, Bentham recommended: (1) virtual universal manhood suffrage; (2) secret voting; (3) equal electoral districts; (4) the expulsion of placemen; and (5) compulsory attendance at all sessions of Parliament.[47]

Soon after Bentham had published his *Plan of Parliamentary Reform*, Sir Francis Burdett urged him to incorporate his proposals in a bill that could be presented to Parliament.[48] Although at first reluctant to comply with this request, Bentham eventually prepared a set of resolutions, and on June 2, 1818, Burdett introduced them in the House of Commons. The resolutions favoring universal suffrage, the secret ballot, and annual parliaments were viewed by most members of the House of Commons as being absurdly extreme. Even the friends of reform among the Whigs, Brougham, Romilly, and Russell, rejected the Radical resolutions. When the question of reform was finally put to a vote, no one was willing to support the resolutions and 106 voted against them.[49]

The Whig opposition in the House of Commons did not change Bentham's mind about the need for Radical reform. In December, 1819, he published his *Radical Reform Bill*, which included the main points of reform, universal suffrage, annual parliaments, and election by ballot.[50] He refuted the arguments of his friends, who preferred household suffrage, by declaring that the requirement of owning property would disqualify a majority of people. Because of the widespread opposition to his *Radical Reform Bill*, Bentham spent the early months of 1820 writing a defense which he called *Radicalism Not Dangerous*. In this defense of Radicalism he expressed a willingness to comply with the advice of his friends, who preferred household suffrage, but he could not bring himself to abandon the principle of universal suffrage, for it alone could give universal satisfaction.[51]

Bentham's advocacy of Radical reform alienated him from both the Whigs and the Tories at the time when the Poor Laws were again being hotly debated. His conviction that aristocratic influences tended to corrupt all branches of government induced him to give priority to the drastic reform of Parliament. Although Sturges Bourne had applied utilitarian principles to the reform of the Poor Law in 1819, it was not a Benthamite application of utility. The Sturges Bourne Act transferred the authority of levying the Poor Rates to wealthy individuals. Assuming that the self-interest of the rich would lead them to curtail expenditures, Sturges Bourne reapportioned suffrage according to income. By enlarging the voting power of wealthy persons in the Vestries,

Sturges Bourne ran counter to democratic principles at the time when Bentham was making his full commitment to democracy.

One may safely conclude that prior to 1820 Bentham's writings on the Poor Law had received very little attention, and that they had virtually no influence on the formation of national Poor Law policy. The utilitarian spirit which permeated his plan of pauper management was quite hostile to the humanitarian policy which had been adopted by Pitt and his followers. Although the Sturges Bourne Act was a utilitarian remedy for the disease of pauperism, it was not in keeping with Bentham's Radical doctrine.

What had Bentham achieved by 1820, at the venerable age of seventy-two? What had he achieved that would enable his later disciples to become effective reformers? In the first place, he bequeathed to his disciples Radicalism, which was primarily an attitude of hostility toward aristocratic institutions. More than this, he gave them a methodology which enabled them to make a quick diagnosis of social ills and to prescribe a remedy. Most of all, he imparted to them his spirit, a consuming desire for social improvement.

Bentham's method, which was characteristic of the age in which he lived, was to proceed systematically from a self-evident proposition. In his case, utility, man's desire to pursue his own happiness, was a proposition as certain as "the axioms laid down by Euclid."[52] Many persons made different applications of utility, but Bentham, applying it critically to the aristocracy, concluded that the Parliament could pursue only the self-interest of the few against the welfare of the many. Added to the negative side of social criticism was Bentham's utopian element, the greatest happiness for the greatest number. From the greatest-happiness principle he deduced the remedies for all social ills. As a result of his systematic application of utility, his disciples were able to draw from his writings pungent social criticism and to find, in addition to negative criticism, fully detailed plans of social reform.

The disciples inherited from Bentham not only his desire for social improvement but also his intolerance of those who did not possess his superior knowledge. The innate arrogance and impatience of the Radicals were increased by the current opinion that social science was not only possible but already in hand. Bentham's two most famous disciples, James Mill and David Ricardo, did much to expand his doctrine and to extend his influence. One cannot understand the growth and influence of Radicalism without a knowledge of the careers of these distinguished disciples.

NOTES

[1] Elie Halévy, *The Growth of Philosophic Radicalism* (New York, 1949), pp. 251-64. I have used the term 'Radical' to signify the influence of Jeremy Bentham and his principal disciples, James Mill and David Ricardo. The Benthamite Radicals differed from the natural law reformers in that they were willing to enact legislation to harmonize economic interests. I have borrowed Halévy's insight into the contradiction between the natural harmony of interests and artificial identity of interests to show the difference between the two groups of reformers. For this contradiction see *Ibid.*, pp. 498-99.

The literature on Bentham is voluminous and controversial. A standard work is Leslie Stephen, *The English Utilitarians* (London, 1900), Vol. I. A recent philosophical study of Bentham's remarkable career is Mary Mack, *Jeremy Bentham: An Odyssey of Ideas, 1748-1792* (London, 1962). For an analysis of the literature pertaining to Bentham's peculiar ideas on welfare, see Gertrude Himmelfarb, "Bentham's Utopia: The National Charity Company," in *The Journal of British Studies*, Vol. X, No. 1 (November, 1970), pp. 80-126. J. R. Poynter, *Society and Pauperism* (London, 1969), has a chapter devoted to Bentham's ideas on poor relief. For Poynter's estimate of Bentham's influence on the Poor Law of 1834, see pp. 326-29.

[2] *The Works of Jeremy Bentham*, ed. John Bowring (Edinburgh, 1843), I, 227.

[3] *Ibid.*, X, 78-80.

[4] *Ibid.*, I, 1.

[5] *Ibid.*, I, 2; IX, 7.

[6] *Ibid.*, X, 79.

[7] *Ibid.*, X, 80.

[8] *Ibid.*, X, 163-65.

[9] *Ibid.*, X, 281.

[10] Elie Halévy, *England in 1815* (New York, 1949), p. 578.

[11] *Works of Jeremy Bentham*, XI, 97.

[12] *Ibid.*, IV, 37. See also, Elie Halévy, *The Growth of Philosophic Radicalism*, pp. 84-85.

[13] The details of the building can be found in "Panopticon, Postscript I," *Works*, IV, 67-121.

[14] *Works*, IV, 12. See also, Stephen, *The English Utilitarians*, I, 200-206.

[15] *Works*, III, 3.

[16] *Ibid.*, IV, 54.

[17] *Ibid.*, IV, 53.

[18] *Loc. cit.*

[19] *Ibid.*, XI, 99.

[20] 34 Geo. III. Cap. 84. Also *Works*, XI, 148.

[21] *Works*, XI, 150.

[22] *Ibid.*, XI, 96.

[23] *Ibid.*, X, 393.

[24] *Ibid.*, XI, 96-97.

[25] Bentham, "Observations on the Poor Law Bill introduced by the Right Hon. William Pitt," *Works*, XIII, 440-61. Sidney and Beatrice Webb say that the pamphlet was printed for private circulation in 1797, at the time it was written. (*English Poor Law History: Part II: The Last Hundred Years*, I, 35, note #1.) Edwin Chadwick, however, denied that it had been printed. Chadwick edited and published it in 1838, and said that he found it among Bentham's manuscripts. (Bentham, *Works*, VIII, 440.) Sir John Bowring, in his introduction to Bentham's tracts on the Poor Laws, says that it had been

printed but not published before 1838. (*Works*, VIII, 358.) That Chadwick found it in manuscript and had to edit it for publication leads me to believe that it had never been put in a form ready for printing. The "Observations" were written in February, 1797, the larger and more significant work, "Pauper Management," was written in September of the same year and sent to Arthur Young for publication in the *Annals of Agriculture*. It is unlikely that Young would have published "Pauper Management" had he known of Bentham's harsh attack on Pitt's bill.

[26] For Halévy's analysis of Bentham's Poor Law tracts, see: *The Growth of Philosophic Radicalism*, p. 233.

[27] Bentham's attack on Pitt's bill resembled the Poor Law Report of 1834; and the remedy of 1834 was primarily his remedy. Bentham's charges against Pitt were (1) wasteful profusion and (2) careless administration. His remedy, like the remedy of 1834, was a well-administered subsistence and this meant a living standard only slightly above starvation.

[28] *Works*, VIII, 451.

[29] *Ibid.*, 445.

[30] *Ibid.*, 451.

[31] *Ibid.*, 362-68.

[32] *Ibid.*, 365.

[33] *Ibid.*, 369-71. S. E. Finer in *The Life and Times of Sir Edwin Chadwick*, p. 44, says the essence of Bentham's plan was a joint stock company and that Bentham expected the company to be self-supporting. Neither statement is completely accurate. That Bentham never completed that part of the work pertaining to organization shows that he was not very interested in it. While it is true that Bentham expected to make a profit from the efficient management of workhouses, the profit was relative to the existing system of poor rates.

[34] *Works*, VIII, 392.

[35] *Ibid.*, 375.

[36] *Ibid.*, 380-81.

[37] *Ibid.*, 372.

[38] *Ibid.*, 383.

[39] *Ibid.*, 384.

[40] *Ibid.*, 396-98.

[41] *Ibid.*, 401-2.

[42] Although Bentham, in proposing contract-management, was greatly at odds with the Evangelicals, he drew freely upon Count Rumford's *Essays* and upon the *Reports* of the Society for Bettering the Condition of the Poor. (*Works*, VIII, 438.) Bentham continued to seek the help of the Clapham Saints until after the settlement of his Panopticon claim in 1813. His attack upon Sir George Rose and his open advocacy of political Radicalism indicate that he had abandoned all hope of obtaining assistance from the Evangelicals.

[43] *Works*, X, 439.

[44] *Ibid.*, 450-59.

[45] Halévy's statement that Bentham had "an army of disciples" in 1813 is certainly an exaggeration. (*England in 1815*, p. 579.) It is more accurate to say that he had a dozen or more disciples and a small group of admirers. Although the number of persons with whom he corresponded over his long lifetime was large, the number of friends and disciples with whom he corresponded in any given year was small.

[46] *Works*, III, 433.

[47] *Ibid.*, 455.

[48] *Ibid.*, X, 491-94.

[49] *Parliamentary Debates*, XXXVIII, 1118.

[50] *Works*, III, 558.
[51] *Ibid.*, 599.
[52] *Ibid.*, IX, 5.

V

THE ORIGINS OF RADICAL OPPOSITION
Part II. James Mill and David Ricardo

JEREMY Bentham was successful in having as his disciples men of stern moral determination and great intellectual capacity. A score or more of intelligent young men gathered about him, at one time or another, to draw on his fertile knowledge of law. Chief among his disciples was James Mill. For a decade Mill resided with Bentham and served him in the diverse capacities of companion, secretary, advisor, and editorial assistant. More than anyone else, he assimilated Bentham's mass of prolix and unedited materials and reduced them to a state simple and direct enough to be published as articles.

James Mill was born and reared in Scotland. With the financial assistance of Sir John Stuart, a philanthropist, Mill was sent to the University of Edinburgh to be trained for the Presbyterian ministry. He finished his theological studies in 1797, and in the following year, at the age of twenty-five, he was licensed to preach. During the next few years of his life he was more often engaged as tutor than as preacher.[1]

In 1802 Mill migrated to London to venture upon the career of a writer. Prior to meeting Bentham, he acquired experience as a journalist and editor. In 1805 when thirty-three years of age he married Harriet Burrow, a woman of moderate means. To this union was born the following year the first of nine children, and the proud parents named him John Stuart.

Sometime during 1808, Mill met Bentham and this meeting was the beginning of an intimate association that lasted for a decade. For at least part of each of the following ten years, Mill resided with Bentham and derived from him a part of his livelihood. During the early years of this unusual association, Mill used to think of himself as Bentham's "most faithful and fervent disciple" and proudly professed to his master that no one else had taken up his principles so completely and "is so thoroughly in the same way of thinking with yourself."[2] In 1814 when the disciple had reached the age of forty-one and Bentham sixty-six, Mill fully expected to succeed him as the principal utilitarian philosopher. Hopeful of disseminating Bentham's works throughout England, as Etienne Dumont was doing on the Continent, Mill pledged his life to propagating the utilitarian system.[3]

Mill's pledge was not an empty promise. He grasped every opportunity to disseminate and defend utilitarian ideas. In his articles for the *Edinburgh Review* and in William Allen's *Philanthropist*, he propounded Bentham's philosophy of education and legal reform. In 1814, while Mill was fully occupied with the history of British India, he was asked to contribute articles to the "Supplement" of the *Encyclopaedia Britannica.* Although reluctant to take time from his larger work, he accepted the invitation. His articles for the "Supplement" were whipped up in a hurry from materials already at hand, drawn from Bentham's profuse manuscripts.[4] Expecting little response to ideas that had been ignored so long, Mill was astonished when his articles aroused considerable attention.[5]

Mill's most important contribution to the "Supplement" was his article "Government." Macvey Namier, the editor of *Encyclopaedia Britannica*, had many misgivings over the article lest Mill should write in Bentham's profuse style which had been subjected to much ridicule by reviewers. On this point Mill reassured the editor by promising to do nothing more than give a comprehensive outline with the reasons needed to support such a framework.[6] The editor was also eager that Mill should not express the extreme views which had made the Radicals notorious. On the point Mill promised to comply with the editor's wishes by saying "nothing capable of alarming even a Whig." Apparently the article satisfied both the editor and the Radicals, for the Westminister Benthamites reprinted nine hundred copies for free distribution.

In the opening pages of his essay, Mill discussed the purpose of government in terms of Bentham's principle of the greatest happi-

103

ness for the greatest number. Yet he saw that governments were severely limited in promoting happiness, because nature had imposed the law that man should labor for his subsistence.[7] As natural resources are limited and man's desires are unlimited, there is an endless conflict among men for the control of scarce resources. Hence, it is the chief duty of government to prevent the invasion of private property.

After discussing the *ends* of government in a few pages, Mill devoted the bulk of his article to the *means* of achieving the greatest happiness. While he considered the *ends* in the utopian terms of the greatest happiness for the greatest number, he dealt with the *means* of government in the grimmest realism of self-interest. In the application of his hedonistic analysis he derived the principle of corruption, or the tendency of the few to rule for their own benefit. By assuming that the government by a few would always appropriate the wealth of the many, Mill concluded that an aristocracy was inherently corrupt. As an aristocracy could never have any interest identical with the whole community, it must always be against the interests of the whole community. Not only aristocracy in general but especially the British aristocracy, as it was then constituted, had the tendency to rule for the benefit of the few instead of the welfare of the many.[8]

Refusing to praise the British constitution as a balance of monarchy, aristocracy, and democracy, Mill used the traditional concepts of political writers as battering rams against the existing social order. He filled the old bottles with the new wine of egoistic hedonism. According to his analysis, the two primary motives of governors were greed for gain and lust for power. Beginning with this low estimate of human nature, Mill painted a dismal picture of England where the monarch, seeking more power, and the aristocracy, seeking more wealth, were united to invade the property of the people and to deprive them of their happiness. That government existed for the sake of the governed, he thought, was "a proposition wholly indisputable." But this was not the case in England where "the interest of the king and of the governing aristocracy is directly reverse; it is to have unlimited power over the rest of the community and to use it to their own advantage."[9] Thus Mill completely rejected the notion of mixed government which so many patriotic writers had long extolled as a beautiful balance of monarchy, aristocracy, and democracy.

Although keenly resentful of the aristocratic monopoly of political power, Mill, like Bentham, had even a greater passion for improving the government by a thorough democratic reform of the House of Commons. Because the existing governors were misusing their power, it was necessary to establish effective checks over them. To this subject of establishing effective checks on political power, Mill devoted much of his essay. Under the existing system, the only means of establishing effective checks, he thought, was the thorough reform of the House of Commons that would make it truly representative. A truly representative system, one that could check the tendency of aristocracy toward corruption, required a Radical reform of the elective franchise. The franchise should be sufficiently broad so that the interests of the electors would be identical with a majority of the people.[10]

Mill stopped short of Bentham's proposal of universal suffrage. So long as the masses remained uneducated, Mill thought, they could not know their own best interests.[11] Until the people had been properly educated, suffrage should be placed only in the hands of the wisest and most prudent part of the community. Those in control of government "must have the power of setting the fashion and of influencing to a large extent the public mind," and such people were the middle classes, for they were the wisest and most virtuous.[12]

Besides the article on government, Mill used the pages of the "Supplement" to disseminate other Radical ideas. In keeping with the main preoccupation of the time, he urged a drastic reform of the Poor Law. In his article "Beggar," he condemned at length the existing Poor Law. To extirpate mendicity he recommended, as Bentham had done many years before, the building of Panopticon workhouses for the compulsory reformation of beggars. He thought it possible in such workhouses to cultivate the sensibilities of paupers so that they would prefer death to a life of begging.[13]

Mill went beyond the negative measure of suppressing beggars by proposing positive measures for preventing poverty. He endorsed Friendly Societies and savings banks as positive reforms, but like the other political economists of his time he thought the main responsibility for social improvement rested with the paupers themselves. Although reluctant to acknowledge his debt to Malthus, Mill thought it was generally conceded by all economists that in nearly all countries, except the recently discovered lands, "a greater number of human beings is produced than there is food to support."[14] Since a surplus population was the basic cause of poverty, the condition of the paupers could not be improved until they had become morally responsible in limiting their own numbers.

In his article *Colony*, Mill further explored the problem of redundant population. In comparing the British with the Roman colonies, he preferred the latter to the former because they had taken off the redundant population. He conceded rather reluctantly that colonies might be beneficial to Great Britain provided they possessed fertile unoccupied land and were not too far distant to attract British emigrants.[15]

Mill's articles for the *Encyclopaedia Britannica*, it is clear, were economic as well as political in their scope. While relying upon Bentham for his political ideas, he did not depend on him for his economic doctrines. At the time he wrote the encyclopaedia articles, Mill had become an intimate friend of David Ricardo, upon whom he depended for his principles of political economy. It can be said that Mill had two masters and that he served them both equally well as the editor and popularizer of their complex works. His popular versions of Bentham and Ricardo helped in making Radicalism a political force during the 1820's.[16]

Mill was far more than Bentham's disciple; he was at once protege and apostle. No one was more evangelistic than he in making converts to the utilitarian creed, and no doubt his greatest triumph as an apostle was the conversion of Ricardo to the Benthamite cause of good government. Moreover, Mill's influence was decisive in putting Ricardo on the road to intellectual achievement. By introducing him to the Benthamite Radicals of Westminster, Mill provided Ricardo with a community that recognized and applauded his talents. As a friend Mill continuously encouraged Ricardo in the writing of his major work, *The Principles of Political Economy and Taxation*. After this major work had achieved success, Mill insisted that Ricardo acquire a seat in Parliament and become the advocate of the Radical causes of retrenchment and reform.

David Ricardo first gained public attention — or notoriety, as he usually called it — during the bullionist controversy. His first essay in economics was an anonymous letter published on August 29, 1809, in the *Morning Chronicle*. Prior to this venture into political controversy, however, Ricardo had achieved success as a member of the London Stock Exchange.[17]

David Ricardo learned the business of stockbroker as an apprentice to his father, Abraham Joseph Israel Ricardo. David's grandfather, Joseph Israel Ricardo, a Portuguese Jew, was a stockbroker in Amsterdam, where he traded in English funds.[18] In the pursuit of business Abraham settled in London in 1760 to buy and sell on behalf of his Dutch clients who were investing in British funds during the Seven Years War. As a holder of one of the twelve brokerships open to Jews on the London Stock Exchange, he gained a prominent place among the Spanish and Portuguese Jews residing in London.

David was born on April 18, 1772, the third son of Abraham Ricardo's large family. He received his early education in London and then, after the American War had ended in 1783, he was sent to Holland to attend the Talmud Tora, a school attached to the Portuguese synagogue in Amsterdam.[19] Upon David's return to London, his father began to employ him, even at the early age of fourteen, in his business as a stockbroker. So well did he serve his apprenticeship, learning the intricacies of the Stock Exchange and of international trade, that he was able to do business for himself by the time he had reached twenty-one.

About the time David Ricardo entered business for himself, he married Priscilla Ann Wilkinson, the daughter of a London surgeon and a member of the Society of Friends. Ricardo's marriage to a Quaker disrupted his family relations and caused him to secede from the Jewish community. The marriage to a Christian was not the sole cause of his secession from Judaism. Already his rationalism had brought him into fellowship with the Unitarians who were then the intellectual leaders of the London Dissenters. After his marriage he continued his association with the Unitarians, even though his wife attended the Society of Friends.[20]

Ricardo's separation from the Jewish community proved to be no great handicap for his business. When the estrangement from his family threw him on his own resources, his friends came to his financial assistance and enabled him to continue in business as a stockbroker. His social connections with the Quakers and Unitarians undoubtedly helped him to win the confidence of the financial leaders of the City. Once established in business, his early training and native abilities brought him unrivaled success as a member of the Stock Exchange.

Ricardo's knowledge of finance and his concern for those who were investing in government securities induced him to join in the controversy over the high price of gold. Since Ricardo believed that the high price was due to the excessive issue of the Bank of England notes, he urged that the Bank be required to withdraw the excess from circulation; if this were done, he said, "we should soon find that the market price of gold would fall to the mint price. . .and that every commodity would experience a similar reduction. . . ."[21] At a time when the effects of inflation were not clearly understood, he pointed out that everyone on fixed incomes, as well as the public annuitant, suffered from the overissue of bank notes.

Besides his letters in the *Morning Chronicle*, Ricardo published a pamphlet in 1809 entitled *The High Price of Gold as Proof of the Depreciation of Bank Notes*. The controversy which he helped to arouse gained more public attention than he had anticipated. When Parliament met early in 1810, the House of Commons appointed a committee "to inquire into the high price of gold," and its subsequent report prolonged the controversy for several months. The bullionist controversy, which established Ricardo as an authority on finance, brought him to the attention of James Mill and other persons interested in political economy.

James Mill's letter to Ricardo, December 25, 1810, was the first in a correspondence which lasted for fourteen years. From the beginning of their friendship, Mill made it clear that he fully accepted Ricardo's opinion on currency. Although he became Ricardo's disciple in economics, Mill continued to acclaim Bentham as the greatest political philosopher. With the entrance of Ricardo into the arena of economic controversy, Bentham turned his attention more fully to the Radical reform of Parliament. In the Radical campaign for political reform, both Bentham and Mill accepted Ricardo as a worthy ally.

James Mill saw Ricardo as a polemicist who could refute Malthus's defense of aristocratic institutions. For more than a decade Malthus had successfully employed the principle of population to refute the equalitarianism of Radical reformers. So long as England was at war with France, Malthus's principle of population was the best defense of English aristocratic institutions against French Jacobinism.

Although there were differences between Ricardo and Malthus from the time of the bullionist controversy, their differences were publicly recognized during the controversy over the Corn Laws. The friendly correspondence between them, which had originally

108

concerned questions of currency, turned eventually to a discussion of the questions of rent and profit. The fall in the price of corn that came with the prosperity of 1813 and with the prospect of peace in 1814 brought an agitation for restricting the importation of corn. As a result of the agitation, the House of Commons appointed a Committee to consider the question of restricting the importation of corn. The parliamentary debates on the Corn Laws evoked from Malthus two pamphlets defending the Tory policy of protecting agriculture by restricting the importation of grain.

Taking the opposite side of the question, Ricardo rejected Malthus's defense of the Corn Laws. In 1815 Ricardo published a pamphlet entitled, "An Essay on the Influence of a Low Price of Corn on the Profits of Stock: Showing the Inexpediency of Restrictions on Importation. . . ." In this pamphlet Ricardo borrowed Malthus's principle of rent and applied it to all types of capital. "In treating on this subject of the profits of capital," he declared in his introduction, "it is necessary to consider the principles which regulate the rise and fall of rent; as rent and profits, it will be seen, have a very intimate connexion with each other."[22] While acknowledging his indebtedness to Malthus for the doctrine of rent, Ricardo made an entirely different application of the theory of rent. He emphatically denied the necessity of restricting imports. Seeing many advantages in the low price of grain, he could not refrain from rebuking Malthus for defending a policy "inconsistent with the general doctrine of the advantages of free trade."[23]

Ricardo's doctrine of profit, it was clear to Mill, had ideological significance that could be used by the Benthamites against the aristocracy. Bentham had already discovered that the interest of the aristocrat was opposed to the interests of the majority, and now Ricardo discovered "that the landlord is always opposed to the interest of every other class in the community. His situation is never so prosperous as where food is scarce and dear, whereas all other persons are benefited by procuring food cheap."[24]

There was also ideological significance in Ricardo's emphasis on the creative role of the capitalist in ameliorating social conditions.[25] In Mill's estimation, the *Essay* not only corrected the errors in the science of economics but also provided a remedy for the worst abuses in policy.

The Corn Law of 1815, according to Ricardo's analysis, raised the price of food, lowered profits, and increased rents.[26] It was clear from his analysis that only landlords could benefit from the law. The aristocrats in the House of Lords and the landed gentry in the House of Commons, all being landlords, had enacted a law for their own benefit. Thus the passing of the Corn Law in 1815 seemed to confirm the utilitarian doctrine that corruption was inherent in an aristocratic system of government.

The end of the Napoleonic War in 1815 brought about a rapid appreciation in the value of government securities; as a consequence, Ricardo made enormous profits on the funds which he held. This happy turn of events enabled him to retire from the Stock Exchange and devote full time to the career of a political economist. Upon learning that Ricardo had suddenly become a very rich man, James Mill wrote urging him to spend his leisure improving the science of economics. At the same time Mill also urged him to seek a seat in Parliament in order "to improve that most imperfect instrument of government."[27]

Even though fully engaged in writing the history of British India and serving as Bentham's editorial mentor, Mill volunteered his editorial assistance to Ricardo. He promised that he would make "the best thinker on political economy" become also "the best writer." Frankly assuming the authority of schoolmaster, he commanded Ricardo to proceed with his book, arranging it under the headings of rent, profit, and wages. He reassured his hesitant friend with the promise, "If you entrust the inspection of it to me, I shall compel you to make it all right, before you have done with it."[28] Mill's encouragement was a decisive influence in determining Ricardo to undertake the writing of a major work as a rebuttal of what he thought were the errors in Malthus's doctrines.[29]

To achieve his purpose, Ricardo greatly needed Mill's friendly encouragement and editorial assistance. He was not sure of himself as a writer; more than this, he disliked to write. Writing was always such a disagreeable chore that he could not resist laying aside his manuscript whenever friends or relatives knocked at his door. No one understood his inclination to postpone writing better than Mill; for this reason he urged him to push on to a conclusion, think nothing of order, repetition, or style, "regarding nothing, in short, but to get all the thoughts blurred upon paper somehow or other."[30]

110

Gratefully accepting Mill's editorial guidance, Ricardo hastily put his thoughts on paper and sent them to him for criticism. Mill took time from his writing of the *History of British India*, which was near completion, to read and criticize Ricardo's manuscript. His response to the first batch of pages was enthusiastic and extravagant praise, probably calculated to keep Ricardo at his desk: "My opinion may be given in a very few words; for I think you have made out all your points. There is not a single proposition the proof of which I think is not irresistible." Mill made few stylistic changes, for he first wanted to see the work completed: "What I am anxious for is that you should go on, exactly as you are doing, till you have got all your thoughts in this shape upon paper; and have gone over the whole subject. It will then be easy to give you advice about marshalling and separating. And easy for you to put the last hand to a work which will give you immortal honour."[31]

Ricardo responded to Mill's enthusiastic praise with the promise to keep on writing: "How very encouraging your letter is! You really give me hopes that my ardent wish will be attained, that I may produce something which will fairly entitle me to be considered as an improver of the science."[32] While complying with his friend's stern tutorial commands, Ricardo also gratefully acknowledged Mill's editorial assistance: "If I am successful in my undertaking, it will be to you mainly that my success will be owing, for without your encouragement I do not think that I should have proceeded, and it is to you that I look for assistance of the utmost importance to me in the arranging of different parts and curtailing what may be superfluous."[33]

Ricardo kept his promise. He rapidly finished his manuscript and sent it to Mill for correction. Mill was completely satisfied with the sections dealing with taxation: "Your doctrines are original and profound. . . . I embrace every one of them; and am ready to defend them against all the world."[34] That Mill was truly ready to defend his doctrines against the world is, perhaps, the best explanation of his willingness to assist Ricardo in the writing of *Principles of Political Economy and Taxation*. Mill's primary concern was always the formation and propagation of those opinions that would aid Radical reform. It is true that he courted Ricardo's friendship, but Mill was too doctrinaire to cultivate anyone whose opinions differed greatly from his own.

Ricardo's principal applications of economic doctrines were in keeping with the objectives of the Benthamite Radicals. He opposed the Corn Law of 1815, as did they, and he strengthened their position against the landed upper classes by pointing to rent as an unearned income. He added his voice to theirs by demanding drastic curtailment of government expenses. While deploring the extravagance of the upper classes, he praised the capitalists, both shopkeepers and farmers, who saved their money and invested it. Granting freedom to the middle classes to save and invest their income, Ricardo thought, was the best means to improving the real wages of the working classes.

Unfortunately for the working classes, Ricardo's doctrines did not have the social consequences which he had anticipated. He fully expected social improvement to follow from reduction in government expenditures. Rather than improving the social condition of the working classes, Ricardo's *Principles of Political Economy and Taxation* reinforced the natural law opposition to the Poor Law. In the first place, he accepted Adam Smith's doctrine of natural liberty, that prices and wages should be left to find their own level. Moreover, he wished to go beyond Smith by explaining the natural laws which regulate the distribution of the earth's produce among landlords, capitalists, and laborers. In addition to Smith's doctrine of natural liberty, Ricardo assimilated into his own doctrines Malthus's principles of population and rent.

Although greatly indebted to both Smith and Malthus, Ricardo wished to supersede them by discovering the natural laws regulating rent, profits, and wages. Striving for a satisfactory explanation of distribution, he sought to discover those unseen laws which guided the conspicuous activities of the market place. In his eager search, he thought he could set aside the market price as nominal, being only "the temporary effects" of "accidental causes". Let us leave these out of consideration, he said, "whilst we are treating of the laws which regulate natural prices, natural wages, and natural profits, effects totally independent of these accidental causes."[35]

Ricardo's determination to regard the market price as nominal created misunderstanding between him and Malthus. "It appears to me that one great cause of our difference in opinion," he wrote to Malthus, ". . .is that you have always in your mind the immediate and temporary effects of particular changes — whereas I put these immediate and temporary effects quite aside and fix my whole attention on the permanent state of things which will result from them. Perhaps you estimate those temporary effects too highly, whilst I am too much disposed to undervalue them."[36] To this explanation of their differences Malthus replied as follows: "I agree with you that one cause of our difference in opinion is that which you mention. I am certainly disposed to refer frequently to things as they are as the only way of making one's writing practically useful to society. . . . Besides I really think the progress of society consists of irregular movements and to omit the consideration of causes which for eight or ten years will give a great stimulus to production and population or a great check to them is to omit the causes of the wealth and poverty of nations — the grand object of all inquiries in political economy."[37]

The mutual recognition of the differences in their doctrines did not remove the misunderstanding between them, for Ricardo felt obligated to explain natural prices; having done this to his own satisfaction, he willingly left to others the task of distinguishing the temporary from the permanent causes influencing prices and ascribing "the due effects to each." Therefore, in his theory of wages, as in his theory of rent and profit, he gave pre-eminence to the natural price over the market price, to the permanent over the temporary influences.

In Ricardo's analysis, labor, like everything else bought and sold, had a natural price and a market price. The natural price of labor was the amount of wages necessary "to enable the labourers, one with another, to subsist and to perpetuate their race, without either increase or diminution."[38] Although the market price may deviate from the natural price, it has "a tendency to conform to it. It is when the market price of labour exceeds its natural price that the condition of the labourer is flourishing and happy. . . . When, however, by the encouragement which high wages give to the increase of population, the number of labourers is increased, wages again fall to their natural price, and indeed from reaction sometimes fall below it."[39] When starvation and misery had reduced the number of laborers, wages would again rise. Ricardo's grim view of wages, their tendency to fluctuate around the starvation level, was fraught with the harshest social consequences.

After explaining "the laws by which wages are regulated and by which the happiness of far the greater part of every community is governed," Ricardo concluded that wages, like all other contracts, "should be left to the fair and free competition of the market and should never be controlled by the interference of the legislature."[40] Thus Ricardo placed himself in the camp of the natural law reformers who opposed the Poor Law as a violation of the laws of nature. His doctrine of wages led him to voice again the often repeated assertion that the Poor Law aggravated the poverty that it was designed to relieve:

> The clear and direct tendency of the poor laws is in direct opposition to these obvious principles: it is not as the legislature benevolently intended, to amend the condition of the poor, but to deteriorate the condition of both poor and rich; instead of making the poor rich; they are calculated to make the rich poor; and whilst the present laws are in force, it is quite in the natural order of things that the fund for maintenance of the poor should progressively increase till it has absorbed all the net revenue of the country, or at least so much of it as the state shall leave to us, after satisfying its own never failing demands for the public expenditure.[41]

It is clear from this application of his principles that Ricardo desired the ultimate abolition of the Poor Laws, yet he realized that, because of low wages, those laws could not be abolished immediately. "It is agreed by all who are most friendly to a repeal of these laws," he said, "that if it be desirable to prevent the most overwhelming distress to those for whose benefit they were erroneously enacted, their abolition should be effected by the most gradual steps."

What gradual steps would Ricardo have the government take toward the abolition of the Poor Laws? In the first place, he agreed with Malthus that the government should interfere in the conditions of the working classes "to regulate the increase of their numbers, and to render less frequent among them early and improvident marriage. The operation of the system of poor laws has been directly contrary to this. They have rendered restraint superfluous and have invited imprudence by offering it a portion of the wages of prudence and industry."[42]

Ricardo shared the exaggerated fears of the time that the Poor Law expenses were increasing at such a rate as to absorb all the net revenue of the country. "The principle of gravitation," he thought, "is not more certain than the tendency of such laws to change wealth and power into misery and weakness. . . ."[43] So certain was he of this tendency that he denied the right of the poor to relief, lest the burden of the poor rates eventually become more burdensome than all other taxes combined.

Ricardo did more than reaffirm the traditional natural law opposition to the Poor Law. He enlarged the opposition with the new element of Radicalism. Whigs and Radicals were then stridently demanding a sharp curtailment of government expenditures. Ricardo systematized their demands for retrenchment in his principles of taxation. In dealing with taxation he gave primary importance to the place of capital in determining social progress. Inasmuch as demand for labor depended upon the amount of circulating capital, those taxes falling on profits tended to reduce employment.[44] Since all taxes, in his view, discouraged the accumulation of capital, the only wise policy was to keep government expenditures at the exact minimum.[45]

In his analysis of taxation Ricardo pointed out the evil effects of the poor rates. He found the poor rate to be "a tax which falls with peculiar weight on the profits of the farmer, and therefore may be considered as affecting the price of raw produce."[46] Since the tax fell more heavily on the farmer than on the manufacturer, it caused the transfer of capital from agriculture to manufacturing.[47]

The incidence of the poor rates depended somewhat on the stage of economic growth, whether a country be an advancing, a stationary, or a retrograde society. In an advancing society, where agriculture is being extended, the tax would fall in part on the farmer and in part on the consumer. If the poor rate caused a rise in the price of corn, the landlord, upon renewing his leases, would be able to raise his rent. In a stationary or retrograde stage of society, where agriculture was not being extended, the poor rates would be paid by the farmers under their current leases, but upon the expiration of those leases the rates would fall largely on the landlords.[48] Since England was assumed to be in the stage of an advancing society, the levying of the poor rates would move it toward a retrograde society.[49]

Thus Ricardo's analysis lent credence to the reformers' claim that the poor rates would continue to increase until they had absorbed all rent and profit, bringing an end to social progress. Moreover he clearly admonished the legislators to free capitalists; that is, the productive classes, both farmers and manufacturers, for in the freedom to save and invest lay the hope of social improvement. Unfortunately his analysis had the effect of relieving the prosperous middle classes of moral responsibility for the welfare

115

of the lower classes. Although Ricardo was a cheerful, benevolent man, his *Principles*, when added to Malthus's *Essay on Population*, transformed political economy into a "dismal science."

The publication of the *Principles of Political Economy and Taxation* in April, 1817, brought to Ricardo the success which Mill had anticipated for him. The book was favorably reviewed in the *Edinburgh* by John R. McCulloch, who avowed enthusiastic adherence to Ricardian doctrine.[50] After the review appeared the book sold so well that the publisher requested a second edition. The second edition of the *Principles*, with only slight alterations, appeared in 1819.[51]

Mill and Ricardo could now congratulate each other as successful authors. After a decade of exhausting labor Mill completed the fourth volume of his *History of British India*. In December, 1818, it was reviewed in the *Edinburgh*, and in the same issue a new edition of Ricardo's pamphlet, *Economical and Secure Currency*, was reviewed by McCulloch.[52]

Ricardo's preoccupation with economics did not lessen Mill's determination to have him in Parliament as the advocate of the Radical cause of good government. From the time he had learned of Ricardo's retirement from the Stock Exchange, Mill insisted that he seek a seat in Parliament where his "tongue, as well as his pen, might be of use."[53] Knowing Ricardo's inability to conduct a political campaign, Mill instructed him on the purchase of a seat.[54] After Ricardo had finished writing his *Principles*, Mill became more insistent that he use a part of his wealth to advance the cause of good government.[55] At length Ricardo capitulated and promised to purchase a seat in the House of Commons.[56]

Mill acted on the promise at once by negotiating with Henry Brougham for a seat. While bargaining for a rotten borough, Mill, assuming the role of schoolmaster for a second time, instructed Ricardo in the proper manner of Parliamentary debate. During the early months of 1818, the two friends spent much time together, walking and talking politics.[57] In these ambling conversations, Ricardo formulated the principles of Radical reform which he expected to espouse in Parliament. He accepted the Radical theory that the main object of reform was to make government truly representative so that the interests of the governors would be identified with the interests of a majority of the people. He did not go so far as to adopt universal suffrage; but he did seek a suffrage broad enough "to secure the voters against corrupt influence."[58]

116

He did not go so far as to advocate annual Parliaments, but he did believe that elections should be held at least every third year.[59]

In February, 1819, Ricardo entered Parliament and continued to hold a seat until his premature death four years later. While in the House of Commons, he added his voice to those Radical reformers seeking a drastic reduction in expenditures and a thorough reform of the representative system. In the opinion of the Radicals, the Corn Laws, the Poor Laws, and the rotten boroughs belonged to an unenlightened age and supported an inherently corrupt oligarchy.

Ricardo's opposition to the Poor Law was well known before he entered Parliament. Consequently, as soon as he had taken his seat, he was appointed a member of the Poor Law Committee.[60]

His first speech in the House of Commons was in opposition to the Poor Law. He was even more hostile to the Poor Law than was Sturges Bourne, who, as chairman of the Poor Law Committee, had introduced the Poor Rates Misapplication Bill. One feature of this bill was the denial of relief to fully employed persons, such relief being granted as a supplement to wages in support of dependent children. In order to deny relief to able-bodied laborers, Sturges Bourne proposed taking the children from their parents and putting them in schools of industry where they could be educated and set to work. To this proposal Ricardo objected on the grounds that it would add to a redundant population. "If a provision were made for all the children of the poor," he said, "it would only increase the evil; for if parents felt assured that an asylum would be provided for their children, in which they would be treated with humanity and tenderness, there would be then no check to that increase of population which was so apt to take place among the labouring classes."[61] He also pointed out that a consequence of such legislation was to prevent wages from rising above the level of those for a single man; in effect, the bill, if passed, would enact a natural wage at the subsistence level of a single person rather than for a family.

During the years when Ricardo was in Parliament, the Radicals were agreed in condemning the Poor Law as a conspicuous violation of natural liberty. However, they did not agree on the proper remedy. A political leader of the Westminster Radicals outside Parliament, Francis Place, accepted the view that the Poor Law contributed to a redundant population but he did not share Ricardo's belief that the Poor Law should be totally abolished.

117

In 1821 Francis Place undertook a defense of Malthus's principle of population against the objections of William Godwin.[62] While defending the principle of population, Place rejected Malthus's remedies for the evils of a redundant population. Doubting the effectiveness of moral restraint, Place recommended, instead, that the people be educated in the methods of birth control.[63] Unlike Ricardo, he did not deny the right of the poor to relief; nor did he support the view that the poor rates were threatening to devour the profit and rent of the land. Although Place defended the principle of population, he objected violently to Malthus's favorite remedy that children born to future marriages should be ineligible to receive parish assistance.[64]

To obtain a publisher for the manuscript, *Illustrations and Proofs of the Principle of Population*, Francis Place sought Ricardo's help; but the latter was unwilling to give it his full support.[65] While conceding that Place had ably defended the principle of population, Ricardo upheld Malthus's proposed reform of the Poor Law.[66] Mill also followed Malthus in believing that the repeal of the Poor Law was a necessary means of curtailing a redundant population.[67] However much the Radicals may have differed in their attitudes toward the Poor Law, they were agreed in principle that a redundant population was the basic cause of the misery of the working classes.

James Mill set forth his views on the Poor Law in 1821 when he published his *Elements of Political Economy*. He thought of this work as nothing more than a schoolbook for educating young people in the principles of political economy. He had long been sanguine with the hope of writing a book which would teach the new science easily and effectively.[68] When presenting his primer to the public, he professed no new discovery, his only object being a summary of essential principles.

Following Ricardo's *Principles*, Mill gave only slight attention to production in order to emphasize the central problem of distribution. He incorporated into his doctrine the principle of population. The rate of wages, he explained, depended on the proportion between population and employment, or capital, which provided the demand for labor. Since there was a tendency for population to increase faster than capital, there was the inevitable tendency for wages to fall. This argument led him to the conclusion, "that the grand practical problem therefore is to find means of limiting the number of births."[69]

Mill also followed Ricardo in holding that social improvement depended upon a society's ability to accumulate capital faster than the growth of population. To win the race with population, Mill placed his confidence in the prudence and frugality of the middle classes. If distribution were left to natural laws, the greater part of the net produce, he thought, "would find its way into the hands of a numerous class of persons exempt from the necessity of labour and placed in the most favourable circumstance both for the enjoyment of happiness and for the highest intellectual and moral attainments. Society would thus be in its happiest state."[70]

Mill had very little confidence in the ability of the legislature to remove the causes of poverty. The government could not, in his view, prevent the species from multiplying, for it was virtually impossible to reward parents for not having children and even more difficult to punish them for having children. The government, however, could repeal the Poor Law, "the mischievous legislation" which had stimulated the growth of population. The duties of the legislature, therefore, were to direct disfavor against dependence and to educate the people in the economic effects of a rapidly increasing population.[71]

Mill's doctrine of profit, which he had borrowed from Ricardo, was simple and stark enough to alarm both the farmer and the businessman. He viewed profits as what remained to the capitalist after the payment of wages. According to his simple view profits varied adversely to wages. While granting the possibility of capital increasing fast enough to raise both wages and profits, Mill thought such an increase was unlikely. Inasmuch as population "has a tendency to superabound, the active principle of change is on the side of population and constitutes a reason for considering population, and consequently wages, as the regulator."[72]

In his doctrine of taxation, Mill was as stern an advocate of retrenchment as Ricardo had been. He wanted to see all taxes reduced and he thought the poor rates were especially pernicious. Since the poor rates were paid primarily by the farmers who occupied the land, they tended to increase the price of corn, and as the price of corn increased, both wages and profits were diminished.[73]

In summary, Mill's simplified version of Ricardo's *Principles* was directed against the Poor Laws in several ways. He opposed the Poor Laws in general because they interfered with those natural laws regulating profits and wages. He objected to the Poor Laws because they tended to increase population and so aggravate the problem of poverty. Since the poor rates were paid, in part, from profits, they discouraged the accumulation of capital on which social progress depended.

Although Ricardo had originally encouraged Mill to write an economics textbook, he was never enthusiastic about the outcome. Although he found very little in Mill's *Elements* which differed from his own view, he remained noncommittal on the question whether the book succeeded in explaining economics to the uninformed reader.[74]

In keeping with the Radicals' desire to spread the influence of the new science, Mill and Ricardo joined with other interested persons in forming the Political Economy Club. After Ricardo had taken his seat in Parliament, he frequently invited friends to his house to discuss the economic questions which had gained public attention. In the spring of 1821, the friends of Malthus, uniting with the friends of Ricardo, formalized their meetings by adopting a set of regulations drawn up by James Mill.

On April 30, 1821, the Political Economy Club adopted the regulations limiting its membership to thirty and providing for monthly meetings to discuss current economic problems. The members of the new society pledged themselves to regard "the diffusion among others of just principles of political economy as a real and important obligation."[75]

During the last two years of his life, Ricardo was an active member of the Political Economy Club, presiding over its meetings, proposing topics for discussion and participating in the discussions proposed by other members. He always felt at home in the society, and it provided for him a setting where his talents shone the brightest. At the time of his death in 1823, he was, according to John L. Mallet, the Club's "chief light and ornament."[76] For several years after Ricardo's death, Mill continued to participate in the affairs of the Club; when he stopped attending its meetings, McCulloch replaced him as a defender of Ricardo's doctrines against the attacks of Torrens, Senior, and others.[77]

In addition to the founding of the Political Economy Club, James Mill helped to originate the *Westminster Review* as the organ of the Radicals. In 1823 Jeremy Bentham and his friends decided to establish a review as a rival to the Whig *Edinburgh* and the Tory *Quarterly*.[78] Bentham contributed the funds to start the journal and appointed as its editors John Bowring and Henry

Southern. Although Mill was fully employed at the India Office, he was given the important assignment of reviewing periodical literature; this meant, in fact, attacking the *Edinburgh* for its moderate reform and the *Quarterly* for its obstinate opposition to all reform.

Mill's article attacking the *Edinburgh*, which appeared in January, 1824, applied Bentham's utilitarian analysis to the Whigs. Since the Whigs were just as aristocratic as the Tories, they would inevitably use the power of government to promote the interest of the aristocracy over the welfare of the whole community.[79] The aristocrats were, in Mill's opinion, a "sinister interest," having a greater tendency to evil than good; hence, by definition, the major political parties were both inherently corrupt. The corruption did not necessarily extend to all the titled nobility nor to all the families with large fortunes; rather, it permeated only the relatively small number possessing political power "by whatever circumstance, birth, or riches, or other accident. . . ."[80] The sinister influence had permeated the House of Commons, whose members had either bought their seats or had been appointed by aristocrats. In any case, the members were no better than the butlers and stewards on the Lords' estates.

According to Mill's utilitarian analysis, the two political parties were rival sections of a corrupt aristocracy, one section being satisfied with the distribution of the King's favors and the other being dissatisfied. The Tories were the obviously contented ministerial party, while the Whigs comprised the discontented opposition. It was Mill's purpose to explain the motives and conduct of the opposition party. The Whigs, he thought, were trying to discredit the Tories only to gain office. To achieve this end the Whigs had to arouse public opinion against the government without completely alienating the aristocracy; consequently, the Whigs were always compromising their principles to please the aristocrats.[81] To prove this contention, Mill selected excerpts from the past issues of the *Edinburgh* and added a running commentary on the subserviency of the Whigs to the aristocracy.

For several years, from 1824 to 1828, both James and John Stuart Mill contributed articles to the *Westminster Review*. Anticipating success for their journal, the Radicals at first printed three thousand copies, but before long its sales began to fall off, and the *Review* was in need of additional financial support. John Bowring, the editor, to keep it going, sold it in 1829 to Thomas Perronet

Thompson. The transfer of ownership was a victory for Bowring, who had been at odds with James Mill.[82] Thereafter the *Westminster* was conducted primarily as a medium for the opinions of its new owner. It continued, however, to advocate the Radical policy of retrenchment and reform. Despite the clash of personalities and the lack of adequate financial backing, the *Westminster Review* successfully extended the influence of both Bentham and Ricardo.[83]

In spite of Mill's attack on the political attitudes of the *Edinburgh Review*, it continued to be a loyal supporter of the Whigs. Although it never espoused the Radical doctrine of parliamentary reform, the *Review* did adopt Ricardo's economic policies of free trade and retrenchment. Its chief writer on economic questions was Ricardo's disciple, John R. McCulloch, who contributed, during the 1820's, no fewer than forty-four articles on political economy.[84] Under his influence the *Edinburgh* became as stout a foe of the Poor Law as was the *Westminster Review*.

By the time of Ricardo's death, the opposition to the Poor Law had not only reached a mammoth proportion but had grown exceedingly complex. An accumulation of a half-century of agitation, the opposition may best be described as an arsenal of weapons designed to prevent the government from interfering with the wages and working conditions of labor. This opposition became exceedingly complex because of the highly abstract, speculative foundations on which it had been erected. Even though there was little agreement, and even less consistency, among the political and economic theorists who laid these foundations, the theorists were unanimous in opposing the Poor Law as a glaring violation of natural law.

From the time of Adam Smith the natural law reformers had maintained the view that the Poor Law obstructed the mobility of labor and prevented wages from reaching their natural level. That the Poor Law was a logical violation of natural liberty was never doubted by anyone, but Sir Frederick Morton Eden in his remarkable work, *The State of the Poor*, which was published in 1797, could find little evidence that the Poor Law had, in fact, seriously restricted the mobility of labor. What he did find, however, greatly alarmed those occupiers of land on whom the burden of the poor rate fell. Like other persons living through famines and wartime inflation, Eden observed the increase in Poor Law expenditures. He did not explain the increase in terms of inflation, which he did not understand; rather, he explained the increase in terms of what he thought was the escalation inherent in the Poor Law. His observation that the Poor Law aggravated the poverty which it was designed to remedy was certainly an alarming conclusion to his studies. Eden had not merely discovered the principle of escalation inherent in the Poor Law; he also offered as proof of his principle the scale of relief recently adopted by the Berkshire magistrates in their meeting at Speenhamland. It was an ideal case which illustrated the absurdity to which poor relief might be carried; but there is little evidence that the scale was ever carried out, not even at Speen.

In the midst of the gloom of war and famine, Malthus enunciated the principle that population tended to grow at a rate as to outrun subsistence. The Poor Law, he thought, aggravated the tendency of people, especially the tendency of the working classes, to reproduce themselves faster than they could augment the food supply. When his critics insisted that the Poor Law should be continued so long as there remained uncultivated land, Malthus met their argument with his doctrine of rent, demonstrating logically that the more extensive cultivation of land in an old and a mature country like England would lower rather than raise the living standard of labor. Accepting both the principle of population and the doctrine of rent, Ricardo went beyond Malthus and predicted diminishing returns to capital in proportion to the increase of population. In the light of his doctrine, he could take no other position than that of ultimately abolishing the Poor Law. Until the time was more opportune for abolishing the Poor Law, Ricardo contended for the steady reduction of all types of taxation, including the poor rate.

Although the speculation about the pernicious tendencies of the Poor Law had continued for fifty years, the theorists did not agree on the proper remedy. Even if they had been able to agree among themselves, they would have lacked the political influence to enact a drastic reform of the Poor Law. The members of Parliament were alarmed over the increase of poor rates, but they were unwilling to enact legislation derived from speculation, especially legislation that would destroy a venerable and benevolent system of social welfare. Since the political economists were unable to devise an adequate remedy, it remained for the new school of political scientists, the followers of Jeremy Bentham, to provide a thorough reform of the Poor Law in terms of the legal traditions which lawyers could understand and in keeping with the temporising expediencies of party politicians. It remained, therefore, for the Benthamite Radicals, with their perspicacious knowledge of the law, to devise a remedy commensurate with the abuse.

NOTES

[1] Alexander Bain, *James Mill, A Biography* (London: 1882). pp. 20-21. See also Leslie Stephen, *The English Utilitarian*, (London: 1900), II, 1-7.

[2] Bentham, *Works*, X, 481.

[3] *Ibid.*, 482.

[4] Bain, *James Mill*, p. 160.

[5] *Ibid.*, p. 162.

[6] *Ibid.*, p. 189.

[7] James Mill, *Government* (London, 1821), p. 4.

[8] *Ibid.*, p. 7.

[9] *Ibid.*, p. 15.

[10] *Ibid.*, p. 23.

[11] *Ibid.*, p. 29.

[12] *Ibid.*, p. 32.

[13] Bain, *James Mill*, p. 256.

[14] *Ibid.*, p. 258.

[15] James Mill, *Colony* (London, 1821), p. 15.

[16] For a contemporary reviewer's estimate of Bentham's absurd style of writing, see Sydney Smith, *Works*, (New York, 1844), p. 243. When reviewing Bentham's *Book of Fallacies* for the *Edinburgh Review* in 1825, Smith said that the public needed a "Middle-man" between them and Bentham.

[17] Piero Sraffa, *The Works and Correspondence of David Ricardo*, Volume X, *Biographical Miscellany* (Cambridge, Eng., Cambridge University Press, 1955). The principal source of biography is *A Memoir of David Ricardo*, which, according to Sraffa, was written by Moses Ricardo, David's brother, with the assistance of James Mill. *Works*, X, 15.

[18] Sraffa, "Addenda to the Memoir," *Works*, X, 19.

[19] *Ibid.*, 31.

[20] *Ibid.*, 40.

[21] Ricardo, *Works*, Volume III, *Pamphlets and Papers, 1809-1811*, p. 21.

[22] Ricardo, *Works*, Volume IV, *Pamphlets and Papers, 1815-1823*, p. 9.

[23] *Ibid.*, p. 10.

[24] *Ibid.*, p. 21.

[25] *Ibid.*, p. 35.

[26] *Ibid.*, p. 41.

[27] Ricardo, *Works*. Volume VI, *Letters, 1810-1815*, Mill to Ricardo, 23 August 1815, p. 252.

[28] Mill to Ricardo, 9 Nov. 1815, *Ibid.*, p. 321.

[29] Ricardo to Mill, 30 Dec. 1815, *Ibid.*, p. 348. In this letter to Mill, Ricardo stated his central doctrine as follows: "This invariability of the value of precious metals, but from particular causes relating to themselves only, such as supply and demand, is the sheet anchor on which all my propositions are built; for those who maintain that an alteration in the value of corn will alter the value of all other things, independently of its effects on the value of the

raw materials of which they are made, do in fact deny this doctrine of the cause of the variation in the value of gold and silver."

[30] Mill to Ricardo, 14 August 1816, *Works*, VII, 60.

[31] Mill to Ricardo, 18 November 1816, *Ibid.*, p. 99.

[32] Ricardo to Mill, 2 December 1816, *Ibid.*, p. 100.

[33] *Loc. cit.*, p. 101.

[34] Mill to Ricardo, 16 December 1816, *Ibid.*, p. 106.

[35] Ricardo, *Works*, Volume I, *On the Principles of Political Economy and Taxation*, p. 91. I am indebted to the following recent studies of Ricardo's *Principles*: Mark Blaug, *Ricardian Economics* (New Haven, Yale University Press, 1958), Oswald St. Clair, *A Key to Ricardo* (London: Routledge and Kegan Paul, 1957), and Carl S. Shoup, *Ricardo on Taxation* (New York: Columbia University Press, 1960).

[36] Ricardo to Malthus, 24 January 1817, *Works*, VII, 120.

[37] Malthus to Ricardo, 26 January 1817, *Ibid.*, p. 122.

[38] *Works*, I, 92.

[39] *Ibid.*, p. 94.

[40] *Ibid.*, p. 105.

[41] *Ibid.*, pp. 105-6.

[42] *Ibid.*, p. 107.

[43] *Ibid.*, p. 108.

[44] *Ibid.*, p. 151.

[45] *Ibid.*, p. 153.

[46] *Ibid.*, p. 257.

[47] *Ibid.*, p. 259.

[48] *Ibid.*, p. 261.

[49] *Ibid.*, p. 160.

[50] McCulloch to Ricardo, 15 July 1818, *Works*, VII, 280.

[51] Ricardo to Mill, 23 November 1818, *Ibid.*, p. 333.

[52] Mill to Ricardo, 14 January 1819, *Works*, VIII, 10.

[53] Mill to Ricardo, 30 September 1814, *Ibid.*, VI, 138.

[54] Mill to Ricardo, 23 October 1816, *Ibid.*, VII, 86.

[55] Mill to Ricardo, 24 August 1817, *Ibid.*, 181.

[56] Ricardo to Mill, 18 December 1817, *Ibid.*, 228-29.

[57] Ricardo to Malthus, 25 May 1818, *Ibid.*, 263.

[58] Ricardo to Trower, 22 March 1818, *Ibid.*, 261.

[59] Ricardo, "Observations on Parliamentary Reform" and "Defense of Voting by Ballot." *Works*, Volume V, *Speeches and Evidence*, pp. 493-512. According to Professor Sraffa these articles, published after Ricardo's were mock speeches prepared under Mill's tutelage prior to Ricardo's entry into Parliament.

[60] *Works*, Vol. V, p. xxiii.

[61] *Ibid.*, V, p. 1.

[62] Francis Place, *Illustrations and Proofs of the Principle of Population: Including an Examination of the Proposed Remedies of Mr. Malthus and a Reply to the Objections of Mr. Godwin and Others.* (London, 1822). I have used the reproduction (Boston: Houghton Mifflin Co., 1930).

[63] *Ibid.*, pp. 178-79.

[64] *Ibid.*, p. 150. See also, Graham Wallas, *The Life of Francis Place* (New York, Knopf, 1929), p. 165.

[65] Ricardo, *Works*, Volume II, *Letters July 1821-1823*, pp. 52-53.

[66] *Ibid.*, p. 55.

[67] James Mill, *Elements of Political Economy* (2nd ed., London, 1824), p. 59.

[68] Ricardo, *Works*, VII, 107.

[69] Mill, *Elements of Political Economy* (London, 1821), p. 51.

[70] *Ibid.*, 2nd ed., p. 68.

[71] *Ibid.*, p. 60.

[72] *Ibid.*, p. 72.

[73] *Ibid.*, p. 282.

[74] Ricardo, *Works*, IX, 117-18.

[75] "Minutes, 1821-22," *Political Economy Club* (London, 1921), VI, 3.

[76] J. L. Mallet, "Diaries," *Political Economy Club*, VI, 212.

[77] *Ibid.*, 224-25.

[78] Bentham, *Works*, X, 540.

[79] James Mill, "Periodical Literature." *Westminster Review*, I (1824), 210.

[80] *Ibid.*, 212.

[81] *Ibid.*, 222.

[82] John Stuart Mill, *Autobiography*, (New York: Columbia University Press, 1924), p. 91.

[83] Frank W. Fetter, "Economic Articles in the Westminster Review and their Authors, 1824-51," *The Journal of Political Economy*, LXX (December, 1962), 574.

[84] Fetter, "The Authorship of Economic Articles in the Edinburgh Review, 1802-1847," *Journal of Political Economy*, LXI, 3 (June, 1953).

[85] For Mark Blaug's view of McCulloch's attitude toward the Poor Law, see his *Ricardian Economics*, p. 200. The Poor Law which McCulloch favored antedated the humanitarian reforms of Thomas Gilbert. McCulloch wished to return to the Poor Law of 1722 which provided for a workhouse and the farming of the Poor. This was the type of Poor relief proposed by Sir Frederick Eden and which Bentham had adopted in his *Pauper Management*.

VI

THE GROWTH OF RADICAL OPPOSITION
Part I. Rural Unemployment

DURING the decade of the 1820's, the followers of Bentham and Ricardo increased their opposition to the Poor Laws and began to devise a remedy for what they called the disease of pauperism. Drawing upon Ricardo's principles, the Radicals insisted on greater freedom for the tenant farmer to employ his capital on the land. The Radicals firmly held the views that the Poor Laws reduced profits, discouraged investment in agriculture, and subsidized inefficient labor. Despite the persistence of depressed conditions in agriculture, they sought to cut taxes and curtail government expenditures.

The Ricardian analysis had a special appeal for those Liberal Tories who dominated the Government during most of the decade. Of these Liberal Tories only Lord Liverpool had the ability to hold together the several warring factions of the Tory party. During his fifteen years as Prime Minister, he had an inner cabinet composed of the zealous economic reformers.[1] Prominent among the members of this economic cabinet were William Huskisson, Sturges Bourne, Edward Littleton, and Wilmot Horton. Under Liverpool's leadership, the Liberal Tories pursued an economic policy in keeping with Ricardo's principles of free trade, resumption of specie payment, and the curtailment of government expenditures.[2]

For ten years and more after the end of the Napoleonic War, the Liverpool Government was under great political pressure to relieve the distress in agriculture. As farm prices continued to fall, farmers had to abandon their tenancies, landlords had to forego their rents, and rural laborers by the thousands had to seek poor relief in order to subsist.[3] By 1819 business had recovered from the postwar depression, but it was not until 1823 that agriculture began to revive and farmers to adjust to the lower level of prices.[4]

Lacking a theory of the business cycle and having no practicable concept of unemployment, the Tory Government probably aggravated depressed conditions by curtailing expenditures.[5] The Liberal Tories blamed the Poor Laws for both the farmer's lack of capital and the laborer's low wages. The Poor Law policy of giving allowances to large families, it was thought, added to a population already redundant and to the supply of rural labor that had long since outrun the demand. If outdoor relief to able-bodied persons was stopped, the Liberal Tories argued, the supply of labor would adjust to the demand and wages would rise to their natural level.

In the pursuit of a liberal economic policy with respect to labor, the Tory Government repealed the Anti-Combination Laws, which had prevented the organization of labor unions, and abolished the fixing of a minimum wage in the silk industry. The Liberal Tories refused to interfere with working conditions in the factories except to provide protection for children. All these measures were negative in that they repealed old laws requiring enforcement.

The Tory Government, however, did undertake positive measures to curtail the redundant supply of labor. One positive measure was the tightening of the Vagrancy Laws to prevent the migration of workers from Ireland and Scotland. Although the application of the Vagrancy Laws to the Irish and the Scots did not require additional expenses at the national level, it did increase the burden on the poor rates, for the parishes were required to return migrant laborers to their own countries and to pay the cost of transportation. A second positive measure to reduce the supply of labor by subsidizing the emigration of English laborers to the colonies was blocked by the economy-minded Whigs and Radicals.

Throughout the 1820's the Tories supported Sturges Bourne's Poor Law policy which provided for the election of select vestries and the appointment of paid assistant overseers of the poor. The Sturges Bourne Acts of 1818 and 1819 placed the responsibility for administering the Poor Laws on wealthy persons paying the largest proportion of the poor rates. After the wealthiest persons had been elected as the custodians of the poor rates, they were

128

authorized to appoint an assistant overseer who had the duties of administering poor relief. The Government annually circularized the parishes urging the election of select vestries and the appointment of assistant overseers. The Government also required an annual report of the number of places having elected select vestries and the number of places having appointed assistant overseers. The Returns of 1821 showed 2,006 places having select vestries and 2,257 places having assistant overseers.[6] By the end of the decade there were 2,725 places having select vestries and 3,119 places having assistant overseers.[7] It was clear from the small number of places which had elected select vestries by 1830 that the Sturges Bourne Acts had failed to enlist the wealthier payers of the poor rates in the management of the Poor Laws. The Select Vestry Acts undoubtedly enabled some of the larger urban parishes to improve their Poor Law administration and the continued circularizing of the parishes encouraged some to adopt a more efficient management.

The Tory Poor Law policy of the 1820's, as embodied in the Sturges Bourne Acts, was both vigorously defended and stoutly opposed. Among the ablest defenders of the Tory policy was Frederick Page. A resident of Newbury in Berkshire, Page was educated at Oriel College, Oxford. He was called to the bar in 1792 and became a Bencher of the Middle Temple. As the Chairman of the Kennent-on-Avon Canal Company, he became a man of wealth and influence. His distinguished position in the county enabled him to hold the office of magistrate and eventually that of Deputy Lieutenant. On three occasions and in three different parishes he held the onerous office of overseer. He was appointed overseer of the parish of Speen and held the office for three years.[8]

In 1794 Page first undertook the office of overseer out of motives of resentment rather than charity. The owner of a canal whose income had been consumed by the Poor Law assessments, he considered the levy too high and the amount of relief grossly wasteful. When the Berkshire magistrates met in 1795 at Speenhamland and adopted scales of relief in proportion to the size of the family and varying in amount according to the price of bread, Page was outraged by what he thought was an absurdly extravagant scale of relief. He wrote an account of the Berkshire magistrates' meeting and sent it to Sir Frederick Morton Eden who included it verbatim in the first volume of *The State of the Poor.*

In the account of Speenhamland which he sent to Eden, Page charged that the extravagant scale of relief was destroying the independence of agricultural laborers.[10] This hasty judgment, made at a moment of resentment, he later disregarded. His account of Speenhamland marked only the beginning of a long study of indigence and of a life devoted to the relief of destitution. In order to better educate himself, he made several trips to the Continent to study the problems of indigence. After studying the conditions of the poor on the Continent, Page abandoned his previous hostility to the Poor Laws and became a defender of the poor man's right to relief. Although he thought the Elizabethan Poor Law should be reformed, he defended what he thought to be its central principle, that public relief be available for all types of destitution.[11]

In 1822 Page set forth his views in a lengthy pamphlet entitled, *Principles of the English Poor Laws, Illustrated and Defended by an Historical View of Indigence in Civil Society. . . .* Page made it clear in his essay that he was not advocating a system of bread scales.[12] He earnestly defended the laborer's right to relief in times of unemployment. He recognized that the lack of employment was the main source of indigence, and for this reason he took issue with Malthus. Although he conceded Malthus's principle that population was pressing against the limits of subsistence and tending to outrun it, Page insisted that the poor man's right to relief was as basic as the right to property. He assumed also that since the laborer could not foresee the fluctuations in prices and wages, he would be unable to exercise the prudence of delaying marriage and of guarding against a redundant labor supply.[13]

While Page was eagerly defending the poor man's right to relief, Robert Slaney, another Poor Law reformer, was denying that such a right existed. To support his case he selected arguments from celebrated economists including Smith, Malthus, and Ricardo. He tried to show that with the progress of the new science the political economists had grown increasingly hostile to the Poor Laws. Between 1817 and 1827 Slaney published several pamphlets on the Poor Laws, proposing that relief to able-bodied laborers be prohibited; and upon becoming a member of Parliament, he introduced a bill to prevent the granting of relief to laborers in private employment.

Robert Aglionby Slaney was born in 1792 at Hatton Grange in Shropshire. After receiving his education at Trinity College, Cambridge, he studied law at Lincoln's Inn and was called to the bar in 1817. He practiced law until 1826, when he was elected to Parliament for Shrewsbury.[14]

Slaney first became interested in the problems of the working classes during the postwar depression when all types of laborers were out of work. In 1816 he served on the Shropshire County Committee for the Employment of the Poor Destitute of Work.[15] Upon investigating those parishes having the greatest number of paupers, the Shropshire Committee discovered that the mining and manufacturing industries, which contributed the greatest number of workers to the ranks of the unemployed, were assessed very little under the Poor Laws, and that the burden of the poor rates fell consequently on houses and farm land. As a result of this investigation, Slaney understood that such inequities had to be corrected by law; but he also understood that the correction of inequities would not remove the causes of low wages and unemployment.

To find a remedy for low wages and unemployment Slaney turned to the political economists. From his study of the political economists he had made the discovery that the Poor Laws themselves were the main cause of destitution. He learned from Adam Smith that the Poor Laws "contributed to fetter the circulation of labor" and prevented wages from rising to their natural level. He learned from Malthus that the Poor Laws, rather than mitigating the effects of poverty, created "improvidence, idleness, and other vice." From his study of political economy Slaney concluded it was necessary to correct the abuses of the Poor Law and to stop relief payments to all persons except "the naturally impotent."[16]

In 1819 Slaney published a second pamphlet on the Poor Laws with the title, *An Essay on the Employment of the Poor.* In this lengthy treatise on poverty he repeated much of what he had said in the earlier tract and expanded it with a fuller explanation of unemployment. He derived his remedy for unemployment from Ricardo's "late excellent work." He was content to repeat verbatim Ricardo's paradoxical view of the Poor Laws, "instead of making the poor rich they make the rich poor."[17] Following Ricardo's principles of taxation, Slaney concluded that "natural improvement" would occur when the income tax, which had been paid to the government during the war, remained with the people who would invest it more efficiently in the creation of employment. Likewise, he thought if the poor rates were left in the hands of the ratepayers, they would spend the money wisely in the creation of natural employment. Believing that all parish expenditures were essentially wasteful, Slaney opposed both the parish farm and the workhouse as means of creating employment.[18]

Slaney's pamphlet on the employment of the poor gained considerable recognition. When he published a second edition in 1823, the Board of Agriculture awarded him its silver medal.[19] This encouraged him to publish the following year a much larger work which he entitled, *Essay on the Beneficial Direction of Rural Expenditures.* In his new work he continued his attack on the Poor Laws and called for a drastic retrenchment in government expenditures as the best way to create employment.

A whole chorus of voices soon took up Slaney's hue and cry against the Poor Laws, attributing to them low wages, unemployment, and the moral decay of labor. Even distinguished clergymen of the Established Church found in political economy the explanation of immorality. One of the ablest exponents of Ricardian economics was the Reverend Edward Copleston, Provost of Oriel College, Oxford. Copleston contributed two influential tracts to the controversy over the Poor Laws. Following a common practice of the time, he wrote his tracts in the form of open letters addressed to public officials. In 1819 he addressed a letter to Sir Robert Peel, *On the Pernicious Effect of a Variable Standard of Value Especially as It Regards the Condition of the Lower Orders and the Poor Laws.* On the title page he inscribed the central theme of his letter, *Laissez Nous Faire.* He urged Sir Robert Peel to resume specie payment in order to avoid the kind of inflation that had been so damaging to the workers' welfare during the late war.[20] Copleston was able to see the effects of inflation but unable to comprehend the adverse effects of deflation.

Copleston not only deplored the monetary policy which the Tories had pursued during the war but he also condemned "the false humanity which exempts the receiver of parochial relief from the wholesome terrors of a workhouse."[21] The humanitarian reforms of the Poor Laws which Vansittart and the Pittites had enacted were characterized by Copleston as "a system radically vicious tending to corrupt, impoverish, degrade, and disorganize society. . . ." Whatever the Tory Government thought of Copleston's views on the Poor Laws, they rewarded him in 1828 by appointing him Bishop of Llandaff.[22]

As a consequence of the writings of Copleston and other Anglican clergymen, some of the Evangelical humanitarians, and especially the influential members of the Clapham Sect, ceased their long struggle to reform the Poor Laws. The Reverend John Bird Sumner, who had written a major work, *Records of Creation*, in defense of Malthus, was one of the few Evangelicals to receive appointment as bishop. The Mendicity Society, which the Evangelicals had created originally to relieve the destitute, was reorganized during the 1820's as a society to suppress begging.

The Evangelicals at Bath, who had been engaged in welfare work for two decades, abandoned their early relief work during the 1820's and undertook a Malthusian crusade to extirpate pauperism. One of the converts to the new Malthusian morality, William Davis, addressed a pamphlet to the Evangelicals at Bath exhorting them to abandon the futile work of charity. In his *Hints to Philanthropists*, which was published in 1821, he discussed the means of improving the condition of the working classes. Convinced that the immorality of the lower classes was the cause of unemployment, he thought the proper remedy was the education of the poor in the Malthusian virtues of prudence and foresight. As a first step in the improvement of the morality of the working classes, he proposed to repeal the Poor Laws, which he said were adding to "the sum of poverty and misery among the poor."[23]

When the Evangelicals at Clapham ceased to defend the Poor Laws, they left the Radicals free to carry on their campaign with hardly a dissenting voice. The Radical reform of the Poor Laws was first debated in Parliament in 1821 when James Scarlett introduced a bill to correct what he thought were major abuses. His first recommendation was to impose a maximum on relief expenditures, for it seemed to him that the present unlimited provision operated "as a premium for poverty, indolence, licentiousness, and immorality."[24] To achieve his purpose he would establish the current rate of assessment as the maximum beyond which no parish could go. His second recommendation was to deny relief to able-bodied laborers whose claim to public assistance was unemployment. The main object of the bill, he said, was to have the laborer paid a just wage rather than have him depend on the poor rates.

Although Scarlett's bill gained the support of Whigs and Radicals, it was defeated because the Tories were unwilling to relinquish so important a cause as Poor Law reform into the hands of the minority party. As spokesman for the Tory Government, Sturges Bourne accepted the principle of giving relief only to the impotent poor, but he refused to support that part of the bill which set a maximum to Poor Law expenditures. Although the Tories succeeded in defeating Scarlett's bill, they made a major concession by agreeing to deny relief to able-bodied laborers.

Scarlett, moreover, had won a major victory, for he had contributed a new weapon to the arsenal of the Radical opposition to the Poor Laws. Following his lawyer's instincts, he reconstructed the Elizabethan Law by insisting that it had never been the Queen's intention to relieve the able-bodied poor.[25] Reinterpreting the Poor Laws in this fashion, Scarlett concentrated the opposition against the Evangelical reformers who had established outdoor relief for the unemployed laborers as well as for the impotent poor. His Radicalism was carried even further by Michael Nolan, who introduced a bill in 1823 to restore the badging of parish paupers and to farm out the parish poor under the old system of contracts. He also proposed to publish the names of all persons receiving relief. To make it more difficult — and often impossible — to obtain relief, he would require the concurrence of three Justices of the Peace.[26] If his recommendations had been passed by Parliament, Nolan would have repealed several of the most important Poor Law reforms of William Pitt and his followers. As it turned out, the premature bills of Nolan and Scarlett enabled the Radicals to extol the original Elizabethan Poor Law and to concentrate their opposition against Pitt's policy.

During the 1820's the Liberal Tories maintained their doctrinaire attitudes notwithstanding the volumes of information which were collected by Parliament. They continued to believe that the cycle of poor relief was running a relentless course. They thought relief encouraged early marriage, which produced more children needing relief. Assuming that an escalation in the rates was inherent in the system of Poor Laws, a Committee of the House of Commons required the parishes to report annually the amounts of assessments and expenditures. Unlike the investigations undertaken by Sir George Rose, the Committees of the 1820's did not inquire about the number of people receiving relief nor the reasons for their being on relief. While the Liberal Tories were doctrinaire in their attitudes towards the Poor Laws, many of their colleagues in the House of Commons refused to accept political economy as a safe guide to policy. These practical men, some of whom had acquired experience in their own parishes, refused to abolish the Poor Laws.

In order to appraise the growth of Poor Law expenses, the House of Commons appointed annually from 1821 to 1826 a Select Committee on the Poor-Rate Returns. So important was Poor Law reform as a political issue that the most prominent members of both political parties sought places on the Poor Rates Committee. Thomas Courtenay, the Chairman of the Committee, had long been a member of the House of Commons and had often carried administrative responsibility in the Tory Government. As Secretary of the Board of Control he had become familiar with the flow of statistical information connected with the daily operations of his office.[27] Proficient in political arithmetic, he had little liking for political economy. He was consequently at odds with his colleagues, William Huskisson and Sturges Bourne, who were enthusiastic proponents of the new science. As a member of the Poor Law Committee of 1817, he took time to master the vast quantity of statistical information relating to the conditions of the working classes. He was one of the few who recognized that prices had risen much faster than wages during the Napoleonic War. He also recognized that Poor Law expenditures had increased after the war because of fluctuations in trade. He understood that unemployment was seasonal and technological as well as cyclical. Using census data, the price of wheat, and the Poor Law Returns, he was able to conclude: "An accurate allowance for the increase in population and the price of wheat will sufficiently account for the increase in expenditures."[28]

Under Courtenay's direction, the Committee on Poor-Rate Returns made a comparative study of the annual Poor Law expenditures from 1748 to 1820. The Committee found that the amounts levied and spent for relief had increased substantially from 1748 to 1812; that the amounts had fallen during the last two years of the war; and that they had risen again during the postwar depression of 1817-18. After the peak had been reached during the depression, the poor rates began to fall again, and in 1821 the Committee was able to report "that the increase is not now progressive."[29]

In its report of 1822, the Committee on Poor-Rate Returns found that the downward trend in relief expenses had continued during the year ending March 25, 1821. In the same year the

135

Committee studied the relation between the price of wheat and the amount spent on poor relief. Since bread was the staple item of the laborer's diet, it had been assumed the amount of relief varied with the price of wheat; the Committee discovered, however, that relief expenses did not vary in proportion to the rise and fall in the price of wheat.[30]

In its several investigations the Committee on Poor Rate Returns found that "a considerable portion of money which is collected. . .is not applied to any purpose connected with the poor." The Committee, consequently, urged Parliament to separate all other types of local government expenses from poor relief. They especially recommended that the costs of repairing roads be charged to the county rates rather than to the poor rates. Although Parliament did not act upon the Committee's request, the Home Department on its own initiative ordered the parishes to adopt efficient methods of accounting. The administration of relief, however, continued to vary so widely from county to county and from parish to parish that Parliament lacked the information on which it could properly legislate.

As a result of the Poor-Rate Returns for the year ending 25 March 1823, the Committee again had "the satisfaction of reporting a progressive diminution in the amount of the sums levied and expended on account of the poor."[31] Poor Law expenditures had steadily declined for six successive years and had fallen 27 per cent from the peak year of 1817-18. The Committee continued to think it proper to compare the amount of expenditures with the price of wheat, for some members believed that relief expenses varied with the price of wheat. The Committee discovered, however, that during the relief year, ending March 25, 1823, Poor Law expenditures declined 9 per cent and the price of wheat fell 20 per cent. It became even clearer in 1824 that relief expenses did not vary directly with the price of wheat, for in that year Poor Law expenses continued to fall while the price of wheat rose 36 per cent.

Since some Poor Law reformers believed that the high cost of relief in the southern counties was due to the bread scales, the Committee compared the expenditures for the year 1822-23 with the maximum year of 1817-18 and reported the relative decline of expenditures for each county. While the decline for the whole of England and Wales during this period had been 27 per cent, the decline for Berkshire, where the Speenhamland scales had originated, was 46 per cent.

In addition to its study of gross expenditures, the Poor-Rate Committee of 1824 compared the per capita expenditures for the relief year 1822-23 with those for 1812-13, which was the peak year for several of the agricultural counties. Whereas the per capita expenses for England and Wales had fallen from 13s. to 10s., the per capita expenses for Berkshire had fallen from 26s. to 15s. In Sussex, the county with the highest rates, the per capita expenditures had fallen from 32s. in 1812-13 to 22s. in 1822-23. Even though Sussex still had the highest per capita expenditure, its decrease during the decade had been greater than that of any other county except Berkshire. In the esteemed northern counties, Cumberland and Northumberland, where expenses were low, the per capita expenditures during the decade remained virtually unchanged. The county of England with the lowest per capita expenditure (5s.) in 1823 was Lancaster, which was then enjoying a flourishing cotton trade.[33]

The Poor-Rate Returns for the year ending March 25, 1824, did not bear out the Committee's expectation that Poor Law expenditures would increase with the rise in the price of wheat. Even though the price of wheat rose from 41s.11d. in 1822-23 to 56s. 8d. in 1823-24, the costs of poor relief continued to decline. Relief expenditures were lower in 1823-24 than in any other year since 1815-16.[34]

Although the Poor Law expenditures had been decreasing for six years and although the reports of the Committee on the Poor-rate Returns had made it clear that the amount of rates did not fluctuate directly with the price of wheat, the Radicals continued to demand a drastic change in the Poor Laws. They insisted that the Poor Laws not only caused unemployment but also prevented wages from rising to their natural level. To satisfy these demands the Whig leaders in the House of Commons decided to take into their own hands the controversial issue of Poor Law reform. On March 25, 1824, Lord John Russell requested the appointment of a new committee to investigate the practice of paying wages from the poor rates.[35] Russell's original proposal included all types of wages, but at Sir Robert Peel's suggestion, he restricted it to the methods of paying wages to agricultural laborers. Even though the Whigs had initiated the investigation, the leaders of the Tories, Peel, Sturges Bourne, and Western, obtained appointment to the committee. The principal Whig members, in addition to Russell, who became its chairman, were Brougham, Scarlett, and Spring Rice.[36]

137

The Committee on Laborers' Wages, which sat during April and May, 1824, examined thirteen witnesses who were connected, in one way or another, with the administration of Poor Laws. Besides examining witnesses, the Committee circulated questionnaires among magistrates and other county officials requesting information concerning the conditions of employment, the rate of wages, and the methods of paying wages.[37] The questionnaires were sent to 358 places in the forty English counties. The magistrates and other officials were requested to estimate the prevailing conditions and practices in their hundred or division even when these practices varied widely from parish to parish. The replies to the questionnaires provided the Committee with an important body of information concerning the methods of administering relief to able-bodied persons and especially to laborers lacking employment.[38]

The Committee on Laborers' Wages wanted to know in the first place "if any laborers in your district, employed by farmers, receive either the whole or any part of the wages of their labor out of the poor rates?" Of the 382 replies to this question, 64 per cent of the respondents answered either "no" or "rarely."[39] It was clear from the answers to this question and others that the magistrates and other county officials did not generally associate the family allowances, which were paid by the parishes, with the daily or weekly wages paid by the farmers.[40]

The answers to the second question indicated that it was customary for laborers with large families to receive assistance from the parish. The Committee's question was, "Is it customary in your district for married laborers, having children, to receive assistance from the parish rate?" Of the 377 persons replying to the second question, 83 per cent answered in the affirmative. It was clearly the general practice to grant relief according to the size of the family. When the parish provided relief work, either on the roads or in the gravel pits, it was also customary to hire the entire family and to pay relief by the head or the task. Even the amount of work that a man might obtain to earn relief was sometimes rationed according to the size of the family.[41]

The investigation of 1824 disclosed that family allowances, or the relief scales, varied widely from district to district and from parish to parish within the district. The Committee's third question concerned the practice of paying relief according to the size of the family: "Does the family allowance begin when they have one child, or more?" The magistrates were in a position to reply

138

accurately to this question, for they used the scales adopted at the Quarter Sessions when ordering the parishes to relieve certain paupers. Of the 320 officials replying to this question, ninety denied having scales, and twenty-one other respondents claimed they gave relief only to large families or to families in times of illness. In a majority of the districts the magisterial scales were related to the size of the family; but not all the parishes within the districts had adopted the magistrate's scales. In forty districts relief began in some parishes with the first child; in fifty-six other districts relief began with the second child; in seventy districts relief began with the third child; in twenty-seven districts with four or more. These replies indicated that the scales were parsimonious. Some parishes began relief only with the seventh or eighth child. The size of the family was no assurance that relief would be forthcoming, for many parishes took into consideration the ages of the children, excluding those who were employable. The large family most likely to obtain relief was one in which the mother was either pregnant or nursing a baby. Rather than encourage families to seek relief, some parishes offered prizes to large families that were self-supporting.

In addition to family scales, some parishes had bread scales. Although the Committee on Laborers' Wages did not investigate the practice of bread scales, a few officials replied that such scales existed in some parishes. Wherever these scales existed, they were, like family allowances, a rule of thumb, an approximation of need rather than a method of calculating specific grants.

The investigation of agricultural wages in 1824 disclosed not only appalling destitution among farm laborers but also extensive unemployment, especially of a seasonal variety. The venerable system of roundsmen and the more recent practice of the labor rate were the farmers' methods of meeting the perennial problem of seasonal employment. The Committee's fourth question concerned the roundsmen: "Is it usual for overseers of the poor to send round to farmers laborers who cannot find work to be paid partly by the employer and partly out of the poor rate?" Of the 358 replies to this question, 48 per cent of the districts had continued the practice of roundsmen. There was some evidence in the Returns that farmers were abandoning the system of roundsmen and adopting the labor rate as a fairer way of employing their hands during the winter months.

The Committee on Laborers' Wages attempted to investigate the extent of unemployment in 1824, but it did not succeed in elicit-

139

ing much useful information by the following question: "Has the number of unemployed laborers asking assistance from the parish increased or diminished during the past few years?" To this poorly stated question, 111 officials replied that the number of unemployed workers seeking relief was declining. The replies to this question and to the question on roundsmen indicated extensive seasonal unemployment among agricultural laborers.

That wages were low in rural areas had been notorious since 1795, when Samuel Whitbread introduced his bill in Parliament proposing a minimum wage. Nevertheless, no investigation had been undertaken to determine the rate of wages. The Committee on Laborers' Wages made a feeble attempt to investigate the rate of wages in 1824 with this ambiguous question, "What is the usual rate of wages in your district?" An exact answer to the question was impossible, because rates varied so widely from parish to parish within the district. The rates of wages also varied between skilled and unskilled labor. Those laborers who drove the teams and cared for equipment were of most value to the farmer. If the wide range between skilled and unskilled is reported, what should one conclude about the usual rate? The wages were reported as 12s. a week in the West Riding of Yorkshire, and 6s. and 8s. in the North Riding. In the Bolton division of Lancashire they were reported to be 9s., whereas in Clitheroe they were 12s. to 14s., and in Manchester 12s. The usual wage in Norfolk was 6s. to 9s.; but in the Northampton division, consisting of fifty parishes, the wages were as low as 3s. 6d. The rate of wages as reported by the magistrates and other officials did not accurately indicate the level of family income, since the entire family might be employed during harvest and planting season. Moreover, the skilled laborers, who were the regular hands, were employed throughout the year and some were provided cottages with plots of ground for gardens.[42]

As remedies for low wages and unemployment, the Poor Law reformers of 1824 recommended only a more efficient administration of relief, one which discriminated between the deserving poor and the profligate, between the industrious and the idle. Because the reformers had placed so much confidence in efficient administration as a means of extirpating poverty, the Committee of 1824 asked these questions, "Have select vestries or assistant overseers been established in your neighborhood? If so, what effect have they produced?" To these questions two hundred officials reported that large towns and the more populous parishes had elected select vestries and that about one-fourth of such places had appointed assistant overseers. From these replies one may conclude that large industrial places in Lancashire, the West Riding of Yorkshire, Middlesex, and Surrey had taken advantage of the Select Vestry Acts to improve their Poor Law administration.

The replies to the questionnaires which were circulated by the Committee on Laborers' Wages provided valuable information about the social conditions of rural labor. In addition to the Returns of 1824, Lord John Russell's Committee took copious testimony from thirteen witnesses who were connected with the operations of the Poor Laws. Among the witnesses were clergymen, churchwardens, magistrates, an overseer, and a surveyor of roads, all of whom had been selected to represent different localities and various aspects of Poor Law administration.

The Reverend William Carmalt, a longtime resident of Putney in Surrey, testified concerning the improved administration in his parish.[43] Allowances at Putney were given only to large families and to families in times of illness. In times of unemployment the relief work of wheeling gravel and digging in the pits was designed to be less desirable than private employment. During the four years ending in 1822, while he was managing poor relief, the parish had been able to reduce the number of paupers from 191 to 147. His parish was one of several which had adopted the anti-pauper system designed by Bentham to improve pauper management.[44]

As Lord John Russell was much concerned about welfare in his own county of Bedford, he called several witnesses from that area. The Reverend Philip Hunt, a magistrate at Bedford, reported that inasmuch as wages were only 4s. a week, every family with more than one child got relief, the amount being equal to the cost of maintaining a pauper in the workhouse. The overseer followed the workhouse scale and ignored the magistrate's scales which were determined by the number of the family and the price of bread.[45]

Thomas Todd, a churchwarden at Woburn in Bedford, reported the rate of wages as 10s. for those handling horses; for other types of farm labor the rate was 8s. In addition to their wages, the laborers in some parishes were able to add to their income by gardening the land set aside by the Duke of Bedford for spade husbandry. Relief at Woburn was given to families in sickness and to large families of more than four children.[46]

Thomas Smart, a farm laborer from Eversholt in Bedford, viv- idly described living conditions in his area. He was the father of thirteen children, seven of whom were living at the time of his testimony. During the twenty-eight years of his married life, he had received no relief except for the funerals of his children; and during this time his wages had fallen from 10s. to 8s. a week (they were more in harvest). The family income was supplemented by the mother, when she was able to work, and by the children who began to work at the age of nine. Even the girls went to work as soon as they could find employment. Previously, they had worked in the lace industry but now that the handicraft had ceased, they turned to heavier farm labor. The family had a potato garden which they rented for 50s. a year, a sum equal to six weeks' wages. Thomas Smart thought his condition was above that of most farm labor, yet he could afford no beer and no meat except bacon.[47]

The three witnesses from Bedfordshire, though coming from different occupations, were in agreement about the depressed state of agriculture and the prevalence of low wages. They were also unanimous in denying that poor relief was administered in a way demoralizing to farm laborers.

The living conditions of rural labor in Sussex appeared to be even worse than in Bedfordshire. The Reverend John Pratt, the Rector of Selscombe, testified that the farmers in his district were using the high level of the poor rates as a means of negotiating a reduction in tithes. He was irate that his own living had been cut in half by such negotiations. The clergyman also complained about the farmers' abuse of the Poor Laws. During the winter months they paid no wages to their laborers. Since the burden of the poor rates fell on them, they paid the rates and the parish overseer pro- vided relief in lieu of wages.[48] Pratt's testimony also emphasized the abuse that was everywhere connected with the old system of roundsmen.

A new method, the Oundle Plan, was being adopted by a few parishes as a means of correcting some of the abuses of the rounds- men system. The plan originated in the parish of Oundle in North- amptonshire. There the farmers who were assessed for the poor rates paid the amount of their assessments directly to their labor- ers rather than to the parish overseer. In this way the farmers were able to employ their laborers during the winter months and keep them under their own supervision rather than to return them to the gravel pits and the road work of the parish. The labor rate, the name by which the Oundle Plan was later known, was one attempt to solve the problem of seasonal unemployment that was increasing with decay of the handicraft industries. The labor rate had the advantages of keeping farm labor employed under competent supervision and at work that was meaningful. The farmers liked the plan because it enabled them to keep their best hands throughout the year and to make capital improvements which they could not have afforded otherwise. The obvious objection to the labor rate was that some people who did not employ farm labor were nonetheless assessed under the poor rates to pay the wages of labor. [49]

The principal alternative to the labor rate and the roundsmen was parish road work, but the futility, inefficiency, and brutality of such employment were deeply resented by farm laborers. James McAdams gave a vivid picture of parish road work to the Committee on Laborers' Wages. McAdams had had a long experience as surveyor in the counties of Herts, Essex, Surrey, Lincoln, Hants, and Buckingham. In these counties most parishes were eager to send their pauper laborers to him to be employed on the roads during the winter. As a surveyor for a turnpike trust, which was responsible for building and maintaining roads, McAdams was ordered by the trustees to pay enough wages to free the workers from parish relief. It was his custom to hire the entire family to break, grade, and rake the stones. Boys and girls, ages nine or ten, were paid 6d. a day. Most families, however, were paid by the task. During the early winter months of 1824 there were so many persons unemployed that work had to be rationed. A man was permitted to break six yards of stone each week at a shilling a yard. [50]

McAdams preferred pauper labor to "statute labor," the latter being persons required by law to work so many days a year on the roads. He preferred also to hire the pauper family and to pay them by the task or piece. Those refusing the work at his rates were returned to their parishes. At the time of his testimony in April, 1824, McAdams was paying 10s. a week, the amount, he estimated, on which a small family could subsist. During the spring and summer, many turnpike trusts had to pay as much as 15s. to 20s. a week, the higher rates being paid near London. To avoid paying high wages, McAdams employed men on the roads only during months from October to April. His testimony made it clear enough that the turnpike trusts, as well as the parishes, built and

143

maintained their local and county roads by means of the low wages of the seasonally unemployed rural labor.

During the early months of 1824 unemployment was extensive throughout Suffolk. In the incorporated Hundred of Blything, which included forty-six parishes, the rate of unemployment varied from one-third to one-fourth of the laborers. Depressed conditions required the rationing of work to three days a week and lowered wages to 4s. 6d. This was also the relief scale for husband and wife; families with children received 6d. to 9d. for each child.[51] Although scale of relief over the years fluctuated somewhat with the price of bread, the relief committee which met weekly to determine family allowances did not adhere strictly to the bread scales.

Such were the depressed conditions in the Blything Hundred as reported by the Reverend Anthony Collett, who occupied the Havingham rectory and who had served as a magistrate for several years. He was also a director of the Blything Poor Law Union, which had been incorporated in 1776. The Blything Union spent large sums annually on the employment of its paupers, the expenditures varying greatly with the seasons of the year. The burden of the poor rates was heavy, according to Collett, because the farmers preferred to throw their laborers on the parish rather than pay them wages. They could then use the increase in poor rates as a means of bargaining with their landlords for a reduction in rent.

The testimonies of Collett and the other witnesses appearing before the Committee on Laborers' Wages were an astounding record of rural wretchedness caused by low wages and unemployment. These wretched conditions were confirmed by the replies to the questionnaires circulated among the county officials. The Committee of 1824, however, like the Poor Law Committee of 1817, made little use of the evidence. Rather, they chose to write a doctrinaire report condemning the Poor Laws for causing low wages and the depressed conditions in agriculture.

On June 4, 1824, Lord John Russell presented to the House of Commons his *Report on Labourers' Wages*. Without attempting to summarize the returns from the questionnaires or to generalize from the testimony of the carefully selected witnesses, he delivered a doctrinaire condemnation of the Poor Laws. He explained unemployment in Malthusian terms of a redundant population which was caused by the maladministration of poor relief:

144

"A surplus population is encouraged; men who receive but a small pittance know that they have only to marry and that pittance will be augmented in proportion to the number of their children. Hence, the supply of labour is by no means regulated by demand and parishes burdened with thirty, forty, and fifty labourers for whom they can find no employment and who serve to depress the situation of all their fellow labourers in the same parish."[52]

Lord John Russell's Committee also condemned the Poor Laws for causing the moral decay of farm labor: "By far the worst consequence of the system is the degradation of the character of the labouring class." The Committee reported that the vicious system had so destroyed the moral character of the workingman that "it becomes a matter of indifference whether he earns a small sum or a large one."

The Committee on Labourers' Wages, ignoring the evidence which had been collected, deduced much of their report from their Radical doctrine of labor. The Committee confidently reported that "there are but two motives by which men are induced to work: the one the hope of improving the conditions of themselves and their families; the other the fear of punishment. The one is the principle of free labour, the other the principle of slave labour."[53] Guided by this doctrine of labor, the Committee could confidently report that Poor Laws were destroying free labor and creating slave labor.

The Poor Law reformers, whether Whigs, Liberal Tories, or Benthamite Radicals, were unanimous in blaming the justices of the peace for the maladministration of the Poor Laws. The justices, though good men of good intentions, were condemned as ignorant men, not knowing the consequences of their acts. The justices were accused of having established bread scales and of ordering outdoor relief in such profusion as to encourage idleness and the profligacy of early marriage.[54]

Although the Committee of 1824 were vociferous in their condemnation of Poor Laws, they did not agree on the proper remedy. The Liberal Tories continued to support the Sturges Bourne Act and to rely upon the select vestries and assistant overseers as the best means of improving the administration of relief. Divided among themselves, the Committee could do no more than admonish the magistrates for imposing their scales of relief on the parish officials.

The Committee did not go so far as to forbid "relief to the able-bodied labourers on account of their impotent children" because

145

they feared that such a law might throw "some married labourers entirely upon the parish." In the relief of unemployed laborers, the Committee recommended "that the parish should, if it be possible, provide them with labor less acceptable in its nature than ordinary labour and at lower rates than the average rate of the neighborhood." With complete confidence in the Benthamite doctrine of "less eligibility," they added "that this method has been found practically beneficial in all places where it has been carried into effect."[55]

The *Report of the Committee on Labourers' Wages* was an expression of the growing Radical opposition to the Poor Laws. Some members of the Committee wished to repeal the legislation which had been enacted by William Pitt and his followers. They wanted to stop the payment of relief to able-bodied labourers with large families. They wished to reestablish the old workhouse test in order to distinguish between free labor (natural employment) and slave labor (artificial employment provided by the parish). Under the influence of Ricardo, the Committee viewed unemployment as a problem of capital and labor. According to Ricardo's theory, the amount of capital had to be increased in order to enlarge the demand for labor. Guided by this defective economic theory, the Committee were unable to devise a remedy for the extensive unemployment that prevailed in agriculture. The legislator's inability to deal with the problem of unemployment would lead eventually to the abandonment of the theory which guided the Poor Law reformers of 1824, but that time was in the remote future.

The Committee's recommendations were in keeping with a large and growing school of Radical reformers who were eager to apply the general principles of economics to remedy the disease of pauperism. Bewildered by the complex social conditions under the Poor Law, they sought the clarity and certainty of universal principles. Rather than generalize about specific conditions in the thousands of parishes, they looked for ideal cases to illustrate what they thought were the pernicious tendencies of the Poor Laws.

Popularizers of the new science of political economy were springing up in Parliament and other branches of government. Prominent leaders of both the Whig and Tory parties became members of the Political Economy Club.[56] At the same time, the universities began to establish chairs of political economy; and the professors who occupied them thought it their duty to exhort the public and to advise the government on economic policy.[57] The major political reviews, the *Edinburgh*, *Quarterly*, and *Westminster* gave increasing attention to advocating economic policy.[58]

John Ramsay McCulloch, the disciple of Ricardo, was the foremost popularizer of political economy. During the 1820's the *Edinburgh Review* was the most widely read political journal, and during this decade McCulloch had a virtual monopoly of its economic subjects, writing a total of forty-four articles.[59] Besides the *Edinburgh* articles, McCulloch wrote extensively for the *Scotsman* and contributed to several editions of the *Encyclopaedia Britannica*. He was one of the first economists to make a living by his writing and teaching.

McCulloch published in 1824 his first major work, *A Discourse on the Rise, Progress, Peculiar Objects, and Importance of Political Economy*. An avowed popularizer, he undertook the role of educating the public in the science of political economy. He declared this desire in his Preface, "My object. . .has been to furnish the student of political economy with a general view of the principles on which science is founded."[60] Never lacking confidence in himself or his science, McCulloch was certain that "the errors with which political economy was formerly infected have now nearly disappeared, and. . .it really admits of as much certainty in its conclusions as any science founded on fact and experiment can possibly do."[61]

Accrediting Ricardo with having separated political economy from its former errors, McCulloch did not hesitate to place this achievement on the level with that of Sir Isaac Newton's. McCulloch conceived of science as being a body of general principles deduced by analytical reasoning. His limited view of science led him to reject contemptuously the testimony of practical men and the theorizing which, he said, was based on the narrow foundation of an individual's experience. According to McCulloch, the scientist should draw his theory from the universal experience of mankind.

McCulloch sanguinely expected society, with the aid of political economy, to put an end to pauperism and to bring the nation to a new level of opulence and refinement. An exponent of political economy, he was also an advocate of political science. He was a student of Jeremy Bentham as well as a disciple of David Ricardo. Guided by Bentham's principles, McCulloch believed that he could devise "a scheme of public administration calculated to insure the

147

continued advance of society in the career of improvement." The proper scheme of administration that stimulated invention and industry, he thought, was a more important factor in creating national wealth than either climate or fertile soil.[62]

Although he was a student of Bentham's principles of pauper management, McCulloch warned his readers against confusing political economy with the science of politics. The economic laws of production and distribution, he averred, were the same in every country, at every stage of social development and under every form of government.[63] He also warned against confusing political economy with statistics. It was the duty of the statistician, he thought, to describe the economic condition of a country at a particular time; it was the duty of the economist, however, to discover the causes that brought the country to that condition. In McCulloch's thinking, the political economist stood in relation to the statistician as did the physical astronomer in relation to the mere observer. These and similar views of what made political economy a science led McCulloch to regard lightly such factual information as the evidence collected in 1824 by the Committee on Labourers' Wages.[64]

Convinced that political economy was a reliable body of scientific principles, McCulloch took for himself the role of educating public officials in the best way of creating more wealth. He even assumed the heavy burden of instructing the working classes in the causes of poverty. He wished to teach them Malthus's doctrine that "the population of every country has a natural and constant tendency not only to rise to the level of the means of subsistence but to exceed them. . . ."[65] Although McCulloch saw no danger of population falling below the level of subsistence, he professed the greatest anxiety lest vice and misery should inevitably check the growth of population. In his application of the principle of population, he placed the major responsibility for social progress on the working classes. The great masses of working people must be taught to control their own numbers, for what the upper classes could do for them was "as dust of the balance compared with what they can do for themselves."[66]

In addition to the principle of population, McCulloch wished to instruct the working classes in the laws of wages. He thought it should be understood by everyone that "the market rate of wages is exclusively dependent on the population which the capital of a country, or the means of employing labour bears to the number

148

of laborers." It seemed equally clear to him that wages could not be raised unless the ratio of capital to population was increased. Inasmuch as laborers could do little to increase capital, McCulloch thought they should learn to control their own numbers in order to raise wages.

While adhering to the principle of population, McCulloch repudiated Malthus's *Principles of Political Economy* as being "fundamentally erroneous" and "pregnant with the most pernicious consequences." He especially rejected Malthus's doctrine of a general glut or overload of the market, and he attributed unemployment to a redundant population and a decrease in capital. From this position he attacked the Poor Laws as a cause of decreasing capital, on the one hand, and of increasing the redundant population on the other. The Poor Law policy which he derived from his economic principles had two main features: (1) the elimination of every artificial stimulus to population; and (2) the education of the people in the Malthusian virtues of prudence and foresight.

McCulloch strongly preferred Ricardo's system of political economy to that of Malthus. He attributed to Ricardo the discovery of the laws regulating distribution. According to McCulloch, Ricardo had "carried his researches into every department of the science to correct errors. . .and to elucidate and establish many hitherto undiscovered and most important principles."[67] He avidly accepted Ricardo's doctrine that the worth of commodities, the exchangeable value, "depends exclusively on the quantities of labor necessarily required to produce them." Excluding rent as a cost of production, McCulloch held, as did Ricardo, that profits varied inversely to wages. In taking this position, he shared Ricardo's pessimistic view that as population increased, the price of food rose, and the rise in the price of food necessitated an increase in wages and a decrease in profits.

From Ricardo's principles McCulloch derived the major part of his economic policy, a policy which was hostile to the Poor Laws. In the main, he desired free trade, the retrenchment in government expenditures, and noninterference with private accumulation and expenditure of capital. His recommendations reinforced the policy that was gradually being adopted by the Tory Government; and this deflationary policy probably aggravated the problems of low wages and unemployment.[68]

That McCulloch was beginning to recognize the existence of unemployment resulting from the fluctuations in trade did not deter him from opposing the existing system of Poor Laws. He continued to be a most severe critic of the humanitarian legislation enacted by the Evangelical reformers during the ministries of William Pitt. While opposing the existing method of outdoor relief to the unemployed, he advocated the return to the harsh Poor Law of 1722 which had provided the contract system of pauper management.[69] It is proper to conclude that McCulloch, by his voluminous writings during the 1820's, greatly strengthened the Radical opposition to the Poor Laws. His conception of the new science of political economy encouraged some reformers to disregard the testimony of practical men in favor of general principles. His remedies for pauperism were the more rapid accumulation of capital and the postponement of marriage until one was assured of sufficient income to support his family. While willing to grant relief to certain types of people, McCulloch demanded the discontinuance of welfare to able-bodied persons fully employed and especially the discontinuance of family allowances. Although he had not fully developed his policy of Radical reform by 1824, he had established himself as the major exponent of political economy and a fierce foe of the Poor Laws.

NOTES

[1] W. R. Brock, *Lord Liverpool and Liberal Toryism* (Cambridge, Eng., The University Press, 1941), pp. 191-93.

[2] C. R. Fay, *Huskisson and His Age* (London, Longmans Green, 1950); pp. 81-84.

[3] F. M. L. Thompson, *English Landed Society in the Nineteenth Century* (London: Routledge and Kegan Paul, 1963), pp. 230-31.

[4] G. E. Fussell and M. Compton, "Agricultural Adjustments after the Napoleonic Wars," *Economic History*, Vol. III (February, 1939), 185-87.

[5] Robert Link, *English Theories of Fluctuations 1815-1848* (New York: Columbia University Press, 1959), pp. 185-87.

[6] *Report from the Select Committee on Poor-Rate Return*, Sess. 1821, Vol. 4, 269.

[7] *Abstract of Poor Law Returns*, Sess. 1830-31, Vol. 11, p. 2. These returns may be found in John Marshall, *Digest of all the Accounts of the United Kingdom* (London, 1833), p. 5.

[8] *Gentlemen's Magazine*, (1834) N.S.I., 564; N.S. II, 659. See also the *Dictionary of National Biography*.

[9] Eden, *State of the Poor*, (London, 1797), I, 576-78. Page's account may be found in the one-volume edition by A. G. L. Rogers, pp. 121-24.

[10] Page, *Principles of the English Poor Laws* (Bath, 1822), P. VI. Page says: "the result of his experience in 1795 was communicated to his friend, Sir Frederick Eden, and he inserted it verbatim in his valuable history of the poor, p. 576 to 587 of the first volume."

150

[11] Page, *Principles of the English Poor Laws*, p. 17.
[12] *Poor Law Report*, 1834. Appendix B., Pt. IV, A. No. 39, p. 239. Page denied that relief was granted to able-bodied labourers privately employed. He admitted, however, that allowances were given to families with children to prevent the separation of children from their parents.
[13] Page, *Principles of the English Poor Laws*, p. 98.
[14] *Dictionary of National Biography.*
[15] Slaney, *Some Facts Showing the Vast Berthen of the Poor Rates. . .* (London, 1817), p. 1.
[16] *Ibid.*, p. 39.
[17] Slaney, *An Essay on the Employment of the Poor* (London, 1819), p. 16.
[18] *Ibid.*, p. 46.
[19] William Smart, *Economic Annals of the Nineteenth Century* (London, 1917) II, 181.
[20] Copleston, *On the Pernicious Effect of A Variable Standard of Value. . .* (London, 1819), p. 25.
[21] *Ibid.*, p. 34.
[22] Norman Gash, *Mr. Secretary Peel* (Cambridge, Mass., Harvard University Press, 1961), p. 469.
[23] Davis, *Hints to Philanthropists* (Bath, 1821), p. 3.
[24] *Parliamentary Debates*, N.S., V, 574.
[25] *Ibid.*, p. 595.
[26] *Ibid.*, VIII, 367.
[27] Brock, *Lord Liverpool*, p. 49.
[28] T. P. Courtenay, *A Treatise on the Poor Laws* (London, 1818), pp. 7-8, 108.
[29] *Parliamentary Papers*, Sess. 1821, Vol. 4, 275.
[30] *Report of S.C. on Poor-Rate Returns*, Sess. 1822, Vol. 5, 522.
[31] *Ibid.*, Sess. 1824, Vol. 6, 373.
[32] *Ibid.*, 377.
[33] *Ibid.*, Sess. 1824, Vol. 6, 382-84.
[34] *Ibid.*, Sess. 1825, Vol. 4, 42-46.
[35] *Parliamentary Debates*, N.S., X, 1413.
[36] Smart, *Economic Annals*, II, 249. *Journals of the House of Commons*, Vol. 79.
[37] *Report of the S.C. on Paying the Wages of Labour Out of the Poor Rates*, Sess. 1824, Vol. 6, 401.
[38] *Abstract of Returns Made to the Select Committee. . .* [on] *Paying Wages of Labour out of Poor Rates*, Sess. 1825, Vol. 19, 363.
[39] John H. Clapham, *An Economic History of Modern Britain* (Cambridge, Eng., the University Press, 1926). I, p. 123. Professor Clapham has misinterpreted the first question; he says "relief was given only in cases of disablement or other exceptional need or that it was only given very rarely." The officials, I think, understood wages to mean the actual payment to their laborers. They were not thinking, as Professor Clapham seems to be, of the abstract concept of the proportion of economic income going to the laborers.
[40] Mark Blaug, "The Myth of the Old Poor Law and the Making of the New," *Journal of Economic History*, XXIII (June, 1963), 159. Professor Blaug's suggestive article repeats Clapham's misunderstanding of the Returns of 1824. Although I agree with some of his conclusions, the article is marred by serious errors of fact. The questionnaire of 1824 was not sent to the Parishes, as he says (p. 159). He further confuses the Allowance System with the Speenhamland policy. His assumption that the farmers were more prosperous in years of bad harvests is surely false. (p. 155). The Committee of 1824 cer-

tainly did not confuse the roundsmen system with the labor rate, as Blaug says they did (p. 160).

For the conditions of agriculture during the 1820's, see: Fussell and Compton, *Economic History*, III (February, 1939), 190-204.

[41] *Parliamentary Papers*, Sess. 1824, Vol. 6, 411-15.

[42] *The Returns of 1824* and the *Evidence* collected by the Committee on Labourers' Wages constitute the best sources of information relating to the administration of the Poor Laws. Although these sources have to be used with caution, they are worthy of further study. The data on wages especially should be critically reviewed.

[43] *Parliamentary Papers*, Sess. 1824, Vol. 6, 416.

[44] *Ibid.*, 419.

[45] *Ibid.*, 436.

[46] *Ibid.*, 452.

[47] *Ibid.*, 457.

[48] *Ibid.*, 451.

[49] *Ibid.*, 452.

[50] *Ibid.*, 412-15.

[51] *Ibid.*, 457-65.

[52] *Ibid.*, 405.

[53] *Ibid.*, 406.

[54] *Ibid.*, 407.

[55] *Ibid.*, 408.

[56] *Political Economy Club* (London, 1821), VI, 358-60.

[57] R. K. Webb, *Harriet Martineau* (New York: Columbia University Press, 1960), p. 105.

[58] Frank W. Fetter, "Economic Controversy in the British Reviews," *Economica*, (November, 1965), pp. 424-37.

[59] D. P. O'Brien, J. R. McCulloch: *A Study in Classical Economics* (New York, 1970), p. 19. Between 1818 and 1837 McCulloch wrote a total of seventy-eight articles for the *Edinburgh Review*, and seventy of these were contributed before the passing of the new Poor Law in August, 1834. For Professor Frank Fetter's identification of the *Edinburgh* articles, see *Journal of Political Economy*, LXI (June, 1953), 249-53.

[60] McCulloch, *A Discourse on. . .Political Economy. . .* (Edinburgh, 1824), p. i.

[61] *Ibid.*, p. 9.

[62] *Ibid.*, p. 19.

[63] *Ibid.*, p. 74.

[64] *Ibid.*, p. 75.

[65] *Ibid.*, p. 57. O'Brien, *J. R. McCulloch*, p. 316, thinks that McCulloch had abandoned Malthus's principle of population by 1828; but it is clear from the 1830 edition of *Principles* that he was still Malthusian in his chapter on "Population." As late as 1830, McCulloch still held the doctrine that "poverty was the spur of civilization" (pp. 224-25), and he continued to oppose foundling hospitals (p. 233). O'Brien further concludes that McCulloch's change in attitude came shortly after Nassau Senior's attack on Malthus. It is true that Senior's explanation of the concept of "tendency" permitted some modification of Malthus's doctrine by recognizing countervailing influences. But Senior continued to believe, at least to the time of his own *Principles* of 1836, that the population principle was a scientific discovery comparable to Newton's. At the time of the correspondence with Malthus, Senior was proud to obtain a response from the great man who had already achieved national renown. It is clear that Senior wrote his Malthusianism into the *Poor Law*

Report of 1834. Mistakes concerning Senior, Malthus, and McCulloch result from O'Brien's misinformation about the different contexts of thought, policy, and conditions.

[66] McCulloch, *A Discourse on. . .Political Economy* (1824), p. 61.

[67] *Ibid.*, p. 65.

[68] O'Brien, *J. R. McCulloch*, pp. 319-20, has fully documented McCulloch's opposition to the Poor Laws prior to 1826 and has successfully refuted Mark Blaug's statement: "McCulloch had never adopted the Malthusian attitude to public relief." (*Ricardian Economics*, p. 200). McCulloch's argument that the old Poor Law had checked the growth of population was Malthus's defense of the principle of population when he discovered from the censuses that England's population was not growing as fast as the population of Scotland and Ireland, where there were no Poor Laws. He used this argument before the Committee on Emigration to support government subsidies for emigration provided the vacated cottages were torn down.

[69] *Ibid.*, pp. 324-31. O'Brien has also documented McCulloch's changing attitude toward the Poor Law after 1826. McCulloch was not in favor of the humane system of welfare, as O'Brien contends, but favored the harsh law of 1722 which provided for workhouses under private management. McCulloch, moreover, advocated the granting of power to the landlords, enabling them to tear down cottages in order to check the growth of population. O'Brien has surely exaggerated the importance of McCulloch's changing opinions, for his views were written into the *Poor Law Report* of 1834 (as I shall indicate in Chapter X). That McCulloch later opposed the New Poor Law (as Blaug says on p. 201), because of its administrative centralism and bureaucratic interference, should not lead one to conclude that he favored the law that existed in 1830. Other economists objected to the new Poor Law for the same reasons, but none fully supported the Old Law.

VII

THE GROWTH OF RADICAL OPPOSITION
Part II. Urban Unemployment

THE extensive investigation into the conditions of rural wages and unemployment did not produce legislative fruit. The Poor Law reformers were primarily dependent upon the increase in expenditures to justify the enactment of a new law. Since the principal proponents of reform were members of the Select Committee on Poor-Rate Returns, they were well aware of the continued decline of expenditures since the postwar depression years of 1817 and 1818. Moreover, the continued depressed state of agriculture, which had caused so much distress among farmers and laborers alike, had improved during 1823 and 1824 so that the investigations of the Committee on Labourers' Wages in 1824 had brought unexpected reports of increased employment in many rural districts.

Even though the farmers enjoyed a good harvest in 1824, economic conditions in a majority of counties worsened during the year. When the Committee on Poor-Rate Returns reported in May, 1825, it appeared that the downward trend in Poor Law expenses had come to an end.[1] Twenty-three counties in England and eleven in Wales reported a slight increase, the total increase for England being 1 per cent. The per capita expenses of Sussex were highest and those of Lancashire were lowest.

In addition to the annual returns, the Committee compiled in 1825 a comparative study of per capita relief expenditures for the years 1813 and 1825. Using the population figures for the censuses of 1811 and 1821, the Committee found that whereas per capita expenses for England and Wales in 1813 had been 13s., the per capita expenses in 1825 had fallen to 9s. Inasmuch as population was growing in both census decades, the actual expenses were not as great as the Committee had reported. Certain of the southern agricultural counties, which had gained notoriety for excessive payments during the Napoleonic Wars, had reduced their payments in 1825 below the national average. Berkshire, for example, reduced its per capita expenses from 26s. in 1813 to 14s. in 1825; Bucks reduced its expenses for the same years from 22s. to 17s.; and Wiltshire reduced its expenses from 23s. to 14s. On the other hand, during the same period the exemplary counties of the north, Cumberland, Durham, Northumberland, and Westmoreland had a relatively slight variation in their expenses. The total per capita expenses of the four exemplary counties fell from 33s. in 1813 to 29s. in 1825.[2]

The decline in relief expenditures can best be explained in terms of the general prosperity which the nation enjoyed from 1819 to 1825.[3] Although the harvest of 1825 was good, the financial panic which struck London in May of that year brought a sudden halt to commercial expansion and greatly slowed down the wheels of industry. The panic caused the failure of six London banks and seventy county banks. With the closing of the banks, an unprecedented number of businesses went into bankruptcy.[4]

Although the financial panic was over by the end of the year, the manufacturing industries continued to stagnate during the following year. The cotton industry of Lancashire, in particular, was badly depressed. In Manchester and other places the weavers and spinners, who were employed, expressed their discontent by breaking power looms and spinning frames.

The unemployed textile workers had to turn to the parish for relief. The annual Poor-Rate Returns for the year ending March 25, 1827, clearly indicated the impact of the depression on the cotton industry. The area of the greatest distress was Manchester, where unemployment was both cyclical and technological. Although factory workers were thrown out of work during the depression, the handloom weavers suffered the greatest hardship and were driven to despair by the calamity. As a consequence of these conditions, the relief expenses of Lancashire were increased by 47 per cent over the previous year. Other industrial counties had a much greater increase than did the southern counties which were predominantly agricultural. The relief expenditures for Cheshire increased by 24 per cent; in Leicestershire by 20 per cent; in Nottinghamshire by 19 per cent; and in Middlesex by 10 per cent.[5] A comparative study of the three Ridings of Yorkshire further indicate that the depression of 1826 affected manufacturing more severely than agriculture. While the increase in relief expenses of the North Riding was 6 per cent and in the East Riding 9 per cent, the increase in the West Riding, the home of the woolen industry, was 31 per cent.

Even though the Tory Government had investigated the depression of 1826 and the amount of distress which it had caused, they were unwilling to adopt measures to foster recovery, other than a regulation of the currency. Huskisson and Robinson, who blamed the country bankers for encouraging excessive credit, restricted their issue of one and two pound bank notes.

The Emigration Committee, however, interrupted its proceedings long enough to investigate the extent and character of unemployment. The Select Committee on Emigration had been appointed early in 1826 "to inquire into the expediency of encouraging migration from the United Kingdom." Thinking of unemployment as being the result of a redundant population, the Committee, in its report of May 26, 1826, recommended the subsidizing of emigration as a means of reducing the poor rates.[6] The increase of distress, however, led the Committee to investigate the causes of unemployment in the manufacturing towns.

The Emigration Committee's chief source of information on urban unemployment was a voluntary charitable agency, the London Committee for the Relief of Manufacturing Districts. As on previous occasions, wealthy and benevolent men of London had organized an agency to relieve those districts that were threatened with famine. In some urban slums, such as Bethnal Green, the laborers had to pay the poor rates to relieve the indigent. In times of unemployment such parishes could not possibly pay the costs of relief, for where needs were greatest the ability to pay was least. Recognizing the dire predicament of the slums where the poor were separated from the rich, the London philanthropists organized in 1826 the London Relief Committee. The chairman of the London Relief Committee, who was also the Bishop of Chester, and William Henry Hyett, its secretary, appeared before the Committee on Emigration, and presented vivid accounts of distress in the factory towns. During the summer of 1826 the Bishop of Chester made two visitations of the distressed areas and found that the depression extended over much of Cheshire and Lancashire and had spread into parts of the West Riding of Yorkshire and into the southern parts of Cumberland and Westmoreland. Nearly all the manufacturing districts were included in the areas of his visitations.[7]

The Bishop of Chester was well aware of the wide fluctuations in business activity throughout his diocese. He thought the period of prosperity had come to an end in 1824 when he first came as bishop to the diocese. Upon making his first visitation the next year, he found that economic conditions were worsening.[8] The unemployment, however, was more than cyclical; it was technological as well. The handloom weavers, who were the first to lose their jobs, suffered the greatest hardship. In Bolton alone there were eight thousand handloom weavers, the greater part of whom lacked employment. The handloom weavers living in the villages were worse off than those in the towns, for the weavers in the towns might eventually be absorbed into the powerloom industry. Since the Bishop of Chester could foresee no future employment for the village weavers, he recommended that the government subsidize their removal to the colonies.

William Henry Hyett, the secretary of the London Relief Committee, corroborated the testimony of the Bishop of Chester. The handloom weavers, he thought, could never hope to compete with the powerlooms. As the principal administrator of relief, Hyett was in close touch with the local relief committees in the factory towns. Under his direction a census was taken of the unemployed. In the Hundred of Blackburn, with a population of one hundred and fifty thousand, he estimated that during 1826 some ninety thousand persons had been unemployed.[9] In other districts of the cotton industry he reported similar statistics of unemployment. Largely as a result of his testimony and that of the Bishop of Chester, the Committee on Emigration recommended that the Government grant fifty thousand pounds to enable the handloom weavers to emigrate from the factory towns to Nova Scotia. At the same time, the Committee on Emigration recognized that Irish immigrants would soon fill the houses left by the English emigrants unless some provision were made for the relief of Ireland.[10]

This was not the first time a Tory Government had attempted to solve the problem of unemployment by adopting the expedient of emigration. Inasmuch as Ireland lacked a system of Poor Laws, Lord Liverpool's Government had proposed emigration as a possible remedy for pauperism. When Parliament investigated conditions in Ireland in 1823, Robert Wilmot Horton, the Under-Secretary of State for War and the Colonies, recommended that emigration be tried on an experimental basis. Although Parliament placed the need for retrenchment above almost every other consideration, it appropriated money to subsidize emigration as an experiment in combating poverty.[11] In 1823, 658 persons were sent from Ireland to Upper Canada at a cost of 12,593 pounds. A second experiment was conducted in 1825 when 2,024 persons were shipped from Ireland to Canada at a cost of 43,145 pounds. The primary purpose of these experiments was to demonstrate the practicality of reducing a redundant population.

With the hope of increasing subsidies for emigration, Wilmot Horton obtained in 1826 the appointment of a Select Committee on Emigration. The Committee, over which Wilmot Horton presided, included among its members the Poor Law reformers Lord John Russell, Franklin Lewis, Spring Rice, and Sir Henry Parnell. After sitting for twenty-one days and taking testimony from a score of witnesses, the Committee reported on May 26, 1826, recommending emigration as the proper remedy for the disease of pauperism.

The Committee on Emigration called witnesses who testified of unemployment in rural as well as urban areas and explained it in terms of Malthus's doctrine of redundant population. One of the most prominent of these was Edward J. Curteis, M.P., who had been a magistrate in Sussex for nearly forty years. There was in his district, he said, "a great superfluity of population, that is, of labourers who at the moment are out of employ." Under these conditions it was necessary to supplement wages by granting allowances to families of three or more children and in some areas to families of two or more. However, there was no redundant population during the harvesting of hops, "at which season vast multitudes flock down from London."[12] Although there was ample employment for both men and women during harvest, the influx of Irish laborers, according to Curteis, shortened the harvest and reduced the wages of permanent residents. To remedy the conditions of unemployment, low wages, and increasing poor rates, some parishes in Sussex had raised funds to aid the emigration of the unemployed. The Sussex scheme, however, was unsuccessful because the emigrants preferred to go to the United States rather than Canada; and of those being assisted, one-fourth had already returned home.

A similar scheme of emigration had been undertaken in a hops-growing region of Kent. Thomas Law Hodges, a magistrate residing at Hemsted, informed the Committee on Emigration that he had assisted the surplus laborers to go from his area to New York. A convinced disciple of Malthus, Hodges was of the opinion that once the paupers had been helped to emigrate, their cottages should be torn down to prevent others from filling the vacuum left by the emigrants. At the time of his testimony, he was waiting for the paupers to emigrate so he could "take down twenty-six to thirty cottages. . ., for if we leave the buildings standing, young people seventeen and eighteen years of age and even still younger would marry immediately and thus the evil would continue."[13]

Emigration was also recommended as the proper remedy for crime among the teen-age boys of London. Robert Joseph Chambers, who had been a police magistrate at Southwark for eighteen years, reported to the Committee on Emigration that crime among the teen-agers had been increasing during the period of his magistracy. Since the Apprentice Act of 1815 (56 Geo. III. c. 139) prevented the magistrate from sending apprentices more than forty miles away from the place of their residence, the Metropolis had become overcrowded with such boys. Under these conditions, Chambers thought the proper solution was to subsidize the emigration of London's teen-age boys to the colonies.[14]

It was clear to the Committee on Emigration that it would be futile to aid the emigration of English paupers so long as the Irish laborers were left free to migrate to England. The Bishop of Limerick, who testified about the problems of poverty in Ireland, was a doctrinaire Malthusian. A Bishop who opposed charity, he objected especially to the charitable activities of the London Relief Committee. Although he conceded that charity was useful in arresting famine, he thought "money sent in artificially to Ireland, as contradistinction to the natural order of things. . ., would in a few years leave the peasantry in a worse state than that in which it found them." He wished to see the peasants rely on their own exertions rather than on the casual bounties of charity. Unemployment in Ireland, however, was so great that an immediate remedy was needed. The Bishop thought emigration was the proper remedy for Ireland's unemployed.[15]

While the Bishop of Limerick lamented the plight of the Irish peasants, Sir John Sebright, M.P., on the other hand, testified of the importance of Irish laborers to English agriculture. Sebright was quite willing to have the government transport the English laborers to the colonies, or even to New York, provided Irish laborers were available for the harvests. As the sole owner of an entire parish in Hertfordshire, he was the autocrat of his domain. "I could have perfect control of the population," he declared to the Committee, "and to prevent the space from being filled up again I would, without the slightest hesitation, at once engage to pay a pretty considerable sum per family, per head, for sending those persons out of the country."[16] He was quite ready to pay as much as fifteen pounds a head to rid his parish of "bad characters" and the heads of large families. By apprenticing children and by preventing strangers from obtaining a legal settlement, he thought he could control the population as carefully as he selected his livestock. This perfect control, however, presupposed the continued flow of migrant laborers from Ireland: "The advantage we receive from Irish labourers is very great in harvest, and I am not aware any inconveniences whatever result from them." Sir John had only one slight misgiving about their conduct: "There is one thing they do which may perhaps be deemed prudent; they beg their way home, and get what they can from parish officers on the road, when perhaps they have five or ten pounds in their pockets..."[17]

The evidence given to the Committee on Emigration by Sir John Sebright and the Bishop of Limerick was insufficient to provide a remedy for the pauperism of Ireland. The Committee, and especially Wilmot Horton, the chairman, gave little attention to the evidence, for they had already derived their remedy for pauperism from Malthus's *Essay on the Principle of Population*. On May 26, 1826, prior to investigating urban unemployment, the Committee gave its first report in the House of Commons. Its major conclusion was: "That there are extensive districts in Ireland, and districts in England and Scotland where the population is at the present moment redundant; in other words, where there exists a very considerable proportion of able-bodied and active laborers beyond that number to which any demand for labour can afford employment." As a consequence of a redundant supply of labour, wages had been reduced to a minimum, "which is utterly insufficient to supply that population with those means of sub-

160

sistence and support which are necessary to secure a healthy and satisfactory condition of the community."[18]

The Committee on Emigration further reported "that in England this redundant population has been in part supported by a parochial rate. . ., which threatens in its extreme tendency to absorb the whole rental of the country; and that in Ireland where no such rate exists by law, and where the redundancy is faced in a still greater degree the population is dependent on charity, plunder, and spoliation." It appeared to the Committee that the redundant population tended "to repress the industry and sometimes to endanger the peace of the mother country."

Although most members of the Committee on Emigration acknowledged the prevalence of unemployment — or redundant population, as it was called in Malthusian terms — few members shared Wilmot Horton's sanguine faith in emigration as the proper remedy for the disease. The Benthamite Radicals, the inveterate foes of the Poor Laws, refused to appropriate large sums of money to subsidize emigration. As followers of Ricardo, the Radicals preferred to curtail government expenditures so that more capital would remain in the hands of individuals who could invest it more wisely than the government. Even though Wilmot Horton had derived his belief in emigration from the *Essay on the Principle of Population*, Malthus himself regarded it as a palliative rather than as a remedy for the disease of pauperism.

When Malthus published the sixth edition of the *Essay on the Principle of Population* early in 1826, he restated his previously proposed remedies for pauperism. He had long insisted that all children born to future marriages, a year from the date his reform became law, should be denied public relief.[19] Emigration was, indeed, a palliative compared with so drastic a measure as denying relief to all children born to future marriages. His aim was clearly to abolish to Poor Laws insofar as they affected able-bodied persons. Although he cared little about a policy of emigration for England, he was a forthright advocate of such a policy for Ireland.

On May 5, 1927, Malthus appeared before the Committee on Emigration to make it clear why he rejected a policy of emigration for England and supported it for Ireland. He thought pauperism and unemployment in England could be eliminated by reforming the Poor Laws. He urged the Committee to deny relief to all children born two years after the date on which his reform was adopted.[20] In addition to this, he would have the parishes stop paying the rent of paupers because this mode of relief encouraged early marriages.[21] He approved of those landlords who pulled down cottages as soon as they became vacant, and he proposed further to restrict the supply by taxing the construction of new cottages.[22] Such were the reforms of the English Poor Laws which Malthus preferred.

What of the pauperism of Ireland where there were no Poor Laws? Malthus readily conceded that the evils of a redundant population in Ireland were greater than in England. The habits of the Irish, he thought, aggravated their condition, for they were "satisfied with the lowest degree of comfort, and to marry with little other prospect than to get potatoes for themselves and their children."[23] Although wages were low, they continued to fall; for over-population caused so much crime and destruction of property that new capital would not be introduced until peace and security were restored.[24] Economic conditions in Ireland had thus become so deplorable as to justify legislative interference.

Malthus, therefore, recommended emigration as the most expedient policy for Ireland. He urged Parliament to appropriate funds to finance the emigration of five hundred thousand persons from Ireland to the British colonies.[25] Such a policy, however, would be futile unless measures were adopted simultaneously to prevent the vacated cottages from being reoccupied. To restrict further the growth of population, Malthus proposed to enact laws prohibiting the subletting of land and houses, and that taxes on workers' cottages be assessed to the landlords.[26]

While accepting the expedient of emigration for Ireland, Malthus objected to several measures suggested by other reformers. He certainly rejected the introduction of the English Poor Laws into Ireland. He opposed the cultivation of wasteland as tending to aggravate the conditions of overpopulation. He objected to public works as a method of relieving the lower classes. "I think it relieves them for a short time," he said, "but leaves them afterwards in a condition worse than before."[27] He rejected all bounties to encourage capital investment, because "all those forced modes of employment" tended to stimulate the growth of population.

When the Committee on Emigration gave its *Third Report* on June 29, 1827, it relied heavily upon Malthus's testimony as a scientific endorsement of the policy of emigration. "The testimony which was uniformly given by practical witnesses. . .has been confirmed in the most absolute manner by that of Mr. Malthus, and your Committee cannot but express their satisfaction at finding that the experience of facts is thus strengthened throughout by general reasoning and scientific principles."[28] The Committee shared not only Malthus's scientific principles but also his anxiety lest English laborers should sink to the low level of living on potatoes. Moreover, if the Irish laborers continued to migrate to England, the Committee feared that the English workers would be compelled to live on potatoes instead of bread.

The Committee on Emigration not only wrote Malthus's testimony into their report, but they also endorsed his recommendations for Ireland. They proposed emigration for Ireland and urged that the houses vacated by the emigrants should be pulled down.[29] While the Committee regarded the removal of people and the demolition of houses as in keeping with natural law, they contended that other remedies for unemployment were undue state interference with the natural liberty of individuals. They confidently reported Malthus's opposition to public works and to the cultivation of wastelands as remedies for unemployment. "Your Committee cannot express too strong an opinion," Wilmot Horton declared, "against the idea of regulating by legislation the rate of wages under any conceivable modification."[30]

The problem of unemployment had grown more complex during the years when the Committee on Emigration were holding their hearings. Between the time of the first report on May 26, 1826, and the third report on June 29, 1827, the Committee had investigated the depressed conditions of the cotton industry in Lancashire. While recognizing that unemployment in the textile industry resulted from the changeover to powerlooms and from the periodic fluctuations in the volume of business activity, the Committee, apart from its policy of emigration, could suggest only a moral remedy for cyclical and technological unemployment. Assuming fluctuations to be inevitable, they admonished the workingmen to save a part of their income during the period of high wages so they might survive the hard times of low wages and unemployment. For the workers to conduct themselves otherwise was to commit the Malthusian sin of improvidence. The Committee took the occasion to condemn the Poor Laws for encouraging the laborer's improvidence: "The artisan has considered that he had a perfect right to expend his wages when they were high, without making a provision for the future, inasmuch as the parish was bound to support him whenever the alternation of distress might occur."

As a result of Malthus's influence, the Committee could not think clearly about the causes of pauperism except in terms of overpopulation. Accordingly, they defined redundancy "as a supply of able-bodied and active labourers with their families for whose labour there was no effective demand." The results of redundancy, they concluded, were "to repress industry. . ., creating mendicity, outrage, and diminution of occupation. . . ."[31]

The chief result of the extensive investigation of the Committee on Emigration was to increase the opposition to the Poor Law in several branches of the Government. Civil servants at the Home Office were becoming as formal and rigid in their opposition as were the members of the Board of Trade.[32] Administrative officials were applying the doctrine of natural liberty to the Poor Laws with the same rigor that they had applied it to the Navigation Laws. They treated both bodies of inherited law as antiquated accumulations which ran counter to scientific knowledge. The doctrinaire members of the Home Office, however, did not represent the whole Government any more completely than the Liberal Tories represented truly the Tory Party.

Following the death of George Canning, the traditional Tories, who returned to office in January, 1828, gave little attention to what they were apt to regard as the "mere speculations" of the political economists. Wilmot Horton, the chairman of the Committee on Emigration, who was a Whig member of the Liberal Tory Government, found himself without a place in the Duke of Wellington's Ministry. The new Tory Government was frankly unwilling to spend a million pounds or more to send its laborers from the British Isles to distant parts of the Empire.

The investigations of the Committee on Emigration focused public attention on the rapid increase of vagrancy and mendicity. The investigations indicated that these dual social problems were the products of urban as well as rural unemployment. The social evils long associated with vagrancy and mendicity were aggravated during the 1820's by annual migrations of Irish laborers seeking seasonal employment in England. Driven by the whip of famine, the Irish were willing to work for lower wages than the English laborers could survive on. The new Mendicity Society, motivated by the Benthamite spirit of repression and manipulation, assumed the duty of transporting the laborers through London to the harvest in the southern counties.

The Mendicity Society, acting upon Bentham's principle of less eligibility, attempted to discourage begging by offering employment more distasteful than that available to free labor. Under the guidance of its secretary, William Henry Bodkin, the Mendicity Society provided the less eligible work of stone breaking. Rather than deter the Irish by offering them jobs at stone breaking, the Society attracted more immigrants who considered such work suitable employment.[33]

Inasmuch as the Irish laborers lacked a legal residence in London, they were ineligible for poor relief; their assistance, therefore, came from charitable agencies such as the Mendicity Society. The law which classified them as vagrants required the magistrates to pass them to the nearest seaport, usually Bristol or Liverpool, and the seaport towns returned them to Ireland. From its beginning in 1818, the Mendicity Society had assisted annually from two thousand to four thousand persons. In the year 1826 the Society assisted 3,811 persons, and during the first five months of 1827 it assisted 4,287 persons, mainly Irish migrant laborers who had come to London in search of employment.[34] Since only a minority of the Irish immigrants registered with the Mendicity Society as beggars, the figures do not clearly indicate how many passed through London annually. It was clear, however, that the number of Irish vagrants was increasing at a rate that alarmed the London magistrates and the members of the Mendicity Society.[35]

The number of Roman Catholics who were baptized annually in London probably reflects the number of Irish laborers who had found employment and had taken up permanent residence. The number of baptisms grew from 2,646 in 1819 to 4,437 in 1826. From statistics of baptisms, Bodkin estimated that the number of Roman Catholics in London had increased from 71,442 in 1819 to 119,799 in 1826.[36]

Although the problems of vagrancy and mendicity concerned the Irish laborers primarily, the Scots and the residents of the Channel Isles also had the status of vagrants. The increase in vagrancy, as shown by the Mendicity Society, led to the appointment of a committee by the House of Commons to investigate the operation of the vagrancy laws pertaining to the Irish and Scots. Appointed early in 1828, the Committee on Vagrancy sat for five days interviewing witnesses who were connected with the transporting of migrant workers to English harvests. According to

Jerard E. Strickland, a London magistrate who had the duty of ordering passage for the vagrants from London to Liverpool, the migrant laborers left Ireland during the latter part of May after they had finished planting potatoes. They then went to various places in England to cultivate and harvest crops, and they finally returned to Ireland during October and November, in time to dig potatoes.

Some of the magistrates who passed the Irish as paupers resented doing so, for they knew the migrants were returning home with their summer wages. William Strattham, the town clerk of Liverpool, testified that the migrant laborers frequently sewed money into their clothes in order to be passed as paupers. Sometimes the laborers travelled in groups and paid the passage of one member so he could return safely with their earnings.

The greatest number of Irish vagrants passed through Liverpool, going to Lancashire and bordering counties. A smaller number of Scots, seeking summer employment, were also passed through Lancashire. Over a period of five years, from 1823 to 1827, several towns in Lancashire passed a total of 20,418 Irish vagrants and 1,631 Scottish vagrants.[38] The number of vagrants in Lancashire increased during the depression years 1826 and 1827 when a great number of weavers and spinners were unemployed. In 1826, for example, 7,050 Irishmen and 444 Scots were passed through the Lancashire towns, the total number of vagrants being double the annual average for the earlier years of the decade.

When the Committee on Vagrancy reported to the House of Commons on July 5, 1828, they expressed anxiety over the "increasing irruption of the pauper population of Ireland" at a time when there was unemployment in England. The Committee deplored the great expense in the compulsory removal of the Irish and Scots to their homeland. The members pointed out "the extreme irregularity which the present system operates on different counties." It was certainly true that the western counties had to pay the costs of passing migrant workers from eastern and southern counties which benefited from their labor. Buckinghamshire, for example, in 1828 conveyed 4,904 Irish and Scottish vagrants, and over the previous five years the county had a total of 14,698 paupers.[39] The financial burden fell heaviest on the port cities of Bristol and Liverpool. To correct the irregularities inherent in the Laws of Settlement and Removal required the enactment of legislation extending far beyond the repression of Irish and Scottish migrant laborers.

The English laborers were even more mobile than the Scots and the Irish in their search for seasonal employment. Large numbers of urban workers migrated to the countryside during the harvest to take advantage of high wages, thus reducing the income of permanent farm laborers. The mobility of labor, notwithstanding the Laws of Settlement and Removal, increased the burden of the poor rates in the predominantly agricultural counties. Under these circumstances, the Poor Law reformers, who wished to restrict the migration of the Irish and Scottish laborers, tried also to prevent the movement of English laborers from county to county.

The Sturges Bourne Act of 1819, which classified the Irish and Scots as vagrants in order to remove them, attempted also to restrict the movement of English laborers by requiring a contract of employment for one year rather than for forty days. Thus the natural law reformers of 1819 repealed, in effect, the Pittite legislation which had been designed to increase mobility by relaxing the Laws of Settlement. With the desire of protecting rural labor from the competition of migrants, the Poor Law reformers in 1825 again restricted the mobility of labor by preventing the working classes from obtaining a legal residence by renting a tenement, unless the tenement was a separate house which rented for ten pounds annually.[40]

The new Laws of Settlement failed to accomplish their purpose. Farmers, preferring to hire their hands by the day or by the job, were unwilling to grant a legal residence whether hiring was for forty days or for one year. Rather than increase the burden of the poor rates, which fell upon themselves as the occupiers of land, the farmers hired their permanent laborers for a period just short of a year and thus prevented them from obtaining a settlement. As for obtaining a settlement by renting a separate house worth ten pounds annually, the rise of urban slums with low rentals was evidence that many workers could neither obtain a separate house nor pay ten pounds rent. In the countryside the laborers' cottages rarely rented for as much as ten pounds. The new rigorous Laws of Settlement of 1819 and of 1825 failed both to restrict the movement of labor and to reduce the number of removals.

The growing concern over the increasing number of migrant laborers and over the increasing cost of administering the Poor Laws — the category of "Law, Removals, etc." — led to an important census of the number of persons removed from and received into the counties of England and Wales. Parliament obtained an accounting of the number of removals and receptions for the year ending March 25, 1828. The total number of removals from all the counties was 45,514 and the total received was 39,229.[41] The number of legal contests resulting from removals was 3,071. As one might expect, the greatest numbers of persons being removed, as well as the greatest numbers being received, were in the populous industrial counties of Middlesex and Lancashire. The West Riding of Yorkshire had more persons removed and received than did the other two Ridings taken together. From the fairly even balance between the number of removals and the number of receptions, it appears that much of the movement occurred among neighboring parishes within the counties.[42]

In the same year that the number of persons removed from and received by the parishes was being investigated, the House of Commons appointed a committee to investigate "the employment or relief of able-bodied persons from the poor rates." The Radical reformers were not primarily concerned with either unemployment or the operations of the Laws of Settlement; they were primarily interested in the increasing burden of the poor rates and the interference of the Poor Laws which prevented wages from rising to their natural level. The appointment of the Committee on the Able-Bodied Poor was in accord with the primary interest of the Radical reformers. Presided over by Robert A. Slaney, the Committee included among its members such proponents of Poor Law reform as Peel, Sturges Bourne, Russell, Althorp, Scarlett, and Courtenay.[43] That Slaney should preside over the Committee was ominous. His reputation as a Poor Law reformer had been established in 1817 when he published a pamphlet demanding the exclusion of all able-bodied persons from relief. He was determined to deny relief to the able-bodied persons whom he called "improvident, idle and vicious."[44]

Inasmuch as the Committee on Laborers' Wages had discovered in 1824 that the abuse of making up wages from the poor rates prevailed more widely in certain southern counties than in several of the northern counties, the Committee of 1828 amassed more information contrasting the bad practices of the South with the good practices of the North. The three southern counties selected for study were Wiltshire, Sussex, and Buckinghamshire; the three northern counties studied were Westmoreland, Shropshire, and Northumberland. In the southern counties twenty places, having a total population of 15,628 (census of 1821), were selected for investigation; in the northern counties the nineteen places selected had a population of 16,210 (census of 1821). The Poor Law officials of these selected parishes were required to answer the Committee's questions and to make returns for the year ending March 25, 1828.

The Committee on the Able-Bodied Poor wanted to know the total number of persons relieved during the year, the number of able-bodied men relieved, and the manner in which they were relieved. From the replies to the questionnaire, the Committee found in the three southern counties that 4,077 persons, or 26 per cent of the population, had received relief during the year; whereas in the three northern counties 1,517 persons, or 10 per cent of the population, had been relieved. In the South, 1,241 able-bodied men had received relief; whereas in the North, 216 able-bodied men had been relieved.[45]

The returns made to the Committee on the Able-Bodied Poor indicated that the modes of relief were much the same in both the northern and southern counties. All the counties provided relief for large families; all provided employment on the roads or some form of parish labor; and all paid cottage rent for some families.

Few of the parish officials who answered the questionnaire in 1828 understood relief in the form of family allowances to mean "making up wages from the poor rates." Several places in the South reported "making up wages from the poor rates," a mode of relief which probably meant either the system of roundsmen or the labor rate. In contrast to the practices in the South, none of the parishes in the North reported "making up wages from the poor rates."

The Committee on the Able-Bodied Poor investigated Sussex more thoroughly than any other county, for its per capita relief expenses were higher than elsewhere. The eight places in Sussex, with a population of 8,618, had 2,954 persons, or 34 per cent, on relief. Of the 796 able-bodied men receiving parish assistance, 265 men, or one-third, were granted relief by parish labor. There were some parishes in Sussex that deserved the notoriety which blackened the whole country. Salehurst, for example, with a population of 2,121, had 1,096 persons on relief at some time during the year; and of the 120 able-bodied men on relief, only 13 were relieved by parish work.

When Robert Slaney delivered on July 3, 1828, the "Report from the Select Committee Relating to the Employment or Relief of Able-Bodied Persons from the Poor-Rates," he blamed the Poor Laws for causing redundancy and low wages. Slaney, however, added another explanation of redundancy; "changes in manufacturing methods," he thought, had also caused an increase in redundancy. He departed further from his previously held Malthusian position by denying that the working-class family should be expected to exercise prudent control over its future. "The great fluctuations in the price of food from 1794 to 1821," he said, "render it difficult to calculate accurately the expense of maintaining a family."[46]

Even though Slaney had come to a better appreciation of the causes of poverty, he continued to cling to old remedies. His principle recommendation in the House of Commons was that no payment be made to an employed person for his relief or that of his family. He was fully confident that if the system of family allowances was abolished, wages would rise to their natural level.[47]

Slaney's Parliamentary inquiry into employment and relief of the able-bodied poor was closely associated with the Poor Law reform bill which he had introduced in the House of Commons on June 12, 1827. His bill was a proposal to abolish the payment of wages from the poor rates and to tax the cheap tenements occupied by the working classes. Slaney's bill made little progress during 1827 because it was in competition with Wilmot Horton's plan to subsidize emigration. In the next session of Parliament both Slaney and Wilmot Horton reintroduced separate bills; and the two rival measures were read on the same day, April 17, 1828. The two reformers opposed each other's remedy, even though they were agreed on the causes of the disease.

In debating the bill to prevent the payment of laborers' wages from the poor rates, Slaney greatly strengthened the Radical opposition to the Poor Laws. He reconstructed the 43rd of Elizabeth I by insisting that the original law had never intended to aid the children of employed persons.[48] He further charged that the system of family allowances was badly administered by the justices of the peace. A lawyer proud of his profession, Slaney deeply resented the faulty decisions of the justices who were men often ignorant of the law.

In 1828 Slaney was able to save his bill on laborers' wages from defeat only by referring it to the committee of which he was appointed chairman. With the Tory Government against him, there was little chance of his winning a majority for so drastic a measure of reform. As spokesman for the Government in the House of Commons, Sir Robert Peel did not object to investigating the abuse of the Poor Laws, but he made it clear that he could not accept Slaney's proposed remedy. Peel concluded from the depression of 1826 that unemployment should not be viewed solely as a by-product of surplus population. He acknowledged his perplexity over the increase of unemployment during the previous three years while productivity in both agriculture and manufacturing had been greater than ever before. If unemployment were to be attributed to the Poor Laws, as Slaney had insisted, how could one explain the unemployment in Ireland where there were no Poor Laws?[49] Rejecting Slaney's Malthusian argument, Peel attributed unemployment to the improvements made in machinery, but he was undecided as to "what remedy could be applied against human enterprise and ingenuity." In this state of uncertainty, Peel did not oppose Slaney's bill directly but delayed action by calling for the "fullest deliberation on the question."[50]

When Slaney introduced in 1829 his third bill on laborers' wages, he met even stronger Tory opposition than he had previously encountered. Sturges Bourne, who continued to be the Government's chosen spokesman on Poor Law reform, opposed Slaney's bill as impractical. While conceding that the payment of wages from the poor rates was bad in principle, he thought the system had been acted upon too long to be abolished overnight.[51] The position taken by Peel was much weaker than he had taken the year before; he now virtually abandoned the defense of the Poor Laws, making large concessions to Slaney's arguments.

Although his bill to prohibit the payment of wages from the poor rates was defeated, Slaney had won a major victory in the long war against the Poor Laws. He had greatly strengthened the Radical opponents of public relief by concentrating their attention on the abuse of paying wages to laborers in private employment. He amassed much legal information in his attempt to show that family allowances were contrary to the original Elizabethan Law. He increased the resentment toward the justices of the peace by charging them with ignorance and incompetence, even while praising them as men of good intentions. Thus his major arguments for the defeated bills on laborers' wages became the Radical case that continued to win assent.

The need for Poor Law reform in 1828 and 1829 was less urgent than it had been in the two preceding years of the depression,

171

when the increasing burden of the poor rates had provoked several investigations. Even during the years of depression the poor rates in the predominantly agricultural counties in the South continued to decline, for these were years of good harvests and stable prices for wheat. The industrial counties, especially Lancashire and Yorkshire, which had suffered most during the depression, enjoyed the return of prosperity in 1827 and good times continued through 1829.[52]

The Poor Law Returns for these years reflect the sharp difference between the industrial and agricultural counties. The Poor Law expenditures for the year ending March 25, 1828, showed a decrease of 2 per cent from the previous year for the whole of England and Wales, and the decline of the industrial counties was greater than that for the whole country. The decrease in relief expenses in Lancashire was 17 per cent; in Cheshire, 7 per cent; in Leicester, 6 per cent; in the West Riding of Yorkshire, 9 per cent.[53]

During 1829 the relief expenditures in the industrial counties continued to decline; Lancashire, Cheshire, Leicester, and the West Riding of Yorkshire had decreasing amounts of relief. The several Ridings of Yorkshire reflect the differences between agriculture and industry; the relief expenses in the West Riding declined 3 per cent in 1829, while they were increasing by 3 per cent in the East Riding and by 4 per cent in the North Riding. Despite the downward trend in the manufacturing counties, the total cost of relief for England and Wales during the year ending March 25, 1829, slightly increased. The increase in relief expenses in the agricultural counties came as a result of the bad harvest of 1828. In Berkshire relief expenses increased 10 per cent; in Suffolk, 12 per cent; and in Wiltshire, 10 per cent.[54]

In 1829 another bad harvest occurred, and this calamity coincided with a slackening of business activity. For the first time in five years the relief expenditures of agricultural and industrial counties moved in the same direction. For the year ending March 25, 1830, the total expenditures for England and Wales increased 8 per cent.

The business recession which had come quickly in 1829 was followed the next year by a quick recovery, but agriculture suffered still another bad harvest.[55] Again, the Poor Law expenditures reflected the differences between industry and agriculture. The total expenses for the year ending March 25, 1831, declined; but while the expenses of the industrial counties were falling,

172

agricultural counties were rising. The expenses for the East and North Ridings of Yorkshire increased slightly, while those for the West Riding fell off slightly. Thus in 1830, as throughout the decade of the 1820's, the fluctuations in commerce and manufacturing affected the volume of Poor Law expenditures. It was unfortunate for all who suffered from these fluctuations that the political economists lacked a theory of the business cycle and explained unemployment in Malthusian terms of overpopulation.

The coincidence of the business recession in 1829 with another bad harvest prompted still another investigation of the increasing costs of poor relief. The accounting made of the five-year period ending March 25, 1829, showed an increase in total expenditures for England and Wales. The accounting also revealed that relief expenditures fluctuated from year to year, and the trends varied from county to county, depending upon business conditions and the state of the harvests.

The accounting of 1830 indicated continued improvement in the administration of the Poor Laws. During the first five years of the decade, the Committee on the Poor-Rate Returns made several attempts to improve the parochial system of bookkeeping. That improvement had been made in the system of bookkeeping was acknowledged by the report of 1830. Over the period of five years there had been relatively few defective returns: "no more than 313 such instances occurred in 73,000 returns."[56] The universality of acceptable returns at the Home Office indicated that the more than fifteen thousand Poor Law authorities were cognizant of their legal obligations in administering the Poor Laws.

Further improvements were made in administration by the election of select vestries and the appointment of assistant overseers. Being a permanent paid official, the assistant overseer was more efficient than the annually elected overseer who usually accepted unwillingly the burdensome unpaid office. Many urban parishes had appointed assistant overseers prior to the passage of the Sturges Bourne Act in 1819. According to the Poor Law Returns of 1821, there were 2,006 select vestries and 2,257 assistant overseers. The number of assistant overseers increased annually to 1831, when there were 3,249 such officials. The number of select vestries also increased annually to 1829, when there were 2,736 such parishes; but during the next two years the number of select vestries decreased to 2,535.[57] The northern manufacturing counties took the lead in appointing assistant overseers and in electing select vestries. Lancashire had 202 select vestries and 103 assistant overseers; the West Riding of Yorkshire had 161 select vestries and 160 assistant overseers. The southern agricultural counties, on the other hand, made relatively little use of the Sturges Bourne Act. Bedfordshire, for example, had only eighteen select vestries and thirty-one assistant overseers, and in Buckinghamshire there were only twenty-one select vestries and forty-five assistant overseers.[58]

With the wisdom of hindsight no one would wish to contend that the administrative changes under the Sturges Bourne Act could provide an adequate remedy for unemployment. These changes, however, were symptomatic of the growing belief among Radical reformers that maladministration was the cause of pauperism. The increase of urban unemployment and the rising costs of poor relief renewed the controversy over the Poor Laws. The Reports of the Emigration Committee, recommending the subsidizing of emigration as a remedy for poverty, excited still another plethora of pamphlets defending and attacking the Poor Laws.

The new campaign evoked by the Emigration Committee was significant in that it brought forth a new Evangelical defender of the Poor Laws. Michael Thomas Sadler instilled new courage and determination in those Tories who were the staunch defenders of traditional institutions.

The son of a small landowner, Sadler was born in 1780 at Snelston, in Derbyshire. He was educated in a private school at Doveridge, where he acquired a knowledge of classical language and literature. In keeping with his devout Methodist upbringing, he spent his leisure reading the Bible and other religious literature. At the age of twenty he went to Leeds to join his brother in the business of importing Irish linens.[59] But lacking an aptitude for business, he spent much of his time at Leeds in charitable and religious pursuits. He became a member of the Stranger's Friend Society, and in company with other Evangelicals he visited in the homes of the sick and the poor. As treasurer of the Workhouse Board, Sadler acquired a knowledge of the working classes that engendered a warm sympathy for those who had to bear the burdens of poverty.

In defense of the Poor Laws and in opposition to the Emigration Committee, Sadler projected the major literary enterprise of his life. Because he believed the Reports of the Emigration Committee had been inspired by Malthus, Sadler undertook the enor-

174

mous task of refuting the *Essay on Population*. In this undertaking he was the first among several provincial Evangelicals to reassert the benevolent attitudes of the Society for Bettering the Condition of the Poor and similar humanitarian agencies that had flourished during the first decade of the century. Sadler's Evangelical piety led him to reassert the Biblical conception of Providence. Taking seriously the Biblical injunction to "be fruitful and multiply", he regarded Malthus's principle of population to be brutally harsh as well as sacrilegious.

In 1828 Sadler published a preliminary work on population which he entitled *Ireland: Its Evils and Their Remedies. . . .* In this introductory essay, he attacked the policy of emigration as the improper remedy for the poverty of Ireland. In this essay he also defined his law of population, which was to become the subject of a much larger book. In direct opposition to Malthus's principle, Sadler asserted: "The fecundity of human beings is. . .in the inverse ratio to the condensation of their numbers. . . ."[60]

In 1830 Sadler published his major work, *The Law of Population. . . .In Disproof of the Superfecundity of Human Beings and Developing the Real Principle of Their Increase*. Taking a position opposite Malthus, Sadler denied that either England or Ireland was over populated. His Christian faith led him to accept as his motto the Biblical injunction: "Trust in the Lord and do good; and ye shall dwell in the land and verily thus shalt be fed."[61] Sadler's faith in Providence also led him to deny the Malthusian doctrine that population was held down by the natural checks of disease, famine, and vice. On the contrary, Sadler held that human happiness and prosperity were positive checks against overpopulation. Instead of agreeing with Malthus that the means of subsistence checks population, Sadler insisted that the people produced and controlled the means of subsistence.[62]

Sadler strongly objected to the Malthusian doctrine of moral restraint as a necessary preventive check to population. The masses of people, the laboring poor, he thought, had the pleasures of family life as their chief source of happiness; therefore, to ask the poor man to postpone marriage was to deprive him of major happiness.[63]

Sadler used his principle of population in defense of the Poor Laws. He defended the system of family allowances and outdoor relief as the poor man's right.[64] He not only supported the existing Poor Laws but he also wished to expand their benefits by providing every poor man with a cottage and a plot of land for a garden.[65]

Sadler extended his hostility beyond Malthus to include political economists of various shades of opinion. He charged them with encouraging infanticide by their opposition to foundling hospitals. He also accused them of seeking the repeal of the Corn Laws in order to lower wages.[66] The longer he contemplated the doctrines of political economy the more convinced he became that they were unchristian. His own Christian humanitarianism led him to take a charitable attitude toward the lower classes. He firmly believed that the upper classes had the duty to look after the poor, to supply their needs, and to guard them from oppression. He derived his humanitarianism, in part, from a vision of an agrarian society that belonged to the past; the more the new industrial society of Leeds displaced the old England of his youth, the more tenaciously he clung to it.

Sadler's vociferous attack on the political economists provoked a spate of virulent replies. Malthus, however, did not feel it necessary to defend his principle of population, for he had long before answered his Evangelical critics and had persuaded many of the most influential leaders in London to accept his views. The Liberal Tories, especially those who had proposed a policy of emigration, were embarassed by what they regarded as Sadler's unscientific principles of population. Moreover, the Tories under Canning's leadership, who favored religious toleration for Ireland, keenly resented Sadler's opposition to Catholic Emancipation.

Identifying himself with the Protestant wing of the Tory party, Sadler was a new voice, vehement and eloquent, proclaiming traditional Toryism as the essence of English patriotism. His vigorous defense of the old Toryism brought him to the attention of the Duke of Newcastle, who provided him a seat in Parliament representing the borough of Newark. Sadler took his seat on February 19, 1829, and made his maiden speech on March 17, strongly denouncing the liberal Tory policy of Catholic Emancipation. His defense of the English constitution as Protestant brought him national recognition, and he was no less vehement in his opposition to the reform of Parliament.[67]

With the same fervor that he opposed Catholic Emancipation and the Reform Bill, Sadler defended the pauper's right to relief and the factory children's need for protection. In a very short time he had raised himself up as the main opponent to all types of liberal reform, political, economic, and religious. Free traders, religious dissenters, and Parliamentary reformers assailed him as the arch-reactionary, the inveterate foe of progress. One critic after another, Spring Rice, Macaulay, McCulloch, and Wilmot Horton — to name only the most celebrated — assumed the responsibility of demolishing Sadler's law of population as the kind of unscientific Toryism that stood in the way of progress.

Thomas Spring Rice, a Whig leader in the House of Commons, reviewed unfavorably for the *Edinburgh Review* Sadler's work on Ireland.[68] He identified Sadler as a member of the Italian school of economists who preferred agriculture to commerce. He upheld Malthus against Sadler, and defended the political economists against Sadler's charges of Jacobinism.

Thomas B. Macaulay, who had abandoned the Evangelical faith of his father Zachary, found Sadler's *Law of Population* an object worthy of castigation. He began his review in the *Edinburgh* by saying, "We did not expect a good book from Mr. Sadler; and it is well that we did not, for he has given us a very bad one."[69] Macaulay dealt with Sadler's book on population as a collection of polemical tracts against the political economists. When Sadler undertook a defense of his *Law of Population*, he gave Macaulay a second opportunity of refuting him in the pages of the most influential Whig review. It seemed clear from the heated exchanges between Sadler and Macaulay that the question of population and the Poor Laws had been brought into the arena of partisan politics and would eventually be decided by the abler polemicist.

The person most eager to take up a cudgel against Sadler was Robert Wilmot Horton, who was the proponent of emigration as a remedy for pauperism. Wilmot Horton collected and published the opinions of distinguished economists in defense of his policy of emigration. In his first edition of *The Causes and Remedies of Pauperism*, published in 1829, he included letters from Tooke, Malthus, and Ricardo. A second edition of the same work, published in 1831, included a letter from William Nassau Senior endorsing the policy of emigration. Although Wilmot Horton was unsuccessful in his attempt to establish the policy of emigration, he did succeed in further weakening the Tory defense of the Poor Laws. Moreover, his tactic of marshalling the opinions of the economists set a precedent which the Whigs followed in their later successful assault upon the Poor Laws.

177

The ablest defender of emigration and the most severe critic of Sadler was John R. McCulloch.[70] By 1830 he had become the foremost leader of the Radical opposition to the Poor Laws. McCulloch was greatly alarmed over the redundant population of Ireland and the continuous migration of Irishmen to England and Scotland.[71]

McCulloch readily accepted Malthus's explanation of the surplus population in Ireland. The primary cause of the excess was the system of potato gardens, and the secondary cause was the failure of the landlords to tear down cottages. To enable the government to subsidize the emigration of the Irish to overseas colonies McCulloch proposed to tax the landlords to the extent of four hundred thousand pounds a year. It was not enough, he thought, to transport the paupers from Ireland to the colonies; the government must also see to it that the cottages vacated by the emigrants were torn down so that the vacuum could not be filled up again.[72] To prevent the erection of more cottages, he insisted that a tax of two pounds or more be levied annually on every cottage. Since the potato gardens were the cause of excess population, McCulloch proposed to eliminate the "vicious system" by prohibiting the subdividing of farms.

McCulloch was also rigorous in conducting a campaign against poverty in England. He concentrated his attack on the Poor Law reforms of Thomas Gilbert and the Pittite humanitarians. The greatest abuse, as he saw it, was outdoor relief to able-bodied laborers. By his attack against the humanitarian Tory reforms, McCulloch was able to extol the older Elizabethan Poor Law as a means of inculcating the good habits of frugality and industry. The old Poor Law was, indeed, a means of preventing redundant population.[73] For more than two hundred years, according to McCulloch, the landlords, tenant farmers, and parish officials had been in league to keep down the poor rates and to prevent the growth of population. Prior to the Gilbert reforms, the workhouses McCulloch thought had been a means of deterring the poor from depending upon relief. He not only favored the workhouse as a means of deterrence, but he also expressed enthusiasm for the farming system which had enabled the parish officials to contract their paupers to the employers of labor.[74] The two systems, he argued, had been the effective means of reducing population in England from 1688 to 1770.

178

McCulloch blamed the Poor Law reform of 1795 for the growth of a redundant population and the rapid increase of pauperism. The flood gates of pauperism had been opened in 1795 when the justices of the peace began to grant relief outside workhouses in proportion to the number in the family and price of bread. On the basis of his economic analysis of the Poor Law, McCulloch was able to justify the Benthamite remedy for pauperism. The efficient administration of the Poor Law could cure England of the disease and check the growth of a redundant population. To avoid the plague of pauperism, he thought it necessary to return to the workhouse system which existed prior to 1795. It was necessary, he insisted, to abolish family allowances and to deny relief to able-bodied laborers unless they were willing to come into the workhouse to receive it.[75]

In his *Principles* of 1830, McCulloch fully systematized the Radical opposition to the Poor Law. The core of his Radicalism was the Malthusian principle of population. Closely related to the principle of population was Ricardo's doctrine that the better condition of labor depended upon the accumulation of more capital. McCulloch successfully combined his economic analysis with the Benthamite principles of workhouse deterrence. He accepted the Radical reinterpretation of the Poor Law, praising the original Elizabethan law and blaming the more recent Pittite reforms for the profusion of outdoor relief. Although willing to relieve the able-bodied unemployed poor, McCulloch would do so by transforming poorhouses into prisons.

Along with other Radicals, McCulloch had changed his mind about the Laws of Settlement. By increasing the residency requirements to five years or longer, he would enable the landlords to curtail the movement of labor, especially the migration of Irish laborers to England. He would also invest the landlords with greater power over the administration of the Poor Law that they might more effectively limit the growth of population. By tearing down cottages and refusing to build new ones, he thought the landlords would be the most effective means of reducing a redundant labor supply. Like other Radicals, McCulloch was willing to use legislation to reinforce the natural self-interest of the landlords, their reluctance to pay the poor rates.[76]

NOTES

[1] *Parliamentary Papers*, Sess. 1826, Vol. 3, 69.

[2] *Ibid.*, 79.

[3] Gayer, Rostow, and Schwartz, *The Growth and Fluctuation of the British Economy 1790-1850*, Vol. I, 171-72.

[4] Smart, *Economic Annals 1821-1830*, p. 298.

[5] *Parliamentary Papers*, Sess. 1828, Vol. 21, 639.

[6] [First] *Report from the Select Committee Appointed to Inquire into the Expediency of Encouraging Emigration from the United Kingdom, 1826.* p.3.

[7] *Third Report from the S.C. on Emigration. . .1828*, p. 237.

[8] *Ibid.*, p. 243.

[9] *Ibid.*, pp. 245-48.

[10] *Second Report from the S.C. on Emigration. . .*, 1827, pp. V-VI.

[11] [First] *Report from the S.C. on Emigration. . .*, pp. 8-9.

[12] *Ibid.*, p. 114.

[13] *Ibid.*, p. 136.

[14] *Ibid.*, p. 83.

[15] *Ibid.*, p. 143.

[16] *Ibid.*, p. 124.

[17] *Ibid.*, p. 125.

[18] *Ibid.*, p. 3.

[19] Malthus, *Essay on the Principle of Population*, Sixth Edition, 1826, II, 338.

[20] *Third Report from the S.C. on Emigration. . .*, Q. 3254, p. 315. Malthus's testimony on May 5, 1827 runs from question 3186 to 3434, pp. 311-27.

[21] *Ibid.*, Q. 3362, p. 323.

[22] *Ibid.*, Q. 3369, p. 323.

[23] *Ibid.*, Q. 3306, p. 319.

[24] *Ibid.*, Q. 3389, p. 324.

[25] *Ibid.*, Q. 3381, p. 324.

[26] *Ibid.*, Q. 3326, p. 320.

[27] *Ibid.*, Q. 3343, p. 321.

[28] *Ibid.*, p. 9.

[29] *Ibid.*, p. 12.

[30] *Ibid.*, p. 30.

[31] *Ibid.*, p. 3.

[32] C. R. Fay, *Huskisson and His Age*, pp. 84-89.

[33] [First] *Report from the S.C. on Emigration. . .*, Q. 2363, p. 217.

[34] *Third Report from the S.C. on Emigration. . .*, Appendix No. 7, p. 580 is an extract of the *Ninth Report of the Society for Suppression of Mendicity.*

[35] *Ibid.*, p. 590. See Appendix No. 7 for the numbers of Irish paupers in London from 1821 to 1827.

[36] *Ibid.*, Appendix No. 8 is an estimate of the growth of the numbers of Irish Catholics in London from 1819 to 1826.

[37] *Report from the S.C. on Laws Relating to Irish and Scotch Vagrants*, p. 9.

[38] *Ibid.*, p. 4.

[39] *Ibid.*, p. 3.

[40] Nicholls, *History of English Poor Laws*, II, 198. The new law was 6 George IV. C. 57.

[41] *Abstract of Returns showing the Number of Persons Received into and Removed out of their Respective Parishes. . . . Parliamentary Papers*, Sess. 1829, Vol. 182, 4-5.

[42] Mitchelson, "The Old Poor Law in East Yorkshire" in *East Yorkshire Local History Society*, 1853, p. 9. Sidney and Beatrice Webb, *History of the Old*

Poor Law, p. 347, have exaggerated the number of removals and the cost of appeals. They have also given inadequate attention to the modifications of the Laws of Settlement from 1800 to 1834.

[43] H. of C. *Journal*, Vol. 83 (1828), 382.

[44] Slaney, *Some Facts Showing the Vast Burthen of the Poor's Rates. . . .* 1817, p. 39.

[45] *Parliamentary Papers*, Sess. 1829, Vol. 21, 95.

[46] *Report from the Select Committee on the Poor Laws Relating to the Employment of Able-Bodied Persons from the Poor Rate, Parliamentary Papers*, Sess. 1828, Vol. 4, 142.

[47] *Ibid.*, p. 147.

[48] *Parliamentary Debates*, New Series, *XVIII*, 1531.

[49] *Ibid.*, 1544.

[50] *Ibid.*, 1545.

[51] *Ibid.*, XXI, 1050.

[52] Gayer, Rostow, and Schwartz, *The Growth and Fluctuation of the British Economy*, I, 173.

[53] *Parliamentary Papers*, Sess. 1829, XXI, 99.

[54] *Ibid.*, Sess. 1830, XXXI, 49.

[55] Smart, *Economic Annals, 1821-1830*, pp. 466-67. Also, Gayer, *et. al., Op. Cit.*, I, 225.

[56] *Parliamentary Papers*, Sess. 1830-1831, XI, 4-6.

[57] *Ibid.*, p. 2.

[58] John Marshall, *Digest of all the Accounts of the United Kingdom*, p. 5.

[59] J. T. Ward, "Michael Thomas Sadler," *University of Leeds Review*, Vol. VII, (1960), pp. 152-59.

[60] M. T. Sadler, *Ireland: Its Evils and their Remedies. . .*, p. vii.

[61] R. B. Seeley, *Memoir of the Life and Writings of Michael Thomas Sadler*, p. 34.

[62] Howard Mackey, *Humanitarian Opposition to the Economists on the Poor Law and Factory Legislation* (unpublished dissertation, Lehigh University, 1955), p. 98.

[63] M. T. Sadler, *The Law of Population*, I, 339.

[64] *Ibid.*, I, 347.

[65] Seeley, *Michael Thomas Sadler*, p. 585.

[66] Sadler, *Law of Population*, I, 62.

[67] Ward, *Op. Cit.*, 153.

[68] *Edinburgh Review*, No. 100 (Jan., 1830), pp. 344-51.

[69] *Ibid.*, No. 102 (July, 1830), p. 297.

[70] *Ibid.*, No. 98 (June, 1829), pp. 301-14; also, O'Brien, *J. R. McCulloch*, p. 331.

[71] *Ibid.*, No. 89 (Dec. 1826), p. 54; O'Brien, *op. cit.*, p. 335.

[72] *Ibid.*, p. 71.

[73] *Ibid.*, No. 94 (May, 1828), pp. 303-4.

[74] *Ibid.*, p. 311.

[75] *Ibid.*, pp. 327-29.

[76] O'Brien, *op. cit.*, p. 330, thinks there was "a strong element of humanitarianism in McCulloch's later approval and defence of the old Poor Law. . . ." This is surely a misunderstanding of the existing system of welfare. O'Brien also says on p. 330 that all McCulloch thought necessary was a return to the "pre-1782 system." If O'Brien had taken the time to read the *Poor Law Report* of 1834, he would have found that this attitude was an essential part of the Radical opposition to the humanitarian legislation of the Evangelical reformers.

VIII

THE GROWTH OF RADICAL OPPOSITION
Part III. The Riots of 1830

THE three successive bad harvests from 1828 to 1830 greatly aggravated the problems of rural unemployment. The sullen discontent of rural laborers burst into rioting during August, 1830. The jobless workers not only put the torch to the ricks of grain, as was their custom, but also to the farmers' houses and barns.[1] Beginning in Kent, the violence spread to the neighboring counties; wherever the rioters went, they destroyed threshing machines.

As a consequence of the rioting, the House of Lords undertook an extensive investigation of the Poor Laws. The Lords' Committee, which was presided over by Lord Salisbury, conducted its inquiry from December 7, 1830, to April 22, 1831.[2] It took testimony from thirty-six witnesses, including several magistrates and ten clergymen. In order to discover the causes of the riots, Lord Salisbury questioned the witnesses on rural wages, unemployment, and the administration of the Poor Laws.[3]

The witnesses were virtually unanimous about the existence of unemployment and the deplorably low level of wages. All types of unemployment existed throughout the southern counties, including seasonal, cyclical, and technological. Nearly everywhere rural laborers were suffering from the disappearance of handicraft industries which had formerly flourished but could no longer compete with machine production.[4]

182

Another type of technological unemployment was caused by the enclosure of the open fields. Following wet seasons which destroyed the harvests in the low-lying clay lands, there was no capital available for draining and hedging. When such fields were sown in grass, they afforded very little employment.

Seasonal unemployment plagued rural areas after machines had destroyed household industries. Women and children, who had previously been a part of the family economy, could no longer find employment.[5] In many rural areas the threshing of grain was the principal winter employment, and in a few places the threshing machine was displacing men, although it had not yet come into general use. Poor harvests meant a lack of work for those who relied upon threshing for their winter employment. It was a common practice for farmers to keep their best hands employed throughout the year. The carters and threshers were regarded as regular hands and the rest of the laborers as occasional hands. Many of these casual laborers were thrown upon the parish for relief during the winter months and at other periods of inclement weather. Even with employment the occasional laborer could not support a family on wages of ten pence or a shilling a day.

The low wages paid to casual farm laborers do not fully describe the appalling misery of their existence. When the normal variations of the season deprived them of employment at subsistence wages, their only recourse was to parish relief work. Parish officials provided the able-bodied paupers with work on the roads and in the gravel pits. Relief work was sometimes a bizarre punishment for the failure to find other employment; sometimes the paupers' children were put to work on the road gathering dung after the horses for fertilizer; sometimes men themselves were harnessed to carts to pull loads of stone.[6] Although such extreme cases of parish brutality must have been rare, they were probably as frequent as the cases of parish generosity which some reformers supposed characterized the rural parishes in the southern counties. It was almost universal in the southern counties to set the paupers to digging in the gravel pits, spreading stones, and other forms of labor on the county roads.

If the Berkshire magistrates had relief scales, the overseers and the farmers who paid wages and administered relief ignored them.[7] The farmers saw to it that the paupers working on the roads were paid less than the regular workers employed in the fields; they normally paid less to the unskilled than to the skilled, and those who worked on the roads were usually the least skilled. Thus the principle of less-eligibility was a commonplace practice in many rural areas.

Such were the economic conditions in the southern counties that caused the riots of 1830. It was clear to the magistrates who testified before the Lords' Poor Law Committee in 1831 that the lack of employment and the character of relief work underlay the discontent that caused the rioting. The magistrates had taken the initiative in urging the farmers to increase wages and to employ their hands more fully with meaningful work. In order to employ labor more fully on the farms, some parishes had initiated a labor rate which had been recommended in 1824 by the Committee on Laborers' Wages. Under the labor-rate plan the farmers could hire more casual labor during the winter seasons and pay them wages instead of paying poor rates to the parish.[8]

While some parishes were resorting to the labor rate as the proper remedy for unemployment, other parishes preferred to adopt some plan of land allotments. The Sturges Bourne Act had enabled the parishes to purchase as much as twenty-five acres of land to sublet as gardens to their able-bodied paupers. This plan of allotment was in keeping with the practice of many farmers who supplied garden plots for their regular hands. In many parishes, therefore, such gardens, especially when planted in potatoes, supplemented the farm laborer's income.[9]

Although a majority of the witnesses before the Lord's Committee advocated either a labor rate or land allotments as remedies for rural unemployment, some among them recommended the subsidizing of emigration as the proper remedy. One of these witnesses was Thomas Law Hodges, M.P. for the county of Kent and also one of the magistrates. For nearly a decade Kent had been subsidizing emigration, Hodges said, as a means of ridding the county of surplus population. Most of those who took advantage of this opportunity migrated to the United States, found employment, and were able to repay the money lent to them. Unfortunately, while some of the parishes were paying their laborers to emigrate to foreign lands, it was necessary for the farmers to hire Irish migrant laborers to help harvest the hops.[10] At least one witness, Richard Spooner, saw the absurdity of subsidizing emigration while Irish and Scottish migrants were being hired to harvest the crops. He also made the observation — probably the correct one — that any voluntary system of emigration would carry off the best laborers.[11]

Although the House of Lords' Committee collected much testimony on rural unemployment, their only purpose was to reform the Poor Laws. Some members of the Committee had already reached the conclusion that proper methods of relief were an adequate remedy for employment. Like the House of Commons' Committee on Laborers' Wages in 1824, they compared the Poor Law administration of selected northern counties with the notoriously bad administration of certain southern counties. When Robert Slaney, one of the most persistent advocates of Poor Law reform, appeared before the Lords' Committee, he denounced the southern practices of family allowances and making up wages from the rates. Moreover, he now regarded these practices as illegal and contrary to the purpose of the original Elizabethan Poor Law.[12]

Inasmuch as riots had occurred in several places in Sussex and as the county had become notorious for the worst type of Poor Law administration, the Lords' Committee called six of its thirty-six witnesses from that county. The six witnesses from Sussex included two overseers, one magistrate, one clergyman, one steward, and one pamphleteer. John Barton, who had won distinction as a Malthusian reformer, attributed the riots in Sussex to low wages but also thought that low wages were the result of redundant population and low morals.[13] Barton acknowledged the lack of employment for women and children, and he also observed that men had to seek employment on the roads because farmers could not afford to cultivate their lands at the prevailing price for wheat.

The six witnesses from Sussex agreed upon the economic conditions that underlay the discontent in their county. One of the most experienced of these witnesses was Thomas Partington, chairman of the Quarter Sessions in the eastern division of the county, who had been a magistrate for twenty-five years. In his testimony before the Lords' Committee, he estimated that one-fourth of the residents in his parish of Hamsey lacked full employment. Those lacking employment worked for the parish digging and breaking flint. In providing relief work it was the usual practice of the parishes in his division to hire the whole family at task work. The amount of relief work needed varied greatly from parish to parish, depending on the quality of the soil and the size and location of the farms. In the parishes under the South Downs, for example, the farms were large and the soil good; but in the Weald, where land was poor and the farms small, wages were low and many persons unemployed. Because of depressed economic conditions,

185

some of the land in the Weald, which had been cultivated during the Napoleonic War when prices were high, had been subsequently returned to grass and could be used only for sheep.[14]

In many parishes of the western division of Sussex agriculture was as badly depressed as in the eastern division. The Reverend George Wells, who resided near Steyning on the border of the Weald, reported to the Lords' Committee that some of the clay soil was so poor that it produced nothing in wet seasons. Because of the failure of harvests during recent seasons, the farmers were unable to employ labor.[15]

The two overseers from Sussex confirmed the depressed economic conditions described by Wells and Partington. According to Richard Holloway, an overseer in the parish of Shipley, the farmers of the Weald suffered severely during wet seasons. The drains had to be cleaned every year, and the farmers could not afford to have them cleaned after a harvest had failed.[16] Inasmuch as the third successive harvest had failed in 1830, the farmers, according to Holloway, were worse off than they had ever been in his district.

Thomas Turner was the acting overseer, as well as the surveyor of roads, for the parish of Sompting. Although many parishes in Sussex were more badly depressed than his, Turner found it necessary to employ people grading roads and leveling hills. For such work he paid a single man eight pence a day while regular hands on the farm received two shillings a day. Since these working conditions had brought on the riots of 1830, many parishes, he said, had adopted the practice of employing laborers on the farms by means of the labor rate.[17]

Another witness, John Cameron, a steward on an estate at Cowdray, testified that much of the land of the parish was so poor that it was kept under cultivation only to provide employment. Many farms in his area, for lack of adequate drainage, could not grow wheat. As a means of preventing further rioting, he proposed a labor rate that would fix wages at ten shillings a week.[18]

Agricultural conditions similar to those in Sussex prevailed in neighboring Hampshire and Kent, where rioting had also destroyed ricks of grain and other farm property. The riots, however, did not occur in the northern counties which had long been celebrated for their superior administration of the Poor Laws. The peaceful conduct of rural labor in these areas was attributed to the superior administration. Since it was assumed that the northern counties were

186

free of abuse, the Lords' Committee called only one witness to present evidence on the superior conditions of the North. John Grey, a magistrate for North Durham and also the owner of land at Midfield Hill in Northumberland, confidently testified of the superior conditions in his area.[19] In his region there were few people on relief because a whole family could still find employment. Moreover, at times of harvest there was a scarcity of hands. It was certainly clear from his testimony that agriculture, living standards, and social customs were quite different from those in Sussex. In addition to high wages and full employment, the laborer had his house and garden free of rent and pasture enough for a cow. In the North most of the farms were large with much land sown in grass, such conditions requiring fewer hands than the types of farms in Kent and Sussex. The Lords' Committee could not but conclude from Grey's testimony that the Poor Laws were better administered in the North because fewer hands were coming to the parish for employment.

Sussex and Northumberland, having widely different economic conditions, adopted methods of poor relief in keeping with those conditions. Judging from the evidence presented to the Lords' Committee in 1831, methods of poor relief differed not only from county to county but also within counties according to economic conditions. The Lords' Committee found seasonal unemployment everywhere in rural areas and more unemployment in districts of heavy clay soils than in regions of lighter sandy soil, more in the lowlands than the highlands, more on wheat farms than dairy farms.

While methods of poor relief differed in many respects, the Lords' evidence of 1831 pointed to the general practice of family allowances. Although granting relief in some proportion to the number in the family was a common practice in all counties, the amount of relief and the method of administering it differed from place to place. The majority of parishes were willing to aid large families with several children too young to work. Many parishes began relieving families with three or four children; a few began relief with the first or second child, while other parishes, especially in the North, refused relief until the arrival of seven or eight children.

In some parishes the family allowance was used only in connection with relief work to determine the rate of pay. Other parishes preferred to hire the whole family and pay by the task. In a few places the parish work was rationed; and in virtually all parishes the amount earned fell below the wages of farm labor in regular employment.

Family allowances, or payment by the head, were also used by the parish official to determine the amount of relief to be paid families who resided outside the place of their legal settlement. Many parishes preferred to grant allowances to large families who had migrated to find employment and who lacked a legal residence in the place of their employment. Some urban parishes, especially in the older parts of London, paid family allowances or other forms of relief, even though they had few resident paupers, and sometimes none.

Although the House of Lords' Committee had amassed evidence showing extensive rural unemployment, they did not investigate methods of increasing employment. As their primary purpose was to reform the Poor Laws, they anticipated finding ways of improving administration that would reduce the cost of relief. Their comparison of the northern counties with the southern showed their preference for the former over the latter. That they called as witness a magistrate, who had already successfully applied Bentham's principles of pauper management, indicated their willingness to undertake some scheme of dispauperization. For this reason, they gave their full attention to John T. Becher's pauper experiments at Southwell.[20]

The Reverend John T. Becher, the incumbent of the parish of Thurgarton, had been the chairman of the Newark division of Nottinghamshire for twenty-four years and a magistrate active in Poor Law administration for thirty-eight years. As a magistrate he had resisted the humanitarian reforms adopted during the time of William Pitt. During the war years when prices were rising, he had objected to both the Berkshire and the Norfolk scales.[21] In 1808 when most parishes were transforming their workhouses into poorhouses and resorting to methods of outdoor relief, Becher persuaded Southwell, where he was the presiding magistrate, to erect a new workhouse on the principle of deterrence. The new workhouse, moreover, was "constructed and governed" in accordance with Bentham's principles of "inspection, classification, and seclusion." Built to accommodate eighty-four paupers, the workhouse was incorporated with Bentham's ideas of inspectability, with a lodge at the center and wings extending on each side.[22] To improve further its pauper management, Southwell appointed Paul

Bauser Assistant Overseer in 1812, and he continued in the office for sixteen years.

When the postwar depression caused extensive unemployment in the Newark division of Nottingham, the Duke of Newcastle urged the magistrates to set a minimum wage; but Becher, rather than interfere with wages, preferred to subsidize emigration to the Cape of Good Hope, and with his help some two hundred persons were able to emigrate.[23] After the return of prosperity in the early 1820's, Becher resolved to cut relief expenses to the minimum. At the parish of Thurgarton, with a population of 330, there was in 1827 one pauper, a widow who received sixpence a week.

The parish of Southwell, also, was successful in reducing its relief expenditures during the 1820's. The acting overseer at Southwell from 1821 to 1824, George Nicholls, succeeded in reducing gross expenditures from 2,254 pounds to 760 pounds.[24] Since these expenditures included rents, salaries, lawyers' and doctors' fees, little relief could have been paid except to the impotent poor. Even the expenses of the workhouse, during Nicholl's term in office, were reduced from 410 pounds in 1821 to 142 pounds in 1823. In the year ending March 1, 1828, total relief expenses were 830 pounds, and of this amount how much actually went to paupers is uncertain. In that year there resided at Southwell forty-seven permanent and four occasional paupers, not counting children. The relief payments at Southwell probably did not exceed those at Thurgarton where, on March 1, 1828, one elderly blind man received one shilling a week from the parish and three widows received three shillings each.[25]

In 1823 John Becher was able to extend his anti-pauper system by incorporating the Thurgarton Hundred under the Gilbert Act. On October 6, 1823, he sent a circular letter to the principal landlords and occupiers residing within ten miles of Southwell, inviting them to undertake the formation of a Gilbert Union. When the landlords and occupiers of the Thurgarton Hundred met on October 31, they accepted Becher's principle of deterrence and agreed to relieve able-bodied paupers in the workhouse. During the following year the workhouse was constructed to accommodate the forty-nine parishes of the new union. Contrary to Gilbert's humane purposes, the new workhouse was intended to deter persons from seeking relief. It was designed according to Bentham's principles of classification and inspection.[26] To manage the new workhouse the Thurgarton Hundred hired a governor, matron, chaplain, surgeon, and treasurer. The able-bodied poor who applied for relief were set to work breaking stones, shoveling gravel, and doing tasks intended to drive paupers off the relief rolls. As such work was paid by the task and at rates lower than regular employment, it had the desired effect of keeping people off relief. Although the workhouse had been built to house seventy-one persons, it had only fifty-four paupers in 1827; of this number, twenty-three were men, seventeen were women, and fourteen were children.

John Becher defined his anti-pauper system in Bentham's terms of "secluded restraint and solitary discipline." The system, "together with our simple and yet sufficient diet," he declared, proved to be so repugnant to the poor that they soon left the workhouse. When Becher came before the Lords' Committee in 1831, he testified that his anti-pauper system was working so well that Southwell was giving no relief outside the workhouse to able-bodied paupers.[27]

Although Becher's anti-pauper system at Southwell was the most fully developed and thorough in its deterrence, there were other Poor Law officials who were equally determined to dispauperize their parishes. The Reverend Thomas Whately, incumbent of the parish of Cookham, which included half the town of Maidenhead in Berkshire, had adopted an effective system of dispauperization. His system of deterrence had reduced relief expenses from 3,133 pounds in 1819 to 835 pounds in 1831, but he had made such reductions by driving from the parish sixty-three families who had previously required relief.[28]

Among the dispauperizing magistrates who appeared before the Lords' Committee in 1831, none was more determined to uproot poverty than Thomas Walker. Before his appointment as police magistrate in London, he had gained distinction for his suppression of paupers. In 1817 he had served as overseer in Manchester and had succeeded in reducing relief expenditures even during the postwar depression. From Manchester he went to the parish of Berry Pomeroy, where he led a campaign to repress paupers. His successful war against paupers in Devonshire brought him to the attention of London officials, and they appointed him magistrate of the Lambeth Street Police District. His District included some of the most impoverished areas of London. In the slums of East London he found laborers who claimed there were no jobs, but he simply would not believe them. He was able to reduce expenditures by insisting that relief be refused to paupers until they had submitted to a workhouse test. He further cut expenses by refusing to issue passes to Irish migrant workers. His general attitude was that it would be better if there were no Poor Laws at all, and some of his practices indicated that he ignored the law as much as possible. When Lord Salisbury cross-examined him on his attitude toward the law, Walker admitted that he was acting illegally.[29]

In spite of the time and attention given to investigating the anti-pauper schemes which were flourishing in several different counties, the members of the House of Lords Committee were unwilling to recommend dispauperization as the proper reform of the Poor Laws. While the members recognized the existence of rural unemployment, they did not agree on its causes. Some members of the Lords' Committee accepted Malthus's explanation that a surplus population made the supply of labor exceed the demand. One member, the Duke of Richmond, favored voluntary migration as the proper means of ending unemployment. Lord Salisbury, who had presided over most of the sessions of the Poor Law Committee, rejected the notion of a redundant population and repudiated also the anti-pauper system. When presenting the Committee's Report to the House of Lords on March 4, 1831, Salisbury recommended land allotments that would provide the parish poor with gardens.[30] The motion for land allotments was supported by Lord Stanhope, one of the most active members of the Committee, but the Duke of Richmond insisted that the chairman's recommendations did not represent the majority view of the Committee. The proposal of land allotments as the proper remedy for unemployment found support among the Whigs as well as the Tories. Lord Althorp and Spring Rice, on behalf of the Whig Government, proposed a bill authorizing the parishes to purchase as much as fifty acres of land and to set poor people to work on it.[31]

There were a few Tories in the House of Commons who wished to go far beyond the Whig plan of land allotments. On October 11, 1831, Thomas Michael Sadler introduced a bill proposing that the government subsidize the building of houses for the poor on land with a garden plot of not less than one-quarter acre.[32] After his bill had been drastically modified in committee, it enabled the parish to enclose as much as fifty acres of crown land that lay within its boundaries. The parish, if it chose to enclose the land, might then lease it to parish laborers in lieu of other kinds of relief.[33]

The debates on Sadler's bill marked a revival of Evangelical interest in the Poor Laws. In the following year John Weyland's bill sought to enlarge the scope of the previous land allotment acts. He wished to authorize any parish which had been enclosed by an act of Parliament to rent land to its cottagers. Weyland estimated that under the four thousand acts of enclosure many allotments had already been made. He wished, however, to extend the system of allotments to all parishes to enable them to purchase land and sublet it to the landless cottager. When Weyland's bill ultimately became law it authorized the parishes, but did not require them, to purchase land for their cottagers. The parishes, for the most part, were unwilling to assume such responsibility. While there were many parishes where landlords provided allotments for the cottagers on their estates, the farmers who controlled the parishes were unlikely to carry out the provisions of the new law.[34] The new law, however, was amended, forbidding parishes to build cottages on parish land. Thus Parliament wrote into the new law Malthus's assumption that a dearth of cottages was the best check on population.[35]

The debates on the land allotment acts revealed a broad diversity of opinion on the best mode of attacking rural unemployment. If the traditional Tories wanted to set the people to work on the land digging their existence from the soil, the Liberal Tories, imbued with the spirit of Malthus, preferred to reduce the surplus population by a policy of subsidizing emigration. An increasing number of Whigs, now in office for the first time in several decades, wished above all else to strike at Tory power by cutting government spending and reforming the system of representation on both the local and national level. The Whigs could provide only a political solution for economic problems; among the Whigs the Benthamite Radicals stood out as the most zealous of reformers. These Radicals opposed government supported employment as "artificial and calculated to raise up and retain a larger number of labourers in a district than there is legitimate employment for; and consequently, by such excess of supply over demand, to lower the price of labour to an amount incompatible with social or physical well-being."[36]

The Benthamite Radicals, as well as other political economists, were even more strongly opposed to the labor rate than to the land allotment acts. They regarded the labor rate as a direct interference with the natural law of wages; they therefore opposed

Lord Winchilsea's bill. The Earl of Winchilsea, who resided in Kent, proposed the labor rate as the best means of preventing riots.[37] The purpose of his bill, he explained, was to allow the farmers to employ their hands during the winter season, paying them their usual wages. The amount paid in wages during the off-season would then be credited to the farmers against their assessment to the poor rates. At the same time, the farmers could make necessary repairs to their property, repairs that could not be made in bad seasons for lack of capital.

Lord Winchilsea's labor rate bill, like the whole question of Poor Law reform, was caught up in the revolutionary agitation over Parliamentary reform. The Whigs, who took office on November 17, 1830, having matured no Poor Law reform of their own and being more badly divided on the question than the Tories, preferred to postpone action by appointing a committee to investigate the laws once more. When Lord Salisbury requested such a committee on November 29, 1830, Lord Grey, on behalf of the new Whig ministry, supported his request. The appointment of the Lords' Poor Law Committee in 1831 caused the postponement of Lord Winchilsea's labor rate bill.[38]

After the House of Lords had finished its investigation, Lord Winchelsea, on June 27, 1831, reintroduced his labor rate bill.[39] The Whig Ministry, still deeply embroiled with the Parliamentary Reform Bill, again forestalled the Poor Law question by appointing a Committee of investigation. As justification for further delay, Lord Althorp professed a lack of confidence in the committees that had already collected information on the subject. All the gentlemen who had come before the committees, he declared, had "preconceived opinions on the subject." Althorp proposed to appoint a Commission that would conduct "an inquiry on the spot to find out the different effects of the different systems as they existed in different parishes throughout the country."[40]

When Lord Salisbury pressed the Whigs for action in the Upper House, Lord Brougham repeated what Althorp had said in the Commons: it was the Government's intention to appoint a Commission.[41] Until the Whigs had matured their own plan of reform, they were willing to accept the labor rate as a temporary measure of relief; the life of the new law was limited to March 25, 1834, when the Commission was to bring its report.[42]

In at least one respect the Whigs were prepared to alter the Poor Laws before they had received the Commission's report; they were

193

as eager to change the system of representation on the local as on the national level. Several Whig reformers strongly objected to the Sturges Bourne Select Vestry Act. A system of voting which proportioned political influence according to wealth was clearly not in keeping with the spirit of popular representation embodied in the Great Reform Bill. Under the Sturges Bourne Act, which the Tories continued to support, the wealthier rate payers might accumulate as many as six votes in the parish election of vestrymen. John Cam Hobhouse, the Westminster Radical, introduced in 1831 the Whig measure which made it possible for local parishes to elect their vestries by a popular ballot.[43]

The intense excitement aroused by the controversy over the Reform Bill in 1831 made possible the passage of the Hobhouse Vestry Act. Demonstrations were held in the largest parishes of London to petition Parliament for the passage of the bill. At St. James, Westminster, one of the largest metropolitan parishes, the Radical reformers urged the parishioners not to pay the poor rates until the select vestry had been abolished.[44] At a similar meeting in the large parish of Marylebone, with the Radical Joseph Hume presiding, the parishioners resolved not to pay the rates imposed by the select vestry. The spirit of rebellion spread to Bath, where irate citizens would not allow the parish officials to sell property distrained for not paying the rates.

When the petitions from the parishes favoring Hobhouse's vestry bill reached the House of Commons, the Tory opponents of the measure, led by Sir Charles Wetherell, proposed a motion of censure, charging that the refusal to pay taxes was a treasonable conspiracy. The Whigs, however, were able to defeat the motion of censure owing to the general enthusiasm for the Great Reform Bill.

When the Whig vestry bill was introduced in the House of Lords, it evoked extensive debate and arguments similar to those used for and against the Great Reform Bill. At the second reading of the bill on October 11, 1831, Lord Melbourne supported it on behalf of the Government, and the Duke of Wellington led the Tory opposition to the measure.[45] A Tory amendment which would have extended the Sturges Bourne Act to all the metropolitan parishes was defeated fifty-four to thirty-six, and this defeat prepared the way for the passage of the Vestries Act extending popular representation to local government.

The debates on the Vestries Act of 1831 revealed the growing influence of the Benthamite Radicals. Although Joseph Hume in the Lower House and Henry Brougham in the Upper House had fallen short of Bentham's Radicalism, they both advocated drastic political changes that went beyond the moderate reforms of the Whigs. In their zealous quest for political liberty, they revealed also how doctrinaire they had become. Joseph Hume, in particular, showed the inflexible limits of his principles in the debates on the Truck Act. E. J. Littleton's bill, which passed its third reading on October 5, 1831, prohibited the payment of wages, in certain industries, in kind, specifying that wages be paid only in money. Joseph Hume, however, objected to the measure as unnecessary legislative interference. Fortunately, there were few members in the House of Commons as doctrinaire as he; on his motion to postpone the third reading of the truck bill, he was defeated by a vote of sixty-one to four.[46]

The growth of Radical opposition to the Poor Laws in Parliament revived Jeremy Bentham's interest in his own work on *Pauper Management Improved*, which he had published thirty-two years before. Satisfied that the principles of central inspection and contract-management which he had propounded for the Panopticon were receiving at last the attention they deserved, he determined to instruct his disciples in other plans for reforming the Poor Laws. For the further education of his disciples he resorted to writing the history of his struggle to build the Panopticon. Now in his eighty-second year, he related in his memoirs the long and futile struggle to obtain the government's approval of the principles of the Panopticon and their application to prisons and workhouses.

Bentham entitled his memoirs, "History of the War between Jeremy Bentham and George the Third."[47] At the beginning of the memoir Bentham recommended his long treatise, *Pauper Management Improved*, "the work to which this brief, and it is hoped, not altogether uninstructive nor uninteresting history is designed to serve as an introduction. . . ." Although Bentham had abandoned the hope of bringing prisoners under his plan of contract-management, he made it clear that he still hoped to apply his principles to the management of paupers. He reminded his disciples that the Panopticon principles of "lodgement, maintenance, and employment of prisoners" had been originally devised for "persons of the unoffending class."

The major principles of the Panopticon which Bentham wished to apply to paupers were (1) central inspection and (2) contract-management. The foremost principle was efficient public inspec-

tion, or in his own words, "universal and constant inspectability
. . .inspectability of the inspectors by the eye of the public opinion tribunal. . . ."[48]

Bentham's second principle of Poor Law reform was contract-
management. He had long believed that, to achieve an efficient
Poor Law system, the unpaid officials — the trustees — should be
replaced by paid officials whose duties would coincide with their
interests. The old Poor Law officials, the trustees, Bentham
thought, were functionaries by patronage whose interests did not
coincide with duty.[49]

Bentham made it clear in his memoirs that he regarded the reform of the Poor Laws as an essential utilitarian reformation of
society. According to the principle of utility a man must pursue
his own happiness, avoiding pain and seeking pleasure. Whatever
brought happiness to the individual was his interest. It followed
from the principle of utility, as both James Mill and Bentham had
been proclaiming for more than a decade, that the interests of the
aristocratic few could never coincide with the interests of the
majority. On the national level the aristocracy, in pursuit of their
own interests, had already corrupted the House of Commons; and
on the local level the appointees of aristocrats, were demoralizing
the poor by encouraging idleness and improvidence. This aspect
of local government, Bentham concluded, needed reform as much
as did the House of Commons.

Bentham's principles of pauper management came to be ac-
cepted by his disciples as a great scientific discovery which consti-
tuted the proper remedy for the perennial disease of pauperism.
The Radicals were already the most determined foes of the Poor
Laws and the most persistent advocates of drastic reform. Edwin
Chadwick, who took the lead in the reform of 1834, did so in
Bentham's name and in keeping with the spirit and principles of
Pauper Management Improved.[50]

While the Radicals were depending on Bentham for their remedy for the disease of pauperism, they relied upon others for their
diagnosis. The political economists had already diagnosed the
disease in terms of increasing population and declining capital investment. The riots of 1830, which seemed to confirm their principles, elicited from the leading political economists a number of
pamphlets explaining the causes of the riots and prescribing
remedies to prevent future outbursts. When Nassau Senior published in 1830 his *Three Lectures on the Rates of Wages*, which he

had already delivered at Oxford University, he added a preface entitled "On the Causes and Remedies of the Present Disturbances."

Nassau William Senior was born in 1790 at Compton Beauchamp, in Berkshire. The son of an Anglican clergyman, he received his education at Eton and Magdalene College, Oxford. At the age of twenty-three he began the study of law at Lincoln's Inn, and six years later he began the practice of law. Although preoccupied with a busy legal career, his interest in the Poor Law turned his attention to the study of political economy. When Oxford University created, in 1825, its first chair in political economy, Senior was appointed to occupy it. Since the occupant of the chair was required to publish a lecture every year, Senior dutifully complied and published in 1827 his *Introductory Lecture on Political Economy*. Other lectures were produced annually before he published the *Three Lectures on the Rate of Wages*.

In the Preface to his *Lectures*, Senior proposed a remedy for the riots of 1830. He was completely confident that the science of economics could provide a remedy for pauperism, which had caused the disturbances. An adequate remedy, he thought, must comply with the "proposition that the rate of wages depends on the extent of the fund for the maintenance of laborers, compared with the numbers of laborers to be maintained."[51] The proposition, as stated by Senior, seemed so self-evident that he felt no need to discuss it at length. His overweening confidence in his principles prompted him to formulate a hasty remedy for the suppression of disturbances. His solution was to increase the wage fund by raising the productivity of labor. On the one hand, industry should be liberated to allow every man to pursue his own interests; on the other hand, all taxes should be reduced to the minimum. Senior strongly objected to the poor rates on the grounds that they were a burden to both the master and the workman, and he objected to the Poor Laws, in general, because they made wages a matter of right rather than one of contract between master and men.

Senior explained the causes of the riots of 1830 in terms of the maladministration of the Poor Laws in the southern counties, which had destroyed the proper relationship between employer and labor. In the southern counties, he asserted, the Poor Laws were destroying free labor; just as slaves were paid according to their needs rather than their services, so English free laborers were being paid family allowances rather than wages.[52]

Although expressed in the scientific language of political economy, Nassau Senior's attack on the Poor Laws was, in fact, scarcely less inflammatory than the diatribes of the working class. Not only were laborers being reduced to slavery, but also property owners were being ruined by the Poor Laws. Like Malthus, Senior could engender sympathy for the upper as well as the lower classes; the ruin of the upper classes, he thought, was even worse than that of the lower, for the upper classes have further to fall and the ruin of the upper classes "is sudden and irretrievable."[53]

Nassau Senior's *Three Lectures on the Rate of Wages* was reviewed in the *Edinburgh Review* by John R. McCulloch. However much McCulloch differed with Senior in understanding political economy, he agreed with him in placing the blame for the riots on the improper administration of the Poor Laws. McCulloch, moreover, agreed with him on the principle that labor, like other commodities, should be left to seek its own price in the market. The Poor Laws were to be condemned, therefore, for interfering with the natural laws regulating wages. While praising Senior's doctrine of wages, McCulloch condemned Sadler for attributing economic difficulties to the deflation resulting from the resumption of specie payment.[54]

McCulloch's views in 1831, as one might suppose, differed very little from those which he had held in 1828 when he wrote his major article on the Poor Laws. He was, in fact, content to state the earlier article verbatim. He was still convinced that the Poor Laws, as administered in the southern counties, caused idleness and improvidence among rural laborers. To restore tranquility in these counties, he urged the government to transport the surplus laborers to the colonies and to tear down the cottages which they evacuated. He would also reform the Poor Laws by abolishing outdoor relief to able-bodied laborers. Although McCulloch recognized the existence of urban unemployment that came with fluctuations in trade, he thought it necessary only to teach the laborers to be patient and courageous. Since the safety of the country depended upon the conduct of the working classes, he recommended "the diffusion of sound instruction" among them. The doctrines which he desired to teach the working classes were the laws regulating population and wages.

McCulloch enhanced his prestige as an economist by publishing in 1830 a second edition of *The Principles of Political Economy*. As the professor of political economy at the University of London and as the principal writer of economic articles for the *Edinburgh Review*, McCulloch had only Senior as a rival. Malthus, whose doctrine of gluts had been summarily rejected, had little to add to what he had already said on emigration and the Poor Laws. McCulloch's preeminence in political economy enabled him to propagate widely the Radical reform of the Poor Laws. In the second edition of his textbook, he restated the radical program which he had proposed in his *Edinburgh Review* article on the Poor Laws. In general, his policy was to use the Poor Laws as a means of checking population and deterring poverty; the essence of his policy was the principle of deterrence which had been incorporated in the law of 1722. At that time the workhouse was used as a shield to protect the poor rates and as a humiliating test to prevent people from seeking relief.[55] McCulloch clearly preferred this policy of 1722 to the humanitarian reforms of William Pitt and others who had transformed the workhouse into a place of refuge for those who had none to care for them. The same humanitarian reforms were designed to encourage the Justices of the Peace to grant outdoor relief to paupers in their own homes. McCulloch's Radical reforms, which he set forth in his textbook, were both a repudiation of Pitt's humanitarianism and a reinstitution of workhouse deterrence. "All, in fact, that is necessary is to revert to the regulations established previously to 1795, to abolish every vestige of the allowance system, and to enact that henceforth no able-bodied labourer shall have a legal claim to relief unless he consents to accept it in a workhouse."[56] The deterrence principle had previously been celebrated by Sir Frederick Morton Eden in his famous work on the *State of the Poor* and by Jeremy Bentham in his *Pauper Management Improved*. Bentham, in particular, had set forth in exhaustive detail a plan of making the workhouse less desirable than the meanest private employment. Bentham's principles of pauper management were restated by McCulloch in 1830; in every workhouse, he said, "strict discipline, scanty fare, and hard labour" should be endorsed as a means of removing idle and disorderly persons from the relief rolls.

Whereas earlier political economists Adam Smith and Ricardo wanted to abolish the Poor Laws as an interference with the natural laws, McCulloch wanted to preserve them as a positive check on the growth of population. The landlords and tenants who levied the rates and administered the laws, he thought, had the necessary interest and authority to check population by tearing down laborers' cottages and by refusing to build new ones.[57]

McCulloch's book, *Principles of Political Economy*, was reviewed in the *Edinburgh Review* by Walter Coulson, who took the occasion to write another pamphlet on the riots of 1830. Coulson concluded from the smoking ruins of barns and corn ricks that farm laborers needed more knowledge of political economy, for the insurrection had been the result of "vulgar errors about wages and machinery."[58] At such a crisis as this, Coulson thought, McCulloch had done a great public service by publishing "a good elementary political economy."

By training and experience Coulson could readily apprehend the political significance of McCulloch's *Principles*, just as James Mill had seen the political significance of Ricardo's *Principles*. A Benthamite and a friend of James Mill, Coulson had distinguished himself as a lawyer. Although he had not written widely on economic subjects, he had served as the editor of a liberal newspaper, the *Globe and Traveller*. That Coulson, a former amanuensis of Bentham's, was selected to review McCulloch's book indicated that the *Edinburgh* reviewers had come to look with more favor on Bentham's *Pauper Management Improved* as providing the proper reform of the Poor Laws.

Even though McCulloch's *Principles* treated the whole range of economic subjects, Coulson devoted his attention to the two chapters on "Population" and "Poor Laws." He praised Malthus's principle of population as one of the most revealing achievements of philosophy; the only intelligent way of viewing the Poor Laws was according to the principle of population, "whether they tend to regulate in a beneficial manner the increase in the number of people, always ready, as we have seen, to outrun the increase in capital."[59]

Coulson fully agreed with McCulloch that the most urgently needed reform of the Poor Laws was the denial of relief to the able-bodied. By building workhouses and adhering to Bentham's principle of less-eligibility, Coulson was confident that the growth of population could be curtailed and wages increased.[60]

Coulson's review marked McCulloch as both the ablest Radical opponent of the Poor Laws and as the reformer who had formulated a policy based upon both political science and economics. Coulson recognized McCulloch's achievement as combining the economics of Malthus and Ricardo against the Poor Laws and as finding in Bentham's *Pauper Management Improved* the proper remedy for their defects. McCulloch's radical remedy was, in brief, to deter poverty by making relief within the workhouse as disagreeable as a term in prison. The workhouse test, then, was to be a means of distinguishing between the idle and industrious poor, between those worthy and unworthy of relief. Thus by the magic of an administrative reform, population was to be controlled, and wages increased.[61]

The riots of 1830 had given a new urgency to the reform of the Poor Laws. The investigation conducted by the House of Lords Poor Law Committee revealed the close connection between unemployment and the disturbances in the southern counties. Some members of the Lords' Committee, seeking an immediate remedy for rural unemployment, proposed parish land allotments and the labor rate as proper means of relieving unemployment. The Tories, who went out of office in 1830, could not agree on the best method of dealing with unemployment; some preferred land allotments, others preferred subsidies for emigration, while still others preferred the labor rate. The Whigs had been out of office so long that they could not formulate a policy, and they were too much embroiled in the reform of Parliament to give attention to the reform of the Poor Laws. They were willing, therefore, to accept the Tory proposals of land allotments and the labor rate as temporary expedients. Meanwhile, they would appoint a Commission to investigate the Poor Laws and postpone action on this divisive question until the Great Reform Bill had passed.

NOTES

[1] J. H. Clapham, *An Economic History of Modern Britain*, I, 139; J. L. and Barbara Hammond, *The Village Labourer*, Chapters XI, XII; E. J. Hobsbawn and G. Rude, *Captain Swing*, (New York, 1968), Chapters X and XI.

[2] *Parliamentary Debates*, 3rd ser., Vol. I, 687.

[3] *Report from the S. C. of the House of Lords appointed to Consider of the Poor Laws with Minutes of Evidence. . .Parliamentary Papers*, Sess. 1831, Vol. 8, p. 321.

[4] *Ibid.*, See testimony of Richard M. Bacon, p. 115, and the Rev. James Beard, p. 9. I have attempted to summarize the economic conditions as found in the evidence; many other witnesses bore testimony similar to that cited.

[5] *Ibid.*, See Richard Holloway, p. 30; and Robert Chick, p. 57.

[6] *Ibid.*, See the Reverend Henry Fouli's testimony, pp. 74-75.

[7] *Ibid.*, See Edward Simeon, pp. 281-82, and George Harrison, p. 89.

[8] *Ibid.*, See Charles Wetherall, p. 42.

[9] *Ibid.*, See Lord Stanhope, p. 203.

[10] *Ibid.*, p. 14.

[11] *Ibid.*, p. 158.

[12] *Ibid.*, p. 145.

[13] *Ibid.*, p. 188.

[14] *Ibid.*, pp. 62, 65.

[15] *Ibid.*, p. 107.

[16] *Ibid.*, p. 38.

[17] *Ibid.*, p. 88.

[18] *Ibid.*, p. 102.

[19] *Ibid.*, p. 133.

[20] *Ibid.*, pp. 214-60. John Becher testified on March 11 and 14; his testimony was the most lengthy of any witness before the Lords' Committee.

[21] *Ibid.*, p. 215.

[22] John Becher, *The Anti-Pauper System*, (London, 1828), p. 2. Also, see J. D. Marshall, "The Nottinghamshire Reformers and their Contribution to the New Poor Law" in *Economic History Review*, 2nd ser., Vol. XIII, No. 3 (April, 1961), 254-57.

[23] *Third Report from the S. C. on Emigration*, p. 401.

[24] Becher, *Anti-Pauper System*, p. 37. This was the George Nicholls who wrote the history of the Poor Laws.

[25] *Ibid.*, p. 40.

[26] *Ibid.*, p. 15.

[27] *Report from S. C. of the House of Lords on the Poor Laws*, p. 222.

[28] *Ibid.*, pp. 172-86.

[29] *Ibid.*, p. 82. For other cases of Benthamite dispauperizing schemes, see the testimony of Joseph Francis Faithful, pp. 266-68, and Francis Pym, pp. 316-33.

[30] *Parliamentary Debates*, 3rd Ser., III, 11.

[31] 1 and 2 Will. IV. C. 42.

[32] *Parliamentary Debates*, 3rd Ser., VIII, 498.

[33] 1 and 2 Will. IV. C. 59.

[34] *Parliamentary Debates*, 3rd ser., XI, 288.

[35] George Nicholls, *History of the English Poor Laws*, III, 202-3.

[36] *Ibid.*, II, 203. Sir George Nicholls, for example, still held to this view as late as 1854 when he wrote his famous history of the Poor Laws.

[37] *Parliamentary Debates*, 3rd Ser. I, 371-75.

[38] *Ibid.*, I, 603, 687-90.

[39] *Ibid.*, IV, 358.

[40] *Ibid.*, IX, 1099.

[41] *Ibid.*, IX, 1144.

[42] 2 and 3 Will. IV, C. 96. As this was a temporary measure Nicholls did not think it was necessary to comment on it.

[43] *Parliamentary Debates*, 3rd Ser., IV, 501, V, 310. See Webb, *Old Poor Law*, p. 274.

[44] *Ibid.*, VIII, 699.

[45] *Ibid.*, 831.

[46] *Ibid.*, 8-9.

[47] John Bowring, ed., *Bentham's Works*, XI, 97.

[48] *Ibid.*, 102.

[49] *Ibid.*, 103.

[50] In 1838 Sir Edwin Chadwick printed and circulated Bentham's tract, "Observations of the Poor Bill," as a defense of the New Poor Law. When Sir

John Bowring, Bentham's literary executor, published the major edition of his works, he pointed out in his introduction that many provisions of the Poor Law Amendment were identical to Bentham's plan of pauper management. See Volume VIII, 358.

[51] Nassau Senior, *Three Lectures on the Rate of Wages*, p. IV.

[52] *Ibid.*, p. VI.

[53] *Ibid.*, p. VII.

[54] *Edinburgh Review*, No. 105 (March, 1931), p. 44.

[55] McCulloch, *Principles of Political Economy*, 2nd Ed., p. 411.

[56] *Ibid.*, p. 420; O'Brien, *J. R. McCulloch*, p. 330. For my comment on O'Brien's views, see p. 402, note 76.

[57] *Ibid.*, p. 421.

[58] *Edinburgh Review*, No. 104 (January, 1831), p. 337.

[59] *Ibid.*, p. 346.

[60] *Ibid.*, pp. 351-52.

[61] J. R. Poynter, *Society and Pauperism*, pp. 304-5. Poynter fails to understand that McCulloch wanted to revert to the law of 1722 in order to use the workhouse as a deterrent.

IX

THE RADICAL INVESTIGATION
OF THE POOR LAWS IN 1832

WHO were the Radicals of 1832 bold enough to undertake the drastic reform of the Poor Laws? They were a small group of politicians, statesmen, and intellectuals who shared the legislative principles of Jeremy Bentham and the economic doctrines of David Ricardo. Their common heritage gave them coherence and a sense of direction. This remarkable group of men formed a temporary union of economists and political scientists. Although the union was as unstable as a marriage made in Hollywood, it had some remarkable results. The Radicals had a major responsibility for the passing of the Reform Bill, the abolition of slavery, the amelioration of the factory system, and the reform of the Poor Laws.

James Mill, above others in the group, had successfully combined the economics of Ricardo with the politics of Bentham. A disciple of both men, he propagated their teachings through his own writings. His activities in Westminster politics inspired his followers with a desire to participate in practical affairs. Through the agency of the Political Economy Club, of which he was a founder, the Radicals associated with the political-economy minded leaders of the Whig government and consequently exerted an influence far beyond their numbers.

During the 1820's John R. McCulloch's influence among the Radicals was second only to that of James Mill. McCulloch continued to advocate Ricardo's principles in the Political Economy

Club after James Mill ceased to attend the meetings and before John Stuart Mill had become a member. As the principal writer for the *Edinburgh Review* on economic questions, he helped to formulate the Whig policy on the Poor Laws. He was one of the strongest exponents of using the Poor Laws to control the growth of population and to spur on the industry of the working classes; one of those who wanted the workhouses returned to the place they had occupied prior to 1795 when they were supposed to have been the means of checking the growth of the poor rates. Even though he continued to hold the doctrine of natural liberty as the central principle of his science, he had become increasingly convinced that the Poor Law could not be entirely abolished but might properly be used to curtail excess population and reduce the redundant labor supply.

McCulloch can be regarded as the voice of the Edinburgh Whigs who were well represented in the House of Commons by Joseph Hume and Henry Brougham. Although Hume and Brougham were too arrogant to be agreeable colleagues, they were so industrious and well informed that they became indispensable to the Whigs. When the Whig Ministry was formed in 1830 Brougham, who was disliked and mistrusted by the Whigs, was created a peer and sent to the Upper House as the Lord Chancellor.

There were other reforming Whigs who may be regarded as a part of the Edinburgh contingency. A few aristocratic Whig families, at the turn of the century, preferred what they regarded as the enlightened education of the Scottish universities to the more traditional teaching at Oxford and Cambridge. Prominent among the Whigs of Scottish training were Lord John Russell, Thomas Spring Rice, and Lord Lansdowne. These men had the common experience at the University of Edinburgh of sharing Dugald Stewart's lectures in moral philosophy and political economy.

Comparable to the Scottish contingency of the Whigs was the Liberal faction of the Tory party. During the 1820's the Liberal Tories, those seeking to apply economic principles in shaping economic policy, exercised greater leadership in the ministry of George Canning. Just as there were prominent Whigs serving in the Tory Governments of Canning and Goderich, so there were Liberal Tories who eagerly joined Lord Grey's Government in 1830.

While the Liberal Tories were exercising a larger leadership in the Governments of Canning and Goderich, the defenders of the traditional Poor Laws, Lords Bexley and Harrowby, were disregarded as advisors on economic policy. The Ultra-Tories, who had championed the Poor Laws along with the other existing arrangements in Church and State, suffered a decline in political influence when Wellington and Peel accepted Catholic emancipation. The passing of the Reform Bill in 1832 further weakened the Ultra-Tories and especially impaired the reputations of those Bishops who had voted against the measure in the Upper House.

Because of the fragmented condition of both major political parties in 1832, the Poor Laws, as reformed by the Tories under the younger William Pitt, were virtually defenseless. The Evangelicals, the "Saints" who had done so much to ameliorate the condition of the working classes, were as badly divided and disorganized as were the political parties. The London leaders, members of the Clapham Sect, had already abandoned the reform of the Poor Laws as one of their righteous causes. As shown in the many volumes of the *Christian Observer*, the metropolitan Evangelicals had turned their attention from the defense of public relief to the promotion of private charity and education as the best methods of coping with the complex problems of pauperism. Although the Christian promoters of benevolent causes were divided on several issues of the day, they could still unite in the national agitation to abolish colonial slavery. But even in this crusade, the provincial Evangelicals in Birmingham and Manchester were exercising an independent leadership and employing methods of their own designing. In the case of factory legislation, the centers of the agitation for reform were in the new industrial areas of Lancashire and Yorkshire. The recognized spokesman in the House of Commons for the provincial Evangelicals was Thomas Michael Sadler. He was at once the best-known defender of the Poor Laws as well as the champion of factory legislation. Although Sadler had made many enemies by his opposition both to Catholic emancipation and to the Reform Bill, he was able to obtain a committee of the House of Commons to investigate factory conditions. After a long and arduous investigation, he introduced a bill in keeping with the humanitarian reforms endorsed by the Evangelicals of Leeds. When he was defeated during the election of the first reformed Parliament, the northern Evangelicals obtained Lord Ashley to be their exponent of factory legislation in the House of Commons. The Whig Government, however, was reluctant to leave so vital a question in Tory hands, and appointed its own Factory Commission to counteract Sadler's investigation. On the basis of its recommendations, the Whigs introduced a factory bill, which was unacceptable to Lord Ashley. The Whigs, then, were clearly opposed to Sadler on questions of both the Poor Laws and factory legislation.

The Factory Commission was one of three royal commissions appointed by the Whig Government to conduct mammoth investigations into social, political, and economic conditions. In addition to the Factory Commission and the Poor Law Commission, the Whigs also appointed a Royal Commission to investigate municipal corporations.

The commission of inquiry was a well-established procedure by 1832, having been used many times by previous Tory Governments. No fewer than sixty commissions had been appointed between 1800 and 1832.[1] It was the first time, however, that a commission had been appointed to investigate the Poor Laws. Those Whigs making the decision to investigate by commission had faith in the new sciences of legislation and political economy. To many of the Whigs, as well as to the Radicals, it seemed possible that "Bacon's dream of an inductive philosophy based upon a careful preparation of factual evidence was becoming a reality in the realm of social affairs."[2] Some of the Radicals held a firm belief that the commission could be used to disseminate scientific knowledge among the industrious classes. That others regarded the commission as a useful instrument of political propaganda did not hinder the aspirations of those who wished to educate the working classes in the principles of political economy.

The Radicals who undertook the investigation of the Poor Laws were conscious of the proper methods of investigating social and economic conditions. They had before them the supreme model of Adam Smith's *Inquiry into the Nature and Causes of the Wealth of Nations*. In his article, "Of the Expense of the Institutions for the Education of Youth," Smith explained the proper method of moral philosophy: the moral philosophers should collect the maxims of prudence and morality and connect them together "by one or more general principles from which they were all deductible, like effects from their natural causes."[3]

Adam Smith's method of investigation was implicit in his work and probably would not have become explicit without the systematic exposition of Dugald Stewart. In developing scientific methods of investigation Stewart had great influence; he not only gained preeminence as a teacher of moral philosophy at the University of Edinburgh, but he also gained fame as one of the early professors of political economy.[4]

Dugald Stewart was born in 1753 at Edinburgh, where his father, Matthew Stewart, was a professor of mathematics at the University of Edinburgh. In addition to an early training in mathematics, Dugald studied political economy under Adam Ferguson and then went to the University of Glasgow in 1771 to study moral philosophy with Thomas Reid, who had been appointed to succeed Adam Smith. The following year he returned to Edinburgh to teach mathematics. He was appointed professor of mathematics in 1775 and continued to teach that subject until his appointment as professor of moral philosophy in 1785 to succeed Adam Ferguson. After teaching this subject for twenty-four years, he resigned in 1809 to spend the rest of his life publishing and republishing the several editions of his lectures on moral philosophy. The last volume of his edited works, *The Elements of the Philosophy of the Human Mind*, appeared in 1827, just a year before his death. His works continued to be in such demand after his death that they were edited and published in 1855 by William Hamilton.

During his long career as a teacher, he educated more than three thousand students, and before his death, he had the pleasure of seeing many of them rise to places of public leadership. Among those attending his lectures on political economy were Sydney Smith, Francis Horner, Henry Petty, Francis Jeffrey, Henry Reeve, Macvey Napier, and Henry Brougham.[5] Stewart thus contributed substantially to the education of several leaders of the Whig party and to the editors of the *Edinburgh Review*.

Dugald Stewart's influence on his students was practical and moral. He imparted to them his faith that they too could contribute to scientific knowledge and apply science to the solution of social problems. He inspired his students, moreover, to believe that Adam Smith had achieved a social science as reliable as the physical discoveries of Kepler and Newton.[6]

In expounding Adam Smith's method of investigation, Dugald Stewart developed his own theory of knowledge based upon observation and induction. By observation he meant the common experience of scientists and philosophers in all ages and places. Only the wisdom of the philosophers, the maxims of the ages, could supply the factual data on which to build a social science. Once maxims had been systematically arranged according to a few connecting principles, a science could be achieved.[7] Even history, if written by a philosopher, "could be made to yield the necessary materials for the construction of a Newtonian science of man."[8]

In teaching Adam Smith's *Wealth of Nations*, Dugald Stewart persistently took the position that he was expounding a social science as reliable and useful as mechanics and physics. In the Preface to his *Dissertations*, first published in 1815, he informed his readers that he would confine his observations to metaphysics, ethics, and political philosophy. He went on to explain metaphysics as the philosophy of the human mind and political philosophy as "the modern science of political economy."[9] In the *Elements of the Human Mind*, he further defined philosophy in Smith's own words, "the science of the connecting principles of nature."[10] The science of political economy he regarded as an invisible chain, like the law of gravity, which bound together all disjointed objects and incoherent events and introduced order into the chaos of appearances.

What was Smith's principle, or natural law, which, in Stewart's opinion, was to be placed alongside Newton's law of gravity? It was a principle of psychology, a universal motive, the desire of every man to better his condition. "It has long been an established principle among the most judicious and enlightened philosophers that, as the desire of bettering our condition appears equally from a careful review of the motives which habitually influence our conduct and from a general survey of the history of our species to be the master spring of human industry. . . ."[11]

During his long career as a teacher of moral philosophy, Stewart was continually thrown on the defensive by statesmen, legislators, and common law barristers who rejected his doctrines as being too speculative. In developing his polemics against this constant criticism, he grew increasingly hostile to several groups of practical men whom he regarded as bad theorists. He readily assumed that all men who dealt with the subject matter of political economy were necessarily theorists. When barristers, shopkeepers, and country gentlemen attempted to generalize from their limited and circumscribed experience, they became bad theorists who hindered the growth of scientific knowledge.

Stewart grew increasingly militant against practical men. He especially regarded the political arithmeticians as being among the most unreliable practical men, for they continued to defend the Corn and Navigation Laws against the doctrine of natural liberty. He likewise opposed the statisticians, for they "invariably encour-

age a predilection for restraints and all the other technical combinations of an antiquated and scholastic policy. . . ."[12]

In his defense of Adam Smith's doctrine of natural liberty,
Stewart taught his students to distrust practical men who relied
upon the narrow range of facts common to their experience. True
science, which is drawn from the general interest of the human
race, Stewart thought, must always add to the sum of human
happiness; in contrast to the general utility of science, a knowledge of particular facts "tends only to disturb our tranquility."[13]

The true social scientist, according to Stewart, would proceed
in the same manner that Newton investigated the physical world.
In his *Outline of Moral Philosophy*, a student's handbook, Stewart
laid down these methods of scientific investigation. The first step
is "to ascertain the simple and general laws on which the compli-
cated phenomena of the universe depend". After obtaining these
laws, we may then reason concerning the effect resulting from any
given combination of them. In the former instance we may be said
to carry on our inquiries in the way of analysis; in the latter that of
synthesis — or in Bacon's words, "scala ascensoria and desensoria."[14]

While encouraging his students to undertake the investigation of
social conditions, he warned them against the errors that hinder
scientific progress in all areas. The principal errors were "a habit of
abstract thought uncorrected by experience and a habit of unenlightened practice without the aid of general principles. . . ."[15]
The latter error was more common than the former; it was an
error made often by practical men who would consider only established institutions as the basis for their conclusions. The political
scientist, Stewart argued, should not limit himself to the experience derived from established institutions but should reason from
the known principles of human nature. While admitting there were
dangers from hasty speculation, he thought these were not so great
as the difficulties arising from "an unenlightened veneration for
maxims which are supposed to have the sanction of time in their
favour." The social scientist, he insisted, should avoid not only the
venerable maxims but also "the danger of dwelling too much on
details and rendering the mind incapable of those abstract and
comprehensive views of human affairs which can alone furnish
the statesman with fixed and certain maxims for the regulation of
his conduct."[16]

In the light of Dugald Stewart's teaching, one can better understand the careers of such Radical reformers as Joseph Hume and

Henry Brougham. Brougham's remarkable career was very largely influenced by the knowledge which he brought with him from Edinburgh. His scientific curiosity remained unsatiated throughout his career as political reformer, and he always thought of himself as a promoter of scientific knowledge.[17]

Although lacking Brougham's forensic abilities, Joseph Hume was no less certain of his own intellectual superiority. His doctrinaire intransigence prevented his rising to the leadership of the Radical faction in the House of Commons, but his thorough knowledge of law and political economy enabled him to remain the most persistent champion of Radical reform for nearly two decades. As it turned out, the intellectual independence of the Parliamentary Radicals prevented anyone from asserting leadership over them.[18]

If James Mill had been able to buy a seat in the House of Commons, he might have become the leader of the Parliamentary Radicals. Lacking that affluence, he remained their leader outside Parliament until his death in 1836. As one of Dugald Stewart's students, James Mill paid tribute to the formative influence of his teaching. "The taste for the studies which have formed my favourite pursuits and which will continue to do so to the end of my life, I owe to him."[19] In his major works, Mill attempted to apply Stewart's methods of inquiry. In his multi-volume *History of India*, he applied Stewart's method of "conjectural history."[20] When writing his last major work, *Analysis of the Phenomena of the Human Mind*, Mill paid still another tribute to Stewart's influence.[21]

Although Mill first learned political economy from Stewart's lectures of Edinburgh, he departed from those practical doctrines to become increasingly abstract and deductive in his reasoning. While striving to make the principles of political economy as clear and concise as the axioms of mathematics, Mill encountered the growing hostility of men who accused him of being too speculative. In defense of his method, Mill restated on numerous occasions Stewart's polemic against practical men. To the end of his life he continued to wage war on practical men, insisting, as Stewart had done three decades earlier, that practical men were merely bad theorists, deriving their theory from established institutions and the limited range of their own experience. Mill saw no inherent conflict, however, between theory and practice, and he continued to believe that "good abstract principles are the accumulated results of experience presented in an exceedingly condensed and concentrated state."[22]

Richard Whately's views on the methods of political economy were quite similar to those of James Mill. As professor of moral philosophy at Oxford, Whately had revived the teaching of logic at the University during the 1820's. He had taught Nassau Senior moral philosophy, encouraged his first lectures on political economy, and then succeeded him when Senior accepted a similar chair at King's College, London University. The two Oxford scholars continued to collaborate in the attempt to improve the methods of the social sciences.[23]

Both Senior and Whately became advisers to the Whig Government on questions of economic and social policy. In 1831 Lord Melbourne, at the Home Office, appointed Senior to investigate labor unrest and the following year made him one of the Poor Law Commissioners. At about the same time, the Whig Government elevated Whately to the Archdiocese of Dublin and a year later appointed him to head an investigation of pauperism in Ireland. The Archbishop's predilection for the new disciplines of social science induced him to appoint the first professor of political economy at the University of Dublin.

In his *Elements of Logic*, Whately regarded political economy as a science more like physics than like geology: in essence, one of deductive reasoning, not one of massive factual data resembling geology. In his enthusiasm for political economy as a science, Whately compared the discoveries of Smith and Malthus with those of Sir Humphry Davy. The two greatest political economists, according to Whately, had established the science of political economy on facts open to the observation of everyone; their genius lay in the exercise of judgment as to the degree of evidence in their premises and in the skills with which they combined premises to reach previously unthought of conclusions.[24]

Whately and Senior were conscious of themselves as the founders of the new science of political economy at Oxford. They were also aware that the chief opponents of their science were those practical men, politicians and common law barristers, who reason from the evidence of their confined experience, not from the universal experience of men in other times and places.[25]

On the grounds of scientific procedure, Senior and Whately opposed the traditional method of investigation used by Parliamentary committees of inquiry. They insisted that the House of Commons' collection of facts from history and statistics led to no theory or to an erroneous one. The correct investigations of poverty, they thought, should show an acquaintance with the leading principles of political economy. The investigator should always begin his inquiry by asking the central question about the creation of wealth rather than the insulated questions about poverty.[26]

According to the methods of Senior and Whately, the investigation into the poverty and pauperism of England and Ireland should be undertaken only by those men who were acquainted with the principles of political economy.[27] The learned opinion of the political economist was to be given precedence over the testimony of such practical men as the overseer of the poor and the justice of the peace who were responsible Poor Law officials. To what extent the Whig Government acted upon the advice of Senior and Whately is difficult to say, but it is clear that several of the Poor Law Commissioners and the Assistant Commissioners serving under them were political economists who held doctrinaire, Radical attitudes toward the Poor Laws.

At the time the Poor Law Commissioners were conducting their investigations of poverty, the young John Stuart Mill was attempting to appraise the reliability of the methods of such an undertaking. During the years 1830 and 1831 Mill wrote his first book on economics, *Essays on Some Unsettled Questions of Political Economy*.[28] He was unable, however, to find a publisher for the *Essays* until 1844, after he had achieved unexpected success with his *System of Logic*. The essay on method, which he thought the most important of the group, was published before the others, in the *London and Westminster Review*.[29] Although the essay on method, rewritten in 1833, had no influence on the Radical investigation of the Poor Laws, it clearly shows many of the scientific attitudes that prevailed at the time.

John Mill had gone as far as he could with the logic inherited from his father. This early training left him stymied by the unresolved paradox of the difference between logical discovery and physical discovery. In developing his logic of the social sciences, John Mill remained frustrated for five years, unable to progress beyond the methods of Stewart and Whately. When William Whewell published, in 1837, his *History of Inductive Science*, Mill was still at the impasse he had reached five years before. Whewell's *History*, as Mill says, enabled him to cross the threshold into a better understanding of the inductive sciences.[30]

213

Mill's essay on method, published first in 1836, was entitled, "On the Definition of Political Economy and on the Method of Philosophical Investigation in that Science." After he had advanced in his understanding of scientific method, he republished the essay with the title, "On the Definition of Political Economy and on the Method of Investigation Proper to It." As he progressed further with his logic, he was able to discern more clearly the differences between the social and the physical sciences.

John Mill first undertook the writing of the essay on method in order to correct some of the logical mistakes which he had been taught by his father. He differed with him, for example, on the definition of political economy, denying his assertion that "political economy is to the state what domestic economy is to the family." John asserted the view that "political economy is really... a science; but domestic economy is an art."[31] Yet he agreed with his father in regarding political economy as an abstract science. It reasoned from assumptions, not from fact; and like geometry, it was built on hypotheses. Such a science, he thought, was essentially paradoxical inasmuch as its first principles, or its fundamentals, were the last to be discovered.[32]

John Mill was especially hopeful of bringing to an end the long war which his father and other political economists had waged against practical men. He thought the ancient feud between men of theory and men of practice was "one of the greatest misfortunes of modern times." "The separation of theory from practice — of studies of the closet from the outward business of the world — has given a wrong bias to the ideas and feelings of the student and of the man of business."[33] Mill determined to end the feud between theory and practice in order to improve both science and policy. The best policy-maker, in his view, was the statesman with a knowledge of science and a broad practical experience.

Although Mill thought the essay on the scope and method was the most important of his five early essays on political economy, he hesitated to publish it so long as his father lived. When his father died in 1836, John felt "exempted from the restraints and reticences" which filial gratitude had imposed on him.[34] After being freed from the elder Mill's influences, John came to regard his father as the last eighteenth-century man, as one of the last intellectual representatives of the Scottish enlightenment. In the same vein, it might be said that the Radical reforms of the 1830's,

214

the Reform Bill and Poor Law Amendment Act, were the long-delayed achievements of eighteenth-century men.

The persons appointed to serve on the Poor Law Commission belonged to two diverse groups who may be viewed as the dignified members and the effective members. The dignified members, who were busy in other occupations, lent their prestige and credibility to the Commission. The three dignified members were John Bird Sumner, Bishop of Chester; Charles James Blomfield, Bishop of London; and William Sturges Bourne, Tory member of the House of Commons. In books, pamphlets, published speeches, and Parliamentary testimony, these three members had recorded their opposition to the existing Poor Laws. Sumner, the most distinguished of the three, was the author of a Malthusian treatise, *Records of Creation*.[35] He was as famous for his political economy as for his theology at the time he was elevated to Bishop of Chester to succeed Blomfield, who had been elevated to the See of London. While serving as the Bishop of the great industrial Diocese of Chester, Blomfield appeared before the Committee on Emigration in support of government subsidies for emigration as a remedy for redundant population.[36] Sturges Bourne, who had presided over the Poor Law Committee of 1817, was the principal Tory exponent of Poor Law reform in the House of Commons.[37]

The effective members of the Commission, the fact-finders and reporters, were drawn chiefly from a small circle of London intellectuals, either from the political economists, the friends of Nassau Senior, or from the Benthamite lawyers, the friends of Walter Coulson. Senior, the most active member of the Commission, had already built up a lucrative legal practice and had become the chief economic adviser to the Whig Government.[38] Like Senior, Walter Coulson was a member of the Political Economy Club and a trained lawyer. In addition to his experience as a conveyancer, he had been an editor and had served as one of Bentham's several secretaries.[39]

During the years of the Poor Law inquiry, the Political Economy Club stood as a shadow government for economic policy. Members of the Whig Government, with primary responsibility for economic affairs, were also members of the Political Economy Club. Lord Althorp, leader in the House of Commons and Chancellor of Exchequer, had been a member of the Club since 1823. Charles Poulett Thomson, Vice-President of the Board of Trade, was elected to membership in 1828. The successor to Althorp as Chancellor of the Exchequer, Thomas Spring Rice, was elected to the Club in 1832. Six of the seven members elected from 1832 to 1834 were associated, in one way or another, with the investigation of the Poor Laws. One of the six new members, Edwin Chadwick, was elected in 1834.[40]

Although not a member of the Poor Law Commission when it was first formed, Edwin Chadwick was appointed a member in April, 1833. Prior to his appointment, however, he had served as an Assistant Commissioner; but unlike the other Assistants, he was paid a retainer's fee and was able to give his full time to the investigation.[41]

Edwin Chadwick, whose influence on the Poor Law Commission was second only to that of Nassau Senior, was one of the last of Jeremy Bentham's converts and one of his ablest and most devoted disciples.

Born in 1800 in a village near Manchester, Edwin was the son of James Chadwick, a friend and follower of Tom Paine.[42] Edwin received his first education in an elementary school at Longsight near Manchester. After moving to London at the age of ten, he received further education at the hands of private tutors in classical and modern languages. His legal education began at the age of fifteen when his father placed him in an attorney's office. In 1823 he was admitted to the Society of the Inner Temple to continue his reading for the Bar. While studying law, he made a meager living as a reporter for the *Morning Herald*. Although a diligent student of law, he struggled hard for several years to gain recognition as a journalist. When he was admitted to the Bar at the age of thirty, he was an editorial assistant to Albany Fonblanque for the *Examiner*.

While still a law student and struggling journalist, Chadwick became acquainted with the Benthamites, Doctors Neil Arnott and Southwood Smith. His association with these physicians made him familiar with the social problems of sanitation and public health. He also became a member of the Utilitarian Society, which had been formed by John Mill and other younger Benthamites.[43] At the home of George Grote, where the Utilitarians frequently met, Chadwick joined in debating the great questions of political economy.

As an exponent of Utilitarianism, Chadwick wrote an article on insurance, which was published in 1828 by the *Westminster Re-*

view. The article came to the attention of Nassau Senior, who invited him to contribute to the *London Review*, a journal which he and Whately had recently founded. To this invitation, Chadwick responded with two articles, one on medieval French charities and the other on law enforcement and penal reform.[44]

As a consequence of the article on penal reform, Jeremy Bentham invited Chadwick to become his secretary. Early in 1831 Chadwick accepted the invitation that made him a member of the venerable philosopher's household. Serving as Bentham's secretary was a rare opportunity but also a lamentable experience, for it proved to be the last year of the old man's life. Chadwick spent these twelve months nursing him through his last illness. In gratitude for such faithful service, Bentham rewarded him with a small legacy.[45]

Bentham had been blessed with longevity, enabling him to complete his mammoth *Constitutional Code*. After thirty years of deviating from his main objective and after writing scores of memoranda applying Utilitarian principles to the pressing problems of the day, he had finally succeeded in bringing his writings together in a systematic whole. He was able, therefore, to bequeath much more to Chadwick than the legacy specified in his will. He left a rich storehouse of remedies for all the social and political diseases which still plagued society at the time of his death.

With the enthusiasm of a youthful convert, Chadwick accepted Bentham's prescriptions for the social ills that had baffled other reformers. He adopted as his own Bentham's schemes of reform, including national agencies of inspection and control. He determined to follow Bentham's principle of substituting contract-management, or paid public officials for trustee management of the aristocratically-appointed justices of the peace. He was one of the few who fully understood and readily accepted the Radical principles of pauper management. As one of Bentham's last disciples, he regarded the old philosopher's "History of the Long War with George III" as a last commission to effect a Radical reform of the Poor Laws.

That Chadwick had accepted Utilitarian principles before his appointment as Bentham's secretary was made clear in his *Westminster Review* article on insurance. The article showed more than a familiarity with the actuarial basis for life insurance; it was more than a defense of Friendly Societies. A substantial part of the article was a digression of four pages criticizing the methods followed by the House of Commons in investigating social and economic conditions. In proposing new methods for conducting scientific investigations, Chadwick revealed his knowledge of the principles propounded in Whately's *Logic*.[46] In deploring the conservatism of practical men, he quoted Dugald Stewart's polemic against them. Practical men were to be ruled out of court as reliable witnesses and were to be regarded as a source of bad theory. Good theory, he insisted, is derived from connected and well-ascertained facts "more comprehensive by far than the sum of mere routine is likely to possess."[47]

Chadwick showed himself to be a champion of those scientific methods which Senior and Whately strove to improve and publicize. A proper investigation must be guided by the principles of political economy and politics. The theory of natural liberty, with its corollary principles, should provide the general outline, the framework, for a survey of social conditions. True principles would serve as connecting links, joining together a vast body of factual material, illuminating some events and throwing others into shadow. True principles would throw into shadow the testimony of practical men, the magistrates, overseers, and churchwardens. True principles, moreover, would illuminate the testimony of men accustomed to broad generalizing and become the basis for developing better theory. Such were the methods of investigation which were widely accepted at the time the Poor Law Commission was appointed, and some of the Commissioners regarded the Poor Law Inquiry as the first scientific investigation of social conditions.

Before they had appointed the Assistant Commissioners, the Commissioners began the collection of what they regarded as the most important part of their evidence. With the aid of the clerks in the Home Office, they sent questionnaires and letters of instructions to several hundred local officials in a carefully selected group of town and country parishes.[48] The queries were sent out shortly after the appointment of the Commission and were being returned during the summer months of 1832. The answers to these questions supplied many case studies for future investigation by the Assistant Commissioners.

The tasks of framing the questions and selecting the persons to whom they should be sent proved to be more complex than the Commissioners had foreseen. Their questions evoked such a variety of answers that the Commissioners had to alter the rural questions twice. As originally framed the questions were so doctrinaire that they could not be answered. Since the questions were designed to evoke opinion as well as fact, many replies were too discursive to be tabulated. Some of the questions, moreover, assumed the existence of factual data which many of the rural parishes had never recorded. Other questions evoked lengthy explanations from some respondents and categorial replies from others; indeed, the rural questions baffled the local officials as much as their answers perplexed the Commissioners.

In addition to the doctrinaire bias inherent in their methods of investigation, the Commissioners' vision was distorted by the Radical opposition to the Poor Laws that had accumulated since the Report of 1817. Their bias determined what places were chosen for their examination. Like the Radical reformers of the 1820's, they assumed that conditions were worse in agricultural areas than in industrial areas. They further assumed that bad Poor Law administration caused the distress, and that the superior administration in the northern counties accounted for the better conditions of the working classes. Guided by this doctrinaire view of the southern and northern counties, the Commissioners intensively investigated a few counties in each area to show the inherent tendencies of good and bad administration. This bias caused them to neglect or scarcely touch a majority of the counties.

Because the Commissioners assumed that the Poor Laws were generally well administered in the towns and cities, they investigated urban conditions less thoroughly than rural areas. Although only one set of questions was sent to the towns, the replies could hardly be reduced to a usable body of information. The same set of questions, often controversial, was sent to a wide variety of persons, including magistrates, overseers, churchwardens, guardians, landowners, and occupiers. Some of the respondents, lacking sources of information, could only estimate conditions; other respondents, having jurisdiction over a wide area, as in the case of a magistrate, gave answers which sometimes contradicted the replies of parochial officials.

In addition to circulating the town and rural questions, the Commissioners drew up instructions for the Assistant Commissioners.[49] After determining the scope and character of the investigation, they left the task of writing the instructions in the hands of Nassau Senior.[50]

The instructions to the Assistant Commissioners outlined the scope of the investigation, defined the procedures to be followed, and suggested the conclusions that they were expected to reach. In general, the instructions reasserted the conclusions reached by the Poor Law Committee of 1817. Before the Assistants had begun their investigation, the Commissioners declared their intention of returning to the administration of the Poor Laws that had existed prior to 1795 and of reestablishing the workhouse as a shield for the rates. They clearly intended to retain the 43rd of Elizabeth I as a necessary means of limiting the number of laborers, for they thought the original Poor Law had achieved "the adequation of their numbers to the demand for labour."[51]

The Commissioners further indicated in 1832 that they had no intention of eliminating relief for the impotent; but they were already determined to modify the bastardy laws. They expressed the opinion that the Poor Laws "operate as a punishment to the father, a pecuniary reward to the mother, and a means by which the woman obtains a husband, and her parish rids itself of parishioners." Although aid to the impotent was not to be eliminated, the Assistants were instructed to discover "the degree in which the public provision for sickness and old age interferes with the exercise of prudence."[52]

The Commissioners concentrated their attention on relief to able-bodied persons employed by individuals. They regarded the allowance system in all its forms, whether roundsmen, labor-rate, or bread scales, as their primary target. Seeking to discredit outdoor relief, they instructed the Assistant Commissioners to determine what effects the allowance system had on "the industry, habits, and character of labourers, the increase in population, the rate of wages, the profits of farming, the increase or diminution of farming capital, and the rent and improvement of land."[53]

Recognizing the existence of unemployment, the Commissioners accounted for it in terms of the corrupting influence of poor relief. They required their Assistants to "distinguish between those cases of redundant population in which there are more labourers than could be profitably employed at the existing prices of produce, although the labourers were intelligent and industrious and the farmers wealthy; and those in which the redundancy is occasioned either by the want of capital among the farmers, or by the indolence or unskilled habits of the labourers."[54] Thus committed to the belief that the Poor Laws stimulated a redundant

220

population, the Commissioners were unable to escape from a moralistic explanation of unemployment.

The Commissioners were not unaware of the assumptions which underlay their investigations. There were two general inquiries, they said, "to which each specific inquiry may be made subservient. One is the great question. . .how far the proprietors of land and capital appear to have the power and will to create, or increase or render secure, the prosperity and morality of those who live by the wages of labour." A lesser assumption was that the Poor Law, before 1795, had been the means of creating "the industry, orderly habits, and the adequation of their numbers to the demand for labour, which within the memory of man distinguished the English labourers." They further assumed that the Poor Law, as administered after 1795, caused "the idleness, profligacy, and improvidence, which now debase the character and increase the numbers of the population of many of the southeastern districts. . . ."[55]

The other great question, according to the Commissioners, was "how far the evils of the present system. . .are diminishing, stationary, or increasing." They recognized that the pauperism could be extirpated only "with immediate local suffering." "If, however, the present evils, oppressive as they are, appear to be diminishing, or even to be stationary, it may be more prudent to endure them, than to encounter the certain inconvenience, and the probable hazard, of any extensive change." While the Commissioners delegated to the Assistant Commissioners the heavy duty of determining the extent of pauperism, they had already concluded, even before they had appointed the Assistants, that the disease had spread so far that it could not be stopped by "mere palliative amendments."

The instructions prepared by the Commissioners were so extensive, abstruse, and unrealistic that the Assistant Commissioners could not follow them except in broad outline. Moreover, because they were unpaid, "few fit persons" could be found who would undertake such difficult and onerous duties. The few zealous reformers who volunteered their services were assigned districts too large to "make a full or even cursory inquiry of each parish." Each assistant was permitted to select the parishes in which he might collect "those facts from which some general inference may be drawn and which form the rule rather than the exception."[56]

Appointed in August, 1832, the Assistant Commissioners were requested to have their reports ready by the end of November that they might be presented to Parliament in January of the following year. As only a few of the Assistants had met the deadline, Lord Melbourne, on December 3, sent an urgent letter requesting them to report promptly. Several reports reached the Home Office by the end of December, some came in during January, and others in February. It was not until March 19, 1833, that the Commissioners were able to present a preliminary report to Lord Melbourne.[57]

The Commissioners also decided to publish the results of their preliminary investigation in a popular form, not merely for the benefit of the many new members of the reformed Parliament but for the education of the public as well. Published in octavo, rather than the usual folio form, the early report was entitled, *Extracts from the Information Received by His Majesty's Commissioners as to the Administration and Operation of the Poor Laws*. The *Extracts* were widely circulated as an ordinary book and were reviewed by journals and newspapers.[58]

The Commissioners expected their report to be a means of educating the working classes in political economy and in preparing them to accept a drastic reform of the Poor Laws. Although the Commissioners were not prepared to submit their final report, they had already made up their minds to go beyond "palliative amendments," for they had discovered "proof that the maladministration, which was supposed to be principally confined to some of the agricultural districts, appears to have spread over almost every part of the country, and into the manufacturing towns — the proof that actual intimidation, directed against those who are, or are supposed to be unfavourable to profuse relief, is one of the most extensive sources of maladministration, — and the proof that the evil, though checked in some places by extraordinary energy and talents, is, on the whole, speedily and rapidly progressive."[59]

In preparing the preliminary report for the opening of Parliament, the Commissioners found it necessary to work in great haste. As the tardy reports came in from the Assistants, the Commissioners sent them to the printer without attempting to summarize or systematize them. The result was that they published sixteen separate and conflicting reports. To save further time, they constructed beforehand an elaborate index of the subjects about which they expected to receive information. Standing in the place of a table of contents, the index was derived from the instructions which they had previously given to the Assistants at the time of their appointments. Inasmuch as the instructions had not proposed a remedy for abuses, it was necessary for the Commissioners to index the report of one of the Assistants separately, giving to it such a preponderance that the evidence in the other reports was distorted.

Two of the seven Commissioners, Nassau Senior and the Reverend Henry Bishop, supplemented the reports of the Assistant Commissioners by undertaking their own investigations. Together they went to Royston, Herts, where some of the population were also resident in Cambridgeshire. At Royston they collected information showing the evil consequences of the interference by the Cambridge magistrates. By making a separate inquiry the two Commissioners were able to discredit the report of the Assistant Commissioner, Alfred Power, who had made a friendly appraisal of the Cambridgeshire magistrates.[60]

The evidence against magisterial interference was incorporated in the report of John W. Cowell, a roving Assistant Commissioner, who was given special assignments to supplement the reports of the other Assistants. When the Commissioners adopted the principle of less-eligibility as the remedy for pauperism, they sent Cowell into Nottinghamshire to investigate Becher's anti-pauper system at Bingham and Southwell.[61]

The Commissioners selected other pieces of evidence which they inserted in the *Extracts*. From the hundreds of replies to the rural queries, they published only two, the answers returned from Lenham, Kent, and from Ticehurst, Sussex. Both were strong cases of bad management. They inserted also the results of their investigation of the bankrupt parish of Cholesbury, Berks, "thinking its history might afford an instructive example."[62] The Commissioners selected the atypical cases of Ticehurst, Lenham, and Cholesbury from among fifteen thousand places because they illustrated the ultimate tendencies inherent in the existing Poor Law administration.

The *Extracts* were full of strong cases selected by the Assistant Commissioners to prove what most of them had assumed to be true in principle. Several of the Assistant Commissioners were Malthusians, thoroughly obsessed by the fear of a redundant population and a rapidly growing pauperism. Some assistants shared Ricardo's fear that the rapid growth of poor relief was devouring capital and preventing the farmers from employing labor. All the assistants would probably have agreed with Adam Smith that the Poor Laws violated the principles of natural liberty.

Although the Assistant Commissioners generally opposed the Poor Law, they were far from agreeing among themselves what abuses were the most objectionable. While most of the reports were doctrinaire, some were carefully factual, explaining destitution in terms of economic conditions. Among the latter was the report of John Wilson, which analyzed pauperism as an economic condition rather than a moral disease.[63]

In his report on the conditions in the county of Durham, Wilson disregarded what the Radical reformers had assumed to be true since 1817. He rejected the assumption that the better economic conditions of Durham, as compared with Sussex, resulted from superior Poor Law administration. He reported the allowance system to be in operation in the north, but not as extensively as in the south. "Comparative exemption from the evil in the Northern Counties has been imputed by some as a merit of their inhabitants. They ascribe it to good management. I ascribe it to good fortune," he said. "In the northern division of Northumberland, comparative thinness of population attributable in some degree to the hinding system of hiring laborers — in the district of the Tyne and Wear, employment given by collieries, etc., — in South Durham, indeed throughout the county, recent public works have deferred the evil day of public maintenance. Let anyone of these causes cease to act in its present extent. . . . What ensues? — The process of the southern counties — a process hitherto escaped in many places by mere accident — a process actually commenced in the southern part of this favoured region."[64]

Wilson, moreover, recognized the existence of several kinds of unemployment and that destitution was closely associated with it. He even acknowledged that the survival of an industrial town, such as Darlington, during a depression required some form of relief. He explained why many parishes in the north were free from seasonal employment; because of labor shortages, many farmers provided board and room for the unmarried workers and cottages for men with families. In both cases the laborers had their subsistence even though the work fluctuated with the seasons.

Another Assistant Commissioner, Gilbert Henderson, understood the economic relationship between destitution and unemployment. Technological unemployment caused destitution in Lancashire where the spinning and weaving of cotton cloth were being done increasingly on machines driven by steam engines. "The poor rates," Henderson explained, "have been greatly augmented by the transition from hand to power-loom weaving. The vicissitude affects the whole of the Salford and Blackburn hundreds, which comprise three-fifths of the population of the county, and partially felt in the other hundreds."[65]

Henderson's report also covered the economic conditions of Liverpool and Manchester. In his analysis of these industrial and commercial centers, his competence in statistics and accounting enabled him to make a reliable appraisal of conditions. He knew enough about parochial accounts to separate relief expenses from "payments made for county, highway, and church rates." He was able to comprehend that the best statistical measure of social welfare, in terms of available data, was the rate of relief per capita of population. Using this index he compared the costs of relief in Lancashire with national expenditures. Finding the highest expenditures for the county at Garstang, he investigated the parish and discovered the high costs were due to unemployment resulting from the failure of a print works.

Henry Stuart, Assistant Commissioner for Suffolk, supplied invaluable information with respect to the union of parishes and the management of paupers in workhouses. The Blything Hundred of Suffolk, under a Local Act of Parliament passed in 1764, incorporated forty-six parishes under one board of guardians. The Blything corporation, however, was unable to overcome the persistent unemployment which prevailed after the end of the Napoleonic War. "It is to be lamented," Stuart reported, "that no effectual means have been discovered to bring relief to the unemployed. . . ."[66]

Another Assistant Commissioner who explained destitution in terms of economic conditions was J. W. Pringle. After investigating Carlisle, Cumberland, he recognized the existence of seasonal unemployment, for the number of casual paupers doubled during the four winter months. In some of the neighboring rural parishes, he found that the ancient practice of contracting the poor had survived.[67]

The four assistant Commissioners, Stuart, Pringle, Wilson and Henderson, who had described the economic basis of destitution, made few recommendations for remedial legislation. These four reports, however, were ignored by the Commissioners who continued to concentrate their attention on the abuses of Poor Law administration in the southern counties.

The worst abuses were to be found in the Home Counties and those bordering the Channel. The Commissioners extensively investigated Sussex and drew more examples of bad administration from it than from any other county. One Assistant Commissioner, Ashurst Majendie, was sent to investigate East Sussex and sections of Kent where the riots had originated in 1830. He selected the parish of Lenham, Kent, to show "the effects of a local redundancy of population, a lavish scale of relief, and a general want of control in forcing land from cultivation." His survey of East Sussex, however, added little new information to what the House of Lords' Committee had learned in 1831. Yet Majendie confidently reported the doctrinaire conclusion: "It is most satisfactory to observe in this and all other cases where the allowance system has been abolished that the condition of the labourers has been materially improved."[68]

Charles H. Maclean, another Assistant Commissioner, surveyed West Sussex and parts of Surrey. Although he found much evidence of seasonal unemployment in rural parishes, he concluded only that one of the worst defects of pauper management was the absence "of the wholesome influence of a resident proprietor." His and other reports from several southern counties indicated that no adequate employment could be found during the winter months except digging gravel and road work, conditions which had caused the riots of 1830.

Compared with the exhaustive coverage of Sussex, the investigation of many other counties was so superficial as to be unreliable. The report of Charles P. Villiers consisted of six parishes selected from the four large counties of Warwick, Worcester, Gloucester, and Devon. From a hasty survey of the places, chosen apparently for their accessibility to a tourist's itinerary, Villiers' main conclusion was: "The facts connected with them serve to show the degree in which pauperism may depend upon the administration of the law and the evils which follow from the exercise of power by ill-qualified persons."[69]

The district assigned to D.O.P. Okeden covered parts of Oxford, Wilts, and Dorset. From these counties he chose six places to illustrate good and bad management. By bad management he meant the interference of the magistrates; by good management he meant the oversight of a clergyman who was interested in the material as well as the spiritual life of the parish. Hasilbury Bryan, in Dorset, was chosen because the Reverend Henry Walter was an example of a "rector of great intelligence and the most correct views on the working of the Poor Laws."[70] The parish of Calne, Wilts, on the

226

other hand, was badly managed because it paid no attention to the character of those who received relief. More Crichel, Dorset, was an example of good management, for here there were two resident landowners who had refused to build cottages for thirty years with the beneficial results that there were not enough able-bodied paupers to maintain the county roads. While Okeden was thoroughly Radical in condemning the Poor Laws, his proposed remedies were hardly the sort that Parliament could pass into law.

The Assistant Commissioner for Stratfordshire, D. C. Moylan, might have written his report without leaving his residence in Lincoln's Inn. A barrister, he had only a lawyer's analysis of the Poor Laws. The 43rd of Elizabeth I, he thought, intended only to relieve "the lame, impotent, old, blind," and within this original intent, it was a good law. His principal remedy was a general reform of the Law of Settlement which would confer legal residence only at the place of birth.[71]

Henry and Redmond Pilkington jointly explored the operations of the Poor Laws in the counties of Derby and Leicester. They selected two places in Leicestershire "to illustrate. . .the effects of the worst administration of the Poor Laws in full operation."[72] At Hinckley they found that so much capital had been consumed by the poor rates that "total ruin must ensue not only to farmers but to landlords themselves, unless the government should take their case into consideration. . .and make alteration in the Poor Laws." Their conception of remedial legislation, however, did not extend beyond the recommendation of the Gilbert Union at Shardlow, which had effectively used the workhouse test as a means of keeping down the rates.

Charles H. Cameron and John Wrottesley, who were already serving the government as members of the Charity Commission, investigated only the allowance system in Buckingham. They selected portions of their evidence "to illustrate the effect produced upon the habits of the labouring population, by the way in which parish relief and wages are distributed among them." They reported having found bread scales in every parish except Aylesbury.[73] They denounced the allowance system as confidently as they rejected the doctrine "that destitution, however produced, constitutes a claim to be supported by the community."[74]

By the middle of January, 1833, after nearly all the reports of the Assistant Commissioners had been received, the Central Commissioners came to realize they had succeeded only in condemning Poor Law abuses without providing feasible remedies for such abuses. Although Lord Melbourne had instructed the Assistant Commissioners to select examples of good and bad management, the majority of cases chosen illustrated only the defects of the existing system. The Commissioners, consequently, had little more to recommend to the Whig Ministers than the Sturges Bourne Act, the Tory policy since the Poor Law Report of 1817. As they could not propose a Tory measure to a reformed Parliament, the Commissioners adopted as their own and recommended the only report of the sixteen which had boldly suggested a remedy for the abuses which were so fully condemned.[75]

Of the seventeen Assistant Commissioners whose reports were published in the *Extracts*, only Edwin Chadwick proposed a clear remedy for the disease of pauperism. His report was based on Bentham's principles of pauper management; his main proposal was indoor relief in a Benthamite workhouse as a substitute for outdoor relief and as a means of eliminating family allowances. He also recommended contract management, or salaried officials, for unpaid magistrates and overseers of the poor.

Chadwick thought his extensive investigation had established the principle of less-eligibility, which underlay the Benthamite science of dispauperization. His achievements seemed so remarkable to the Commissioners that they published the whole of his report, which ran for 138 pages or almost one-third of all the *Extracts*.

Chadwick felt obliged to defend the length of his report inasmuch as he had disregarded Lord Melbourne's letter requesting the Assistant Commissioners to write brief reports. He defended its unusual length on the grounds that London comprised one-eleventh of the population and paid one-seventh of all relief expenses.

Chadwick, moreover, felt justified in presenting a report which overshadowed the reports of all the other assistant Commissioners. He was convinced that he alone had the right diagnosis of pauperism and that he alone had verified the principle of less-eligibility. In a subsequent article for the *Edinburgh Review*, he defined less-eligibility as follows: that the pauper's "situation on the whole shall not be made really or apparently so eligible as the situation of the independent labourer of the lowest class."[76] By establishing this principle he thought he had thrown new light on the disease of pauperism: "Not only every prevalent doctrine as to the condition of the working classes," he said, "but every prevalent doctrine as to the measures to be adopted as specifics for the disease of pauperism were proved to be unsound."[77]

Chadwick was convinced that outdoor relief to able-bodied laborers was contrary to the principle of less-eligibility. Family allowances, he declared, were "the vital evil of the system." On this point he was always emphatic, "relief to the able-bodied on terms more eligible than regular industry" causes pauperism, deterioration of labor, the decrease in capital, and the destruction of property. In 1836 Chadwick could feel certain that he put to rest all "further speculations on the remedies for the moral plague" and had reduced theory to practice so that a cure had been set "in operation on a vast scale."[78]

If Chadwick had become exceedingly proud of his achievement by the time he wrote his article for the *Edinburgh Review*, he was no less sanguine with expectation when he began his investigations in 1832: "It appears to me," he reported to the Commissioners, "that the force of the temptation to pauperism and crime can be duly estimated. . .only by means of a close inquiry. . .into the condition and modes of living of the independent and hard-working classes as compared with those, who without labour or with less labour are supplied with the fruits of labor."[79] The longer he investigated the principle of less-eligibility the more convinced he became of its validity: "The importance of the relative view of the condition of the pauper and the independent labourer is indicated by every witness who had much experience in parishes or districts affording wide fields for observation."

According to Chadwick's conception of verification, it was necessary to explore many types of working conditions, in cities as well as rural areas, in other countries as well as in England. To satisfy these standards, he surveyed agricultural labor in Berkshire as well as urban labor in London; and as further proof of his principle, he incorporated in his evidence the testimony of experts in the United States, from the cities of Boston, New York, and Philadelphia, and from the rural area of Louisiana.

Berkshire was the ideal county in which to compare the conditions of paupers and independent laborers, for it was the home of the Speenhamland bread scales. It had long been assumed by the Radical reformers that Speenhamland had stimulated the growth of pauperism, encouraged improvident marriages, increased the number of bastard children, and subsidized a redundant population. Because Berkshire had been subjected to so much hostile criticism, there arose in the vicinity of Reading a group of reformers who were experimenting with Bentham's principles of dispauperization. The most famous of the Berkshire reformers was the Reverend Thomas Whately, the resident clergyman of the parish of Cookham, which included a part of the town of Maidstone. His experiments, along with those of H. Russell, a justice of the peace, were comparable to the anti-pauper system of Becher and the Nottingham reformers. As their testimony was already a public record, Chadwick had only to incorporate it into his evidence and draw the proper inferences from it.

Chadwick took a short tour of Berkshire, accompanied by Frederick Page, to interview the principal reformers. Experiments in dispauperizing were being conducted at Swallowfield where Russell, the resident magistrate, had ordered the discontinuance of the allowance system. A similar situation existed at Burghfield where the Reverend H. C. Cherry had likewise abolished allowances. Chadwick thought the success of these experiments could be measured by the decline in the number of improvident marriages producing pauper children. He was able to obtain from Russell and Cherry the relevant statistics for the years 1810 to 1831, and on the basis on these figures he made the following report: "It will be seen that at Burghfield, out of the 115 marriages, 20 were improvident, and that 54 pauper children were the product of these improvident marriages." The discontinuance of the allowances in 1829, Chadwick concluded, had brought an end to the improvident marriages which produced pauper children. Although the evidence returned from Swallowfield was less clear than that from Burghfield, Chadwick reached the same conclusion: "Similar effects had been produced by the allowance system at Swallowfield. . ., by the abatement of the cause, the effects have ceased."[80]

In the larger and more complex parish of Cookham, it was impossible to make a distinction between provident and improvident marriages. "But the removal of the bounty on improvident marriages afforded by the allowance system," Chadwick declared, "has been attended by a marked check to population." At Cookham, moreover, bastardy had been reduced by "the plan of allowing the mother one shilling a week, and giving her the alternative of the workhouse."[81]

That Chadwick had found an effective method of checking the growth of population, improvident marriages, and bastardy carried great weight with the Commissioners. Although Chadwick himself, along with other Radicals, had rejected Malthus's view that population in civilized countries was pressing against the means of subsistence, he did accept Malthus's moral attitude toward the Poor Laws. He agreed with Malthus that the maladministration of welfare was the principal cause of pauperism. He thought, moreover, that the moral decay of the working classes could be measured by their lack of continence, foresight, providence, industry, and frugality. Pauperism itself was, in his view, a Malthusian disease signifying the moral degeneration of the working classes.

In the survey of agricultural labor, Chadwick made much use of the information supplied to him by J. Tidd Pratt, who was already gaining recognition as the "minister of self-help to the whole of the industrious classes."[82] As the certifying barrister for the Savings Banks and as the first National Registrar of Friendly Societies, Pratt was able to supply him with information on the conditions of independent laborers. From the surprisingly large number of agricultural laborers who were members of Friendly Societies and depositors of Savings Banks, Chadwick drew this conclusion: "That labourers have new means of obtaining as much of necessaries and comforts as at any former period, if not more, i.e., that their wages will go as far, if not farther than at a time known to the present generation."[83]

Chadwick's examination of urban working-class conditions was far more extensive than his study of rural labor. In his survey of London, he used the same methods that were used in the study of agricultural labor. He took the testimony of a few witnesses whose opinions were already a matter of public record. The testimony of four principal witnesses, William Benett, Charles Mott, William Stone, and Thomas Walker, provided nine-tenths of the evidence of his report; indeed, the testimony of the Reverend William Stone extended over twenty pages and that of Charles Mott ran on for thirty pages. The testimony of these two witnesses was given more space than that of all the other witnesses in London because they demonstrated for Chadwick the validity of the principle of less-eligibility.

Thomas Walker, the stipendiary magistrate for the Lambeth Street District, was set forth by Chadwick as a good example of a paid public official who had successfully deterred crime and pauperism; William Benett, magistrate for the Worship Street District, on the other hand, exemplified the deleterious effects of an interfering official. From the testimony of these two witnesses, Chadwick inferred a close relation between crime and pauperism: "For in all the more populous districts I have found that the bad management of workhouse and the bad management of prison react on each other and both exercise a pernicious influence on the morals and condition of the labouring classes." [84]

Prior to becoming a London police magistrate in 1829, Thomas Walker had been a Poor Law administrator at Stretford, in the parish of Manchester. He had also served in the same capacity for Berry Pomeroy, in Devonshire. He was a strong advocate of repressive measures. Because he thought it necessary to deter pauperism, he refused to carry out the provisions of the Poor Law. When he appeared in 1831 before the Lords' Poor Law Committee, he was rebuked by Lord Salisbury, its chairman, for refusing to administer the law. [85]

In the Worship Street District, William Benett willingly assumed the duty of supervising the parochial officials in their administration of relief. As he interpreted the 43rd of Elizabeth I, the parishes were obligated to set the poor to work, but since there was no employment to be had, it was necessary to relieve the paupers with money. Benett was not only a defender of the Poor Law but also a severe critic of the Poor Law Commission and its procedures. He strongly objected to Chadwick's methods of taking testimony, charging that witnesses were examined in private before only one Commissioner and that evidence was taken *ex parte* and not on oath. He accused Chadwick of calling only witnesses who were known to be strongly biased against magistrates. He further accused him of stating opinions as facts and hearsay evidence as proof. He objected to Chadwick's selecting events from a period of fourteen years without specifying the dates of the events. As most of the answers of witnesses were given to leading questions, Benett wanted to know from the Commissioners "how then can the motives, the discretion, or the judgment of a magistrate be even questioned on such slight and inadmissable evidence?" [86]

Benett's strictures never changed Chadwick's mind about the pernicious influence of magisterial interference nor persuaded him to return to the tedious and inconclusive methods of common law inquiry. His comparative study of workhouses and prisons disclosed what he regarded as the startling evidence that the diets of those institutions were superior to the food consumed by ordinary soldiers and independent laborers. When reporting this information, Chadwick made the following observation: "It should be borne in mind that every penny unnecessarily spent on the pauper operates as a bounty on imposition and crime and a discouragement to industry, forethought, and frugality. . . ."[87]

Another of Chadwick's preferred witnesses was the Reverend William Stone. While Thomas Walker was gaining notoriety for refusing to pass the Irish migrants through London, William Stone became celebrated as a clergyman who objected to all charitable activities in the Metropolis. He especially objected to charitable endeavours aiding migratory laborers from Ireland. "Armies of this degraded and almost brutish populace refuse to leave our neighborhood," he declared in the evidence collected by Chadwick. "I have had so much experience of this fact in my parish, and feel so persuaded of the impossibility of improving the moral or temporary condition of an indigent Irishman that I almost sicken at the sight of one."[88]

William Stone became the Rector of Christ Church, Spitalfields, in July 1829. When he first arrived in the parish he intended to cooperate with the charity organizations which were then busily engaged in the relief of the unemployed silkweavers of Spitalfields. A year after his arrival, however, he turned against the charity organizations because he had become convinced that charity was a second poor rate which made the clergyman a perpetual overseer. As a preacher of Malthusian morals, Stone sought to extirpate the sin of improvidence, "the great improvidence being marriage, I mean a marriage contracted without means either in possession or reasonable expectation of providing for four children as a result of the marriage."[89]

That Chadwick had already made up his own mind about deleterious effects of charity was clear in the questions which he asked Stone. He seemed to be fascinated by the Ricardian paradox; "as poor relief created the poor, so charity created its recipients." In his summary statement to the Commissioners, Chadwick reported the discovery of this fact: "In every district the discontent of the labouring classes appears to me to be proportional to the money dispensed in poor rates or in voluntary charity."[90] He was still convinced of his scientific discovery when he wrote his Poor Law article in 1836: "The result of this experimentation was that the present system of charity tends to create the distress which it proposes to relieve, but does not relieve all the distress which it creates."[91]

The only witness examined by Chadwick more extensively than Stone was Charles Mott. "I have thought it my duty to submit for consideration the whole of his examination," Chadwick explained to the Commissioners, because Mott had had "the most extensive practical experience I have met with." Granting the correctness of his explanation, one needs to ask why the Commissioners alloted more space to a description of the Lambeth workhouse than to fifteen thousand other places in England. The answer to this question seems to be that Mott's experience was a verification of the measures proposed by Chadwick and adopted by the Commissioners as a proper remedy for pauperism.

Charles Mott was a contractor for the maintenance of the poor at Lambeth. He first obtained the contract in 1829. His management had been so successful in reducing the costs of poor relief that the parish awarded him a new three-year contract on November 29, 1932. At the same time, he was holding a contract for the management of the poor in the Newington parish of Gosport. In addition to his pauper business, he was the principal proprietor of the Peckham House Lunatic Asylum, where he maintained the lunatics sent to him from forty parishes. For twelve years he had devoted himself to the maintenance of the poor in accord with Bentham's principles of pauper management. Trained as a merchant and employed as a shopkeeper, he became aware of the inefficient management carried on in his own parish. "From what I then saw of general parochial management," he said to Chadwick, "it occurred to me that I might serve myself whilst I served the public by contracting for the management of paupers, as well as or better than they were then managed, and at a cheaper rate."[92]

Charles Mott was doing at Lambeth and Gosport what Bentham had dreamed of doing thirty years before; namely, managing paupers more efficiently than they were then being managed by unpaid parish officials and the justices of the peace. Like Bentham, Mott understood that efficiency was a matter of careful bookkeeping to determine the minimum amount of food necessary to keep the inmates healthy. Success was measured in half-ounces of food; for, as he pointed out to Chadwick, seven hundred half-ounces of food wasted three times a day "would make a very formidable difference." He had discovered this principle of success upon becoming manager of the paupers of Newington parish. When he first took over the job, he found the kitchen scales so dirty that they did not balance — a small neglect which had ruined the former manager.

As a disciple of Bentham, Charles Mott favored contract management to trusteeship. "A contractor, for his own interest," he testified to Chadwick, "will attend more closely than any parish officer, however well-intentioned, can be expected to attend to the interest of others." True to his Utilitarian principle, Mott shared his Lambeth contract with his superintendent, Drouet, so that he, too, would "have an interest in good management."[93]

Efficient management could be achieved, according to Mott's testimony, only in large workhouses that required the united support of many parishes. Lambeth, for example, with eighty-seven thousand people could afford one large efficient establishment, whereas the City of London (within the walls) having fifty-five thousand people relieved its paupers in ninety-six different parishes. The City of London was so divided by conflicting parochial jurisdictions that it would have been impossible to build a workhouse large enough to apply Bentham's principle of classification.

Bentham's principle of less-eligibility presupposed a workhouse commodious enough for the separation of the sexes, separation of children from the adults, the able-bodied from the impotent, and the independent laborer from the indigent. Without this extensive classification, the condition of paupers could not be made less attractive than that of the lowest paid laborer. In Mott's experience, Gosport was the only place where the pauper's diet had been successfully made lower than the independent laborer's.

Charles Mott concluded his long testimony with a dire prediction. If pauper maintenance were not made less eligible than the condition of the independent laborer, he foresaw the time fast approaching when the slum conditions in Bethnal Green would overtake all the parishes of London; "the pauper population becoming too great for the industrious classes to bear, industry paralyzed, rents diminishing, property absorbed, and all sinking down to a pauper level."[94]

Chadwick concluded his report with Mott's testimony which he presented to the Commissioners as verification of the principle of less-eligibility and as evidence in favor of those institutional changes necessary to carry the principle into effect. Although he summarized his report with what he called "inferences to be drawn from the large body of evidence which I have now stated," he did nothing more, in fact, than restate the Radical case against the Poor Laws and Bentham's proposed remedies for the existing abuses.

The Radical case against the Poor Laws included the traditional criticisms drawn from the political economy textbooks of Smith, Malthus, and Ricardo. In his summary, Chadwick restated Smith's criticism that poor relief diminished the wages-fund from which the laborer's subsistence had to be paid, and that the Law of Settlement prevented the distribution of laborers according to the demand for labor. Following Ricardo's principles, Chadwick held that the poor rates were rapidly escalating, destroying the property of landowners and the capital of the employers of labor. Like other Radicals, Chadwick agreed with Malthus that the Poor Laws were destroying "the industry, forethought, and honesty of labourers," at the same time they were increasing their numbers. However much Chadwick was influenced by the teaching of political economy, his opposition was based chiefly on Malthusian morals, for he thought the costs of relief were "trifling when compared with the moral effects which I am deploring."[95]

Although Chadwick magnified the evils of the existing system, he was confident that he had discovered the proper remedy. His main recommendation was the workhouse under "a rigid administration and contract management." It was the embodiment of his principle of less-eligibility, which enabled him to draw "a broad line between the independent labourers and the paupers." Relief within the house would be substituted for outdoor relief to the able-bodied. This drastic reform, he thought, "would tend powerfully to promote providence and forethought, not only in the daily concerns of life, but in the most important of all, marriage." But none of these wholesome changes could be effected unless "the administration of the Poor Laws should be entrusted as to their general superintendence, to one Central Authority with extensive powers; and as to their details, to paid officers acting under the consciousness of constant superintendence and strict responsibility."[96]

When Chadwick made his report on January 24, 1833, he recognized that the Commissioners had no legislative program to correct the abuses which were so roundly denounced by the other Assistant Commissioners. He further perceived that he had formulated a legislative program which the Commissioners could adopt and recommend to Parliament. When later writing for the *Edinburgh*

Review, he explained his own role in the creation of the Poor Law Amendment Act of 1834: "One of the Commissioners' reports contained an exposition of the principles of the chief remedial measures which were afterwards adopted." [97]

Nassau Senior was one of the first Commissioners to recognize and appreciate the importance of Chadwick's achievement. For that reason, Senior proposed and obtained his appointment to the Commission. Henceforth there would be a division of labor between Senior, the economist, and Chadwick, the political scientist. Following the principles of political economy, Senior would condemn the abuses inherent in the existing Poor Law system and leave to Chadwick the heavy responsibility of constructing a new system based upon Bentham's science of legislation.

The division of labor between Senior and Chadwick rested on what they regarded as a methodological difference between political economy as a science of wealth and legislation as a science of welfare. "The great science of legislation. . .," Senior wrote in 1836 in his *An Outline of the Science of Political Economy*, "requires a knowledge of general principles supplied by political economy but differs from it essentially in its subject, its premises and conclusions." The scientific legislator, according to Senior, "drew his premises from an infinite variety of phenomena, supported by every degree of assent, from perfect confidence to bare suspicion, and its expounder is enabled, and even required, not merely to state general facts, but to urge the adoption or rejection of actual measures or trains of action." [98]

The method of the political economist, as conceived by Senior, was quite different from that of the scientific legislator: "his premises consist of a very few general propositions, the result of observation, or consciousness, and scarcely requiring proof or even formal statement, which almost every man, as soon as he hears them, admits as familiar to his thoughts or at least included in his previous knowledge; and his inferences are nearly as general, and if he has reasoned correctly, as certain, as his premises. Those which relate to the nature and production of wealth are universally true. . . ." [99]

Chadwick granted priority to Senior both as economist and as logician. When explaining his own achievement as a scientific legislator, he was content to quote Senior's statement on methodology of the sciences of political economy and legislation. He further explained the scientific method of his Poor Law investigation in these words: "We may ask how extreme an inquiry does it not require to determine what is the relative condition of a whole class of people; and when the principles are undoubted, what a mass of evidence is requisite to convince a whole nation."[100]

Undue confidence in the reliability of his method excited Chadwick into making excessive claims for his achievements. His mistaken methods led him into the error of accepting opinions as facts and in preferring witnesses who could translate their experience into the abstract thought of accepted theory. The mistaken method caused him to err in setting aside the evidence of some witnesses as the unenlightened testimony of practical men. "The state of the fact," he said, "on all the main points as to the condition of the population and causes of pauperism were found on detailed examination to be at all points essentially different from the prevalent notion of them." The facts which he thought he had disproven were the existence of general unemployment, the influence of trade cycles on distress, and the economic basis of destitution. He felt sure that the facts arrayed in his evidence showed "the cases of blameless distress in trade are as rare as unavoidable or blameless poverty." Although Chadwick conceded the existence of "dangerous congestions of pauperism in particular places," he thought there was "no real or general surplus beyond the average demand for employment throughout the year." He reached this conclusion because he found that "the apparent surplus of population gave way under numerous variations of circumstances, where the parish was made the hardest taskmaster and the worst paymaster within the district."[101]

Chadwick, however, was not alone in attributing pauperism to the immorality of the working classes. The Commissioners also hailed his evidence as proof of the "degree in which the existing pauperism arose from fraud, indolence, and improvidence."

In 1836 both Senior and Chadwick were standing on the threshold of a better understanding of the differences between the social and physical sciences. But while standing on this threshold they assimilated to themselves the certainty and prestige of the physical sciences without fully comprehending the imprecision and unpredictability of their own knowledge. They were physicians performing surgery prematurely on the body politic. Both reformers, however, were aware of their methods and hopeful of improving them. But neither was aware of the defects of an economic theory that prevented their seeing the consequences of unemployment and trade cycles. Both men were still clinging to the wages-fund theory of employment. In the following year, 1837, William Whewell published his *History of the Inductive Sciences*, which enabled John Mill to cross the threshold where he had halted for five years and to resume work on his *System of Logic*. Eventually Senior and Chadwick would likewise come to a better understanding of more reliable scientific methods, but meanwhile they continued to defend the amended Poor Law as their greatest achievement.

The defective methods of investigation and the prevailing faults of economic theory, one may conclude, greatly misled the Poor Law Commissioners in 1832 and distorted their vision of working-class conditions. Their easy assumption of the readiness of their scientific knowledge induced them to write a doctrinaire report in 1834 which disregarded a great amount of contrary evidence directly bearing on the conditions of the laboring classes. The bias of their report not only obstructed the progress of social welfare during the remainder of the century but has also continued to impede the writing of the social history of the period.

Sidney and Beatrice Webb in their great work on *English Poor Law History* have pointed out the bias of the Commissioners and their Assistants.[102] We have attempted in this chapter to go beyond their charge of bias and to explain more fully the nature and extent of the bias and how it distorted the vision of social conditions.

R. H. Tawney in *Religion and the Rise of Capitalism* declared the Report of 1834 to be "wildly unhistorical".[103] We have tried to show why it should continue to be so regarded by the historians writing in the second half of the twentieth century. In the next chapter on "The Passing of the Poor Law Amendment Act," we shall attempt to picture social conditions under the old Poor Law, using some of the evidence collected by the Commissioners in 1832 and 1833 but disregarded by them in their Report of 1834.

Much attention has been given in this chapter to the *Extracts*, because they were more widely circulated and published in a form readily assimilated. It is probable that the *Extracts* had a greater impact on the reading public than did the many volumes of evidence published in the unmanageable folio volumes. The Commissioners' instructions to the Assistants, which were published along with the *Extracts*, reveal the presuppositions with which they began the investigation and show their determination at the outset to recommend drastic measures. That they published Chadwick's report in full and accepted his proposals in their final report further indicates that a majority of the Commissioners had already made up their minds in favor of the extensive reform of the existing Poor Laws.

NOTES

1 Hugh M. Clokie and Joseph W. Robinson, *Royal Commissions of Inquiry* (New York, Oxford University Press, 1938), pp. 58-59.

2 *Ibid.*, p. 67.

3 Adam Smith, *The Wealth of Nations* (New York: The Modern Library, 1937), p. 724.

4 John Veitch, "A Memoir of Dugald Stewart," in his *Collected Works*, Edited by William Hamilton, (Edinburgh, 1854), vol. X, xxii-xxxix. Also, Leslie Stephen, *The English Utilitarians* (London, 1900), vol. I., 143-62.

5 Stewart, *Collected Works*, Vol. X, li.

6 *Ibid.*, II, 235.

7 *Ibid.*, Vol. X, xcvii.

8 Donald Winch, ed., *James Mill: Selected Economic Writings* (Chicago: University of Chicago Press, 1966), p. 8.

9 Stewart, *Collected Works*, I, 22.

10 *Ibid.*, III, 250.

11 *Ibid.*, III, 332.

12 *Ibid.*, III, 334.

13 *Ibid.*, II, 520.

14 *Ibid.*, II, 7.

15 *Ibid.*, II, 231.

16 *Ibid.*, II, 222.

17 William Chester New, *The Life of Henry Brougham to 1830*, (New York: Oxford, 1961), p. 6.

18 John Stuart Mill, *Autobiography* (New York: Columbia University Press, 1924), p. 136.

19 Alexander Bain, *James Mill* (London: Longmans, Green, 1882), p. 16.

20 *James Mill: Selected Economic Writings*, p. 3.

21 James Mill, *Analysis of the Phenomena of the Human Mind* (London, 1829), I, 59.

22 *James Mill: Selected Economic Writings*, p. 367.

23 *Dictionary of Political Economy* (London, 1901). Whately reviewed Senior's *Introductory Lecture on Political Economy* in the *Edinburgh Review*, Vol. 48, (Sept. 1828), 171-85.

24 Richard Whately, *Elements of Logic* (Ninth edition; Boston, 1852), pp. 280-84. The first edition appeared in 1826; the fourth in 1831.

25 Richard Whately, *Introductory Lectures on Political Economy* (4th ed. 1855), pp. 43-44. Lecture IX. "Mode of Pursuing Study in the Science" was included in the fourth edition of *Elements of Logic*. The *Introductory Lectures on Political Economy* were delivered at Oxford in 1831.

26 Whately, *Political Economy*, (London, 1832), p. 147.

27 *Ibid.*, p. 149.

28 J. S. Mill, *Autobiography*, pp. 126-27.

[29] *London and Westminster Review*, vol. XXVI (October, 1836).

[30] *Autobiography*, p. 145; also see Mill, *System of Logic*, "Preface to the First Edition." In his *Collected Works*, Volume XII, *Early Letters*, p. 179.

[31] John S. Mill, *Collected Works: Essays on Economics and Society*, edited by J. M. Robson. (Toronto, University of Toronto Press, 1965), Vol. IV, 313.

[32] *Ibid.*, 311.

[33] *Ibid.*, 334.

[34] *Autobiography*, p. 144.

[35] See Chapter II, p. 18.

[36] See Chapter VII, p. 4.

[37] See Chapter III, pp. 32-35.

[38] See Chapter VIII, pp. 20-21.

[39] John Mill, *Autobiography*, p. 61. For Coulson's review of McCulloch's *Principles*, see *Edinburgh Review*, No. 105, (March, 1831). For my comments, Chapter VIII, pp. 24-25.

[40] *Political Economy Club* (Centenary Volume, London, 1921), vol. VI, 358-60.

[41] S. E. Finer, *The Life and Times of Sir Edwin Chadwick* (London, 1951), p. 49.

[42] R. A. Lewis, *Edwin Chadwick and the Public Health Movement* (London, Longmans, Green, 1952), pp. 5-7.

[43] John Mill, *Collected Works*, XII, 20.

[44] Lewis, *Edwin Chadwick*, p. 10.

[45] Finer, *Sir Edwin Chadwick*, p. 31.

[46] *Westminster Review*, IX (April, 1828), 390-94.

[47] *Ibid.*, p. 417.

[48] *Report from H. M. Commission for Inquiring into the Administration and Practical Operation of the Poor Laws.* (1834), "Statement of Proceedings," p. 1.

[49] "The Instructions to the Assistant Commissioners" are found in the *Poor Law Report*, "Supplement" No. 3, pp. 248-55. They may also be found in the *Extracts*, pp. 411-26.

[50] Senior to J. A. L. Quetelet, August 21, 1832. In this letter Senior says he is sending "a little pamphlet of my own called 'Instructions to Assistant Poor Law Commissioners'." Quoted in Samuel Leon Levy, *Nassau Senior, the Prophet of Modern Capitalism*, p. 398, footnote 296. Sidney and Beatrice Webb, *English Poor Law History Part II: The Last Hundred Years*, Vol. I, p. 90. The Webbs say the *Instructions* were printed but not published; they were without bias; and Chadwick was the author. The Webbs were wrong on all these points; or they may have been talking about another set of instructions, as Levy suggests.

[51] *Extracts from the Information Reviewed by His Majesty's Commissioners As to the Administration and Operation of the Poor-Laws* (London, 1833), p. 425. The outline presented in the instructions contained the main heads of *Report* except for the Radical remedies as proposed by Chadwick. The Radical case against the old Poor Law which appears in the *Report* was written into the instructions. See *Poor Law Report*, pp. 249, 255.

[52] *Extracts*, p. 415.

[53] *Ibid.*, p. 417.

[54] *Ibid.*, p. 418.

[55] *Ibid.*, p. 425.

[56] *Ibid.*, p. 412.

[57] *Ibid.*, p. v. The preliminary report was signed by the Bishop of London, the Bishop of Chester, Sturges Bourne, Nassau Senior, Henry Bishop, Henry

Gawler, and Walter Coulson.

[58] Edwin Chadwick, "The New Poor Law," *Edinburgh Review*, LXIII (1836), 505. Chadwick says the Commission acted upon Brougham's suggestion that the preliminary reports be published in a popular form.

[59] Commissioners' letter to Lord Melbourne, March 19, 1933, *Extracts*, pp. iv-v.

[60] *Extracts*, pp. 374-83.

[61] *Ibid.*, Cowell's report was dated February 25, 1833, pp. 397-99.

[62] *Extracts*, p. 86.

[63] Halévy, *A History of the English People*, II, 123. The sure-footed Halévy, still the preeminent historian of the nineteenth century, stumbled over John Wilson. He says "Wilson's report is devoid of interest." He further finds "this strange report, extremely meager in its information and entirely negative in its conclusions" and declares that "Wilson was deliberately doing his best to betray the confidence of the group to whom he owed his place on the Commission." Halévy much preferred Cameron to Wilson, for Cameron closely followed the Radical line.

[64] *Extracts*, p. 169.

[65] *Ibid.*, p. 339.

[66] *Ibid.*, p. 157.

[67] *Ibid.*, p. 405.

[68] *Extracts*, p. 1.

[69] *Ibid.*, p. 158.

[70] *Ibid.*, p. 102.

[71] *Ibid.*, pp. 195-99.

[72] *Ibid.*, p. 183.

[73] A more reliable estimate of conditions can be found in the *Poor Law Report*, Supplement No. 1, p. 209. If one compares supplement no. 1 with the reports of the Assistant Commissioners appearing in the *Extracts* and in the *Appendix A*, one will understand how readily they allowed opinion to take precedence over fact.

[74] *Extracts*, p. 80.

[75] There were sixteen reports from eighteen assistant Commissioners and from Henry Bishop, a Commissioner. Ultimately there were twenty-eight assistants whose reports appeared in *Appendix A*.

[76] *Edinburgh Review*, LXIII (April, 1836), 499.

[77] *Ibid.*, p. 503.

[78] *Ibid.*, p. 504.

[79] *Extracts*, p. 226.

[80] *Ibid.*, p. 237.

[81] *Ibid.*, p. 240.

[82] P.H.J.H. Gosden, *The Friendly Societies In England* (Manchester, University of Manchester Press, 1961), p. 10.

[83] *Extracts*, p. 236.

[84] *Ibid.*, p. 241.

[85] See chapter VIII, p. 12.

[86] *Poor Law Report* (1834), Appendix A. Pt. III, p. 121.

[87] *Extracts*, p. 268.

[88] *Ibid.*, p. 294.

[89] *Ibid.*, p. 287.

[90] *Ibid.*, p. 333.

[91] *Edinburgh Review*, LXIII, 495.

[92] *Extracts*, p. 305.

[93] *Ibid.*, p. 310.

[94] *Ibid.*, p. 332.
[95] *Ibid.*, p. 338.
[96] *Ibid.*, p. 339.
[97] *Edinburgh Review*, LXIII, 505.
[98] Senior, *Political Economy*, p. 2.
[99] *Ibid.*, p. 3.
[100] *Edinburgh Review*, LXIII, 490.
[101] *Ibid.*, 498.
[102] S. and B. Webb, *English Poor Law History* Pt. II, 84-85.
[103] Tawney, *Religion and the Rise of Capitalism*, p. 225.

X

THE RADICAL REFORM OF THE POOR LAWS

THE Radical reform of the Poor Laws was based upon the investigation and recommendations of the Poor Law Commission. The Report of the Commission, which was presented to the House of Lords on February 21, 1834, was divided into two distinct parts. The first part attempted to verify the Radical case against the existing system of welfare. It exposed and condemned what the Radicals considered to be abuses inherent in the existing Poor Laws. The second part comprised the remedial measures which became eventually, although in a modified form, the Poor Law Amendment Act. As a whole, the Report was a division of labor between Nassau Senior, the economist, and Edwin Chadwick, the political scientist, the former writing the first part and the latter writing the second.

While Senior and Chadwick were the authors who put the materials in a final form, they were in reality the compilers of Radical criticisms and proposed reforms that had been circulating for more than a decade. The Report was, in fact, the work of many hands, the Commissioners and their staff, the Assistant Commissioners, the Whig Ministers, the staff of the Home Department, and the many members of Parliament who had long struggled to improve social conditions. This work of many hands, like Rumford's soup, contained many ingredients.

244

A theory of welfare permeated the entire Report. The theory included the concepts: the poor, poverty, indigence, and pauperism.

The most general term, and one in widest circulation, "the poor" included all persons who, lacking property and profession, had to work for a living or who, unable to work, became dependent upon charity or relief for their subsistence. "The poor" included most of the laboring population. The ambiguity of the term, which Chadwick and others deplored, did not prevent people from using it. One need not penetrate the jungle of social history very far to hear such expressions as "we must not pauperize the poor" or "the poor will not permit the poor to be imprisoned in workhouses." Confusion adhered to the term because it was applied to both the independent and the dependent poor. The independent poor, the great mass of every population, were the bulwark of society, for they were the producers of goods and services. The dependent poor were the "paupers."

In the language inherited from the eighteenth century, the dependent poor comprised the impotent as well as the able-bodied. Rogues and vagabonds, old and young, the lame and the blind, the lunatics and the insane were packaged in a gross bundle called the dependent poor. The Commissioners thought they had made progress in 1834 when they used the concept "indigent" instead of dependent poor. They defined indigence as "the state of a person unable to labour, or unable to obtain by his labour, the means of subsistence."[1]

The eighteenth-century concept of "poverty" was predominant in the Commissioners' thinking. They continued to think of poverty as "the spur of civilization." According to the doctrine of natural liberty, as set forth by Adam Smith, "all men have the desire of bettering our condition, a desire which comes with us from the womb and never leaves us till we go into the grave."[2] While all men had this economic motive, the laboring classes were motivated by the necessities of food, clothing, and shelter. In the Poor Law Report, poverty was defined as "the state of one who in order to obtain a mere subsistence is forced to have recourse to labour." Chadwick was more explicit in his *Edinburgh Review* article, when he explained poverty as "the natural, the primitive, the general and the unchangeable state of man; and as labour is the source of wealth, so is poverty of labour. Banish poverty, you banish wealth."

Chadwick agreed with the Commissioners in viewing indigence, not poverty, as the central problem of social welfare: "Indigence, therefore, and not poverty is the evil, the removal of which is the proper object of the Poor Laws. Indigence may be provided for — mendicity extirpated; but all attempts to extirpate poverty can have no effects but bad ones."[3]

In Chadwick's thinking, the concept was derived from the doctrine of natural liberty. As all men strive to better their condition, poor men at the lowest levels of employment strive to obtain their subsistence. Inasmuch as the Poor Laws weakened the will to struggle for subsistence, they violated natural law. From the doctrine of natural liberty, Chadwick derived his principle of less-eligibility, namely, "that the condition of the person relieved at the public expense must be made less eligible on the whole than the person living on the fruits of his own labour...."[4]

Another concept of social welfare permeating the Poor Law Report was pauperism. It was regarded as a social disease. Just as cholera was the plague of urban populations, so pauperism was a contagion spreading among the lower orders, reducing the industry of the laboring classes, causing the withdrawal of capital, and bringing the whole society to stagnation. According to this diagnosis, the cause of the disease was the improper administration of the Poor Laws. Bread scales and family allowances, the converse of less-eligibility, were destroying "the industry and morals of the laborers."[5]

After conducting their investigation, the Commissioners summarized their views as follows: "We have seen that one of the objects attempted by the present administration of the Poor Laws is the repeal *pro tanto* of that law of nature by which the effects of each man's improvidence or misconduct are born by himself and his family."[6]

The concept "pauperism" was derived from Malthus's principles of population. In his views, the positive checks on population were war, famine, disease, and crime; the preventive check was moral restraint, providence, and forethought. The provident laborer, remaining continent, postponed marriage until he earned enough to support a family. By exercising forethought, the individual would save enough to provide for the casualties of illness and accident as well as the certainty of old age. Pauperism was the obverse of moral restraint; it was the failure to exercise the preventive check on population. The ravages of pauperism could be measured by the number of marriages producing pauper children; more exactly, it could be measured by the number of illegitimate children and their unwed mothers on relief.

Chadwick especially thought pauperism must be suppressed, for it had caused "the demoralization of the labouring classes, the deterioration of their labour, and the reduction in the demand for their employment. . . ."[7] As Chadwick conducted his investigation, he became increasingly confident that he had discovered not only the right diagnosis of the disease but also its proper remedy. His remedy for pauperism was the rigorous application of the principle of less-eligibility. In this survey he discovered that the remedy had already dispauperized certain parishes in Berkshire. His enthusiasm for the new science of dispauperization led him to devote much of his final report to the Berkshire experiments. He took time to define what he meant by the term: "dispauperized is used to indicate that a check has been given to the evils of abusive mode of administration rather than that those evils have been fully extirpated."[8]

After explaining the procedures of their investigation, the Commissioners gave considerable time to the reinterpretation of the history of the Poor Laws. Their reconstruction of the system followed the lines already laid down by Sir James Scarlett in the debates of 1821 and 1823: "It is now our painful duty to report that in the greater part of the districts, which we have been able to examine, the fund, which the 43rd of Elizabeth directed to be employed in setting to work children and persons capable of labour but using no daily trade and in the necessary relief of the impotent, is applied to purposes opposed to the letter and still more to the spirit of that law and destructive of the morals of the most numerous class and to the welfare of all."[9]

In their reinterpretation of the Poor Laws the Commissioners made plain their intention of returning to the workhouse system which the Pittite reformers had abandoned. They extolled the workhouse law which had been adopted in the reign of George I and denounced the humanitarian reforms of George III. The repeal of the 36th of George III was their main objective. The Commissioners did not deny the benevolent intentions of the Pittite reformers; they merely charged them with the inability to understand the consequences of their good intentions. They declared the 36th of George III to be "the great and fatal deviation from our previous policy. The 43rd Elizabeth never contemplated as object of relief, industrious persons." Without condemning Pitt's followers, the Commissioners condescended to excuse them: "But we must not judge them according to the knowledge which we have acquired in the dear-bought experience of 40 years."[10] But Chadwick, in particular, was less willing to excuse them; he had a clear opinion of the humanitarians, "those good persons whose hearts are larger than their heads."[11]

The Commissioners did not rest the case against the Pittites solely on "the dear-bought experience of 40 years." They were confident that their own recommendations were in keeping with political science. Their first scientific principle was that every man should be free to better his condition; their second principle, derived from the first, was that parish officials should be guided by their own interests in assessing rates and administering relief. The good law of George I which had established workhouses and the contract system was in keeping with scientific principles. "But things were not left to take their own course. Unhappily no knowledge is so rare as the knowledge when to do nothing. It requires an acquaintance with general principles, a confidence in their truth, and a patience with the gradual process by which obstacles are steadily but slowly surmounted, which are among the last acquisitions of political science and experience."

Inasmuch as Sturges Bourne was a member of the Commission, it is not surprising that the Commissioners endorsed the Poor Law Report of 1817. They repeated the ominous warning of the Committee over which Sturges Bourne had presided: "That unless some efficacious check were imposed. . ., the amount of the assessment would continue to increase until at a period more or less remote. . .it should have absorbed the profits of property on which the rate might have been assessed, providing thereby the neglect and ruin of the land. . . ."[12] The Commissioners thought the Sturges Bourne Act (59 Geo. III C. 12) had provided "an efficacious check," but only a temporary one. According to their calculation, the growth of the rates had been checked until 1824, but thereafter they resumed their upward spiral. By this endorsement of the natural law doctrine of inherent escalation of the rates, the Commissioners assimilated into their Report the major arguments that had been used against the Pittite reforms.

Once the Commissioners had established the legal and scientific basis for their Report, they proceeded with the major task of exposing the abuses in the operations of the existing system. By the operations of the Poor Laws they meant the form in which relief was given, the kinds of people receiving it, and the effects of relief on the recipients. Indoor and outdoor relief was granted to both the impotent and the able-bodied poor. Outdoor relief might be granted in money or in kind. Frequently rents were paid; less frequently relief came in the form of food and clothing. Outdoor relief might also take the form of allowances to families, parish employment, or made-work privately supervised, such as the roundsmen or labor rate.

The central abuse of the system, as seen by the Commissioners, was outdoor relief to the able-bodied. Like all Radical reformers, whether economists or political scientists, they were fully committed to the abolition of outdoor relief to able-bodied persons in private employment. The Commissioners reported having found in many parishes people on relief "who are professed to be without employment." As the term "unemployment" did not exist in their vocabulary and as their theory explained only a redundant labor supply, the Commissioners discounted the poor man's professions of unemployment: "In still larger numbers of instances the relief is given on the plea that the applicant has not been able to obtain work. . .and is entitled to receive from the unlimited resources of the parish what he has not been able to obtain from a private employer."[13]

Guided by Malthusian theory, the major objectives were to restrict the growth of population and to restore labor to private employment. The Commissioners, therefore, objected to all the expedients of temporary employment. They were critical of the several schemes of employment improvised by parish officials. The chief sources of parish employment in rural areas were the repairing of roads and the digging of gravel. The Commissioners ridiculed this kind of work: "But it is now usual to give a large weekly sum and to force the applicants to give up a certain portion of their time by confining them to gravel pits or some inclosure or directing them to sit at a certain spot and do nothing. . . ."

Since employment on the roads and in the gravel pits had contributed to the riots of 1830, the farmers in many areas adopted the system of labor rates as a means of placating hostility. This emergency measure provided meaningful employment under normal supervision. The farmers agreed to pay the usual wages during slack seasons and the amount paid in wages would be credited to them against their poor-rate assessment.[14] Although this scheme, along with higher wages, seemed to have aided the pacification of the riot-torn areas, the Commissioners objected to it on the grounds that it interfered with the normal demand for labor and that it shifted to others the burden of the rates.

Another form of rural employment, antedating the labor rate, was the roundsman system. According to this practice, the overseer sent the applicant for relief around to the occupiers of the parish, who, if they had any odd jobs to be done, hired the pauper at wages fixed by the parish. Part of the wages was paid by the parish and part by the farmer. This practice had been subjected to so many abuses for such a long period of time that the Commissioners could join generations of reformers who had condemned it.[15]

Of all the forms of outdoor relief, the Commissioners considered family allowances to persons in private employment to be the worst. This practice violated their firmly held principles of political economy. It prevented wages from rising to their natural level. The allowance gave more to the married man than to the single, thus determining wages according to needs rather than services. It interfered with the normal demand for labor by holding laborers in areas where their services were no longer needed. According to Malthusian principles, the family allowance subsidized large families, encouraged early marriages and added to a redundant labor supply. Family allowances, therefore, were regarded as gross maladministration of the Poor Laws; proper administration, on the other hand, would restrict population, curtail the labor supply, equalize supply and demand, raise wages to their normal level, and pay laborers according to their services.

The term "allowance" was as generic as the word "relief." The charitable practice of assisting large families even antedated Elizabeth's time. It was as commonplace to feed people by the family as it was for the farmer to feed cattle by the size of the herd. The best measures of a family's needs were its size and age, and at the same time the measure of its possible income. The magistrate could call the family before him and award relief according to the obvious circumstance, and by the same simple counting there would be no need for relief in seasons of employment.[16] The most compelling need was that of the large young family in which the wife was constantly pregnant or nursing her infants. A halcyon heritage from subsistence agriculture decreed that the five-year-old children could be profitably employed under family supervision.

250

This heritage brought with it the venerable practice of relieving large families, beginning with the third or fourth child, especially when the children were under ten years of age. The fortunate family was one with children above ten years who could contribute substantially to the family income.

When the Commissioners issued "Instructions" to their Assistants, they already had before them many replies to the Rural Queries. They had learned from these replies that the term "allowance" had different meanings in diverse parts of the country and for various classes of respondents. In some places allowance meant nothing more than relief; in others it meant relief to an employed person "on the account of his children." If an employed person received relief on his own account, the allowance was called "payment of wages out of the rates." When the Commissioners came to write their Report, however, they notified their readers that they would use "allowances" to mean "parochial relief afforded to those who are employed by individuals at the average wages of the district." By thus semanticizing "allowance" in keeping with their proposed remedy, they were able to magnify the abuse which they wished to uproot. But they did so at the cost of misrepresenting the evidence that they had so laboriously accumulated.[17]

Every student of welfare should want to know about the condition of the impotent poor, the old and the young, the sick and the infirm. The student will find very little information about such people in the Poor Law Report of 1834. In a few pages the Commissioners passed over the host of people who were being benefited most by the Poor Laws. "The outdoor relief to the impotent. . .," they said, "is subject to less abuse. . . ." They also found, "even in those places distinguished by the most wanton parochial profusion, the allowances to the aged and infirm are moderate."[18]

Inasmuch as the Commissioners had concentrated their attack on outdoor relief to the able-bodied, they devoted little time to indoor relief. They failed to recognize that the humanitarian reformers had transformed the old workhouses into poorhouses as residences for the homeless. Because the Commissioners had already decided to reestablish workhouses to deter paupers from the rates, they passed over the experience of the eighteenth-century reformers who had abandoned them. They also neglected the evidence pertaining to the urban workhouses created under Local Acts and the union workhouses provided by the Gilbert Act. The Commissioners were content to criticize all such establishments for "the absence of classification, discipline, and employment, and for the extravagance of allowances."[19] Since these workhouses were not managed according to Bentham's principles, they were presumed to be maladministered.

The cardinal proof of maladministration was the heavy burden of expenditures, which the Commissioners found to be "steadily and rapidly progressive." They conceded, however, that expenses had been higher in 1818 than in 1832, and explained the difference as follows: "But it is to be remembered, 1st, That the year ending the 25th of March, 1818, was a period of extraordinary distress among the labouring classes, especially in the manufacturing districts, in consequence of the high price of provision, unaccompanied by a corresponding advance in wages; 2dly, That in the year ending the 25th of March, 1832, the price of corn was lower by one-third than in 1818 and that of clothes and of the other necessaries of life lower in a still greater proportion; so that, after allowing for an increase of population of one-fifth, the actual amount of relief given in 1832 was much larger in proportion to the population than even that given in 1818, which has been considered as the year in which it attained its highest amount. . . ."

If the Commissioners had had more faith in their statistics, they might have made a fruitful study of the fluctuations in the rates since 1815, but they had more faith in their axioms than in their arithmetic. They discounted their own statistics by concluding: "That the statement of the mere amount directly expended, whether estimated in money or in kind affords a very inadequate measure of the loss sustained by those who supply it. A greater part of it is incurred not by direct payment out of the rates, but by the purchase of unprofitable labour."[20]

In the section of the Report called "Objections to Amendment," the Commissioners reviewed the self-interests of three classes of people who were defending the existing system. The laborers defended the Poor Law because "it always gives them easy work" and they never have to seek it. From the laborer's point of view, "the government has undertaken to repeal, in his behalf, the ordinary law of nature: to enact that children shall not suffer for the misconduct of their parents. . ., that no one shall lose the means of his comfortable subsistence whatever be his indolence, prodigality, or vice. . . ."[21]

The Commissioners also thought that some employers would defend the Poor Laws because it enabled them "to hire and dismiss labourers according to their daily or even hourly want of them, to reduce wages to the minimum or even below the minimum of what will support an unmarried man and to throw upon others a payment of a part, frequently of a greater part, and sometimes the whole of the wages actually received by the labourers."

The proprietors, however, were castigated by the Commissioners for acting on benevolence rather than self-interest. The great landlords, who made and administered the laws, were too noble and well-meaning to remedy a deplorable situation. The Commissioners concluded that some among the upper classes "seem to have acquired habits of thinking and feeling and acting which unfit them to originate any real and extensive amendment, or even to understand the principles on which it ought to be based." [22]

In their review of the effects of the Poor Laws on proprietors, employers, and laborers, the Commissioners cited the bankrupt parish of Cholesbury, in Bucks, to illustrate the ultimate tendency of the rates to devour property. The existence of one bankruptcy in fifteen thousand parishes was, to be sure, no reason for reform; but the tendency, which it exemplified, did provide adequate grounds.[23] Although anxious about the effects of the Poor Laws on property, the Commissioners were even more concerned over the moral decline of the working classes. Their foremost objective was to restore "that law of nature by which the effects of each man's improvidence or misconduct are borne by himself and his family." [24]

In that first section of the Report dealing with practical operations of the Poor Laws, the Commissioners set forth the form of relief and the types of persons receiving it. In the second section dealing with administration, they described "the persons by whom relief is awarded" and "the persons at whose expense it is given." Although there were many types of administrators and many kinds of ratepayers, the Commissioners arrayed most of their evidence against the magistrates.

Throughout the Report the Commissioners assumed that the magistrates administered relief under the influence of their own superior standard of living and were, on that account, guilty of profusion. In the vocabulary of the Report, the magistrates' corruption meant profusion, not malfeasance. There were cases of malfeasance among the overseers, and petty frauds were sometimes committed by members of the vestries. But these kinds of

253

corruption were deemed insignificant when compared with the profusion of the magistrates. Profusion was the central abuse of administration, and it was identified with outdoor relief to laborers. The Commissioners, therefore, were primarily concerned with the magistrates, whose jurisdiction they had already determined to eliminate.

From the time of Elizabeth I, the primary responsibility for administering relief was vested in the parish officials, the overseers of the poor. The overseers were unpaid officials, elected to serve for one year. If the person elected refused to serve, he could be fined for such refusal. Farmers usually filled the office in rural parishes, and shopkeepers were frequently elected in the towns. It was an onerous office with unpleasant and unpopular duties. Few men sought it. The overseer had long been the object of criticism, and the Commissioners merely repeated perennial complaints: "Neither diligence nor zeal are expected from persons on whom a disagreeable and unpaid office has been forced and whose functions cease by the time they have begun to acquire knowledge of them. . . ."[25]

The Commissioners were less critical of assistant overseers, who were paid, permanent officials. Many towns and large urban parishes incorporated under Local Acts had not only permanent, paid overseers, but also other salaried officials performing duties associated with welfare. The Gilbert Unions were created for the purpose of combining parishes, building poorhouses, and applying the methods of efficient management that had already been developed by the urban corporations. The Sturges Bourne Act further extended the new principles of management to all places which chose to elect vestrymen. The majority of places that had reorganized under the new law appointed assistant overseers.

The Radical reformers of 1832 were well aware of the new methods of management that had been developed in urban corporations and the Gilbert Unions. With Sturges Bourne serving on the Commission, many Radical reformers assumed that the principles of the law which bore his name would be made national and compulsory. When the Assistant Commissioners were appointed, they were instructed to investigate the operations of select vestries and the performance of the assistant overseers. In their individual reports, the Assistant Commissioners reported favorably on Poor Law management under the Sturges Bourne Act and recommended that its principles be extended to other areas. The Commissioners, however, disregarded the recommendations of their Assistants, for by the time of the final Report, they had already decided to vest complete authority in a central board. The Commissioners, therefore, found it necessary to condemn the assistant overseers along with the annually elected officials: "A more perfect state of subserviency can scarcely exist," they declared, for "a profuse and corrupt vestry" have no difficulty in finding "a willing instrument for their purpose."

While the overseers had the duties of collecting the rates and distributing relief, the authority for assessing the rates and controlling expenditures rested with the vestry. At the time of the Radical investigation of 1832, there were three types of vestries: open, closed, and select.

The open vestry, existing from the reign of William and Mary, was broadly representative, comprising all rate-payers of the parish. Some of the urban parishes were large and unwieldy and had become the arena of political conflict. The closed vestry, prevalent in many rural areas, was narrowly co-opted and controlled by the Established Church. Members of the select vestry were elected by the ratepayers, some of whom had several votes in proportion to the amount of rates paid.

The Commissioners conceded much to Sturges Bourne and the Tory landlords by extending the principle of selectivity to all constituent Poor Law authorities. They went even beyond the Sturges Bourne Act by granting right of multiple voting by proxy to landlords. The mystery of this decision becomes virtually inscrutable when one realizes that the landlords, unless they were also occupiers, did not pay the poor rates.

Why this drastic change in policy at the same instant that the passing of the Great Reform Bill had increased enthusiasm for popular representation? The Commissioners decided to give multiple voting rights to landlords in order to achieve a more efficient management. They had learned from their principles of political economy that the landlords contributed indirectly to the rates by reducing their rents to their tenants. The Commissioners, therefore, thought it unwise to deny voting rights to "a great part of the principal contributors to the fund." The practice of excluding the landlords from the control of the relief fund had, in their view, tended only to vest control "in an irresponsible body, many of whom should have little interest in its permanent diminution." The elimination of the landlords' restraining influence in the assessment of rates had allowed the vestries to become "the most irresponsible bodies that ever were entrusted with the performance of public duties or the distribution of public funds." [26]

Although the Commissioners found fault with the existing overseers and the vestries, they reserved their severest indictment for the magistrates. Their determination to cashier the magistrates was explicit in the Instructions to the Assistant Commissioners, who were directed to "collect facts and opinions as to the practicability and expediency of exonerating the magistrates, wholly or partially, from their jurisdiction with respect to relief. . . ." [27] The magistrates were blamed for the system of outdoor relief to the able-bodied and for the profusion associated with bread scales. The ordering of relief was the abuse of "interference," and ordering relief according to bread scales was the abuse of extravagance or "profusion". In the vocabulary of Radical reform, both terms signified corruption and maladministration. Thus it happened that the Speenhamland scale became the model of both profusion and interference. [28]

The Speenhamland scale first entered the reform literature through the pages of Sir Frederick Eden's *State of the Poor*, where it was exhibited as an example of extravagance. The Commissioners excerpted Eden's account of Speenhamland and reprinted it in their Report. [29] In addition to Eden's account, they reprinted material from the *Poor Law Report of 1817*. Their Report restated Lacoast's testimony about the extravagant scale at Chertsey, Surrey. Lacoast had testified that the Chertsey scale, two quartern loaves for each member of the family, was so extravagant that it had attracted paupers from neighboring parishes. The Chertsey scale, which was less than the Speenhamland, granted relief only after the price of flour reached one shilling fourpence a gallon. When the price of flour went to two shillings a gallon, the relief of a family of four was two shillings. [30] The existence of many such diverse scales should indicate how little influence the Speenhamland scale had on parishes in other counties.

The Commissioners incorporated in their Report other sparse fragments of evidence confirming the existence of bread scales. Although instructions had been given to all the Assistant Commissioners to search for the origins of the deplored practice, there was little information forthcoming. Assistant Commissioner MacLean reported that the magistrates in the western part of Sussex had used bread scales during the famine of 1800, but the scale gave only sixpence for each member of the family when the price of flour was two shillings a gallon. In the search for origins in Warwickshire, Charles Villiers found that bread scales had originated during the famine years and had been one of several expedients to meet the emergency.

Notwithstanding the sparse evidence uncovered by their investigation, the Commissioners exhibited the Speenhamland scale as the model of magisterial profusion. They preferred Speenhamland to the legal scales which had been imposed on all magistrates by Parliament and were in general use. The first of these, the militiaman's scale, was imposed on the magistrates at the beginning of the war against the French Republic as an aid to the recruitment of volunteers. When the war was resumed in 1803, the scale was reimposed. It required the overseer "to pay weekly to the wife and each child of the militiaman an allowance equal to the ordinary price of one day's husbandry labour in the district but the allowance is never to be less than one shilling." If the militiaman were killed in action, his family would be paid a pension from the poor rates. Although the Commissioners did not propose to abolish the payment of pensions from the poor rates, they could not refrain from criticizing them. "They are not made in reward of the father's services but according to the number and assumed wants of the family...." [31]

The practice of pensioning the widows of militiamen was extended to other women; and in many places widows were granted pensions of one shilling to three shillings a week. If she also had dependent children, she received one shilling sixpence for each child. For some reason, a grant of two shillings was made to illegitimate children, a practice which the Commissioner stoutly disapproved.

More widely prevalent than the militiaman's scales was the one imposed on the magistrates in 1815. The new scale required the magistrates to award the pauper three shillings a week or an amount equal to three-fourths of that necessary to maintain him in the workhouse. Subsequently, the Sturges Bourne Act of 1819 restricted the power of the magistrates to order relief but perpetuated the scale. Another money scale widely prevalent, shown by the investigation of 1832, and one frequently adopted in populous urban parishes was the award of sixpence for husband and wife and one shilling sixpence for each child under ten years of age.

In the presence of so many types of scales, why did the Commissioners object chiefly to bread scales? In the first place, this model of profusion had been the big weapon in the arsenal of reform, demonstrating the incompetence of the gentry to control expenditures. In the second place, the bread scales were a contradiction, for by tying the amount of relief to the price of bread they gave a snowball effect to the growth of expenditures. The logical implication was clear: the scarcer the bread, the higher the price; the higher the price, the more profuse the relief.

Although the Commissioners concentrated their opposition on the bread scales, they objected to all magisterial Poor Law jurisdiction. Unguided by wholesome self-interest, magisterial interference "tended to destroy all vigilance and economy on the part of those who receive it." Because the magistrates were men of fortune and high social standing, they were unable to understand the needs of the paupers who applied to them for help.[32]

After spending nearly a third of their Report censuring the magistrates for interference and profusion, the Commissioner concluded with an apology, exonerating the magistrates from any charge of malfeasance: "They have exercised the powers delegated to them by the poor laws not wisely, indeed, or beneficially, but still with benevolent and honest intentions." But benevolence and good intentions did not justify their jurisdiction. The Commissioners professed the inability to conceive of a more "dangerous instrument. . .than a public officer, supported and impelled by benevolent sympathies, armed with power from which there is no appeal, and misapprehending the consequences of its exercise."[33]

Two doctrinaire abuses emerged from the pages of the Poor Law Report. The first was outdoor relief profusely administered. The second abuse was the interference of the magistrates who were incompetent to understand or control pauperism.

Two minor abuses were deeply submerged in the Report in order not to divert attention from the main issues. The minor abuses were the Laws of Settlement and Bastardy.

From the time of Elizabeth I, it had been assumed that a person was legally settled at the place of his birth or where he had resided for three years. Much of the litigation over residence resulted from the law of Charles II which enabled the parish to remove a person within forty days of arrival lest he become an applicant for relief. Although the intention was to remove anyone likely to become chargeable, this law, in fact, provided grounds for a settlement after forty days residence. To prevent a pauper from obtaining a legal residence, the parish frequently instigated procedures to remove him before he became chargeable. Settlements might be acquired on grounds other than birth and residence. Traditional provisions of common law gave settlement to persons inheriting estates and to wives whose husbands had legal residence. The Laws of Settlement were relaxed during the reign of William and Mary by granting legal residence to persons serving in a parish office for a year and paying the poor rates.[34]

Early criticism of the Laws of Settlement came from Adam Smith, who argued that such laws hindered the mobility of labor and thereby prevented wages from reaching their natural level. The younger William Pitt invoked Smith's authority in support of humanitarian reform. Attempting to ameliorate the harsher aspects of the law, the humanitarian reformers denied to the parish the power to remove anyone before he became chargeable.[35] This humane law eliminated such unseemly litigation as the removal of a pregnant woman to prevent the child from obtaining a settlement. The humanity of this law was acknowledged by the Commissioners, and it was one of the few Poor Laws enacted during Pitt's ministries which they endorsed.

The Commissioners, however, had no intention of repealing the Laws of Settlement. They were resolved to retain the Laws of Settlement to control the movement of English laborers and to protect the English market from the influx of Scotch and Irish migrants. By making the Laws of Settlement more rigorous, the Commissioners felt they were reinforcing the laws of nature: "when things are left to their natural course, the agricultural labourer is generally hired by the year and often passes his whole life on the same farm."[36]

The desire to check the growth of population also led to the strengthening of the Laws of Bastardy. The existing laws, difficult to enforce, placed primary responsibility on the man. They enabled the magistrates to make orders of filiation on the testimony of the woman, and such orders were sometimes made on her testimony alone.

The Commissioners' opposition to the existing Bastardy Laws was almost compulsive: "These laws place at the mercy of any abandoned woman, every man who is rich enough to give security." So long as relief was given according to the number of children, they thought the existing Poor Laws also encouraged bastardy: "To the woman, therefore, a single illegitimate child is seldom an expense and two or three are a source of positive profit."[37]

Relatively little of the vast body of evidence collected by the Commissioners pertained to the minor abuses of bastardy and settlement. Most of it concerned the major abuses of outdoor relief and the extravagance of the magistrates. There were several kinds of evidence collected by the Commissioners and published as Appendices to the Report, of which replies to the Rural and Town Queries comprised the largest part. These returns were digested and published in seven folio volumes running several thousand pages. The reports and findings of the twenty-eight Assistant Commissioners filled three more volumes.[38] Two volumes of the Appendix were devoted to the investigation of vagrancy and the labor rate. Reluctant to leave any source of information unexplored, the Commissioners collected evidence through the Foreign Office pertaining to relief practices of other countries. This foreign intelligence filled still another weighty volume.

The Commissioners considered the returns from the Rural and Town Queries to be the most valuable part of their evidence because of "the number and variety of persons" who answered them.[39] The places selected for interrogation were extreme cases of good and bad management, those notorious for bad management taking precedence over those known for good management. Good and bad counties had long been identified by per capita expenditures and by the proportion of rates to the rent. Traditionally, the worst administered were the southern counties, Dorset, Hants, Sussex, and Kent; the best administered were the northern counties, Cumberland, Durham, Westmoreland, and Northumberland. Another broad distinction was made between town and country administration. Since the best administered parishes were in the towns, they were not investigated so extensively as the rural parishes.[40]

As the Commissioners were interested in collecting opinions as well as facts, they sent the questionnaires to a variety of people. They questioned professionals, lawyers, surveyors, and clergymen who were not directly associated with Poor Law administration. Questionnaires were sent to deputy lieutenants and magistrates, who replied for divisions of counties. Some questions went to incorporated parishes and unions, but most went to the parochial officials, overseers, assistant overseers, churchwardens, and vestry clerks. In many instances the local officials of the same parish gave contradictory answers to the questions. After receiving conflicting answers, the Commissioners instructed their Assistants to cross-examine persons who had returned such replies and to obtain vouchers of actual practices. The questionnaires sent to the rural parishes were so frequently misunderstood that the Commissioners circulated three different versions of the questions.[41] That replies to the three different sets of questions were compiled together did not trouble the Commissioners, for they were seeking opinions as well as facts.[42]

The immense bulk of the returns from the Rural Queries so overwhelmed the Commissioners that they were able to make little use of them. They professed that about half of the replies were of no value and served only to encumber the useful matter. But they "were unwilling to incur the responsibility of selection." It must be added, they were also unwilling to incur the responsibility of pointing out which half was useful matter and which was cumbersome.[43]

Since the Commissioners' primary objective was to prevent the magistrates from ordering outdoor relief, they attempted to discover the extent of this practice and of other relief methods in rural areas. Rural Queries 24 and 25 concerned the existence of scales and allowances:

> Query 24. Have you any and how many able-bodied labourers in the employment of individuals receiving allowances or regular relief from your parish on their own account, or on that of their families; and if on account of their families, at what number of children does it begin?
>
> Query 25. Is relief or allowance given according to any and what scale?

The answers to Queries 24 and 25, pertaining to scales and allowances, indicated the existence of several types of scales in different parts of England. Of 1,195 places replying to Queries 24 and 25, 28 per cent had no scales, 22 per cent had fixed money scales, 20 per cent had bread scales, 21 per cent had family scales, and 9 per cent had no one on relief or relieved paupers only in the workhouse. Those places having money or bread scales also relieved their paupers according to the size and age of the family. The general practice was to relieve large families with several children under ten years of age, beginning with the third or fourth child.[44]

After reading hundreds of replies, one must conclude that some sort of scale was generally used by the parish whether the pauper

261

was privately employed, or employed by the parish, or unemployed. Scales had a variety of meanings. Some respondents understood scales to mean only bread scales, while others thought they meant only published scales. Rarely did any respondent identify bread scales with Speenhamland.[45] The replies further indicate that parsimony, not profusion, was the general practice, whether the parish had a fixed money scale or a sliding bread scale.

Rural Queries 39 and 40 pertained to the extent of allowances and the attitudes of local officials toward them:

> Query 39. Can you state the particulars of any attempt which has been made in your neighborhood to discontinue the system (after it has once prevailed) of giving to able-bodied labourers in the employment of individuals parish allowance on their own account or that of their families?

> Query 40. What do you think would be the effects, both immediate and ultimate, of an enactment forbidding such allowance, and thus throwing wholly on parish employment all those whose earnings could not support themselves and their families?

Of the 929 replies to Query 39, 58 per cent of the respondents acknowledged having allowances; 42 per cent reported having none. Of the 897 replies to Query 40, 490 respondents favored continuing family allowances; 265 wished to eliminate them. The complexity of the question left 142 persons undecided whether to continue or eliminate allowances. Many places having allowances defended them on the grounds either that wages were too low to support a large family or that the parish could not supply enough jobs for the unemployed.[46]

Closely connected with scales and allowances were the questions about magisterial interference. By Rural Queries 43 and 44 the Commissioners hoped to collect evidence to prove the interference of the magistrates:

> Query 43. Is relief or allowance generally given in consequence of the advice or order of the magistrates, or under the opinion that the magistrates would make an order for it if the application were made to them?

> Query 44. What do you think would be the effect, immediate and ultimate, of making the decision of the vestry or select vestry in matters of relief final?

Of the 870 replies to Query 43, 484 places reported having magisterial interference; 367 denied having interference; and nineteen evaded answering the question directly. The replies to this question provided some of the evidence sought by the Commissioners. The magistrates were, indeed, exercising a wide jurisdiction over the ministry of parish relief. Many places, however, had no interference. The townships of Cheshire and Northumberland managed their local affairs independent of the magistrates; and in sparsely settled areas the magistrates were often too remote to curtail the farmers' parsimonious control of parochial affairs.[47]

The replies to Query 44 indicate that where the magistrates had the greatest influence, they were highly esteemed. Of the 967 replies to this question, 559 wished to continue pauper appeals; 316 preferred to discontinue them; and ninety-two were undecided. Even a majority of local officials, the clergy and the overseers, thought it necessary to continue appeals in order to protect paupers from the farmers who not only employed them but also determined the amount of their relief in seasons of unemployment.[48]

The Commissioners' case against the magistrates did not rest on the charge of mere interference; rather, their charge was interference on the side of extravagance. The ordering of profuse relief was the significance of the Speenhamland bread scales; the replies to the rural questions, however, failed to substantiate the charge of profusion.

Speenhamland did not exist at Speen. Among the respondents to the Rural Queries was Frederick Page, a deputy lieutenant of Berkshire and a magistrate at Speen. If any magistrate knew the meaning of Speenhamland, it must have been Page, for he had originally sent the account to Sir Frederick Eden and had condemned it as extravagant.

What was the situation at Speen in 1832? In reply to Query 39 Page declared: "There never has been any parish allowance given to labourers in the employ of individuals, to enable the latter to pay lower wages. I should even say that it was never proposed, as the leading members of the select vestry are known to be decidedly against such a plan."[49] Although Page denied the existence of allowance in-aid-of-wages, he acknowledged the granting of relief to large families according to the original Berkshire scale.[50]

The replies to the Town Queries yielded even less evidence than the Rural Queries to support the charge of magisterial profusion.

Like the questions sent to the county parishes, the Town Queries were not meant to be an impartial exploration of urban welfare. Rather, they were intended to establish extreme cases of good and bad administration, cases already well known to Poor Law reformers. More questionnaires (148 of 365) were sent to Middlesex than to any other county; more to the London parishes within-the-walls than to the well-managed populous parishes incorporated under Local Acts. Of the eighty-four questionnaires sent to the whole of London, seventy-two went to the City-within-the-walls whose parishes had already lost their paupers to surrounding areas with cheap housing. The urban questionnaire included questions on outdoor relief to the able-bodied, the jurisdiction of magistrates, and the types of scales used in granting relief:

Query 30. Is allowance or regular relief out of the workhouse given by your parish to any able-bodied mechanics, manufacturers, labourers or servants?

Query 31. Is the relief or allowance given on the advice or order of the magistrate? Or under the opinion the magistrate would make an order if application were made to him?

Query 32. Is it given according to any and what scale? Is it given to any persons wholly employed by individuals, on the grounds that their wages are insufficient to maintain their children?

Of the 365 replies to Query 30, 206 places (56 per cent) granted allowances to able-bodied persons; but a majority of these places granted relief to labourers only when unemployed. The remainder in 159 places (44 per cent) provided only work relief for able-bodied persons lacking private employment.[51]

Of the 314 respondents to Query 31, 176 reported having magisterial interference; 138 reported having none. Very few urban magistrates, however, ordered relief according to bread scales. Of the 322 replies to Query 32, 213 places denied having scales, fifty-two places relieved large families, forty places had a fixed money scale, nine places had bread scales, and eight places provide only work relief for the able-bodied paupers.[52]

The Town Queries 31 and 41 were derived from the Commissioners' assumptions about wages and the condition of labor. Influenced by the doctrines of political economy, they frequently thought of the wages as one of the abstract portions distributed

264

among the agents of production. They viewed wages as being paid from a fixed fund, and from the same fund, relief to laborers must also be paid. If relief or wages were paid from the farmer's or businessman's capital, those enterprisers would be unable to hire the normal number of labourers.

The Commissioners, moreover, assumed that the entire family should be employed, and that a large family could subsist only if several members earned an income. Query 38 asked what the annual income would be of the "average man" with "an average amount" of employment; and Query 39 asked what his wife and four children might earn, fourteen, eleven, eight, and five. The few replies to such ill-conceived questions indicated only that a man's wages could not support more than a family of four or five children.[53]

The preoccupation with the doctrines of political economy so obscured the Commissioners' vision that they lost sight of seasonal unemployment in both town and country. The evidence contained in the Appendices to the Report point to the existence of several kinds of unemployment, cyclical, structural, technological, and seasonal. Appendix D contained evidence against the labor rate, which was condemned as mismanagement of the Poor Laws. The labor rate was, in fact, a serious attempt to employ farm labor during winter months at regular pay and under normal supervision. Appendix D, therefore, should be regarded as proof of extensive rural unemployment.[54]

Appendix E, containing the results of the investigation of vagrancy, provides much useful information on both seasonal and structural unemployment. The Radical reformers were determined to stop the flow of Scotch and Irish laborers into England. The thirteen thousand vagrants who passed through Preston during 1832 were, for the most part, going to work in English harvests. In addition to the Scots and the Irish, there were English laborers on the tramp looking for work. From September 15 to October 11, 1832, 626 English vagrants, who passed through Preston, represented sixty-one different trades.[55]

The final reports of the Assistant Commissioners filled three volumes of Appendix A. Several of the Assistant Commissioners described social conditions in a manner that would do credit to a present-day economic historian, but the majority were Radical reformers collecting cases to illustrate their preconceived objectives.[56] Their preconception of unemployment was that a surplus population had been created by the magistrates' ordering of profuse relief. These highly selected cases were further selected by the Commissioners' staff and inserted between the lines of their Report, which had been written well in advance of the publication of Appendix A.[57]

While all the reports of the Assistant Commissioners were directed against the abuses of the existing system, the remedies for the abuses were derived primarily from Chadwick's investigations of London and Berkshire. His drastic remedies were prescribed for the disease of pauperism which he diagnosed as Malthusian redundancy. Yet nowhere in England was structural unemployment more conspicuous than in that area of the Metropolis, St. Martin's parish, Bethnal Green. The rebuilding of the City to make room for institutions of finance and commerce had swept paupers beyond the walls into parishes where jerry-built tenements arose to receive them. In like manner, as Spitalfields was reconstructed, the destitute silkweavers were dispersed to the cheap housing of Twig Folly.[58]

The slums of London, full of conspicuous misery, appalled Chadwick. When he came to Bethnal Green to interrogate Acting Overseer Bunn, he was told: "Yesterday, 4,144 individuals were relieved in the house, and of these five out of six were weavers or connected with the weaving trade." Bunn further informed Chadwick that six thousand to seven thousand persons were relieved every week.

How did Bunn explain the indigence of Bethnal Green? He pointed out to Chadwick that it was caused by the repeal of protection for silkweavers' wages: "The chief decline in wages took place eight years ago when the piece book, or fixed scale of wages, was done away with. Wages immediately after fell in consequence of excessive competition between men and masters as well."[59]

Similar testimony was given by Richard Gregory, the parish treasurer of Christ Church, Spitalfields: "There are now few weavers in Spitalfields comparative to what were. The larger proportion of them have, within the last thirty years, gone to Bethnal Green and Shoreditch. . . ." Such testimony, however, was passed over by Chadwick as the "chronic complaints" heard for twenty years.[60]

With the reconstruction of the City and Spitalfields, what happened to the Laws of Removal and Settlement? The overseer of Shoreditch, for example, could not return paupers to the City or

Spitalfields, where there were no houses to receive them. Unable to remove paupers, he appeared daily with a hundred or more before the magistrate of the district, William Benett, who ordered their former parishes to relieve them. Resenting such magistrate's interference, the parish officials of Spitalfields refused to obey his orders. Under Chadwick's guidance, one of the local board of governors, Brushfield, continued to defy Benett's orders. The testimony resulting from this controversy provided Chadwick with his best example of an interfering magistrate.

Under the influence of political economy, Chadwick strove to discredit those explanations of economic conditions which ran counter to his principles. Influenced by the same inadequate principles, the Commissioners reviewed and rejected remedies which would appear to present policy makers as the best solutions for their welfare problems. They rejected, for example, a national rate, which would have provided an adequate source of revenue. A national rate would also have eliminated the Laws of Settlement and have increased the mobility of labor. After considering the advantages of a national rate, the Commissioners could not bring themselves to adopt it. They concluded that it was a wrong principle for the government "to promise subsistence to all, to make the government the insurer against illness, misfortune, and vice. . . ."[61]

The Commissioners rejected the proposal of land allotments to agricultural laborers, unless the allotments were made by the landlord or his tenant. With equal firmness they opposed the labor rate. Although willing to concede its temporary success, they thought "the ultimate effects of a labour rate. . .must be to destroy the distinction between pauperism and independence."[62]

The unifying principle of the Commissioners' recommendations was less-eligibility. The essence of the new science of dispauperization was to make the condition of the pauper less pleasant than the condition of the lowest paid laborer. The strict application of the principle, they thought, would have the following effects: Paupers would be converted into independent laborers; poor rates would fall; wages would rise; improvident marriages would be reduced; laborers would become more content; and crime would be diminished.

Guided by the principle of less-eligibility, the Commissioners repealed the humanitarian legislation that had been in effect for forty years. Their first recommendation, the most important of

267

the twenty-two, abolished outdoor relief to able-bodied laborers and their families, except in cases of illness. Assistance to large families was disallowed. Henceforth, the unemployed, male and female, must enter a workhouse to obtain relief.

So drastic and harsh a measure could be justified only as a means of preventing national calamity. The Commissioners regarded pauperism as a national calamity, a contagious disease that had to be extirpated. Alarmed by the growth of population and appalled by the increase of misery, they thought it their duty to stop the downward spiral of moral degeneration. They therefore willingly imposed suffering on a great number of people for the sake of national progress and the health of future generations.

To enforce so drastic a measure, the Commissioners effected a revolution in local government by transferring jurisdiction over welfare from the magistrates to a central board of commissioners. They pronounced the magistrates to be men of good intentions, but unable to understand that they were augmenting the miseries which they intended to relieve. It was the essence of their radicalism to transfer political power from the country gentlemen to urban professionals trained in law, economics, and political science.

The authority and responsibility vested in the Central Board were extraordinary. Heretofore legislation enabled the parishes to act; the new law would compel them to do so. The old law encouraged local initiative and was flexible enough to allow adaptation of policy to diverse economic conditions. The new law, seeking uniformity for its own sake, placed the parishes under national control. Even remote villages with sparse population were made to bear the scrutiny of a central inspector. Vested in the Central Board was the authority to compel parishes to unite in order to build workhouses. The Commissioners not only recognized, but also justified, the Radical reform of local government: "The extent of the powers and duties must be measured by the extent and inveteracy of the existing evils, and by the failures, or worse than failures, of the measures by which the removal has been attempted."[63]

The chief institution for dispauperizing the working classes was the workhouse. The new workhouse was to be constructed according to the design of the Panopticon. It embodied the Benthamite principles of classification, separation, and seclusion. Such principles were not devoid of humanity, for they were intended to promote the health and morals of the inmates. The harshness of

268

the scheme was depriving paupers of liberty, luxuries, and the ability to communicate with one another.[64]

The Commissioners recommended the scheme notwithstanding the eighteenth-century experience with workhouses and houses of industry. The Gilbert Act of 1782 had enabled parishes to unite in order to build workhouses; but the workhouses had been so unsuccessful that the humanitarian reformers transformed them into poorhouses.[65]

The two major recommendations concerning the magistrates' ordering of outdoor relief were supplemented by two minor ones. The minor recommendations related to bastardy and settlement. To establish effective control over a redundant population, the Commissioners thought it necessary to restore rigor to the Laws of Settlement. They hoped to effect tighter control over the movement of labor by eliminating all grounds for settlement except birth.[66]

To achieve a more effective control over population, the Commissioners, moreover, thought it necessary to deter improvident marriages producing pauper children. An obviously improvident parent was the mother of an illegitimate child. To deter bastardy the Commissioners recommended the repeal of previous legislation which had shifted the burden of supporting a bastard from the mother to the putative father. They revised the law by placing responsibility on the mother and denying relief to her child.[67]

Although the Commissioners were harsh in their deterrence of pauperism, they were sanguine in expecting beneficial consequences to flow from their proposed legislation. They anticipated a rise in wages high enough to provide a standard of comfort and security. They expected laborers to be able to make better use of the institutions of self-help, such as education, savings banks, and Friendly Societies. They showed their faith in the individual's desire of bettering his condition by authorizing the parish to make loans to persons wishing to emigrate.[68] Their faith was also written into the ninth recommendation, which authorized relief to able-bodied laborers to be made as a loan and recoverable by attachment of wages.[69] In making this recommendation, as in so many others, the Commissioners disregarded their evidence. The replies to Rural Query 41, concerning the making of loans under the Sturges Bourne Act, disclosed that few parish officials had attempted to administer relief as a loan and that the few who attempted it were unsuccessful.[70]

269

The Commissioners were reluctant to reform the system of poor rates even though they had discovered that the existing method of rating was "in the highest degree uncertain and capricious." The rates were so inequitably assessed that they varied from one-fifth of the rent to full actual value. In many places property had not been re-evaluated for a half-century. Another inequity was the rating of the occupier rather than the owner. Since paupers paid no rates, many urban tenements with low rents remained unrated. These inequities in the assessment of the rates were left untouched because the Commissioners thought it unwise to increase the revenues for welfare.[71]

On February 21, 1834, Lord Melbourne presented the Poor Law Report in the House of Lords imploring the Lords to give it their "serious consideration." On the same day in the House of Commons, Lord Althorp, while debating the question of agricultural distress, promised to benefit agriculture by reducing the poor rates, "the growth of which would swallow all the surplus property of the country. . . ."[72]

The course of events during the ensuing session prevented Parliament from giving the Poor Law Amendment Bill the attention which so complex a body of legislation deserved. The energies and interests of the members of Parliament were fully absorbed by the political issues of religious liberty and the repeal of the Union with Ireland. The insistent and even violent demands for the redress of religious grievances and for a more liberal government in Ireland disrupted the Whig ministry and precipitated the resignation of Lord Grey before the Poor Law Amendment Bill had been debated in the House of Lords.

On April 17, Lord Althorp introduced the Poor Law Amendment Bill in the House of Commons. Chancellor of the Exchequer and Whig leader in the House of Commons, Althorp conducted the Bill successfully through all its difficult stages. It was not to be treated as a Whig measure, and there was to be no opposition from the Tory leaders.[73] With the tacit support of Sir Robert Peel, Lord Althorp could adopt a disarming attitude of conciliation and compromise.

The Poor Law Amendment Bill, as explained and defended by Althorp, was not strictly a welfare measure. It concerned the able-bodied laborer more than the impotent poor. Its purpose was to bring the labor supply in line with demand, and so raise wages. To transform the pauperized working classes into a happy labor force,

270

it was necessary to stop outdoor relief to able-bodied laborers and their families. Though harsh at first, the curtailing of outdoor relief would have desirable consequences, "a very short time would elapse after the removal of assistance before wages would rise to an equivalent amount, and as soon as that was the case the situation in which labourers would be placed would be infinitely preferable to that in which they at present stood." [74]

While defending the new Poor Law in terms of economic doctrines, Althorp acknowledged that he did not go as far as "strict political economists" would have him go: "Political economy implied that every man be left to supply his own subsistence, by his own labour — that he must know what his family cost — that he alone should provide for them and that he ought to make provision for calamities which sickness and misfortune might bring upon him out of his previous savings." But Althorp did not fully agree; he stood somewhere between the doctrines of political economy and the attitudes of religion and humanity which convince us, "that the support of those who were really helpless and really unable to provide for themselves was not only justifiable but a sacred duty imposed on those who had the ability to assist the distressed." [75]

Lord Althorp was willing, nevertheless, to repeal the 36th of George III which he recognized as a humane law. It had been introduced to benefit the laboring population "whose interests and welfare they now most destructively opposed." A law thus based on "a very humane principle had been productive of the most baneful effects."

Lord Althorp stood within a long legislative tradition of Poor Law reform. Most of his arguments had been used by the reformers of the 1820's. He paid little attention to the principle of less-eligibility. When explaining the workhouse principle, he referred to Cowell's investigations rather than to Chadwick's. He was politically wise in saying little about London and Berkshire, for Chadwick had aroused great antagonism in those areas.

The outraged country gentlemen of Berkshire found in John Walter an able defender of rural practices under the old Poor Law. Equally motivated by a sense of outrage were William Cobbett and Sir Francis Burdett. George Delacy Evans, one of the few members who professed to having read the Report, objected to it because it assigned the wrong causes for "the demoralization and misery which existed." [76] Sir Samuel Whalley, a guardian of St. Maryle-

271

bone, defended the methods of the urban corporations under the Local Acts. That the "three-tailed Bashaws" of the Central Board had been empowered to repeal eight hundred Local Acts, embracing a century of experience, filled Sir Samuel with incredulity but did not leave him speechless.

It was unfortunate that several of the newly elected members of the Reformed Parliament were so inexperienced that their efforts were frustrated by the rules of procedure. Joseph Brotherton, of Salford, expressed the view that "the fluctuations in the trade of the county" would make it "impolitic to exclude able-bodied laborers from relief." G. R. Robinson, from Worcester, added his opinion that in a stagnant period hundreds of thousands of unemployed people would have to be dealt with and there would never be enough workhouses to enclose them. Unfortunately, his resolution to promote beneficial employment was lost in the technicalities of procedure.[77]

George Poulett Scrope, the principal economic writer for the *Quarterly Review*, emerged during the debates as an able leader of the opposition. Well informed about economic conditions and the operations of the Poor Laws, he identified himself with the working classes and made an earnest plea for their right to relief. He defended the old Poor Laws but not allowances in-aid-of-wages. As a political economist he opposed all interference with wages, but he also agreed with Robinson that unemployment was a major cause of destitution. He was, therefore, opposed to shutting up the poor in "workhouse gaols".[78]

The opponents of the Poor Law Amendment Bill were in an exceedingly difficult position. Lacking experienced leadership, they opposed the Bill for different reasons. They were overwhelmed, moreover, by the mass of evidence, which no one professed having read completely. George Grote, as becoming to the future historian of Greece, acknowledged having read Appendix A. Thomas Attwood jested that the evidence contained twenty-one billion facts and that anyone doubting it could go count them for himself.[79] William Cobbett added a similar comment; he thought no one had read one-twentieth of the evidence and to do so would take 365 days.

Despite the difficulties of their position, the opponents of the Poor Law Amendment Bill continued to resist the measure through each stage of the committee. They had a field day in attacking the workhouse scheme by proposing oblique amendments that embarrassed Althorp and his supporters. An amendment to forbid the building of treadmills in the workhouse had to be defeated. Another amendment compelled the Whigs to defend the Commission's power of separating husband from wife and parents from children. Althorp's only defense of so harsh a proposal was to promise that separations would be the exception and not the rule.

Lord Althorp made a major concession to the opposition by greatly expanding the "emergency clause." Inasmuch as the Bill had made inadequate provision for the impotent poor, the aged, the infirm, and the orphan, Althorp had to shelter them under the "emergency clause." The parish overseers and guardians were empowered to relieve the impotent poor upon making such recommendations to the Central Board. The "emergency clause" became Althorp's escape hatch. It was expanded to include even the able-bodied: "the overseers or guardians of any parish or union shall deem it advisable that relief should be given to any able-bodied person, wholly or partially in the employment of any person or persons, it shall be lawful for such overseers or guardians to make a statement and to report to the said Commissioners the special circumstances which in their judgment render such relief expedient."[80]

Legislation so comprehensive as the Poor Law Amendment Bill did not completely satisfy its supporters any more than it merited the undivided opposition of its foes. The Whigs had paid a high price for Tory support by their concessions to Sturges Bourne. They granted to the absentee landlords the privileges of accumulative voting by proxy. In the age of the Reform Bill, the Benthamite Radicals were not expected to support a principle as undemocratic as accumulative voting. Under the leadership of Hume, Grote, and Torrens, the Radicals were able to eliminate accumulative voting for occupiers but not for the landlords.[81]

Although Sir Robert Peel and the Duke of Wellington had committed themselves to the support of the Poor Law Amendment Bill, many of their Tory followers showed their discontent by voting for the Labourer's Employment Bill, which included the principles of a labor rate. When the Bill was introduced on March 25 by Sir Charles Burrell, it gained the support of Lord Stanley, who was still a member of the Whig Government. By the time the Bill had reached its second reading, the Whig Ministry had been disrupted by the Irish Questions, and Stanley and three other Ministers had resigned. To defeat the Tory dissidents and to bol-

273

ster the tottering Government, Lord Palmerston spoke against the Labourer's Employment Bill. He stigmatized the proponents of a labor rate as bad theorists. His speech contained little more than the traditional polemic for political economy. What the proponents of the labor rate called "practical principles," he declared, were nothing more than bad theory "founded on their own narrow and particular experience." [82]

Political economists, whether Whig or Tory, could be counted on to oppose the principle of a labor rate. Poulett Scrope, though a defender of the old Poor Law, opposed the labor rate as "nothing more than the allowance system in disguise." Agreeing with Scrope and Palmerston, Robert Torrens viewed the labor rate as a bad remedy based on a wrong principle: "Nothing could be worse than accumulating idle labourers in a parish and deducting from the productive industry of others to support them. If there were a surplus of labourers in a parish, the proper way to deal with them would be, if they could not be employed on the land, to apply them to the increase of trade and commerce of the country."

Although the Labourer's Employment Bill, at its second reading, won a minority of only thirty-six in the House of 116 members, its Tory supporters had increased the hostility to the Whig Ministry. On June 6, Lord Althorp made his most important concession to the opposition by denying to the Central Board the power to compel the building of workhouses: "Although it had been recommended in the Report that the Commission should have power of building workhouses, his Majesty's Government would not consent to give them that power." [83]

At the third reading of the Poor Law Amendment Bill its opponents were able to muster only a minority of fifty against its passage. Nevertheless, they had served a useful purpose. They had alerted the country to the grave defects of the new Poor Law. They had clearly defined the issues which would grow into a movement more violent than any opposition that ever arose against the old Poor Law. They had foretold what would happen when the stagnation of trade — that was to come in 1837 — created more unemployed than could be enclosed in a workhouse. They had, indeed, prepared the way for the later Chartist revolt which would be fomented by Stephens and Oastler.

On July 1 Lord Grey introduced the Poor Law Amendment Bill in the House of Lords. But before it reached its second reading,

274

Grey had resigned and the reins of government had passed into the hands of Lord Melbourne.

At the second reading of the Poor Law Bill on July 21, Lord Brougham made the major speech in its defense. He exulted in the Bill as though it were his personal triumph. He fully endorsed the Poor Law Report as "admirable in all respects," and in keeping with scientific principles of investigation. He had high praise for Chadwick's report which he regarded as the scientific verification of less-eligibility: "That they who toil should not live worse than the idle," appeared to Brougham to be "as self-evident as if a man were to say two and two make four and not fourteen. . . ."[84]

Although Brougham celebrated the Report and defended the Poor Law Bill, he was not in full agreement with either. He was still a natural law reformer who preferred the doctrines of Adam Smith and Malthus to the later economics of Ricardo, Mill, and McCulloch. He much preferred the Scottish system of welfare to the English. He opposed homes for the aged and foundling hospitals, for such institutions, whether private or public, destroyed providence, foresight, and prudence. While applying the natural law doctrines of Smith and Malthus to charitable institutions, he disagreed with the Radical reformers who thought the Poor Laws could be used as a means of checking the growth of population. Such an application of the law would eventually "encourage improvident marriages."[85]

Lord Brougham, moreover, disagreed with the Radical reformers who wished to restore the spirit and intention of the 43rd of Elizabeth. He thought the Elizabethans knew virtually nothing about economics: "those who formed the statute of Elizabeth were not adept in political science — they were not acquainted with the true principles of population — they could not foresee that a Malthus would arise to enlighten mankind upon the important branch of science — they knew not the true principle upon which to frame a preventive check to the unlimited increase of the people."[86]

In order to check the growth of population, Brougham thought it necessary to stop subsidizing large families and to start financing emigration. He would also check the growth and movement of populations by modifying the Laws of Settlement and Bastardy. Although he preferred settlement by birth only, he would support a settlement by residence of an adequate length.

Lord Brougham reserved his strongest aversion for the Laws of Bastardy which made both male and female responsible for the support of an illegitimate child. His observations on female morality outraged the Bishops. But Brougham had full confidence in his utilitarian analysis of female sexuality; in brief, the calculation of interests, not her passions, was decisive in a woman's being seduced.[87]

Henry Phillpotts, Bishop of Exeter, led the attack on the Poor Law Amendment Bill in the House of Lords. Knowing that he could not defeat a measure supported by the leaders of both parties, he sought to arouse opposition to it and to undermine confidence in the Poor Law Report. He concentrated his attack on the proposed changes in the Laws of Bastardy. He refused to accept Brougham's observations, and he rejected the declaration in the Report, "that the virtue of female chastity does not exist among the lower orders."[88]

In replying to Phillpotts, the Bishop of London defended the Commissioners' Report but did not feel responsible for all that was written in the separate reports of the Assistant Commissioners. Although Blomfield did not condone the statement on the lack of female virtue among the lower orders, he dismissed Chadwick, who had made it, with a mild reprimand: "he had a style of writing which perhaps indicated a certain degree of warmth — not to say precipitancy — which now and then led him to conclusions somewhat beyond what the premises would warrant."[89]

Bishop Phillpotts' opposition to the bastardy clauses reduced somewhat the burden placed on the mother of an illegitimate child. The amended Bill passed its third reading on August 8, but it was passed against the protests of those who wished to record their defense of female virtue among the lower orders. Other Lords entered protests against shutting up people in workhouses who lacked employment or had insufficient wages to support their families.[90]

When the Poor Law Amendment Bill finally passed, it contained two major and two minor provisions. The major provisions corrected what had long been regarded as the gravest abuses of the old Poor Law. Both abuses were embodied in law enacted under the younger William Pitt, the 36th of George III, which enabled the magistrates to order outdoor relief to all types of needy people, even to employed laborers with large families.

The first major reform under the new Poor Law stopped all outdoor relief on a specified date, June 1, 1835. Except in cases of emergency, it required able-bodied paupers to enter a workhouse to obtain relief. Indoor relief was to be administered in such a fashion as to make it less desirable than the worst condition of the independently employed laborer. The second major reform was the transfer of jurisdiction from the magistrates to a Central Board of Commissioners. Henceforth, effective control over public relief rested with the national government. Whereas previous legislation had enabled the parish to act, the new Poor Law compelled them to act.[91]

The Central Board of three permanent Commissioners had the authority to appoint Assistant Commissioners as supervisors over local officials. The Central Board could direct certain parishes to unite in order to build workhouses and administer relief more efficiently. The new unions elected guardians who were the responsible officials on the local level, the parish vestry having retained only the function of assessing and collecting the rates. The guardians and the vestrymen were henceforth to be elected by the occupiers who paid the rates and by the landlords who owned property in the parish. Permanent salaried officials were appointed by the guardians to replace the previous unpaid, annually-elected overseer. Other paid officials, the governors and matrons of the workhouse, a treasurer and a surveyor, were appointed by the guardians, but subject to removal by the Central Board.

The new Poor Law, consequently, had great political significance. By transferring jurisdiction from the magistrates to the Central Board, it reduced the Tory influence exercised through the Gentry and the Established Church. At the same time it created a new source of patronage sufficient to reinvigorate the Whigs.

The two minor provisions in the new Poor Law modified the Laws of Settlement and the Laws of Bastardy. The new Law of Settlement was designed to provide a permanent residence for rural laborers and to protect the English labor market from Irish and Scottish migrants. The new Law of Bastardy placed primary responsibility on the mother for the support of her illegitimate child.

The new system of welfare was founded upon the investigation and recommendations of the Poor Law Commission. The purpose of the Commission was to point out the abuses of the old system and to recommend remedies for those abuses. The final Report, by and large, was the product of a division of labor between Nassau Senior, an economist, and Edwin Chadwick, a political scientist.

Most of the information collected by the Assistant Commissioners under Senior's supervision condemned the existing Poor Laws as violation of the natural laws of political economy. The creation of a new system on the ruins of the old was mainly Chadwick's achievement. He created the new system of welfare in keeping with the principle of less-eligibility and laid the foundations of what he thought was a science of dispauperization.

The new Poor Law was proposed as a remedy for the disease of pauperism, a Malthusian disease of over-population and moral decline resulting from the failure to exercise providence and foresight. The maladministration of the Poor Laws, or the magistrates' ordering of profuse relief, had aggravated the disease and thwarted the natural desire of every man to better his condition.

The new Poor Law, to some extent, satisfied the political economists who believed in the natural harmony of interest. It removed those obstacles that had thwarted the operation of natural law. At the same time, the new Poor Law satisfied the political scientists who believed legislation should be used to promote artificially the harmony of interests. Thus the contradiction inherent in utilitarian thought was overcome in the passing of the Poor Law Amendment Act.[92]

NOTES

[1] *Report from His Majesty's Commissioners for Inquiring into the Administration and Practical Operation of the Poor Laws*, p. 127. The Report and Appendices are found in *Parliamentary Papers*, 1834, Vols. XXVII-XXXVIII.

[2] Adam Smith, *The Wealth of Nations* (ed. by Edwin Cannan, Modern Libary), p. 324.

[3] *Edinburgh Review*, LXIII (1836), 501.

[4] *Ibid.*, p. 490.

[5] *Poor Law Report*, p. 41.

[6] *Ibid.*, p. 44.

[7] *Edinburgh Review*, LXIII (1836), 504.

[8] *Appendix A.*, Pt. III, p. 23.

[9] *Poor Law Report*, p. 8.

[10] *Ibid.*, p. 71.

[11] *Edinburgh Review*, LXIII (1836), 501.

[12] *Poor Law Report*, p. 37.

[13] *Ibid.*, p. 12.

[14] J. D. Marshall, *The Old Poor Law, 1795-1834*, p. 14. Marshall has confused somewhat the labor rate with the roundsmen practice.

[15] *Poor Law Report*, p. 19.

[16] John Clapham, *Economic History of Modern Britain*, I, 357. Dorothy Marshall in *The English Poor in the 18th Century* found the practice of allow-

ances before 1795.

17 *Poor Law Report*, pp. 12-13.

18 *Ibid.*, p. 24.

19 *Ibid.*, p. 29.

20 *Ibid.*, p. 31. The doctrine of escalation of the rates was adopted in the period 1815 to 1820 by the natural law reformers who did not consider the rates in real terms of the price of wheat. If they had compared the increase in expenditures with the cost of living, or with the increase of other government expenditures, they probably would not have adopted the doctrine.

21 *Ibid.*, p. 34.

22 Elie Halévy, *The Growth of Philosophic Radicalism*, pp. 430-32, for an exposition of the Radical doctrine of self-interest as applied in Bentham's *Constitutional Code* and how Bentham used legislation to harmonize interests.

23 *Poor Law Report*, pp. 37-38. In a half dozen different places in the *Extracts, Report, and Appendices*, the Commissioners celebrated this notorious parish.

24 *Ibid.*, p. 44.

25 *Ibid.*, p. 55.

26 *Ibid.*, p. 61.

27 *Extracts*, p. 421.

28 S. and B. Webb, *The Old Poor Law*, pp. 178-79. The Webbs on this point are more extreme than the Commissioners. E. J. Hobsbaum and George Rulé, *Captain Swing*, p. 13. These authors are not yet ready to abandon the Hammonds' conception of Speenhamland although they recognize some modification has to be made. See John L. and Barbara Hammond, *The Village Labourer*, pp. 181 ff. J. R. Poynter, *Society and Pauperism*, p. 80, finds that Speenhamland "was only one of a host of complementary or conflicting remedies which won the favour of the magistracy."

29 *Poor Law Report*, pp. 68-69. The Speenhamland scale was a table showing that the weekly income of the family should be in keeping with its size, including as many as seven children, and in proportion to the price of a gallon loaf of bread ranging from one shilling to two shillings. This scale created a sensation because of its profusion. Scales were not unusual, but the Speenhamland scale was regarded by Eden as an absurdity. Its extravagance exceeded credibility; for example, when the price of bread reached two shillings, as shown on the scale, a family of seven children was supposed to have an income of twenty-five shillings a week, an amount two or three times as much as winter wages of an ordinary farm laborer.

30 *Poor Law Report*, p. 70.

31 *Ibid.*, p. 71.

32 *Ibid.*, p. 76.

33 *Ibid.*, p. 84.

34 *Ibid.*, p. 85.

35 35 George III, cap. 101.

36 *Poor Law Report*, p. 86. J. D. Chambers and G. E. Mingay in a recent book, *The Agricultural Revolution 1750-1880*, p. 119, argue that the Laws of Settlement reduced the freedom and independence of labor. This is Adam Smith's argument; but Eden, with more facts, observed that the Laws of Settlement had not greatly hindered the mobility of labor.

37 *Poor Law Report*, p. 93.

38 I have included the Reverend Henry Bishop and Edwin Chadwick among the Assistants, even though they were also Commissioners. Bishop did much work in the field; Chadwick was made Commissioner after he had written the report published in the *Extracts*.

[39] *Poor Law Report*, p. 1. See also p. 207 for the introduction to the "Supplement."

[40] The Answers to the Rural Queries filled five volumes of the *Appendix*; the answers to the Town Queries filled two volumes.

[41] *Appendix B*, Pt. I, p. 1.

[42] The replies to the Rural Queries must be used with great caution. Professor Mark Blaug has recognized some of the difficulties in using these returns, but I think the difficulties are even more serious than he has supposed. His pioneer work has pointed the way to what may be done with these materials in reconstructing the social history of this period. See the *Journal of Economic History*, XXIV (1964), 229-37.

[43] *Appendix B.*, Pt. I, p. 10.

[44] Replies to Queries 24 and 25 are found in *Appendix B.*, Pt. III. As many respondents gave only one answer for both questions and in the briefest form, it is often impossible to determine the actual practice. It must be remembered that there were three different editions of Query 24; Query 25 was not altered. It must also be remembered that the respondents did not always reply for the parish where they resided; the replies sometimes pertained to a district or a township.

[45] Speenhamland was a scale of family income by which need could be measured. It was used by the magistrate when the pauper applied to him after the parish overseer had refused to relieve him. The scale could be used to deny relief as well as to grant it. If the scale had been used as a strict measure of relief during the 1820's, expenditures would have fallen drastically; had the scale been used extensively during the famine years of 1795, 1799, 1800, many parishes would have become bankrupt. It was a rule of thumb less useful than a head-count.

[46] *Appendix B.*, Pt. IV, Vol. 33.

[47] *Ibid.* Pt. IV includes Queries 38-45 in Volume 33 of the *Parliamentary Papers*.

[48] *Ibid.*

[49] *Appendix B.*, Pt. IV, p. 239.

[50] Page defended the Sturges Bourne Act. He served as Chadwick's guide in Berkshire. See *Extracts*, p. 235.

[51] *Appendix B.*, Pt. III, Vol. 36.

[52] *Ibid.* Parts III, IV, and V are found in Vol. 36.

[53] *Ibid.*

[54] *Parliamentary Papers*, Vol. 38.

[55] *Ibid.*, Vol. 39, p. 29.

[56] The majority of the Assistant Commissioners explained economic conditions in terms of bad administration. Only five or six assistants took into view the several types of unemployment. What the present-day economist would call unemployment the Radicals explained as overpopulation resulting from subsidies to children. For a recent useful review of economic conditions and the literature pertaining to it, see J. D. Marshall, *The Old Poor Law*, pp. 37-42.

[57] For the Commissioners' account of their procedure, see *Poor Law Report*, pp. 1-3.

[58] *Appendix A* has three parts; Part I is in *Parliamentary Papers*, Vol. 28; Parts II and III are in Vol. 29. Part III contains Chadwick's final report.

[59] *Appendix A*, Pt. III, p. 109.

[60] *Ibid.*, p. 115. Chadwick put the testimony of an unnamed witness in a footnote to refute Gregory.

[61] *Poor Law Report*, p. 100.

[62] *Ibid.*, p. 127.

[63] *Ibid.*, p. 192.

[64] *Ibid.*, p. 172.

[65] The Commissioners recommended a return to the eighteenth-century type of workhouse, notwithstanding the evidence of the Assistant Commissioners against it. Assistant Commissioner Stuart investigated Suffolk, the county having the widest experience with Gilbert Unions and workhouses. After an extensive survey of the Gilbert system, he reported the following conclusions: "Although the workhouse was the great recommendation of the system at the outset, yet after it had been some years in operation, it was discovered that the benefits to be derived from it had been generally overrated; profit from it there was none. . . ." (*App. A.*, 355). He confirmed what many other officials reported: that it cost more to maintain paupers in public institutions than in private residences.

Arthur J. Lewis, another Assistant Commissioner who had investigated the western counties, Salop, Hereford, and Monmouth, supplied information against the feasibility of workhouses. Monmouth, which lacked workhouses, had the lowest rates of the three counties. Hereford had abandoned its workhouses because it was more expensive to maintain the poor inside than out. In the northern division of Salop, the parishes had united to maintain their poor in common workhouses. The houses at Ellsmere and Oswestry were of ample dimension and under large-scale management. Lewis's report provided the following appraisal of the Salop experience: "The original founders of the establishments were, indeed, so sanguine as to their utility that they imagined that able-bodied paupers. . .would yield a surplus fund. These golden dreams, as might have been expected, have never been realized. The labor of paupers is, in fact, a loss to the establishment." (*App. A.*, 659).

[66] Recommendation XIV repealed all grounds for settlement except birth. Parliament modified the Recommendation by providing settlement by occupying a tenement and paying the poor rates for a year. 4 and 5 Will. IV. c. 76, S. LXVI. See Nicholls, II, 278.

[67] Recommendations XX and XXI. These recommendations were modified by Parliament. The new Laws have made it possible for an overseer or a guardian, if the child became chargeable, to apply to the Quarter Sessions and the Court determined the father of an illegitimate child and made him responsible for its support. For the complexity of this law, see Nicholls, II, 278-79. No fewer than eight Sections of the New Poor Law pertained to the regulation of bastardy.

[68] Recommendation XXII.

[69] *Ibid.*, IX. Also, *Poor Law Report*, p. 190.

[70] *Appendix B*, Pt. IV.

[71] See Nicholls, II, p. 308 for subsequent legislation, the Parochial Assessment Act of 1836.

[72] *Hansard*, 3rd ser., XXI, 661.

[73] *Ibid.*, XXIII, 842.

[74] *Ibid.*, XXII, 882-83.

[75] *Ibid.*, 877-78.

[76] *Ibid.*, XXIII, 805.

[77] *Ibid.*, XXIII, 969. For a hostile view of Robinson, see Thomas MacKay, *A History of the English Poor Law* (New York, 1900), p. 134. MacKay's chapter is "The Passing of the Bill."

[78] *Ibid.*, p. 1326.

[79] *Ibid.*, XXIV, 314.

[80] *Ibid.*, 428.

[81] *Ibid.*, 332.

[82] *Ibid.*, 157.

[83] *Ibid.*, 313.

[84] *Ibid.*, XXV, 219.

[85] *Ibid.*, 223.

[86] *Ibid.*, 229.

[87] *Ibid.*, 249. For Malthus's influence on Lord Brougham, see Arthur Aspinall, *Lord Brougham and the Whig Party*, p. 229.

[88] *Hansard*, 3rd ser., XXV, 591. The statement by Chadwick is in the *Report*, p. 195. J. R. Poynter, *Society and Pauperism*, p. 323, thinks the debate was "a somewhat unseemly squabble between two Bishops."

[89] *Hansard*, 3rd ser., XXV, 596.

[90] *Ibid.*, 1096-99.

[91] For the growth of centralism during the 1830's see: David Roberts, *Victorian Origin of the British Welfare State*, Chapter 3.

[92] Halévy, *The Growth of Philosophic Radicalism*, p. 498. I have tried to use Halévy's insight into "the double way in which they [the Radicals] understood the identification of interests." For a sympathetic exposition of the new Poor Law, see Thomas Mackay, *A History of the English Poor Law*, pp. 146-55.

CONCLUSION

WE have surveyed the three different groups of reformers who attempted to improve the English Poor Laws during the decades from 1785 to 1834. The first group, the Evangelical humanitarians, sought to ameliorate the conditions of indigent women, children, the sick, and the elderly. Their method was to relieve individuals without giving much thought to the causes of their destitution.

The Evangelical humanitarians successfully repealed the law of 1722 which compelled paupers to seek relief in workhouses under the management of private contractors. They transformed the workhouses into poorhouses as residences for the sick, the aged, the orphan children, and other persons having no one to care for them who were unable to care for themselves. They instituted a policy of outdoor relief, granting financial assistance to all persons having their own residence and someone to care for them. In keeping with this benevolence, they provided aid for large families, usually those having three or more children under ten years of age.

Besides increasing benefits to the able-bodied and the impotent poor, the reformers of William Pitt's time made it easier for laborers to move to places of employment. They successfully relaxed the Laws of Settlement by prohibiting the removal of persons without legal residence until they had applied for relief. They prohibited the removal of sick persons, including pregnant women, and families having a sick member. The parish officials were also forbidden to remove members of Friendly Societies. By enlarging means of obtaining a legal residence, the Pittite reformers further improved the mobility of labor.

The humanitarians were especially solicitous for the welfare of pauper apprentices. They restricted the removal of pauper children from places of their birth and increased the premiums paid to masters accepting pauper children as apprentices. They assumed a guardian's interest in the apprenticing of chimney sweeps and enacted factory legislation to protect children apprenticed to the new factory owners. The Evangelicals, moreover, successfully promoted new institutions of self-help, including savings banks and Friendly Societies. They made their greatest effort in providing new facilities for educating the poor. Although they were primarily interested in the moral and religious education of the poor, their efforts mark the beginning of a national system of elementary education.

While promoting institutions of self-help, the humanitarians had the cooperation of the natural law reformers, who were the proponents of the new science of political economy. Guided by Adam Smith's principles of free trade, the natural law reformers opposed the Poor Laws as interference with the laws of wages and as preventing the individual from pursuing his own interests.

A central aspect of Adam Smith's economic liberalism was the assumption that all men have the desire to better their condition. The natural law reformers believed that self-interest was a better guide for the legislator than was benevolence. During the postwar depression, when relief expenditures had reached a peak, Sturges Bourne and other Liberal Tories of Lord Liverpool's ministry institutionalized the self-interest of the ratepayers as a check on Poor Law expenses. Under the Poor Law of 1819, the parishes were enabled to organize select vestries, which granted multiple votes to the rich in proportion to the amount of rates paid. The select vestries, moreover, were authorized to hire paid overseers to supervise relief and to reduce expenditures. The great fallacy of the natural law reformers was to attribute the increase of relief expenses to the Poor Laws themselves rather than to the unemployment that came with the end of the Napoleonic War.

T. R. Malthus's principle of population greatly increased the natural law opposition to the Poor Laws. Assuming that population tended to outrun subsistence, Malthus held the view that the Poor

284

Laws subsidized a surplus population. Although reluctant to abolish the Poor Laws immediately, he sought to restrict them by denying relief to infants born a year after his law had been enacted. Failing in this major effort to reform the Poor Laws, he was able, nevertheless, to persuade many reformers that unemployment resulted from a redundant population. Malthus's principle of moral restraint, prudence and forethought, placed the burden of economic progress on the working classes. The laborers must refrain from marriage until they were able to support a family; they must take thought of the future and withhold from current income, however meager, savings against the inevitable day of old age, sickness, and death.

Malthus also blended economics with politics. His willingness to defend the interests of the landlords by advocating the Corn Law of 1815 alienated him from other political economists. When he wrote his textbook on political economy in 1820, his principles went unheeded and his explanation of the postwar depression was ignored. As a consequence of Malthus's defense of the Corn Laws, the economic textbooks of Ricardo, James Mill, and McCulloch provided the guiding principles for the Liberal Tories, the Whigs, and Radicals of the 1820's. During the decade preceding the Poor Law reform of 1834, the Radicals succeeded in combining the economics of Ricardo with the political science of Jeremy Bentham.

James Mill was a disciple of both Ricardo and Bentham. His synthesis of Benthamite politics and Ricardian economics is what Elie Halévy has called "philosophic radicalism." The Radical reformers continued to use the natural law arguments against the Poor Laws, but unlike the natural law reformers, the Radicals were willing to legislate the harmony of interests. As political scientists, it was their forte to devise remedial legislation for the disease of pauperism which they thought threatened the progress of society. In their diagnosis, pauperism originated with the humanitarian legislation of Pitt's time. They regarded the Evangelical reformers as men of benevolent intentions but ignorant of the consequences of interfering with the laws of nature. The Radicals preferred the pre-1795 Poor Laws to the humanitarian legislation of the following decade and regarded the workhouse scheme of 1722 as the best method of cutting relief expenses.

According to the Radical diagnosis, pauperism was a disease infecting the whole society, reducing the industriousness of the working classes and causing their moral decline. With the intention

285

of restoring able-bodied paupers to their previous industriousness, the Radicals consciously adopted harsh means. As Bentham had proposed in his early scheme of pauper management, the Radicals committed themselves to the deterrence of paupers. They deterred the pauper by depriving him of his liberty and by separating him from his friends and family. According to the principle of less-eligibility, the conditions in the workhouse must be made less agreeable than the living conditions of the lowest paid person in private employment. A policy so harsh in its conception could not be effectively administered in many parts of England, especially in times of economic depression.

With the wisdom of hindsight, the student of social policy can better understand why the several groups of reformers of the early nineteenth century failed in their attempts to ameliorate the conditions of the working classes. Some of the reformers continued to hold the eighteenth-century doctrine of poverty as "the spur of civilization." This doctrine, which emphasized motivation more than condition, left little place for the analysis of the causes of destitution. The nineteenth-century concept of pauperism added to the confusion inherent in the earlier discussions of destitution. Under the influence of Malthus and the law of population, the early nineteenth-century reformers viewed pauperism as a social disease, a degradation of the working classes, that resulted from excessive outdoor relief. They too readily concluded that unemployment was the result of a redundant population. Never fully understanding the causes of unemployment, whether cyclical, structural, seasonal, or technological, they were unable to provide adequate remedies for destitution. They could not, of course, foresee that free enterprise would not provide adequate housing for people of low income, nor could they foresee that the Friendly Societies would fail to provide security for manual laborers in times of sickness, old age, and death. Finally, the reformers failed to improve conditions because they lacked exact information about the numbers of indigent people, whether casual or permanent, indoor or outdoor, young or old, sick or unemployed. With improved knowledge of the twentieth century and the wisdom of experience have come old-age pensions, health insurance, public housing, and many other social benefits that characterize the welfare state.

BIBLIOGRAPHY

These lists include the principal items in the footnotes and are designed to indicate the scope and character of materials on which the study is based. The place of publication is London unless otherwise noted.

GOVERNMENT PUBLICATIONS

Parliamentary Debates:

Cobbett's Parliamentary History of England from 1066 to 1803. 36 vols., 1806-1828.
Cobbett's (after 1812) *Hansard's Parliamentary Debates.*

Parliamentary Papers:

Abstract of Returns Relative to the Expenses and Maintenance of the Poor. 1804.
Minutes of Evidence. . .[on] Mendicity and Vagrancy in the Metropolis and Its Neighborhood. 1815.
Report from the S. C. on the Poor Laws. 1817.
Second Report and *Third Report.* 1818.
Report from the S. C. of the H. of L. on the Poor Laws. 1818.
Abstract of Returns Relative to the Expense and Maintenance of the Poor. 1818.
Report from S. C. on Poor Rate Returns. 1824, VI; 1825, IV; 1826, III.
Report from S. C. on Labourers' Wages. 1824, VI.
Abstract of Returns Made to the S. C. . . .[on] Paying Wages of Labour out of Poor Rates. 1825, XIX.
Report from the S. C. Appointed to Inquire into the Expediency of Encouraging Emigration from the United Kingdom. . . . 1826.
Second Report, 1827. *Third Report,* 1828.

An Account of the Society for the Refuge of the Destitute, Specifying the Greatest Number of Males and Females at Any Time in the Establishment .... 1827.

Report from the S. C. Relating to the Employment of Able-bodied Persons Assisted from the Poor Rates. 1828, IV.

Abstract of the Returns of the Number of Poor Persons Belonging to Several Parishes Relieved or Assisted from the Poor Rates. . . . 1829, XXI.

Abstract of Returns Showing the Number of Persons Received into and Removed out of Their Respective Parishes by Virtue of Any Order of Removal. . . . 1829, XXI.

Report from the S. C. on Laws Relating to Irish and Scotch Vagrants. 1828.

Abstract of Returns of the Amount of Money Levied and Expended for the Relief of the Poor. 1830, XXXI.

Amount of Money Levied for Poor Rates and County Rates in England and Wales and Payments thereout for the Relief of the Poor at All the Several Periods for which Returns Have Been Required by Parliament; Also the Average Price of Wheat at Every Such Period. 1830-31, XI.

Report from the S. C. of the H. of L. Appointed to Consider of the Poor Laws; with Minutes of Evidence. . . . 1831, VIII.

Abstract of the Returns of the Amount of Money Levied and Expended for the Relief of the Poor. . .in the Year Ending 25 March 1831. 1832, XLIV.

Report from S. C. on the Present State of Agriculture, With Minutes of Evidence. . . . 1833.

Extracts from the Information Received by His Majesty's Commissioners as to the Administration and Operations of the Poor Laws. (8 vol.) 1833.

Report from His Majesty's Commissioners for Inquiry into the Administration and Practical Operation of the Poor Laws. 1834, XXVII-XXXIX.

REPORTS OF SOCIETIES

The Reports of the Society for Bettering the Condition and Increasing the Comforts of the Poor. 6 vols., 1797-1815.

The Economy of an Institution Established in Spitalfields, London, for the Purpose of Supplying the Poor with Good Meat Soup. . . . 1799.

General Report of the Committee of Subscribers to a Fund for the Relief of the Industrious Poor Resident in the Cities of London and Westminster. 1800.

Reports of the Society for the Suppression of Beggars. Edinburgh, 1813-1829.

The First Report of the Committee of the Fish Association for the Benefit of the Poor. 1813.

Report of the Association Formed in London. . . for Benefit of the Manufacturing and Labouring Poor. 1813.

Report of the Committee for the Relief of the Industrious Poor at Spitalfields. 1816.

Report for the Directors of the Town's Hospital of Glasgow on the Management of the City Poor, the Suppression of Mendicity, and the Principles of the Plan for the New Hospital. Glasgow, 1818.

CONTEMPORARY BOOKS AND PAMPHLETS

Aiken, John, *Life of John Howard*, 1792.

Allen, William, *Life of William Allen, with Selections from His Correspondence.* 3 vols. 1846-47.

_____ Plans for Diminishing the Poor's Rates in Agriculture. 1833.

Arbuthnot, Charles, Correspondence of Charles Arbuthnot. ed. by A. Aspinal, Camden Series, LXV, 1941.

Baker, James, The Life of Sir Thomas Bernard. 1819.

Becher, J. T., The Anti-Pauper System. . . . 1828.

Bell, Andrew, The Madras System, or Elements of Tuition, Comprising the Analysis of an Experiment in Education at the Male Asylum, Madras. . . . 1808.

Bentham, Jeremy, The Works of Jeremy Bentham, ed. by Sir John Bowring, 11 vols., Edinburgh, 1843.

_____ Jeremy Bentham's Economic Writings. ed. by W. Stark, 3 vols., 1952-54.

_____ The Collected Works of Jeremy Bentham. ed. by J. H. Burns: Vols. I and II, Correspondence, by L. S. Sprigge, 1968.

Bernard, Thomas, Outline of Measures for the Improvement of the Character and Condition of the English Poor. 1805.

_____ Letter to the Bishop of Durham on the Measures now before Parliament for Promoting and Encouraging Industry and for the Relief and Regulation of the Poor. 1807.

_____ The New School: Being an Attempt to Define the Principles, Details, and Advantages. 1809.

Brydges, Sir Egerton, Arguments in Favour of Relieving the Able-Bodied Poor by Finding Employment for Them. . . . 1817.

Butcher, E. E., (ed.) Bristol Corporation of the Poor: Selected Records 1696-1834. Bristol, 1932.

Buxton, Thomas Fowell, The Distress in Spitalfields. 1816.

Chalmers, Thomas, The Influence of Bible Societies on the Temporal Necessities of the Poor. Edinburgh, 1817.

_____ On Political Economy in Connexion with the Moral State and Moral Prospects of Society. 1832.

Clarkson, William, An Inquiry into the Causes of the Increase of Pauperism and the Poor Rates and the Proposition for Equalizing the Rates. 1815.

Colquhoun, Patrick, The State of Indigence and the Situation of the Casual Poor in the Metropolis. 1799.

_____ A Treatise on the Police of the Metropolis. 1800.

Copleston, Edward, A Letter to the Right Honorable Robert Peel. . . .on the Pernicious Effects of a Variable Standard of Value Especially as Regards the Condition of the Lower Orders and the Poor Laws. Oxford, 1819.

Copleston, Edward, Second Letter to Sir Robert Peel on the Causes of the Increase of Pauperism and on the Poor Laws. 1819.

Courtenay, Thomas P., Letter to. . . .William Sturges Bourne, Chairman of the Select Committee of the House of Commons for the Consideration of the Poor Laws. . . . 1817.

_____ A treatise on the Poor Laws. 1818.

Curwen, J. C., Speech in the H. of C. on May 28, 1816 on a Motion for a Committee Taking into Consideration the State of the Poor Laws. 1816.

Davis, William, Hints to Philanthropists, or a Collective View of the Means for Improving the Condition of the Poor and Labouring Classes of Society. Bath, 1821.

Eden, Sir Frederick Morton, The State of the Poor: Or an History of the Labouring Classes in England from the Conquest to the Present Period. . . . with Parochial Reports Relative to the Administration of Workhouses and Houses of Industry. . . . 3 vols., 1797.

Ensor, George, An Inquiry Concerning the Population of Nations. 1818.

Field, John, Correspondence of John Howard, the Philanthropist. 1855.

Gilbert, Thomas, *A Scheme for the Better Relief and Employment of the Poor.* 1764.

____ *Plan for the Better Relief and Employment of the Poor; for Enforcing and Amending the Laws Respecting Houses of Correction and Vagrants.* 1781.

____ *Supplement to Mr. Gilbert's Plan and Bills for the Relief of the Poor.* 1787.

Gisborne, Thomas, *An Enquiry in the Duties of Men in the Higher and Middle Classes of Society in Great Britain. . . .* 2 vols. 5th ed., 1800.

Greville, Charles, C.F., *Journals of the Reigns of George IV and William IV.* 3 vols., 1874.

Hanway, Jonas, *Letters on the Importance of Preserving the Rising Generation of the Labouring Part of our Fellow Subjects. . . .* 2 vols., 1766.

____ *The Soldier's Faithful Friend, Being Moral and Religious Advice to Private Men in the Army and Militia.* 1766.

____ *An Earnest Appeal for Mercy to the Children of the Poor. . . .* 1766.

____ *The State of Chimney Sweepers' Young Apprentices. . . .* 1773.

____ *Virtue in Humble Life: Containing Reflections on the Reciprocal Duties of the Wealthy and Indigent, the Master and Servant. . . .* 1774.

____ *The Defects of Police, the Cause of Immorality. . . .* 1775.

____ *Solitude in Imprisonment, with Proper Labor, and a Spare Diet, the Most Humane and Effectual Means of Bringing Malefactors to a Right Sense of their Condition.* 1776.

____ *The Citizen's Monitor: Shewing the Necessity of a Salutary Police. . . .* 1780.

____ *A Sentimental History of Chimney Sweepers in London and Westminster. . . .* 1785.

____ *A Comprehensive View of Sunday Schools. . . .* 1786.

Hershel, John F. W., *Preliminary Discourse on the Study of Natural Philosophy.* 1830.

Horton, R. Wilmot, *The Causes and Remedies of Pauperism. . . .* 1830.

____ *Correspondence Formed for Investigating the Most Efficient Remedies for the Present Distress among the Labouring Classes in the United Kingdom.* 1830.

Howlett, J., *The Insufficiency of Causes to which the Increase of the Poor and the Poor Rates Have Been Ascribed. . . .* 1788.

____ *Examination of Mr. Pitt's Speech. . . .Relative to the Condition of the Poor.* 1796.

Hume, Joseph, *An Account of the Provident Institution for Savings Established in the Western Part of the Metropolis.* 1816.

Jerram, Charles, *Considerations of the Impolicy and the Pernicious Tendency of the Poor Laws.* 1818.

McCulloch, John R., *A Discourse on the Rise, Progress, Peculiar Objects, and Importance of Political Economy. . . .* Edinburgh, 1824.

____ *The Principles of Political Economy: with a Sketch of the Rise and Progress of the Science.* 2nd ed., 1830.

Malthus, Thomas Robert, *An Essay on the Principle of Population. . . .* Several editions, 1798, 1803, 1806, 1807, 1817, 1826.

____ *Additions to the Fourth and Former Editions of an Essay on the Principle of Population.* 1817.

____ *An Investigation into the Cause of the Present High Price of Provisions.* 1800.

____ *A Letter to Samuel Whitbread. . .on the proposed Bill for the Amendment of the Poor Laws.* 1807.

Malthus, Thomas Robert, *Principles of Political Economy Considered with a View to their Practical Application.* 1820.

_____ *A Summary View of the Principle of Population.* 1830.

Marcet, Jane, *Conversations on Political Economy; in which the Elements of that Science are Familiarly Explained.* Philadelphia, 1817.

Marshall, John, *Digest of all the Accounts of the United Kingdom.* 1833.

Martin, Matthew, *Letter to the Right Hon. Lord Pelham on the State of Mendicity in the Metropolis.* 1803.

Martineau, Harriet, *Illustrations of Political Economy.* 9 vols., 1831-1833.

_____ *Poor Laws and Paupers Illustrated.* 2 vols., 1833-34.

Mill, James, *Elements of Political Economy.* 1st ed., 1821; 2nd ed., 1824.

_____ *Essays on Government, Jurisprudence, Liberty of the Press, Prisons and Prison Discipline, Colonies, Law of Nations, and Education.* Reprinted from the *Supplement to the Encyclopaedia Britannica*, 1821.

_____ *Analysis of the Phenomena of the Mind.* 1829.

_____ *A Fragment on Mackintosh. . . .* 1835.

_____ *Selected Economic Writings.* ed. by Donald Winch, Chicago, 1966.

Mill, John Stuart, *Collected Works*, ed. by F. E. L. Priestly. Vol. IV, *Essays on Economics and Society*, Vols. XII and XIII, *Earlier Letters of John Stuart Mill, 1812-1848.* Toronto, 1963-67.

_____ *A System of Logic.* 8th ed., New York, 1900.

_____ *Autobiography.* New York, Columbia University Press, 1924.

Nicholls, George, *Eight Letters on the Management of our Poor. . . .* Newark, 1822.

Owen, Robert, *Report to the Committee of the Association for the Relief of the Manufacturing Labouring Poor.* 1817.

Page, Frederick, *Principles of the English Poor Laws. . . .* Bath, 1822.

Place, Francis, *Illustrations and Proofs of the Principle of Population.* ed. by Norman Himes, Boston, 1930.

Paley, William, *Principles of Moral and Political Philosophy.* 1785.

Pitt, William, *Heads of Mr. Pitt's Speech. . .Relative to the Relief and Maintenance of the Poor, the Encouragement of Industry, and the Diminution of the Poor Rates.* 1797.

Pugh, John, *Remarkable Occurrences in the Life of Jonas Hanway.* 1787.

Ricardo, David, *The Works and Correspondence of David Ricardo.* ed. by P. Straffa and M. Dobb, 10 vols. Cambridge, England, 1951-1955.

Rose, George, *A Brief Examination into the Increase of the Revenue, Commerce, and Manufacturers of Great Britain from 1792-1797.* 1799.

_____ *Observations on the Poor Laws. . . .* 1805.

_____ *Observations on Banks for Savings.* 1816.

Rumford, Benjamin, Count, *Essays Political, Economical, and Philosophical.* 1797.

Sadler, Michael Thomas, *Ireland: Its Evils and their Remedies. . . .* 1828.

_____ *The Law of Population; a Treatise. . .in Disproof of the Superfecundity of Human Beings, and Developing the Real Principle of their Increase.* 1830.

Senior, Nassau William, *An Introductory Lecture on Political Economy.* 1827.

_____ *Three Lectures on the Rate of Wages, with a Preface on the Causes and Remedies of the Present Discontent.* 1830.

_____ *A Letter to Lord Howick on a Legal Provision for the Irish Poor. . . .* 1831.

_____ *An Outline of the Science of Political Economy.* 1836.

_____ "Remarks on the Opposition of the Poor to the Poor Law Act," *Edinburgh Review*, (October, 1841).

Senior, Nassau William, *Historical and Philosophical Essays.* 1865.

_____*Correspondence and Conversations of Alex de Tocqueville with Nassau William Senior, from 1834 to 1859.* 2 vols., 1872.

Slaney, Robert, *Some Facts Showing the Vast Burthen of the Poor Rates.* . . . 1817.

_____*An Essay on the Employment of the Poor.* 1819.

_____*Essay on the Beneficial Direction of Rural Expenditures.* 1824.

Smith, Adam, *An Inquiry into the Nature and Causes of the Wealth of Nations.* ed. by Edwin Cannan. New York, 1937.

Stewart, Dugald, *Collected Works.* ed. by William Hamilton, 10 vols., Edinburgh, 1854.

Strickland, George, *A Discourse on the Poor Laws of England and Scotland* . . . . 1827.

Sumner, John Bird, *A Treatise on the Records of the Creation and on the Moral Attributes of the Creator.* . . . 1816, 6th ed. 1850.

Tooke, Thomas, *A History of Prices and the State of Circulation from 1792 to 1856.* New York, 1928.

Townsend, Joseph, *Dissertation on the Poor Laws.* 1785.

_____*Observations on Various Plans Offered to the Public for the Relief of the Poor.* 1788.

Weyland, John, *A Short Inquiry into the Policy, Humanity and Past Effects of the Poor Laws.* . . . 1807.

_____*Observations on Mr. Whitbread's Poor Bill, and on the Population of England.* . . . 1807.

_____*The Principle of the English Poor Laws Illustrated from the Evidence Given by the Scottish Proprietors.* . . . 1815.

_____*The Principles of Population and Production.* . . . 1816.

Whately, Richard, *Introductory Lecture on Political Economy Delivered at Oxford in the Easter Term 1831.* 4th ed., 1855.

_____*Thoughts on Secondary Punishments, in a Letter to Earl Grey.* 1832.

_____*Elements of Logic.* 4th ed., 1831; 9th ed., 1852.

Whewell, William, *History of the Inductive Sciences.* 2 vols., 3rd ed., 1858.

Whitbread, Samuel, *Substance of a Speech on the Poor Laws.* . . . 1807.

Wilberforce, William, *A Practical View of the Prevailing Religious System of Professed Christians in the Higher and Middle Classes in this Country, Contrasted with Real Christianity.* 1797, 15th ed., 1824.

_____*The Correspondence of William Wilberforce.* ed. by Robert and Samuel Wilberforce. 2 vols., 1840.

Young, Arthur, *The Autobiography of Arthur Young, with Selections from his Correspondence.* 1898.

MODERN AUTHORITIES

Anschutz, Richard P., *The Philosophy of J. S. Mill.* Oxford, 1953.

Ashton, T. S., *The Industrial Revolution, 1760-1830.* 1948.

_____*An Economic History of England in the Nineteenth Century.* 1955.

_____"The Standard of the Workers in England, 1790-1850." *Journal of Economic History, Supplement,* IX (1949).

Aspinal, Arthur, *Lord Brougham and the Whig Party.* Manchester, 1929.

_____*Politics and the Press.* 1949.

_____(ed.), *Three Nineteenth Century Diaries.* 1952.

Bain, Alexander, *James Mill, a Biography.* 1882.

Beales, H. L., "The New Poor Law." *History,* XV (1931).

Blaug, Mark, *Ricardian Economics.* New Haven, 1958.

Blaug, Mark, "The Myth of the Old Poor Law and the Making of the New," *Journal of Economic History*, XXIII (June, 1963).
_____ "The Poor Law Report Re-examined," *Journal of Economic History*, XXIV (June, 1964).
Bonar, James, *Malthus and His Work*. 1885.
Boner, Harold A., *Hungry Generations: the Nineteenth Century Case against Malthusianism*. New York, 1955.
Bowley, Marian, *Nassau Senior and Classical Economics*. 1937, reprinted by Augustus M. Kelly, 1949.
Brebner, J. B., "Laissez Faire and State Intervention in Nineteenth Century Britain," *Journal of Economic History*, VIII (1948).
Briggs, Asa, *The Age of Improvement*. 1959.
Brock, William R., *Lord Liverpool and Liberal Toryism*. 1941.
Brown, Ford K., *Fathers of the Victorians: The Age of Wilberforce*. Cambridge, England, 1961.
Burrow, J. W., *Evolution and Society*. Cambridge, England, 1966.
Cannon, Edwin, *A History of the Theories of Production and Distribution in English Political Economy from 1776-1848*. 1893.
_____ *The History of Local Rates in England*. 1896.
Chambers, J. D., *The Workshop of the World, British Economy from 1820-1880*. 1961.
_____ and G. E. Mingay, *The Agricultural Revolution 1750-1880*, 1966.
Clapham, John H., *Economic History of Modern Britain*, 3 vols. 1927.
Clark, George Kitson, *An Expanding Society, Britain 1830-1900*. Cambridge, England, 1967.
Clive, John L., *The Edinburgh Review 1802-1845*. 1957.
Clokie, Hugh M. and Joseph W. Robinson, *Royal Commissions of Inquiry*. 1938.
Coupland, Reginald, "Wilberforce." Oxford, 1923.
Cowherd, R. G., *The Politics of English Dissent*. New York, 1956.
Deane, Phyllis and W. A. Cole, *British Economic Growth, 1688-1859*. New York, 1962.
Dean, Phyllis, *The First Industrial Revolution*. Cambridge, England, 1965.
Edsall, Nicholas C., *The Anti-Poor Law Movement*. Totawa, N. J., 1971.
Everett, Charles W., *The Education of Jeremy Bentham*. New York, 1931.
Fay, C. R., *Huskisson and His Age*. 1951.
Fetter, Frank W., "The Authorship of Economic Articles in the Edinburgh Review, 1802-1847," *Journal of Political Economy*, LXI (June, 1953).
_____ "The Economic Articles in the Quarterly Review and Their Authors, 1809-1952," *Ibid.*, LXVI (February and April, 1958).
_____ "Economic Articles in the Westminster Review and Their Authors, 1824-1851," *Ibid.*, LXX (December, 1962).
_____ "Economic Controversy in the British Reviews, 1802-1850," *Economica*, (November, 1965).
Finer, S. E., *The Life and Times of Sir Edwin Chadwick*. 1953.
Fussell, G. E. and M. Compton, "Agricultural Adjustments After the Napoleonic Wars," *Economic History*, 1939.
Gash, Norman, "Rural Unemployment, 1815-1834," *Economic History Review*, VI (1935-36).
_____ *The Life of Sir Robert Peel*. Cambridge, Massachusetts, 1961.
Gayer, Arthur D., W. W. Rostow, and Anna J. Schwartz, *The Growth and Fluctuation of British Economy, 1790-1850*. 2 vols., Oxford, 1953.
Gillispie, Charles G., *The Edge of Objectivity: An Essay in the History of Scientific Ideas*. Princeton, N. J., 1960.

293

Gillispie, Charles G., "Science and Technology," *The New Cambridge Modern History*, IX, Cambridge, England, 1965.

Glass, D. V., (ed.), *Introduction to Malthus*, New York, 1953.

Gosden, P.H.J.H., *The Friendly Societies in England 1815-1875*, Manchester, 1961.

Gray, B. Kirkman, *A History of English Philanthropy*. 1905.

Halévy, Elie, *The Growth of Philosophic Radicalism*. French edition, 3 vols., 1901-1904; translated by Mary Morris, 1928; reprinted by Augustus M. Kelly, 1949.

_____ *A History of the English People in the Nineteenth Century*. Vols. I-III, translated from the French by E. I. Watkin and D. A. Barker; 1926-1927; reprinted by Peter Smith, 1949-1950.

Hamburger, Joseph, *James Mill and the Art of Revolution*. New Haven, 1963.

Hammond, John L. and Barbara, *The Village Labourer*. 1911.

Hampson, E. M., *The Treatment of Poverty in Cambridgeshire*. 1934.

Hartwell, R. M., "The Rising Standard of Living, 1800-1850," *Economic History Review*, (April, 1961).

_____ (ed.), *The Industrial Revolution*. Oxford, 1970.

Howse, Ernest Marshall, *Saints in Politics, the Clapham Sect and the Growth of Freedom*. Toronto, 1952.

Himmelfarb, Gertrude, "Bentham's Utopia: The National Charity Company," *The Journal of British Studies*, X, (November, 1970).

Hobsbaum, E. J., "The British Standard of Living, 1790-1850," *Economic History Review*, 2nd ser., X (August, 1957).

_____ and George Rudé, *Captain Swing*. New York, 1968.

Hoffman, Walter G., *British Industry 1700-1950*. Oxford, 1955.

Holyoake, George Jacob, *Self-Help, A Hundred Years Ago*. 1888.

Horne, H. Oliver, *A History of Savings Banks*. 1947.

Hutchins, John Harold, *Jonas Hanway 1712-1786*. New York, 1940.

Hutchison, T. W., "Bentham as an Economist," *Economic Journal*, LXVI (June, 1956).

Jones, Kathleen, *Lunacy, Law, and Conscience 1744-1845*. 1955.

Levy, Samuel L., *Nassau Senior, the Prophet of Modern Capitalism*. Boston, 1943.

Lewis, R. A., *Edwin Chadwick and the Public Health Movement*. 1952.

Link, Robert G., *English Theories of Economic Fluctuations, 1815-1848*. New York, 1959.

McCleary, George F., *The Malthusian Population Theory*. 1953.

Maccoby, S., *English Radicalism 1832-1852*. 1935.

MacDonagh, Oliver, "The Nineteenth Century Revolution in Government," *History Journal*, I (1958).

Mack, Mary P., "The Political Odyssey of Jeremey Bentham." 1962.

Mackay, Thomas, *A History of the English Poor Laws*. 1900.

Mackey, Howard, "Humanitarian Opposition to the Economists on the Poor Law and Factory Legislation," (An unpublished doctoral dissertation, Lehigh University, 1855).

Marshall, J. D., "The Nottinghamshire Reformers and their Contribution to the New Poor Law," *Economic History Review*, 2nd ser. XIII (April, 1961).

_____ *The Old Poor Law, 1795-1834. Studies in Economic History*, prepared for the Economic History Society, 1968.

Marshall, Dorothy, *The English Poor in the Eighteenth Century*. 1926.

_____ "The Old Poor Law 1662-1795," *Economic History Review*, I (1929).

_____ *The English People in the Eighteenth Century*. 1956.

Mathews, R. C. O., "The Trade Cycle in Britain 1790-1850," *Oxford Economic Papers*, New ser., VI (February, 1954).

_____ *A Study in Trade Cycle History: Economic Fluctuations in Britain 1833-1842*. Cambridge, England, 1954.

Mingay, G. E., *English Landed Society in the Eighteenth Century*. Toronto, 1963.

Midwinter, E. C., *Social Administration in Lancashire*. Manchester, 1969.

Mitchell, B. R. and Phyllis Deane, *Abstract of British Historical Statistics*. New York, 1962.

Mitchelson, Noel, "The Old Poor Law in East Yorkshire," *East Yorkshire Local History* (1953).

Myrdal, Gunnar, *The Political Element in the Development of Economic Theory*. Cambridge, Massachusetts, 1943.

Napier, Macvey, (ed.), *Selections from the Correspondence of the Late Macvey Napier*. 1879.

New, Chester W., *Life of Henry Brougham to 1830*. Oxford, 1961.

Nicholls, Sir George and Thomas Mackay, *A History of the English Poor Laws*. 3 vols., 2nd ed., 1898-1900.

Owen, David, *English Philanthropy 1660-1960*. Cambridge, Massachusetts, 1964.

O'Brien, D. P., *J. R. McCulloch: A Study in Classical Economics*. New York, 1970.

Packe, Michael St. John, *The Life of John Stuart Mill*. New York, 1954.

Plamenatz, John, *The English Utilitarians*. Oxford, 1949.

Poynter, J. R., *Society and Pauperism*. 1969.

Prothero, Rowland Edmund, Baron Ernle, *English Farming, Past and Present*. 6th ed., Chicago, 1961.

Rae, John, *Life of Adam Smith*. 1895, reprinted by Augustus M. Kelly, 1966.

Read, Donald, *The English Provinces, c. 1760-1960*. 1964.

Redford, Arthur, *Labour Migration in England 1800-1850*. 1926.

Roberts, David, *Victorian Origins of the British Welfare State*. New Haven, 1960.

_____ "How Cruel was the Victorian Poor Law," *Historical Journal*, VI (1963).

Roberts, Michael, *The Whig Party 1807-1812*. 1939.

Robbins, Lionel Charles, *The Theory of Economic Policy in English Classical Political Economy*. 1952.

_____ *Robert Torrens and the Evolution of Classical Economics*. 1958.

Rose, John Holland, *William Pitt and the National Revival*. 1911.

_____ *Pitt and Napoleon: Essays and Letters*. 1912.

Rose, Michael E., *The English Poor Law*. New York, 1971.

_____ *The Relief of Poverty, 1834-1914*. London, 1972.

St. Clair, Oswald, *A Key to Ricardo*. 1957.

Salaman, R. N., *The History and Social Influence of the Potato*. Cambridge, England, The University Press, 1949.

Schumpeter, Joseph A., *History of Economic Analysis*. New York, 1954.

Seeley, Robert B., *Memoirs of the Life and Writings of Michael Thomas Sadler*. 1842.

Sheppard, Francis H. W., *Local Government in St. Marylebone*. New York, 1959.

Shoup, Carl S., *Ricardo on Taxation*. New York, 1960.

Smart, William, *Economic Analysis of the Nineteenth Century*. 2 vols., 1910, 1917.

Smith, Kenneth, *The Malthusian Controversy*. 1951.

Stephen, Leslie, *The English Utilitarians.* 3 vols, 1900.
Tate, W. E., *The Parish Chest.* 3rd ed., Cambridge, England, 1969.
Taylor, Geoffrey, *The Problem of Poverty 1660-1834.* London, 1969.
Taylor, Overton H., *Economics and Liberalism.* Cambridge, Massachusetts, 1955.
_____*A History of Economic Thought: Social Ideals and Economic Theories from Quesnay to Keynes.* New York, 1960.
Thompson, E. P., *The Making of the English Working Class.* 1963.
Thompson, F. M. L., *English Landed Society in the Nineteenth Century.* 1963.
Thompson, Herbert F., "Adam Smith's Philosophy of Science," *Quarterly Journal of Economics.* LXXIX (May, 1965).
Vernon-Harcourt, G. F., (ed.), *The Diaries and Correspondence of the Right Hon. George Rose.* 2 vols. 1860.
Viner, Jacob, *The Long View and the Short: Studies in Economic Theory and Policy.* Glencoe, Illinois, 1958.
Wallas, Graham, *The Life of Francis Place.* 3rd ed., New York, 1919.
Ward, John T., "Michael Thomas Sadler," *University of Leeds Review*, VII (December, 1960).
_____(ed.), *Popular Movements, 1830-1850.* 1970.
Webb, R. K., *The British Working Class Reader.* 1955.
_____*Harriett Martineau, A Radical Victorian.* New York, 1960.
Webb, Sidney and Beatrice, *English Local Government: English Poor Law History: Part I. The Old Poor Law.* 1927. *Part II. The Last Hundred Years.* 2 vols. 1929.
Williams, Orlo, *Life and Letters of John Rickman.* New York, 1912.
Winck, Donald, *Classical Political Economy and Colonies.* Cambridge, Massachusetts, 1965.
Ziegler, Philip, *Addington: A Life of Henry Addington, First Viscount Sidmouth.* New York, 1966.

PERIODICALS

Annals of Agriculture, 1784-1808.
Annual Register, 1782-1834.
Christian Observer, 1802-1834.
Edinburgh Review, 1802-1836.
Evangelical Magazine, 1793-1834.
Gentleman's Magazine, 1790-1834.
The Pamphleteer, 1813-1817.
Philanthropist, 1811-1815.
Quarterly Review, 1809-1834.
Westminster Review, 1824-1834.

INDEX

Abbot, Charles, 19
Able-Bodied Poor, Committee on, 169
Allowance, *see* Scales of Relief
Althorp, Lord (John Charles Spencer), 270-1, 273
Anti-Combination Acts, 9, 128
Association for Relief and Benefit of Manufacturing Poor, 37
Aspinal, Arthur, 282n.
Barrington, Shute (Bishop of Durham), 15
Bastardy, the law of, 259, 277
Bauser, Paul, 188
Becher, J. T., 188-9
Bennett, William, 232
Bentham, Jeremy, vii, 82-84; and Chadwick, 217; contract management, 85; labor theory, 86; liberalism, 88; memoirs, 195; and James Mill, 98-103; National Charity Company, 91-2; and natural law reformers, 94; Pitt's Poor Law Bill, 89; pauper management, 196; poverty, 90; Radical Reform Bill, 97; reforms of 1831, 195; workhouse principles, 235, 252
Bentham, Samuel, 84
Benthamites, *see* Radicals
Bernard, Sir Thomas, 15-6, 18, 31
Bishop, Henry, 223
Blaug, Mark, 151n.
Blomfield, Bishop Charles, 156-7, 215

Blything Poor Law Union, 144
Bowring, Sir John, 203n.
Briggs, Asa, vii
Brotherton, Joseph, 272
Brougham, Henry (Lord), 205, 275-6
Burdett, Sir Francis, 96
Bourne, William Sturges, 56, 72-4, 215
Business Cycle Theory, the lack of, 128
Business Cycles: depression (1816-18), 54; (1825-26), 156-7; prosperity (1819-24), 155; recession (1829), 172
Buxton, Thomas Fowell, 47n.
Cameron, Charles H., 227
Capper, B. P., 68, 70
Carmalt, Rev. William, 141
Castlereagh, Viscount (later 2nd Marquis of Londonderry), 55
Census of 1801, 19
Central Board of Commissioners, 268, 277
Chadwick, Sir Edwin, 216, Assistant Commissioner, 228-236; and Bentham, 217, 202n.; co-author of the *Poor Law Report*, 277; Commissioner, 237; less-eligibility, 229; on method of investigation, 218, 238; pauperism, 247; on political economy, 236, 267; and Senior, 236-7; wages-fund, 236
Chalmers, the Rev. Thomas, 64

297

Christian Observer, 38-40, 67
Clapham, John H., 151n.
Clapham Sect, *see* Evangelicals
Cobbett, William, 96, 272
Collett, the Rev. Anthony, 144
Colquhoun, Patrick, on poverty and indigence, 40
Commission, Royal, (1832-34), 207, 215-6; assumptions, 221; expenditures, 252; *Extracts*, 222-23; *Geo. I, c. 7* versus *36 Geo. III, c. 23*, 247; "Instructions to the Assistants," 219-21; less-eligibility, 267; magistrates, 268; method of investigation, 207; poverty, 245; population, 249; questionnaires, 218-20, 260-65; *Report*, 244ff.; theory of welfare, 245; unemployment, 220, workhouses, 252, 268
Commissioners, Assistant, 218-20, investigations, 223-27; reports, 228ff.
Copleston, Bishop Edward, 132-33
Cottages, the pulling down of, 7, 162, 179, 200
Coulson, Walter, 200, 215
Counties, southern versus northern, 128, 168-69, 225
Courtenay, Thomas P., 60, 71
Curwen, John C., 54-5
Davis, William, 133
Dispauperization, 267, 278
Dissenters, 43
Eclectic Review, 67
Eden, Sir Frederick Morton, vi, 16-17
Edinburgh Whigs, 205
Emigration: 157-58, 163; as a remedy for pauperism, 160, 163, 184; subsidizing of, 170
Escalation of poor rates, the doctrine of, 17, 32, 57-8, 71, 114, 248, 252
Evangelicals: vi-vii, 2-4, at Clapham, 14, 40; activities, 36-9; contract system, 16, 22; land allotments, 28, 34; magistrates versus parish overseers, 22; as humanitarian reformers, 70, 283; and Malthus, 31-2, 35-6, 38-9, 41, 78; outdoor relief, 10, 14; and Pitt's reforms, 4-11, 15-24; and Sadler's reforms, 174, 206; the Society for Bettering the Condition and Increasing the Comforts of the Poor, 14-5; waning influence, 35, 40, 78, 133
Famine: (1795), 11-12; (1799-1800), 18
Fetter, Frank W., 126n.

Finer, S. E., 100n.
Friendly Societies, 8-9, 69-70
Fry, Elizabeth, 2
Gilbert, Thomas, 4
Gilbert Act, 1782, 5-6
Gilbert Unions, 254
Glasgow Hospital, 63-4
Grey, 2nd Earl, 274
Halévy, Elie, viii, 99n., 100n., 279n., 282n.
Hammond, John L. and Barbara, on Speenhamland, 25n.
Hanway, Jonas, 2-4
Hardwicke, Earl of, 61
Harrowby, Lord (Dudley Ryder), 19
Henderson, Gilbert, 224
Hodges, Thomas L., 159, 184
Hobsbaum, E. J., 201n., 279n.
Horton, Robert J. Wilmot, 158, 170
House of Commons Committees: able-bodied poor, 168; emigration, 157-58, 160, 163; high price of provisions, 18-9; laborers' wages, 138-46; poor laws (1817), 54-9, 72; poor-rate returns, 135-136, 154-55; vagrancy, 166-67
House of Commons Debates, (1818), 72; (1819), 73-4; (1834), 270-4
House of Lords Committees: (1817), 60-1, 75; (1831), 182-91
House of Lords Debates: (1834), 274-6
Howard, John, 2
Howlett, The Rev. John, 13
Humanitarian legislation, the repeal of, 247-48, 267-69, 285
Humanitarians, *see* Evangelicals
Hume, Joseph, 74-5, 195, 211
Huskisson, William, 45
Ireland, 165-66
Jerram, The Rev. Charles, 41
Justices of the Peace (magistrates), 6, 10, 22, 76, 145, 253-54, 264
Laborers, migrant, 167-68
Lancashire, 153, 224
Land allotments, 28, 34, 192
Lansdowne, 3rd Marquis (Henry Petty Fitzmaurice), 205
Less-eligibility, Radical principle of, 93-4, 267
Levy, Samuel Leon, 241n.
Lewis, T. Franklin, 56
Liberal Tories, 127, 134, 192, 205
Littleton, E. J., 195
Liverpool, 2nd Earl, 60-1, 127
Local Acts of Parliament, 6, 254
London, 264-66
London Committee for Relief of Manufacturing Districts, 156-57

Macaulay, Thomas B., 177
Macaulay, Zachary, 38
McCulloch, John Ramsey, 122, 147; and Bentham, 148; contract system, 178; Laws of Settlement, 179; pauper management, 201; and Pitt's reforms, 178; population, 148, 179, 199; pulling down cottages, 179, 200; Radical reforms, 179-201, 204; and Ricardo, 116, 147; unemployment, 198; workhouses, 150, 179, 199
MacLean, Charles H., 226, 256
Magistrates, see Justices of the Peace
Majendie, Ashurst, 226
Mallet, John, 120
Malthus, the Rev. Thomas Robert, An Essay on the Principle of Population, 18-20; on charity, 32; and Godwin, 19; doctrine of gluts, 199; emigration, 161-63; foundling hospitals, 34; on method, 33; morals and theology, 32-33; and Rumford's dietary reforms, 35; poor rates, 32; pulling down cottages, 162; savings banks, 49; and Ricardo, 112-13; wages, 56; and Whitbread, 56
Mandeville, Bernard de, The Fable of the Bees, 23n.
Marcet, Mrs. (Jane), 56
Marshall, J. D., 278n.
Melbourne, 2nd Viscount (William Lamb), 222, 270
Mendicity Society, 164-65
Militia Act, scales of relief, 10
Mill, James, 102, and Bentham, 98, 103; Elements of Political Economy, 118; pauper management, 105; Radical principles, 103-6, 204; and Ricardo, 106-10; and Stewart, 211
Mill, John Stuart, on method, 213-14, 239
Mingay, G. E., 279n.
Minimum wage, 12
Mott, Charles, 234
Moore, Hannah, 2
Moylan, D. C., 227
Natural law doctrines: harmony of interests, i, viii, 378; escalation of rates, 17, 57, 68-9, 71; labor, 2, 7, 9; population, 7, 13, 19, 56; poverty, 2, 7, 40, 46, 78, 245; wages-fund, 17, 20, 58-9
Natural law reformers: 2, 7, 16, 49ff., 59, 72-8, 284; contract system, 16, 95; and Evangelicals, vi, 6, 9, 16-17, 22, 29, 31, 40-2, 53, 78; justices of the peace

versus overseers, 7, 22, 76; and Scottish poor laws, 62, 64; self-interest, 6, 46, 73; workhouses, 7; and Whitbread, 28
Natural law theology, 33, 38-9, 41, 78
New poor law, viii, see Poor Laws
Nicholls, Sir George, 23n., 49
Northumberland, 187
O'Brien, D. P., 152n., 153n., 181n.
Okeden, D.O.P., 226
Old Poor Laws, viii, historians of, 23n.; see Poor Laws
Overseers, Assistant, 129, 254
Page, Frederick, on Speenhamland, 129-30, 150n., 263
Paley, William, 84
Palmerston, 3rd Viscount (Henry John Temple), 274
Panopticon, 85-8
Pauper management, 93, 188, 195
Pauper schools, 59
Pauperism, 245-47
Peel, Sir Robert, 171, 173
Perceval, Spencer, 45
Philanthropist, 41-3
Phillpotts, Henry (Bishop of Exeter), 276
Pilkington, Redmond, 227
Place, Francis, 118
Pitt, William, 4, 8, 10, 14, 22
Political Economy Club, 120, 204, 215
Poor law expenditures, 68-9, 135-37, 154-56, 172-73
Poor law returns, 5, 9-10, 12, 20-1, 25n., 62, 67-70
Poor Laws: 43 Eliz. c. 2 (1601), vii, viii, 1, 22; 13 & 14 Ch. II, c.12 (1662), vii, viii, 1, 2, 5, 10, 22; 9 Geo. I, c. 7 (1722), 1, 2, 5, 10; 22 Geo. III, c. 83 (1782), 4-6; 35 Geo. III, c. 101 (1795), 10; 36 Geo. III, c. 23 (1796), 10; 59 Geo. III, c. 12, 76-8; 4 & 5 Wm. IV, c. 76 (1834), 276-78
Poorhouses, 21, 70, 251
Poor relief methods: contracting (farming), 1, 10, 16; labor rate, 265; make-work, 143-44, 185-88, 264; Oundle plan, 142; roundsmen, 140, 143
Poverty, the Poor, 1-2, 7, 90, 245
Poynter, J. R., 25n., 203n., 279n.
Pratt, the Rev. John, 142
Pratt, J. Tidd, 231
Price, Richard, cost of living index, 13
Radicals (Benthamites): vii, 82, 98, 102-6, 127, 133, 146, 179, 195, 200, 204, 244, 254, 276-78,

285; central inspection, 84, 268, 277; contract-management, 85, 91, 150, 196, 201; escalation of rates, 123; harmony of interests, 99n., labor, 145, 192; less-eligibility, 94; principle of utility, 82-3; workhouses, 92-3, 188, 199, 268

Removals, the number of, 167-68

Ricardo, David, 98, 107-8; corn laws (1815), 110, 124n.; and McCulloch, 116; and Malthus, 112-13; as M.P., 116-17; and James Mill, 106-10; poor rates, 114-15; *Principles of Political Economy and Taxation*, 111-12; and Radical reform, 116-17

Rickman, John, 44-5, 64-5

Riots, 11, 182ff.

Robinson, G. R., 272

Romanticism, and the Evangelical Revival, vi

Romilly, Samuel, 2

Rose, Sir George, 7; Friendly Societies, 8-9; Poor law returns, 20-1; savings banks, 52-3

Rude, George, 201n., 279n.

Rumford, Count (Benjamin Thompson), 11-12

Russell, Lord John, 114, 205

Salisbury, 2nd Marquis, 182

Savings banks, 49-54

Scales of relief: bread, 139, 256, 258, 264; family, 90, 138, 262, 264; militiaman's, 257-58

Scarlett, Sir James (later Lord Abinger), 133, 247

Scotland, Poor Laws of, 52, 62-3

Scrope, Poulett, 274

Sebright, Sir John, 160

Select Vestries, 75, 77, 173-74, 273

Senior, Nassau William, 197, author of "Instructions," 219; and Chadwick, 237-38; co-author of *Poor Law Report*, 277-78; investigations, 223

Settlement and Removal, Law of, viii, 9, 14, 77, 179, 258-59, 279n.

Slaney, Robert A., 130-32, 169-70

Smith, Adam, i, iii, v, 57, 307-11; on Law of Settlement, 9; wages-fund, 17, 57-8, 236

Smith, the Rev. Sydney, 43, on Bentham, 124n.

Society for Bettering the Condition and Increasing the Comforts of the Poor, 14-15, 19

Society of Friends, 41-2

Society for the Suppression of Beggars, 51

Southey, Robert, 44, 65

Speenhamland, 25n., 256, 262-63, 279n., 280; see Scales of relief

Spitalfields Association for the Relief of the Industrious Poor, 37

Spring Rice, Thomas (later Lord Monteagle), 177, 205

Stewart, Dugald, 207; and James Mill, 211-12; on method, 209-10; against practical men, 209; and Adam Smith, 208-10

Stone, The Rev. William, 233

Strangers' Friend Society, 47n.

Stuart, Henry, 225

Sumner, John Bird (Bishop of Chester), 39-40, 133, 215

Surrey, 226

Sussex, 169, 186, 226, 256

Tawney, R. H., 239

Taylor, O. H., i

Tax office, 68

Torrens, Robert, 274

Townsend, the Rev. Joseph, 6-7

Truck Act, 195

Ultra-Tories, 206

Unemployment, 280n.; rural, 127, 139-44, 183; urban, 155-56, 169-70, 172, 264, 266, 272

Utilitarian Society, 216

Utilitarians, viii, see Radicals

Utility, principle of, Bentham's, 83; Paley's, 84

Vagrancy Laws, 128, 265

Vagrants, Irish, 128; Scottish, 265

Vestry, parish, 194, 255

Walker, Thomas, 190, 231

Wages-fund, 17, 57

Wages, in agriculture, 137-146, 170

Webb, Sidney and Beatrice, 23n., 99n., 239, 241n.

Wesley, John, vi

Westminster Review, 120

Weyland, John, 31, 192

Whately, Richard (Archbishop of Dublin), 212

Whately, The Rev. Thomas, 190

Whewell, William, 213

Whigs, the Foxite, 12-13, 22

Whitbread, Samuel, on Malthus, 28; minimum wage, 12; Poor Law Bill, 22

Winchilsea, 8th Earl, 193

Wilberforce, William, 14-16, 19, and Bentham, 89

Wilson, John, 224

Workhouses, 10, 70, 247, 268, 281n.; become poorhouses, 21, 251

Wrottesley, John, 227

Young, Arthur, 90